THE TRANSFORMATION
OF THE CLASSICAL HERITAGE

Peter Brown, General Editor

PUBLIC DISPUTATION, POWER, AND SOCIAL ORDER IN LATE ANTIQUITY

RICHARD LIM

PUBLIC DISPUTATION, POWER, AND SOCIAL ORDER IN LATE ANTIQUITY

UNIVERSITY OF CALIFORNIA PRESS

Berkeley · Los Angeles · London

University of California Press
Berkeley and Los Angeles, California

University of California Press, Ltd.
London, England

© 1995 by
The Regents of the University of California

Library of Congress Cataloging-in-Publication Data

Lim, Richard, 1963–
    Public disputation, power, and social order in late antiquity /
Richard Lim.
        p.   cm. — (Transformation of the classical heritage ; 23)
    Revision of thesis (Ph. D.)—Princeton University, 1991.
    Includes bibliographical references and index.
    ISBN 0-520-08577-9 (alk. paper)
    1. Church history—4th century.   2. Religious disputations—
History.   3. Rome—Intellectual life—History.   I. Title.
II. Series.
    BR205.L56   1991
    270.1—dc20   93-43761
                                                                CIP

Printed in the United States of America
9 8 7 6 5 4 3 2 1

The paper used in this publication meets the minimum requirements of
American National Standard for Information Sciences—Permanence of Paper
for Printed Library Materials, ANSI Z39.48-1984.

For my Mother

CONTENTS

PREFACE AND
ACKNOWLEDGMENTS

This book is the fruit of an attempt to write a social history of public disputations in late antiquity. It took shape gradually, growing from a prospectus for a dissertation that would draw on the stenographically noted debates between Augustine of Hippo and various Manichaeans to illuminate patterns of social relations in Roman North Africa. It soon became clear from my readings, notably in sources bearing on the Christian theological controversies in the fourth-century Greek east, and from edifying conversations with learned friends and teachers, that the value of verbal argumentation itself came under scrutiny in this period, a phenomenon that deserves an explanation. It also became apparent that a social history of public disputation, as opposed to a literary history of the rich and complex ancient dialogue literature, cannot—and should not—be strictly determined by considerations of form or genre. For this reason, I have devised a study that aspires to be neither comprehensive nor exhaustive—both impossible goals in the absence of neat categorical boundaries—but that nevertheless explores the above phenomenon by showing how within various late antique groups the reception and practice of public disputation, as one of many forms of open competition, consistently depended on the principals' underlying notions of authority, group solidarity, and social order. This methodological perspective is the touchstone that guides my choices and treatment of subject matter; it also serves, in no small measure, as the keystone supporting the intellectual structure of the book. While the ancient debates included in my analysis encompass a number of highly complex issues, each of which merits a detailed intellectual history of its own, I generally relate only the most immediately pertinent aspects of the philosophical or theological matters in dispute, focusing instead on their social dynamics and attendant circumstances. I have done this deliberately, partly for the sake of conciseness, seeing that it is beyond the compass of this work to treat the important themes fairly, and partly because I can refer the avid reader who wishes to learn more about the cognitive content of particular debates to the erudite works of others.

*   *   *

In the present work, Chapter 1 sets out the salient cultural parameters surrounding public verbal competition and Graeco-Roman beliefs concerning persuasion and proof in philosophical and religious circles. I discuss the social functions of disputation among pagan philosophical elites, in controversies between Jews and Christians, and among pre-Constantinian Christians, and conclude by considering certain implications of the rise of fourth-century imperial Christianity for the practice of dialectic and for verbal argumentation among Christians.

Chapter 2 explores the institutional culture of Platonist philosophical groups. While historians have long been interested in the rivalry endemic to philosophers of different schools, far less attention has been given to the competition within philosophical coteries. I examine how disputation served as one of several ways to compete for status in the circles of Plotinus, Porphyry, Iamblichus, and philosophical figures discussed in the *Vitae philosophorum et sophistarum* of Eunapius of Sardis. Dialectical disputation allowed the agon to intrude into the philosophical life, often enabling junior philosophers to claim excellence by competing openly with their elders. In this light, the elevation of the status of the philosopher-teacher *cum* holy man may be seen as an effective buffer against rampant strife and contention. Likewise, the subordination of Aristotelian science and logic to Platonic wisdom entailed the implicit ordering of philosophical virtues and claims of knowledge, which helped to domesticate the individualistic and agonistic claims of competitive dialectic.

Chapter 3 documents the social contexts and functions of public debates involving Manichaeans. Disputing others' fundamental philosophical and religious views, particularly beliefs about the origin of evil, enabled Manichaeans to "break the ice" and to reach their intended audience. They were armed with a corpus of controversial writings that helped them pose difficult questions designed to upset their hearers' convictions. The early success of the religion owed much to a fluid cultural landscape and porous group boundaries, notably among the urban intelligentsia; yet this environment of easygoing exchanges threatened the communal solidarity of local groups, whose self-styled leaders soon contrived to restrict this openness to change. In the *Vita Porphyrii* of Pseudo-Mark the Deacon, and in the anti-Manichaean writings of Augustine of Hippo, we discern how the rising power of local bishops was consolidated and strengthened via formal public debates with Manichaeans, debates deliberately staged to forestall the more diffuse and intimate forms of suasion that had brought the Manichaeans much well-deserved success. The ensuing crystallization of a Christian *adversus Manichaeos* literature rigidified group boundaries, fixed normative orthodox and heretical identities, and consequently precluded spontaneous disputation between ordinary orthodox Christians and Manichaean challengers.

Chapter 4 examines the reputations and careers of Aetius the Syrian and Eunomius the Cappadocian, who were called Anomoeans by their detractors because they allegedly believed the essences of the Father and Son to be dissimilar. These two figures, portrayed as Christian dialecticians, were widely feared by contemporaries as formidable public debaters because of their aptitude for constructing sophisms and syllogistic chains. They availed themselves of the channels of social mobility recently opened to men of talent within the context of fourth-century imperial Christianity, their meteoric rise from obscurity demonstrating the role of the *ars dialectica* in social advancement in the late Empire. Their influence with the educated and the powerful generated alarm and consternation among their rivals. These two men, who championed the intellectual and social claims of competitive disputation in Christian theological enterprises, were thought to have popularized certain disputing techniques. While Aetius and Eunomius were viewed with suspicion because they differed from their "orthodox" rivals on points of doctrine, the conflict between the two camps was not just a theological one; they raised issues that sharpened their antagonists' disagreements over ideals, social order, and the construction of authority in the Christian community.

In Chapter 5, I argue that the same circumstances that led to the negative reception of competitive speech also fueled the growth of an apophatic mystical theology that subsequently became central to the Byzantine tradition. The view of the essence of the Deity as a mystery beyond the grasp of human language or conception did not represent a mere passive reception of the Middle Platonic *via negativa* but a response to dialectical questioning, which jeopardized the traditional Christian leaders' position by making it conditional upon *gnōsis*, wisdom or knowledge, thus subjecting them to recurrent and difficult testings by others. The mystification of the divine and the emphasis on silence served as obfuscating strategies to dampen the threatening, perceptibly widespread, phenomenon of curiosity and debate within an expanding and increasingly sophisticated Christian population. I examine this supposition within the contexts of two sets of influential sermons: Gregory of Nazianzus' *Orationes* 27 through 31, his so-called "Theological Orations," and John Chrysostom's *De incomprehensibili natura Dei sermones*, respectively delivered in late fourth-century Constantinople and Antioch.

Chapter 6 shows how views about disputation traceable to fourth-century controversies influenced later representations of the Council of Nicaea, 325 C.E. A preference for hierarchical order shaped the writings of fifth-century Christian writers, who imbued their accounts of the council with many of the concerns and prejudices expressed earlier by the Cappadocians. According to these various historical sources (i.e., the *Historiae ecclesiasticae* of Rufinus of Aquileia, accounts by Socrates Scholasticus and Sozomen, and the *Syntagma* of Gelasius of Cyzicus), a dialectician-philosopher debated the Christian bishops at Nicaea, and the latter were unable to prevail until a charismatic confessor intervened to stop their dialectical melee. The unlearned old man put an end to their futile exchanges by confronting the clever dialectician with the *simplicitas* of the Christian message, and by challenging his opponent to believe in the credal statement he then recited. Miraculously, the dialectician-philosopher was struck dumb and eventually admitted defeat. This story accentuated the virtue of Christian simplicity by contrasting it with the vain deceit of dialectical disputations. The redactional history of this multiform story highlights the *psychomachia* or contest between individualist (competitive) and communal (consensual) forms of authority, and illustrates how various Christian authors reworked the received tradition of a debate in council in light of shifting assumptions about the value of verbal competition in a christianizing society.

Chapter 6 ends with the incipient authority of Christian councils pointedly mobilized against the tradition of competitive dialectic, particularly in the *Liber Dalmatii* from the *Syntagma* of Gelasius of Cyzicus. Chapter 7 carries this story forward by presenting a brief, selective account of the rise of the Christian conciliar tradition and the evolution of procedural conventions to the time of the Council of Chalcedon. Here we see how the growing reliance on a consensual ideology, *consensus omnium*, exhibited by acclamations and traditional authorities, provided an ideological and institutional counterweight to the dynamic *logos*, reasoned speech.

* * *

This book, and the dissertation (Princeton, 1991) on which it is based, would not have been possible but for the generous help and goodwill of many individuals, not every one of whom can be named here. My greatest debt is to Peter Brown and John Gager, who unfailingly sustained me with humane and sage advice, patiently guiding me through what at times seemed an interminable task. Mary Douglas, with her characteristic insight, inspired me to develop ideas about the connection between social bodies and ideologies, and to apply them to the study of historical questions. Martha Himmelfarb, Robert Lamberton, and Elizabeth Clark read the entire manuscript in various stages and offered me much valued advice. Others helped by reading and commenting on elements of the whole: Scott Bradbury, Kate Cooper, Garth Fowden, and Susan Pavloska. They all deserve my warm thanks. I have also been fortunate to have the expert help of Mary Lamprech of the University of California Press and Scott Norton, my copy editor, both of whom worked over the entire manuscript with exemplary care and sympathy. The idiosyncrasies and faults that remain are my own.

I wish to thank the Institut des Études Augustinennes for permission to reprint "Manichaeans and Public Disputation in Late Antiquity," which appeared in an earlier form in *Recherches Augustiniennes* 24 (1992).

Over the years, I have been supported in this work by the generosity of the Mrs. Giles Whiting Foundation; the Group for the Study of Late Antiquity and the Program in the History, Archaeology, and Religions of the Ancient World, both at Princeton University; Smith College; and the Dumbarton Oaks Center for Byzantine Studies, Harvard University, where a brief residence during the summer of 1992 afforded me the ideal setting for making final substantive revisions to the manuscript.

Richard Lim
Northampton, Mass., September 1993

ABBREVIATIONS

The abbreviating conventions adopted in this book are, with slight modifications, based on N. G. L. Hammond and H. H. Scullard, eds., *The Oxford Classical Dictionary*, 2d ed. (Oxford, 1970); H. G. Liddell and R. Scott, *A Greek-English Lexicon*, revised ed. by H. S. Jones (Oxford, 1968); G. W. H. Lampe, *A Patristic Greek Lexicon* (Oxford, 1961); and the index to cited periodicals in *L'Année Philologique*.

AB	*Analecta Bollandiana*
ACO	*Acta Conciliorum Oecumenicorum*, E. Schwartz, ed.
AHR	*American Historical Review*
AJP	*American Journal of Philology*
ANRW	*Aufstieg und Niedergang der römischen Welt: Geschichte und Kultur Roms im Spiegel der neueren Forschung*, H. Temporini et al., eds.
BCH	*Bulletin de Correspondance Hellénique*
BZ	*Byzantinische Zeitschrift*
CAG	Commentaria in Aristotelem Graeca, A. Busse, ed.
CCSG	Corpus Christianorum, series graeca
CCSL	Corpus Christianorum, series latina
CJ	*The Classical Journal*
CMC	*Codex Manichaicus Coloniensis*
Codex Theod.	*Codex Theodosianus*
CPhil	*Classical Philology*
CQ	*Classical Quarterly*
CRAI	*Comptes-Rendus de l'Académie des Inscriptions et Belles Lettres*

CSCO	Corpus Scriptorum Christianorum Orientalium (Louvain, 1903–)
CSEL	Corpus Scriptorum Ecclesiasticorum Latinorum (Vienna, 1866–)
CSHB	Corpus Scriptorum Historiae Byzantinae
DACL	*Dictionnaire d'Archéologie Chrétienne et de Liturgie*
DOP	*Dumbarton Oaks Papers*
GCS	Die griechischen christliche Schriftsteller der ersten Jahrhunderte
GRBS	*Greek, Roman, and Byzantine Studies*
Hist. eccl.	*Historia ecclesiastica*
HSCP	*Harvard Studies in Classical Philology*
HTR	*Harvard Theological Review*
JAC	*Jahrbuch für Antike und Christentum*
JHS	*Journal of Hellenic Studies*
JRS	*Journal of Roman Studies*
JTS	*Journal of Theological Studies*
Lampe	*A Patristic Greek Lexicon*, G. W. H. Lampe, ed. (Oxford, 1961)
LCL	Loeb Classical Library
LSJ	*A Greek-English Lexicon*, H. G. Liddell, R. Scott, and H. S. Jones, eds. (Oxford, 1968)
MEFR	Mélanges d'Archéologie et d'Histoire de l'École Française de Rome
MSR	*Mélanges de Science Religieuse*
n.s.	new series
NPNF	Nicene and Post-Nicene Fathers, second series
OCA	*Orientalia Christiana Analecta*
P. Oxy.	*The Oxyrhynchus Papyri*, A. S. Hunt et al., eds. (1911–)
PBSR	*Papers of the British School at Rome*
PG	*Patrologia cursus completus, series graeca*, J.-P. Migne, ed.
PL	*Patrologia cursus completus, series latina*, J.-P. Migne, ed.
PLRE 1	*Prosopography of the Later Roman Empire I: A.D. 260–395*, A. H. M. Jones, J. R. Martindale, and J. Morris, eds. (Cambridge, 1971)
PLRE 2	*Prosopography of the Later Roman Empire II: A.D. 395–527*, J. R. Martindale, ed. (Cambridge, 1980)
PO	*Patrologia Orientalis*, R. Graffin, F. Nau, eds.
RAC	*Reallexikon für Antike und Christentum*, T. Klausner, ed.
RE	*Realencyclopädie der classischen Altertumswissenschaft*, G. Pauly, G. Wissowa, et al., eds. (Stuttgart, 1893–1978)
REAug	*Revue des Études Augustiniennes*
RecAug	*Recherches Augustiniennes*
REG	*Revue des Études Grecques*

RHE	*Revue d'Histoire Ecclésiastique*
RHLR	*Revue de l'Histoire et de Littérature Religieuses*
RhM	*Rheinisches Museum für Philologie*
RSR	*Recherches de Science Religieuse*
SC	Sources chrétiennes
SP	*Studia Patristica*
SPAW	*Sitzungberichte der preußischen Akademie der Wissenschaften zu Berlin,* Philologisch-historische Klasse
TAPA	*Transactions and Proceedings of the American Philological Association*
TU	Texte und Untersuchungen zur Geschichte der altchristlichen Literatur
VChr	*Vigiliae Christianae*
VP	*Vitae philosophorum*
VS	*Vitae philosophorum et sophistarum*
ZKG	*Zeitschrift für Kirchengeschichte*
ZPE	*Zeitschrift für Papyrologie und Epigraphik*
ZRGG	*Zeitschrift für Religions- und Geistesgeschichte*

ONE

THE DIFFUSION OF THE *LOGOS*

Which possess superior intelligence: animals living on land or animals living in water?

This peculiar subject, one that was "neither vulgar nor devoid of charm," inspired a staged disputation between two friends, Aristomimus and Phaedimus, the former championing the terrestrial animals' claim, the latter the aquatic animals'. In the prologue to his *De sollertia animalium* (On the cleverness of animals), Plutarch suggests that this contest was occasioned by a mild disagreement the evening before, during an inebriated symposium when the issue of the propriety of the hunt—that most aristocratic of sports—was discussed.[1] The protagonists devoted the following morning to their preparations, and when their drinking companions convened at the appointed hour, the referee Autobulus divided them into two camps: those expert in the hunt took up Aristomimus' side; those who lived on islands or by the sea, Phaedimus'.[2]

The debaters cast lots to determine who would be first to deliver his speech (965E). The language and imagery of Greek dicastic law courts pervade the two compelling, learned, and elegant speeches. When the judges—Autobulus and his friend Optatus, an expert on Aristotelian natural science—were called on as if dicasts ($\grave{\omega}$ ἄνδρες δικασταί) to cast their vote (τὴν ψῆφον φέρειν; 965D–E), Autobulus softened the agon by

---

1. Plutarch, *De sollertia animalium* 960B. For another debate that had its origin in a symposium, see Plutarch, *Conviviales quaestiones* 7.8.712D.
2. Plutarch, *De sollertia animalium* 965B, 963B, 965C–E.

effecting a conciliatory resolution of the two positions. He stated that all animals, whether terrestrial or living in water, possessed rational intelligence and must therefore be treated with the requisite consideration (985C). Neither of the contestants was dismayed or surprised to find their hotly contested, opposing positions synthesized by Autobulus to refute critics who would deny rationality to all animals.

The scenario in *De sollertia animalium* may well be a refracted image of the practice of disputation in the Platonic Academy, which Plutarch himself had attended in Athens, though there can be no proof positive for such an identification.[3] Public disputation between friends on subtle intellectual questions was a pastime of the privileged, highly educated adult males who possessed the requisite leisure to examine proposed topics in the shady groves of the Academy, far removed from the dusty bustle of the agora.

This debate could be convincingly portrayed by Plutarch as having reached an amicable resolution because there was no confusion of intellectual with social or professional considerations. The antagonists argued as if for argument's sake; with no prospects of material gain or other advantage, they simply reveled in ludic combat with social peers, continuing the sophisticated yet whimsical conversation of the previous evening's symposium.

This is not to suggest that the debate was taken lightly by the protagonists. The contest itself reeked heavily of lamp oil, of the painstaking study of pertinent writings (960B, 975D). The facade of effortless erudition in the speeches, in which each side proffered a litany of facts with great facility, was indebted to the wisdom enshrined in compendia of ancient works. The foremost authority on which the debaters relied was—to no one's surprise—Aristotle, whose reputation in matters of the natural sciences, particularly the science of animals, was unmatched in antiquity (965D–E). Yet his authority was mediated during the contest by the personal knowledge of the participants, especially Optatus, whose expert grasp of the Stagirite's corpus ensured that no scroll of the *Historia animalium* need be unrolled to check the veracity of the rival arguments (965E).

Plutarch's description of this friendly debate provides a starting point for discussing the ancients' ideals of public disputation, which are impossible to define in the abstract. First and foremost, a disputation was a ritualized verbal contest in which antagonists debated each other while adhering to the rules of a language game, whether of rhetoric

3. See Plutarch, *De E apud Delphos* 386F–87A.

or of dialectic.[4] In the above example, the debate entailed an exchange of reasoned arguments in successive continuous speeches rather than a mutual cross fire, or dialectical interrogation, by the two adversaries. Both forms of debate were common in antiquity.

In addition to its heavy emphasis on traditional textual authority and learned research, the debate was a mobilization of that knowledge arrayed in rival *logoi* (speeches). The construction and application of *logoi* connoted cunning and intelligence, principles of rationality thought to distinguish humans from wild animals.[5] The placid and erudite discussions in Plutarch's *Moralia,* in which witty and polite conversation was mixed with the wine of dialectical rigor, were themselves ideal testaments to the primacy of *logoi.*[6] Many educated Greeks were fascinated by the prospect that *logoi* might become the weapons of choice for people in disagreement, replacing the instruments of violence and compulsion in the ordering of human society.[7]

Asked to characterize a public debate, a Greek might have used an analogy, an antithesis, or both. He might liken a debate to a wrestling match, or a gymnastic contest such as the *pankration,* with its strict rules (*nomoi*). Or he might contrast the debate with a brawl or street fight, the latter resembling ritual contentions in traditional villages in which "each person takes a point or position and repeats it endlessly, either one after the other, or both alone or several at once."[8] Though such activities fulfilled other social functions, they were unseemly and contributed nothing to the resolution of differences per se, because "points of views are rarely developed, merely reasserted. . . . [E]ach keeps yelling his point full voice until, usually, certain voices seem to prevail and the others fade." Educated males such as Plutarch would have made a categorical distinction between the two forms: a debate was an exchange of *logoi,*

4. Two fine, concise introductions to the ancient forms are R. McKeon, "Greek Dialectics: Dialectic and Dialogue, Dialectic and Rhetoric," in C. Perelman, ed., *Dialectics* (The Hague, 1975), 1–25, and P. Hadot, "Philosophie, dialectique, rhétorique dans l'antiquité," *Studia Philosophica* 39 (1980), 139–66.

5. See *De sollertia animalium* 959C. On the perennial importance of cleverness in Greek culture, see M. Détienne and J.-P. Vernant, *Cunning Intelligence in Greek Culture and Society,* trans. J. Lloyd (Atlantic Highlands, N.J., 1978).

6. See the classic study of the genre by R. Hirzel, *Der Dialog: Ein literarhistorischer Versuch,* 2 vols. (Leipzig, 1895). For an exposition of the theoretical distinctions between rational controversy and rational inquiry, see N. Rescher, *Dialectics: A Controversy-oriented Approach to the Theory of Knowledge* (Albany, N.Y., 1977), esp. 46.

7. See Porphyry, *De abstinentia* 1.1.2–3 (Bouffartigue and Patillon, eds., 42).

8. K. Reisman, "Contrapuntal Conversations in an Antiguan Village," in R. Bauman and J. Scherzer, eds., *Explorations in the Ethnography of Speaking* (Cambridge, 1974), 110–24, at 121.

while an unruly argument of the kind described above was mere *thorubos*, tumult and noise, a faux pas in polite intellectual society.[9]

Social class, rules of the game, boundaries—these considerations
informed the ancients' articulated ideals concerning the rational *logos*.
While the expectation that reasoned speech should regulate and harmonize social life was difficult to fulfill, the centrality of the *logos* was
such that, from time to time, it manifested itself in the struggles between
men who did not move in the privileged circles of a Plutarch. In the
world of late antiquity, the superior claim of rational persuasion mod-
erated, in varying degrees, the conflicts between Jews and Christians,
between Christians and pagans, and among various Christian sects.

JEWS, PAGANS, AND EARLY CHRISTIANS IN CONTROVERSY

The fierce rivalry between Jews and Christians from the time of the early
principate gave rise to a large and long-lived polemical literature, much
of it in the genre of the dialogue.[10] The preponderance of this *adversus
Judaeos* material, including the *Argument between Simon the Jew and Theophilus the Christian*, the *Dialogue of Athanasius and Zacchaeus*, and the *Dialogue of Timothy and Aquila*, is so one-sidedly in the favor of the Christian position as to suggest that the writers adopted the dialogue form
merely to dramatize their anti-Jewish arguments.[11] Even so, we can catch
glimpses of the circumstances surrounding the face-to-face debates.

In the late second or early third century, a public debate took place
between a Christian and a Jewish proselyte in a town in Roman North
Africa—or so it was reported by one Christian writer.[12] Under the watch-

9. Plutarch, *Quaestiones conviviales* 7.10.714D: "ταῦτα τοῦ Γλαυκίου διεξελθόντος, ἔδο-
ξαν ἡμῖν ἐπιεικῶς οἱ θορυβώδεις ἐκεῖνοι κατακεκοιμῆσθαι λόγοι"; 9.1.737D: "ταῦτα μὲν
οὖν παρηγόρησεν ἀστείως τὸν θόρυβον". On one occasion, flute music had to be used to
distract a symposium discussion that had turned into an unseemly sophistic squabble:
"εἰς ἅμιλλαν ἀτερπῆ καὶ ἀγῶνα σοφιστικόν" (7.8.713F).

10. See the classic study of the genre, A. L. Williams, *Adversus Judaeos: A Bird's-Eye
View of Christian Apologiae until the Renaissance* (Cambridge, 1935). For a rhetorical analysis
of the pericopes showing debates between Jesus and other Jews in the Gospel of Mark,
see J. Dewey, *Markan Public Debate*, Society of Biblical Literature Dissertation Series, no. 48
(Chico, Calif., 1980).

11. Texts in A. von Harnack, ed., *Die Altercatio Simonis Iudaei et Theophili Christiani
nebst Untersuchungen über die anti-jüdische Polemik in der alten Kirche*. TU 1, no. 3 (Leipzig,
1883); and F. C. Conybeare, ed., *The Dialogues of Athanasius and Zacchaeus and of Timothy
and Aquila* (Oxford, 1898).

12. Tertullian, *Adversus Judaeos*. See critical text and commentary in H. Tränkle, ed.,
Q.S.F. Tertulliani Adversus Judaeos (Wiesbaden, 1964).

ful eyes of a group of spectators and partisan supporters (*partes*), the disputation dragged on for a full day.[13] When toward evening the dust finally settled, the Jewish convert emerged victorious: for the time being, Judaism's claim to represent *verus Israel*, the true Israel, had been tried and found authentic by the ad hoc judges of the debate—its immediate audience—in one corner of the Roman Empire.[14]

What I have surmised as the historical outcome of this debate was not, however, the end of the story, otherwise we should never have learned of the incident in the first place. The Christian retired to lick his wounds and settled on a rematch: not a repetition of the day's disappointing performance, but the composition of a dialogue between a Jewish and a Christian interlocutor. Tertullian's *Adversus Judaeos* was the fruit of this labor.

A dialogue written and published after such an unsatisfactory encounter could "set the record straight" and even turn to one's favor an ambiguous or adverse outcome.[15] By reaching beyond the immediate audience of the disputation, both sides could in effect claim victory by practicing what is known in modern American political parlance as spin-doctoring. Though we are lucky to have Tertullian's side of the story, it would mean that much more if we could also read the account of his apparently triumphant opponent. Such a document was probably never composed, for a winner did not need to labor in writing to immortalize a victory that had already been secured.

The heated controversies between Jews and early Christians involved a proprietary dispute: the authority to attach their own preferred interpretations to biblical scriptures and prophecies. Both groups ac-

13. Tertullian, *Adversus Judaeos* 1.1: "Proxime accidit: disputatio habita est Christiano et proselyto Iudaeo. alternis vicibus contentioso fune uterque diem in vesperam traxerunt. obstrepentibus quibusdam ex partibus singulorum nubilo quodam veritas obumbrabatur." The term *partes* was employed by Tertullian in a technical, forensic sense to refer to litigants in a dispute; see Tertullian, *Adv. Marcionem* 1.20 (CSEL 47:315): "Huic expeditissimae probationi defensio quoque a nobis necessaria est adversus obstrepitacula diversae partis."

14. No appointed judges are referred to in this dialogue. Perhaps here the audience performs the function of determining the outcome. In some literary dialogues, such as Plutarch's *De sollertia animalium*, Methodius' *De resurrectione*, and Minucius Felix's *Octavius*, a member from an intimate circle of friends was asked to judge a "school disputation."

15. Tertullian, *Adversus Judaeos* 1.1: "Placuit ergo, [ut] quod per concentum disputationis minus plene potuit dilucidari, curiosius inspectis lectionibus stilo questiones retractatas terminare." The motive for writing as stated in the *Adversus Judaeos* is surprisingly similar to one expressed in Tertullian's preface to *De fuga in persecutione* 1.1 (CSEL 76:17): "Ibidem ego oblocutus aliquid pro loco ac tempore et quarundam personarum importunitate semitractatam materiam abstuli mecum, plenius in eam de stilo nunc renutiaturus, utpote quam ei tua consultatio commendarat et condicio temporum suo iam nomine iniunxerat."

cepted—though with some notable exceptions, especially in the case of the Christians—the authenticity and authority of the Hebrew bible as holy writ; both embraced the interpretation of sacred texts as a valid method for ascertaining truth. The debates between Jews and Christians became sessions of competitive exegesis in which each side brandished its own catenae, compilations of prooftexts drawn from biblical sources, to advance its religious claims.

Jews and Christians may have contended for the scriptures by means of the scriptures, but they adhered for the most part to the general rules of disputation.[16] The rival parties could engage in this kind of verbal and textual contest mainly because they shared certain fundamental assumptions.[17] Without the common ground of received tradition and shared concerns and interests, they would have had little incentive or opportunity to engage in public disputations.[18]

Yet the Jews and Christians of the Roman Empire did not project their rival claims in vacuo. These predominantly urban dwellers lived in a diverse Hellenistic world, which they shared with a majority population of polytheists or pagans of all stripes. They could not afford to ignore this considerable third party; in fact, each sought, with varying degrees of success, to gain the respect of the gentiles.[19]

Solicitude for this population's goodwill may explain the peculiar nature of the narrative proem of Justin Martyr's *Dialogue with Trypho* (mid–second century).[20] On the one hand, the philosopher, a convert to Christianity, employs the techniques of exegesis to demonstrate that the followers of Christ were the true Israelites, and that scriptural prophecies foretold the coming of Christ.[21] On the other hand, Justin directly emulates Platonic dialogues by setting up the exchanges with a dra-

16. On the prominence of the theme of debate in the Pseudo-Clementine literature, see B. R. Voss, *Der Dialog in der frühchristlichen Literatur* (Munich, 1970), 60–78.

17. See Evagrius, *Altercatio legis inter Simonem Iudaeum et Theophilum Christianum* 1 (E. Bratke, ed., CSEL 45:2).

18. See J. G. Gager, *Kingdom and Community: The Social World of Early Christianity* (Englewood Cliffs, N.J., 1975), 66–92, on the important causal connection between group identity and social conflict.

19. H. Remus, "Justin Martyr's Argument with Judaism," in S. G. Wilson, ed., *Anti-Judaism in Early Christianity II: Separation and Polemic* (Waterloo, Ont., 1986), 59–80, esp. 74–80.

20. For a discussion of the form of this dialogue, see W. Bousset, *Jüdisch-christlicher Schulbetrieb in Alexandria und Rom: Literarische Untersuchungen zu Philo und Clemens von Alexandria, Justin und Irenäus* (Göttingen, 1915), 282ff.; Voss, *Dialog*, 26–39; and M. Hoffmann, *Der Dialog bei den christlichen Schriftstellern der ersten vier Jahrhunderte* TU 96 (Berlin, 1966), 10–28.

21. This question is thoroughly examined by O. Skarsaune, *The Proof from Prophecy: A Study in Justin Martyr's Proof-text Tradition* (Leiden, 1987).

matic preface in which, along a colonnaded avenue of Roman Ephesus, a philosophically trained Jew named Trypho approaches Justin for a discussion of things religious.[22] This proem, which places the writing in the genre of literary and philosophical dialogues, was not included solely as a stylistic ornament. In this brief preliminary exchange, Justin sought to show how the ensuing discussion—which is quite extensive and, arguably, quite tedious—could also have relevance for a readership that was neither Jewish nor Christian. When Trypho and his companions (οἱ μετὰ τοῦ Τρύφωνος)[23] requested a discussion with Justin, who was still proudly wearing his philosopher's cloak, the latter responded by asking the proselyte how he expected to profit by a philosophical discourse. After all, Justin exclaimed, Trypho already held in his grasp the wisdom of Moses the lawgiver and the prophets. Trypho's clever response was clearly designed to appeal to a broad, educated audience:

> Why not? Do the philosophers not fashion their every discourse with regard to the Deity? . . . And do they not continually entertain questions concerning his Oneness and Providence? Is this not indeed the duty of philosophy: to investigate the Deity?[24]

The author needed to assert that this ostensibly domestic quarrel between Jews and Christians was of concern to everyone with a philosophical bent because what followed the proem bore little resemblance to Graeco-Roman philosophical discourse. Justin and Trypho engaged in extensive exegetical fencing, drawing on specific passages from the Hebrew bible to support their own positions and to refute their opponent's. Their contentions over the rightful interpretation of biblical prophecies, acceptable to those familiar with Jewish-Christian debate, would have elicited little understanding from outsiders.[25]

Though Justin the Christian philosopher and apologist sternly op-

---

22. Justin, *Dialogus cum Tryphone* 1.3. Scholars do accept an underlying historical disputation; see S. Krauss, "The Jews in the Works of the Church Fathers," *Jewish Quarterly Review* 5 (1893), 123–30, at 124–25; L. W. Barnard, *Justin Martyr: His Life and Thought* (Cambridge, 1967), 23–24: "The best solution to the literary problem of the *Dialogue* is to postulate an original, historical debate with Trypho which occurred soon after A.D. 132, which Justin subsequently elaborated *c.* A.D. 160, drawing on oral and written testimony material which was known and used in the Church of his Day." The association of the *Dialogus* with Ephesus was made by Eusebius in *Hist. eccl.* 4.18.

23. For references to Trypho's associates, see, e.g., Justin, *Dialogus cum Tryphone* 1.3.

24. Justin, *Dialogus cum Tryphone* 1: "Τί γάρ; οὐχ οἱ φιλόσοφοι περὶ Θεοῦ τὸν ἅπαντα ποιοῦνται λόγον, ἐκεῖνος ἔλεγε, καὶ περὶ μοναρχίας αὐτοῖς καὶ προνοίας αἱ ζητήσεις γίγνονται ἑκάστοτε; ἢ οὐ τοῦτο ἔργον ἐστὶ φιλοσοφίας, ἐξετάζειν περὶ τοῦ Θεοῦ;"

25. See *Acta Iustini* 2 (H. Musurillo, ed., *Acts of the Christian Martyrs* [Oxford, 1972], 43–45, 48–49) on the abrupt change of subject by the magistrate Q. Junius Rusticus as soon as Justin began to expound his religious beliefs.

posed the unthinking acceptance of traditional beliefs by his polytheist contemporaries,[26] he knew well that his own arguments in favor of Christianity were unsatisfactory from the standpoint of philosophical demonstration.[27] It mattered little that he thought Christian truth-claims to be more worthy of trust than philosophical demonstrations or *apodeixeis*, for by his juxtaposition of the two Justin exhibited the standard expectations of proof among those trained in philosophy. Elsewhere, educated Christians who wished to conduct disputations based solely on the authority of scriptures likewise acknowledged their departure from normal philosophical practice, as did an interlocutor in Adimantus' *De recta in deum fide*, who said, "If you wish for there to be a wholly truthful investigation, take leave of philosophical arguments and be persuaded by scriptures alone."[28]

For their part, Greek philosophers ostensibly disapproved of straightforward reliance on authoritative "givens" even as they paid homage to the ancestral wisdom of eminent predecessors. Rational skepticism was by no means practiced by all philosophical polytheists, or even a majority of them. Cicero knew of certain Pythagoreans, for instance, whom he regarded as undesirably dogmatic, because they invoked what "the master said" as their authority in disputation. The orator roundly denounced this practice of justifying one's position *sine ratione*, without rational argument, solely on the basis of unexamined traditional authority, *auctoritas*.[29] Clearly, Cicero was protesting a contemporary trend toward the happy acceptance of dogmatic beliefs.

The same criticisms that Cicero had leveled at the Pythagoreans might be applied in equal measure to Jews and Christians. Christians, in particular, bore the brunt of such polemical assaults because they lacked the protective armor of tradition and antiquity that shielded the Jews from its most grievous blows. According to E. R. Dodds, "Had any

26. For a fruitful discussion of the relation between Justin's truth-claims and the sociology of knowledge, see Remus, "Justin Martyr's Argument with Judaism," 63–66.

27. See the explicit contrast between the two in *Dialogus cum Tryphone* 7.2. On Justin's philosophical background, see N. Hyldahl, *Philosophie und Christentum: Eine Interpretation der Einleitung zum Dialogs Justins* (Copenhagen, 1966), 272–92, and M. J. Edwards, "On the Platonic Schooling of Justin Martyr," *JTS* n.s. 42 (1991), 17–34.

28. Adimantus, *De recta in deum fide* 4.859 (Van de Sande Bakhuyzen, ed., GCS 4 [Leipzig, 1901]: 202): "Εἰ βούλεσθε μετὰ πάσης ἀληθείας τὴν ζήτησιν γενέσθαι, παραιτήσασθε τὰ φιλοσοφούμενα ταῖς γραφαῖς πειθόμενοι μόναις." Adimantus replies: "πεισθῶμεν ταῖς γραφαῖς."

29. Cicero, *De natura deorum* 1.5.10: "Non enim tam auctoritatis in disputando quam rationis momenta quaerenda sunt. Quin etiam obest plerumque iis qui discere volunt auctoritas eorum qui se docere profitentur; desinunt enim suum iudicium adhibere, id habent ratum quod ab eo quem probant iudicatum vident . . . tantum opinio praeiudicata poterat, ut etiam sine ratione valeret auctoritas."

cultivated pagan of the second century been asked to put in a few words
the difference between his own view of life and the Christian one, he
might reply that it was the difference between *logismos* and *pistis*, between reasoned conviction and blind faith."[30] Christians were considered by many contemporary critics to be incapable of rendering a satisfactory defense of their extraordinary beliefs. Some Christians, unable
to prove their claims by scriptures because pagans—who relied on them
only in polemics *against* Christians—would not assent to their authority,
even asserted, after the fashion of the apostle Paul, that the wisdom of
the world was mere foolishness to the faithful. Tertullian, boasting that
credo quia absurdum, self-consciously rejected the standards for demonstrations prescribed by a Hellenistic philosophical koine.[31]

Another of Tertullian's famous dicta was addressed primarily to
other Christians: "What has Athens to do with Jerusalem?"[32] According
to him, Christians ought to desist from attempting to enhance the re-
spectability of their religion by recasting its tenets in Stoic, Platonic, and
dialectical terms. For such was what "heretics" attempted when they

> introduce Aristotle, who instituted dialectic for them, the skill of join-
> ing together and pulling apart, subtle in its opinions, forced in its specu-
> lations, harsh in its arguments, a maker of controversies, an annoyance
> even to itself, investigating everything anew lest there is anything it
> will not have investigated.[33]

Tertullian championed a paradoxical and radically inward-looking
faith: "No one is wise unless he is a believer; no one is great unless he
is a Christian (Nemo est sapiens, nisi fidelis, nemo maior, nisi Christianus)."[34] One ought, in his view, to cultivate simplicity of soul by im-

30. E. R. Dodds, *Pagan and Christian in an Age of Anxiety: Some Aspects of Religious Experience from Marcus Aurelius to Constantine* (Cambridge, 1965), 120.
31. The supposition that Christianity and pagan *paideia* were, in Tertullian's view, mutually exclusive is no longer tenable. For a documentation of the uses of rhetorical techniques and argumentation by Tertullian "the sophist" to support the claims of Christianity, see R. D. Sider, *Ancient Rhetoric and the Art of Tertullian* (Oxford, 1971).
32. Tertullian, *De praescriptionibus haereticorum* 7 (E. Kroyman, ed., CSEL 70 [1942]: 10–11): "Quid ergo Athenis et Hierosolymis? quid academiae et ecclesiae? quid haereticis et Christianis? Nostra institutio de porticu Solomonis est, qui et ipse tradiderat dominum in simplicitate cordis esse quaerendum. Viderint qui Stoicum et Platonicum et dialecticum Christianismum protulerunt. Nobis curiositate opus non est post Christum Iesum, nec inquisitione post evangelium. Cum credimus, nihil desideramus ultra credere. Hoc enim prius credimus, non esse quod ultra credere debeamus."
33. Tertullian, *De praescriptionibus haereticorum* 7 (CSEL 70:9–10): "Arte inserunt Aristotelen, qui illis dialecticam instituit, artificem struendi et destruendi, versipellem in sententiis, coactam in coniecturis, duram in argumentis, operariam contentionum, molestam etiam sibi ipsam, omnia retractantem, ne quid ⟨re⟩tractaverit." The translation in the text is mine.
34. Tertullian, *De praescriptionibus haereticorum* 3 (CSEL 70:4).

bibing the gnomic wisdom of a Solomon, not the clever mental tricks of a Greek philosopher. But Tertullian proposed this hierarchy of knowledge more to dissuade Christians from the elitism and fissiparousness of competitive claims to gnosis than to confute pagans critical of Christian *simplicitas*.[35] The Christian wisdom, the true philosophy, was neither esoteric nor restricted to a privileged few, but was freely accessible to all believers, irrespective of rank or birth. Tertullian's invocation of the ideal of the *via universalis*, as expressed in his *Liber apologeticus* (46), was aptly summed up by Edward Gibbon, who infused in it his own signature prejudices:

> [Formerly,] a chosen society of philosophers, men of a liberal education and curious disposition, might silently meditate, and temperately discuss in the gardens of Athens or the library of Alexandria, the abstruse questions of metaphysical science. The lofty speculations, which neither convinced the understanding nor agitated the passions of the Platonists themselves, were carelessly overlooked by the idle, the busy, and even the studious part of mankind. But after the *Logos* has been revealed as the sacred object of the faith, the hope, and the religious worship of the Christians, the mysterious system was embraced by a numerous and increasing multitude in every province of the Roman world. Those persons who, from their age, or sex, or occupations, were the least qualified to judge, who were the least exercised in the habits of abstract reasoning, aspired to contemplate the economy of Divine Nature: and it is the boast of Tertullian that a Christian mechanic could readily answer such questions as had perplexed the wisest of the Grecian sages.[36]

We may be tempted to accept this portrayal as a valid social description. It is not inconceivable that certain Christian tradesmen in Tertullian's time, in keeping with the Graeco-Roman tradition of the self-taught man known as *autodidaktos* or *theodidaktos*,[37] flouted the prevalent conventions of their society, which stipulated gentlemanly *otium* and social privilege as *conditiones sine qua non* for attaining true elevated knowledge and the competence to discourse on issues concerning the

35. See Tertullian, *Adversus Valentinianos* 2 (CSEL 47:178): "Ideoque simplices notamur apud illos, ut hoc tantum, non etiam sapientes; quasi statim deficere cogatur a simplicitate sapientia, domino utramque iungente: estote prudentes ut serpentes et simplices ut columbae. aut si nos propterea insipientes, quia simplices, num ergo et illi propterea non simplices, quia sapientes? et tamen malim meam partem meliori sumi vitio, si forte: praestat minus sapere quam peius, errare quam fallere. porro facies dei spectatur in simplicitate quarendi, ut docet ipse Sophia, non quidem Valentini, sed Solomonis."

36. E. Gibbon, *Decline and Fall of the Roman Empire* 21.1 (New York, n.d.), pt. 1, p. 680.

37. See a discussion of the inscriptional evidence for οἱ αὐτοδίδακτοι and οἱ θεοδίδακτοι in R. A. Kaster, *The Guardians of Language: The Grammarian and Society in Late Antiquity* (Berkeley, Calif., 1988), 49–50, esp. nn. 65–72.

divine. Still, we can hardly expect that many educated pagans paid them heed, or showed much respect for the ideas expressed.

As far as we know, public disputation with a *pars melior* trained in philosophy was not the most common means by which early Christians attracted adherents to their faith. The literary record abounds with exceptions that prove the rule. It is unlikely that St. Paul debated publicly in the Athenian agora with philosophers and passersby, or delivered a discourse before the council of Areopagus concerning the "unknown God" (Acts 17:16–34), yet the author of Luke-Acts thought it useful to depict the Apostle to the Gentiles in such a light.[38] And the genteel and cultivated discussion in Minucius Felix's *Octavius,* in which Christian and pagan interlocutors engaged in a give-and-take school disputation over the validity of Christian beliefs, was almost certainly entirely fictive, yet its author used the genre of Latin literary dialogue to fashion an apologetic construct to suggest that such discussions *might* have taken place.[39]

Early Christians mainly relied on less exalted and rigorous means, including the use of "inartistic proofs," to defend their faith and persuade potential converts. This emphasis may be due to demography: during this period, Christians and their potential converts hailed from the humbler segments of society, which traditionally had no training in philosophy.[40] As one alert pagan observed:

> Most people are unable to follow any demonstrative argument (ἀπο-δεικτικοὶ λόγοι?) consecutively . . . just as now we see the people called the Christians drawing their faith from parables [and miracles], and yet sometimes acting in the same way [as those who philosophize]. For their contempt of death [and of its sequel] is patent to us every day, and likewise their restraint in cohabitation. For they include not only men but also women who refrain from cohabiting all through their lives; and they also number individuals who, in self-discipline and self-

38. See J. Dupont, "Le discours à l'Aréopage (Ac 17, 22–31), lieu de rencontre entre christianisme et hellénisme," *Nouvelles études sur les Actes des Apôtres* (Paris, 1984), 380–423. Other grand preaching scenes can be found in Acts 13:16–41, 20:18–35, 22:1–21, and 24:10–21, on which generally see U. Wilcken, *Die Missionsreden der Apostelgeschichte* (Neukirchen-Vluyn, 1961; 2d ed., 1963), esp. 87ff. For a more humble (and more plausible) *Sitz im Leben* of Pauline missionary activities, see E. A. Judge, "St. Paul and Classical Society," *JAC* 15 (1972), 19–36, and R. F. Hock, "The Workshop as a Social Setting for Paul's Missionary Teaching," *Catholic Biblical Quarterly* 41 (1979): 438–50.

39. See Voss, *Dialog,* 40–50, and Hoffmann, *Dialog,* 28–39. It was therefore perhaps aimed at appealing to and converting the educated; see J. Wotke, "Der Octavius des Minucius Felix als christlicher λόγος προτρεπτικός," *Commentationes Vindobonenses* 1 (1935): 110–28.

40. See R. MacMullen, "Two Types of Conversion to Early Christianity," *VChr* 37 (1983): 174–92.

control in matters of food and drink, and in their keen pursuit of justice, have attained a pitch not inferior to that of genuine philosophers.[41]

This rendition, by Richard Walzer, from the Arabic of a statement attributed to Galen (in an epitome of Plato's *Republic*) suggests how, despite the lack of logical demonstration of their claims, Roman Christians were admired by as demanding a judge as the illustrious Pergamene physician-philosopher. Though Stephen Gero has shown convincingly that the Arabic passage reflects later emendations by Christian apologists, he concedes that the first part of the statement—concerning the Christians' use of irrational forms of demonstration—may well be original.[42] This strikes me as a fair guess, for an apologetic comment phrased in this concessive fashion would not normally have arisen unless to refute an authentic and widely held criticism. Further, the passage's emphasis on the rationality of religious and philosophical beliefs harmonizes well with the views expressed in many of Galen's undisputed writings, in which he evinces a sincere preoccupation with philosophical demonstration as a necessary guide to important choices in life.

Galen followed the advice of his father, whom he greatly admired, by avoiding attachment to any of the contemporary philosophical and medical *sectae* without thorough and lengthy investigation of their teachings.[43] Galen set great store by the philosophical methods of establishing *epistēmē*, or certain knowledge, by which what was true could be distinguished from what merely appeared to be so; his extremely high standard of proof was outlined in his *De optima secta*.[44] The central question was how to arrive at incontrovertible knowledge (εἰς βεβαίαν γνῶσιν).[45] The Pergamene eventually opted—as did many of his contemporaries—for a deliberate eclecticism, because the certainty he sought ever eluded him.[46]

41. R. Walzer, *Galen on Jews and Christians* (London, 1949), 15–16; his full and helpful discussion appears on 18–74. See also R. L. Wilken, *The Christians as the Romans Saw Them* (New Haven, Conn., 1984), 68–93.

42. S. Gero, "Galen on the Christians: A Reappraisal of the Arabic Evidence," *Orientalia Christiana Periodica* 56 (1990): 371–411, at 404: "The introductory statement, which criticizes the exclusive reliance on non-rational motivations . . . bears the stamp of originality." See also Gero's textual comments on this passage, which draw on other Arabic sources, on 404–11.

43. See texts on Galen's life conveniently collected by P. Moraux in *Galen de Pergame: Souvenirs d'un médecin* (Paris, 1985), 15–16, 42–48. See also R. B. Edlow, *Galen on Language and Ambiguity: An English Translation of Galen's 'De captionibus (On Fallacies)'* (Leiden, 1977), 5.

44. Text in J. Marquardt, ed., *Galen: Scripta Minora* 1 (Leipzig, 1884).

45. Galen, *De optima secta* 2.42 (Marquardt, ed., 1:84). On Galen's theory of knowledge, see M. Frede, "On Galen's Epistemology," in V. Nutton, ed., *Galen: Problems and Prospects* (London, 1981), 65–86.

46. See Wilken, *As the Romans Saw Them*, 73–77.

The question of how others discerned the veracity of their claims had concerned Greek physicians at least since the Hippocratic writings, for they often had to appeal beyond their professional circle for recognition.[47] This concern was in part a reaction against the traditional temple medicines practiced by those who could not, or would not, articulate a rational scientific theory for their *praxeis*.[48] For Galen, appeals to customary usage and established textual authority did not suffice as foundations of true knowledge, whether in the practice of medicine or in other areas of life. Galen, who enjoyed access to libraries and the leisure to cultivate broad-based knowledge, understandably scorned the dogmatism of others, whose positions stemmed partly from the realities of their limited choices. He generally deprecated blind trust in the dictates of an authority or in the accepted wisdom of authoritative texts, including the Jews' reliance on the Laws of Moses, which he otherwise admired.[49]

The charge that Christians were unusually obstinate and unyielding to rational persuasion in matters of faith echoed widely in antiquity. Such a criticism could arguably be applied with justice to the pagans of Galen's time as well,[50] yet to outsiders at least, Christians appeared especially unresponsive to pleas for philosophical demonstration.[51] To sturdy souls convinced that divine revelation was their exclusive birthright, amelioration of their views—the epistemological principle upon which a dialectic of inquiry is predicated—was unnecessary, even undesirable. The proof of their belief rested in their supreme conviction, which they displayed before the world by becoming martyrs in Roman

47. See G. E. R. Lloyd, *The Revolutions of Wisdom: Studies in the Claims and Practice of Ancient Greek Science* (Berkeley, Calif., 1987), 88–102. See especially his nuanced discussion of the implications various kinds of audiences had for the cast of the practitioners' rival truth-claims.

48. See the fruitful discussion of these issues as they surfaced in the preclassical period by G. E. R. Lloyd, *Magic, Reason and Experience: Studies in the Origins and Development of Greek Sciences* (Cambridge, 1979), esp. 37–49.

49. Walzer, *Galen*, 10–11: "They compare those who practice medicine without scientific knowledge to Moses, who framed laws for the tribe of the Jews, since it is his method in his books to write without offering proofs, saying 'God commanded, God spake.'" And on 14–15: "If I had in mind people who taught their pupils in the same way as the followers of Moses and Christ teach theirs—for they order them to accept everything on faith—I should not have given you a definition." On the reception of Moses by pagans, see J. G. Gager, *Moses in Greco-Roman Paganism*, Society of Biblical Literature Monograph Series no. 16 (Nashville, Tenn., 1972).

50. Galen, *De optima secta* 2.43–44 (Marquardt, ed., 1:84–85). On Galen's commentaries on the Aristotelian logical corpus, see Walzer, *Galen*, 78–79.

51. See Porphyry's charge in Eusebius, *Praeparatio evangelica* 1.2. Generally, see S. Benko, "Pagan Criticism of Christianity during the First Two Centuries, A.D.," *ANRW* 2.23.2 (Berlin, 1980), 1055–1118.

arenas. This histrionic bravado, a Christian brand of demonstration, disturbed even the philosophical temper of Marcus Aurelius.[52]

Certain Christians, eager for recognition outside of their own religious community, proposed a more intellectually defensible Christianity, but more often than not their attempts to respond to pagan critiques were regarded by their fellow believers as heretical.[53] Others, such as Clement of Alexandria, proposed the use of philosophical dialectic as a means of differentiating proper from improper Christians.[54]

Another educated pagan found absolutely nothing to commend in Christianity. Unlike Galen, whose rationalist outlook promised at least a degree of openmindedness, Celsus was a resolute traditionalist and apologist for the pagan heritage who based his arguments for polytheism on its greater antiquity and on the sanctity of customary usage. This determined foe of the Christian religion underscored what he regarded as the disturbingly unphilosophical modes of persuasion on which Christians relied to advance their faith:

> In private houses also we see wool-workers, cobblers, laundry-workers, and the most illiterate and bucolic yokels, who would not dare to say anything at all in front of their elders and more intelligent masters. But whenever they get hold of children in private and some stupid women with them, they let out some astounding statements as, for example, that they must not pay any attention to their father and school-teachers, but must obey them; they [the Christians] say that these talk nonsense and have no understanding, and that in reality they neither know nor are able to do anything good, but are taken up with mere empty chatter. But they [the Christians] alone, they say, know the right way to live, and if the children would believe them, they would become happy and make their home happy as well. And if just as they [the Christians] are speaking they see one of the school-teachers coming, or some intel-

---

52. Marcus Aurelius, *Meditationes* 11.3. Generally, see P. A. Brunt, "Marcus Aurelius and the Christians," in C. Deroux, ed., *Studies in Latin Literature and Roman History* (Brussels, 1979), 1:483–519.

53. As did Theodotus of Byzantium and his associates in Rome, who were probably responding to Galen's criticisms; see Hippolytus, *Refutatio* 7.35, and also Eusebius, *Hist. eccl.* 5.28.13 (Lake, ed., 1:520–23): "They have not feared to corrupt divine Scriptures, they have nullified the rule of ancient faith, they have not known Christ, they do not inquire what the divine Scriptures say, but industriously (φιλοπόνως) consider what syllogistic figure (σχῆμα συλλογισμοῦ) may be found for the support of their atheism. If anyone adduced to them a text of divine Scripture they inquire whether it can be put in the form of a conjunctive or disjunctive syllogism. . . ." On similar accusations against later Christians, see Chapter 4.

54. See the discussion of Clement of Alexandria's *Stromateis* in A. Le Boulluec, *La notion d'hérésie dans la littérature grecque, I–III siècles* (Paris, 1985), 2:276–88. See also E. F. Osborn, "Reason and the Rule of Faith in the Second Century AD," in R. Williams, ed., *The Making of Orthodoxy: Essays in Honour of Henry Chadwick* (Cambridge, 1989), 40–61.

ligent person, or even the father himself, the more cautious of them flee in all directions; but the more reckless urge the children on to rebel. They whisper to them that in the presence of their father and their schoolmasters they [the Christians] do not feel able to explain anything to the children, since they do not want to have anything to do with the silly and obtuse teachers who are totally corrupted and far gone in wickedness and who inflict punishment on the children. But, if they like, they [the children] should leave father and their schoolmasters, and go along with the women and little children who are their play-fellows to the wooldresser's shop, or to the cobbler's or the washer-woman's shop, that they may learn perfection. And by saying this they [the Christians] persuade [the children].[55]

Celsus characterized Christians as subversive infiltrators who targeted their efforts at women, children, and old men—people whose powers of judgment were customarily considered deficient—and who won them over by specious arguments and "old wives' tales."[56] In his view, Christians had wrongfully bypassed the dominant authority of the adult males, in particular the *patresfamilias*, by appealing directly to the more gullible segments of Roman society. Christians employed this disgraceful tactic of taking advantage of the legally acknowledged weaknesses (*to asthenes, levitas,* and *infirmitas*) of those compromised by their gender and age because, according to Celsus, they were unable to defend their views before cognoscenti such as himself who possessed *paideia*, good education and moral character, and sound judgment. Since he could not otherwise come to grips with his elusive but seemingly successful adversaries, Celsus composed *Alēthēs Logos* (The true doctrine, c. 178–80), an exposé of Christian fraud using numerous established Jewish arguments, and in so doing threw down a gauntlet. The challenge waited three generations for the Christian intellectual Origen to take it up by composing his famous *Contra Celsum* to refute Celsus' denunciations *seriatim.*

One of Celsus' attacks turned on the plebeian character of Christian literature, unfavorably comparing the *Altercatio Jasonis et Papisci*—an early Christian anti-Jewish dialogue composed by Ariston of Pella following the Bar Kochba Revolt—with pagan literary dialogues.[57] Celsus especially objected to its use of allegory to "explain away" difficult points.[58]

55. Origen, *Contra Celsum* 2.55 (H. Chadwick, ed., *Contra Celsum* [Cambridge, 1953], 165–66).

56. See Origen, *Contra Celsum* 1.9.

57. See Hoffmann, *Dialog,* 9–10.

58. Origen, *Contra Celsum* 4.38, 4.52. On the pagan polemic against Christians' use of allegory on the Hebrew bible, see Eusebius, *Hist. eccl.* 6.19.4 and G. Binder, "Eine Polemik des Porphyrios gegen die allegorische Auslegung des Alten Testaments durch die

Origen admitted Celsus' criticism of the "lowbrow" nature of the *Altercatio*, but argued that the work was directed at simple Christians to bolster their faith.[59] To speak to the *simplices*, a *sermo humilis* was in order,[60] though Origen himself was anything but a simple Christian.[61]

PUBLIC DEBATE AND DISPUTE SETTLEMENT AMONG EARLY CHRISTIANS

In the mid–third century, Origen was among the foremost intellectual luminaries of the Greek east, held in the highest regard not only for his immense learning but also for his ascetic convictions and attainments.[62] Deriving additional charismatic authority from his ministrations to the poor and visits to confessors in the prisons of Alexandria,[63] this young hearer of Ammonius Saccas rapidly gained wide renown among Christians and non-Christians alike.[64] Easily conversant and respected in both intellectual traditions, he "thought it right to examine both the opinions of the heretics, and also the claim that the philosophers make to speak concerning truth."[65]

Origen conducted discussions and debates with an impressive cast of characters, many of whom wished to test (πεῖραν) his knowledge of

---

Christen," *ZPE* 3 (1968): 81–95. For a fairly simpleminded, "do-it-yourself" handbook to Christian allegories, see A. Henrichs and E. M. Husselman, "Christian Allegorizations (P. Mich. Inv. 3718)," *ZPE* 3 (1968), 175–89.

59. Origen, *Contra Celsum* 4.52. On the possible dependence of Origen on Galen, and of the two of them on Paul the Apostle, see R. M. Grant, "Paul, Galen and Origen," *JTS* n.s. 34 (1983), 533–36. On Origen's concern for the *simplices*, see, e.g., G. af Hällström, *Fides simpliciorum according to Origen of Alexandria* (Helsinki, 1984), esp. 23–32.

60. The *locus classicus* for the notion of *sermo humilis* is E. Auerbach's *Literary Language and its Public in Late Latin Antiquity and in the Middle Ages* (London, 1965). See now a parallel discussion concerning the switch from a learned to a colloquial style of writing among Sung Confucianists in China, in D. K. Gardner, "Modes of Thinking and Modes of Discourse in the Sung: Some Thoughts on the *Yü-lu* ('Recorded Conversations') Texts," *Journal of Asian Studies* 50 (1991): 574–603.

61. Origen could certainly speak the language of Aristotle and Chrysippus. On his use of Stoic logic, see L. Roberts, "Origen and Stoic Logic," *TAPA* 101 (1970), 433–44, and J. M. Rist, "The Importance of Stoic Logic in the *Contra Celsum*," in H. J. Blumenthal and R. A. Markus, eds., *Neoplatonism and Early Christian Thought: Essays in Honour of A. H. Armstrong* (London, 1971), 64–78.

62. Eusebius, *Hist. eccl.* 6.2.6–9, 6.3.9–13.

63. Eusebius, *Hist. eccl.* 6.3.3–4.

64. Eusebius, *Hist. eccl.* 6.3.1–3, 6.19.6. See Porphyry's unflattering remarks in Eusebius, *Hist. eccl.* 6.19.

65. Eusebius, *Hist. eccl.* 6.19.12 (Oulton, ed., 2:60–61).

logoi.[66] Slightly before 215, he was politely summoned to an audience with the Roman governor of Arabia, who greatly desired to exchange words with him.[67] His growing reputation caused Julia Mamaea to bring him from Palestinian Caesarea to her court in Antioch to make trial (πεῖραν) of his abilities.[68] Though not certain, it is quite likely that he also held discussions with Jews during his long stay in Palestine.[69] The Alexandrian also debated with heterodox Christians, including followers of Valentinus:[70] Candidus, a certain Bassus,[71] and another Valentinian named Ambrose. This last, who later persuaded Origen to commit his views to writing, was converted after being refuted (ἐλεγχθείς) by Origen in debate.[72]

Origen did not limit his use of *logoi* to debates with religious outsiders, for a full roster of his discussions with other Christians has survived. These accounts are important in that they clearly document the use of public debate as a means for restoring social order and discipline within divided Christian communities.

Origen was especially active in Roman Arabia where, on numerous occasions, he participated in "town meetings" convened to resolve disputes among Christians.[73] One such meeting came about after Beryllus, the bishop of Bostra in Arabia, uttered statements arguing that Christ did not exist before his incarnation, occasioning great offense among other Christians.[74] Origen was given the first chance to enter into dialogue with Beryllus (κάτεισι μὲν εἰς ὁμιλίαν τὰ πρῶτα τῷ ἀνδρί). His

66. Eusebius, *Hist. eccl.* 6.18.2–4 (Oulton, ed., 2:54–55).

67. Eusebius, *Hist. eccl.* 6.19.15; see T. D. Barnes, *Constantine and Eusebius* (Cambridge, Mass., 1981), 83.

68. Eusebius, *Hist. eccl.* 6.21.3–4.

69. On Origen's dealings with Jews and rabbis, see Origen, *Contra Celsum* 1.45, 1.55; and N. de Lange, *Origen and the Jews: Studies in Jewish-Christian Relations in Third-Century Palestine* (Cambridge, 1976), 89–102.

70. On the way in which some of Origen's opponents managed to avoid direct debate with him simply by rewriting his works and then disseminating their own versions, see Rufinus, *De adulteratione librorum Origenous* 7 (CCSL 20:11–12).

71. The debate with Candidus is referred to in Jerome, *Adversus Rufinum* 2.19; the one with Bassus in Origen's *Epistula ad Africanum* in *PG* 11:49A.

72. Eusebius, *Hist. eccl.* 6.18.1 (Oulton, ed., 2:54–55): "Ambrose, who held the views of the heresy of Valentinus, was refuted by the truth as presented by Origen, and, as if his mind were illuminated by light, gave his adhesion to the true doctrine as taught by the church." Origen, according to Jerome, *Ep.* 92.4.1, wrote *Libri in resurrectionis* "quos scripsit ad Ambrosium *dialecticum morem imitans disputandi, in quo sciscitatio est et responsio*" (emphasis mine).

73. On the established custom of inviting foreign arbitrators to settle disputes in and among the Greek city-states, see L. Robert, "Les juges étrangers dans la cité grecque," in his *Opera Minora Selecta* (Amsterdam, 1989), 5:137–54.

74. Eusebius, *Hist. eccl.* 6.33.2.

goal, according to Eusebius, was "to discover what were his opinions, and when he knew what it was that he asserted, he corrected what was unorthodox, and, persuading him by reasoning, established him in the truth as to the doctrine, and restored him to his former sound opinion."[75]

The Caesarean Eusebius claimed to have seen the actual *acta* recording the discussions (διάλεξεις) between the two men.[76] From these and other documents, Pamphilius of Caesarea and Eusebius together edited a volume of *dialektoi Origenous*, of which all but one have perished. Though Origen's debate with Beryllus is not extant, we possess unearthed papyri recording a similar encounter unattested in Eusebius' work.

Once more, the location was Roman Arabia. Around 245, a regional synod was convoked in response to a disturbance (κίνησις) caused by the controversial christological doctrine promoted by a local bishop named Heracleides.[77] Heracleides' dissident theological stance rocked the community, threatening to introduce changes into the congregation's beloved and traditional eucharistic prayer, and brought about considerable social turmoil among the Christians.[78]

Origen was once again called in. As arbitrator, he instituted an *anakrisis*, a cross-examination of the disputing parties aimed at establishing the facts of the case alluded to on the papyri.[79] The preliminary and auxiliary nature of this procedure may explain why the exchanges were not recorded. Origen may also have judged it prudent to exclude from the written *acta* a negotiation held in private, behind stage as it were, so that during the preliminary meeting itself all sides could enjoy the widest latitude in explaining, discussing, and compromising without fear of public disgrace. Otherwise, existing differences might even become more entrenched as protagonists, equating the accommodation of opposing views with public defeat, hardened their positions with defiance.

Much more ceremonial in nature, the public discussions that took place before the assembled congregation comprised the official *acta* of

75. Eusebius, *Hist. eccl.* 6.33.2 (Oulton, ed., 2:86–87).

76. Eusebius, *Hist. eccl.* 6.33.3; also Jerome, *De viris illustribus* 66 (*PL* 23:705).

77. Relevant text and discussion in J. Scherer, ed., *Entretien d'Origène avec Héraclide*, SC 67 (Paris, 1960); *editio princeps* in J. Scherer, ed., *Entretien d'Origène avec Héraclide et les évêques ses collègues, sur le Père, le Fils, et l'âme*, Publications de la Société Fouad Iᵉʳ de Papyrologie, Textes et Documents 9 (Cairo, 1949). Some emendations are offered by R. Merkelbach in "Textkritische Bemerkungen zur 'Debatte des Origenes mit Herakleidas,'" *ZPE* 3 (1968): 192–96.

78. Origen, *Dialogus* 4.17 (Scherer, ed., 62–63).

79. The preliminary interrogation by a presiding magistrate is well-attested in archaic and classical Athens, Sparta, and Rome; see D. M. MacDowell, *The Law in Classical Athens* (Ithaca, N.Y., 1978), 239–42, and E. M. Carawan, "*Erōtesis:* Interrogation in the Courts of Fourth-Century Athens," *GRBS* 24 (1983): 209–26, esp. 211–12n. 10.

the synod. The exchanges followed the model of an interview rather than that of an agonistic debate, and Origen, like the Socrates of Platonic dialogues, gently yet firmly pressed Heracleides to express and defend his own controversial views. The prevailing tone was that of a friendly conversation: the sincere goodwill demonstrated by Origen and his respondents recalls the intimate collegiality of Plutarch's dialogues. An instance of this bonhomie was Heracleides' behavior after he was maneuvered by Origen into saying that the Son was "different from the Father" and hence a second god, a claim that profoundly shocked his audience. Realizing that he had been neatly refuted, he courteously conceded defeat, agreed to never again raise the tricky theological question of christology, and subscribed to (ὑπόγραψαι) Origen's preferred doctrinal formula before the assembled bishops and laity.[80]

The next segment of the papyri describes a session, equally congenial, in which Origen responded to questions from others. The tenor was that of a revered teacher dispensing wisdom to respectful disciples. At the end of the session, these Christians pronounced their complete satisfaction with Origen's views and subscribed to his formulation just as Heracleides had earlier. The process of mending shattered solidarity continued. Origen called on the assembled congregation (ὁ λαός) to witness and act as guarantor of the outcome of these discussions.[81] That Origen was successful in using the vehicle of a public debate to resolve a divisive religious conflict (which could not fail to have social ramifications as well) may be credited to his conciliatory posture and to the deferential attitudes of the other protagonists, who yielded to Origen's demonstration of the truth without intransigence.

Around 247, Origen once again played the key role at a local Christian synod, this one convened to examine the belief that the human soul dissipates at death and reconstitutes at the general resurrection, a view causing commotion within the Christian community. Origen again successfully employed the public debate as a forum for Christian dispute settlement:

> When a synod of no small dimensions was then assembled together, Origen was again invited, and there opened a discussion in public (κινήσας τε λόγους ἐπὶ τοῦ κοινοῦ) on the subject in question, with such power that he changed the opinions of those who had formerly been deluded.[82]

80. Origen, *Dialogus* 4.21 (Scherer, ed., 62–63).
81. Origen, *Dialogus* 4.28–5.7 (Scherer, ed., 62–65).
82. Eusebius, *Hist. eccl.* 6.37.1 (Oulton, ed., 2:90–91). On Origen's views on the correction of errors in others, see Le Boulluec, *La notion d'hérésie dans la littérature grecque,* 2:535–38.

In his repeated attempts to reconcile divided Christian communities, Origen never took for granted an ideal, apostolic *consensus omnium* among Christians; instead, he saw unity as the fruit of constant vigilance. Refuting an accusation by Celsus, Origen confessed with refreshing candor that Christians had never been, even from the beginning, "of one mind." This admission, he said, should occasion no scandal, for "anyone who criticizes Christianity on account of the sects might also criticize the teaching of Socrates; for from his instruction many schools have come into being, whose adherents do not hold the same opinion."[83] When Origen claimed for Christianity the name of philosophy, it was not just to garner prestige but to appropriate the indulgence accorded philosophical sects. Also, Origen wished to represent Christianity as another philosophical *secta* because his own circle operated in some respects as philosophical groups did. Origen's disciple Gregory Thaumaturgus lectured as a philosopher would, freely entertaining questions from his audience and debating with pagan intellectual *agōnistikōs* in an eristic fashion.[84]

Broadly speaking, the influence of rational *logoi* and persuasion extended even to the conciliar proceedings of early Christians. Our discussion concerning Origen suggests that the position of third-century Christians as merely one religious and social group among many enabled relatively unauthoritarian and unregulated colloquia to be used successfully to air and settle internal differences.

This fundamental aspect of pre-Constantinian Christian debates is epitomized by an encounter between Dionysius of Alexandria (d. 264), Origen's pupil, and the Christians in the Arsinoite nome. While bishop of Alexandria, Dionysius received word of a spreading millenarian movement in the Fayum. Upon his arrival at the site of the disturbance, he made inquiries and discovered that the millenarian expectations of the local Christians were justified on the basis of the writings of a Bishop Nepos, whose work on the Revelation of John allegedly inspired wide-

83. Origen, *Contra Celsum* 3.11 (Chadwick, ed., 134–35). Celsus' argument is as follows: "But since they have spread to become a multitude, they are divided and rent asunder, and each wants to have his own party . . ." (*Contra Celsum* 3.12; Chadwick, ed., 135). For Origen's analysis of Christian factionalism, see Le Boulluec, *La notion d'hérésie dans la littérature grecque*, esp. 2:504–7.

84. See Syriac text of *Ad Theopompum* in P. de Lagarde, ed., *Analecta Syriaca* (Leipzig, 1858), 46–64. For a characterization of Gregory's *Dialexis pros Aelianon*, see Basil of Caesarea, *Ep.* 210 (Deferrari, ed., 3:208–9), who described it as an eristic, rather than a dogmatic, writing: "οὐ δογματικῶς εἴρηται, ἀλλ᾽ ἀγωνιστικῶς." See the broader discussion of Gregory Thaumaturgus in Voss, *Dialog*, 86–90, and Hoffmann, *Dialog*, 59–67.

spread eschatological hopes.[85] Accordingly, Dionysius arranged for a public debate between himself and the local Christians, the account of which was given by Eusebius, who narrated it from Dionysius' perspective:

> When I came to the nome of Arsinoë, where, as thou knowest, this doctrine had long been prevalent, so that schisms and defections of whole churches had taken place, I called together the presbyters and teachers of the brethren in the villages (there were present also such of the brethren as wished), and I urged them to hold the examination of the question publicly (δημοσίᾳ τὴν ἐξέτασιν ποιήσασθαι τοῦ λόγου προετρεψάμην). And when they brought me this book as some invincible weapon and rampart, I sat with them and for three successive days from morn till night attempted to correct what had been written.[86]

The debate focused not on the merit of millenarian expectations, which had presumably been the prime cause of offense, but on the authorship of the Revelation of John.[87] In other words, immediate social concerns were addressed in exegetical terms. Dionysius, using scholarly skills clearly attributable to his training by Origen, was able to convince the leaders of the local movement that the text in question was not written by the disciple John and therefore did not deserve the serious consideration the Fayumite Christians were giving it. Yet such an outcome was only possible because Dionysius' debaters abided by the rules of debate that he had set down. The bishop recalled:

> On that occasion I conceived the greatest admiration for the brethren, their firmness, love of truth, facility in following an argument, and intelligence, as we propounded in order (ἐν τάξει) and with forbearance (μετ᾽ ἐπιεικείας) the questions (ἐρωτήσεις), the difficulties (ἐπαπορήσεις) raised and the points of agreement (συγκαταθέσεις); on the one hand refusing to cling obstinately (φιλονείκως) and at all costs (even though they were manifestly wrong) to opinions once held; and on the other hand not shirking the counter-arguments (ἀντιλογίας), but as far as possible attempting to grapple with the questions in hand and master them. Nor, if convinced by reason, were we ashamed to change our opinions and give our assent; but conscientiously and unfeignedly and with hearts laid open to God we accepted whatever was established by the proofs and teachings of the holy Scriptures (τὰ ταῖς ἀποδείξεσι καὶ διδασκαλίαις τῶν ἁγίων γραφῶν συνιστανόμενα).[88]

---

85. Eusebius, *Hist. eccl.* 7.24.6. See now a discussion of this episode in D. M. Frankfurter, *Elijah in Upper Egypt: The Apocalypse of Elijah and Early Egyptian Christianity*, Studies in Antiquity and Christianity 7 (Minneapolis, 1993), ch. 10.

86. Eusebius, *Hist. eccl.* 7.24.6–7 (Oulton, ed., 2:194–95).

87. On a fruitful sociological interpretation of early Christian millenarianism and the Book of Revelation, see Gager, *Kingdom and Community*, 20–65.

88. Eusebius, *Hist. eccl.* 7.24.8 (Oulton, ed., 2:194–95).

This ideal scenario for a debate lasting three successive days was sustained by a common trust in scriptural authorities, by mutual adherence to a code of civility, and by the forswearing of intransigence, so that points of contention could be addressed by questions and answers in an orderly fashion. Dionysius was rewarded for his patient, noncoercive approach to durable consensus with his debaters' open admiration and promise of cooperation:

> In the end the leader and introducer of this teaching, Coracion, as he was called, in the hearing of all the brethren present, assented, and testified to us that he would no longer adhere to it, nor discourse upon it, nor mention nor teach it, since he had been sufficiently convinced by the contrary arguments. And as to the rest of the brethren, some rejoiced at the joint conference, and the mutual deference and unanimity which all displayed.[89]

Aside from this happy ending, a suspiciously satisfactory closure to the story, we do not know whether Dionysius' exegetical debate was successful in quelling what appeared to be a widespread millenarian movement. Dionysius himself harbored enough residual concern to compose *On Divine Promises*, a work designed to counter Nepos' arguments once and for all, because

> if he [Nepos] were present and putting forward his opinions merely in words, conversation, without writing, would be sufficient, persuading and instructing by question and answer (δι ἐρωτήσεως καὶ ἀποκρίσεως) 'them that oppose themselves.' But when a book is published . . . then we are compelled to argue with Nepos as if he were present.[90]

When it emerged that social and religious differences between Christians could be adequately addressed with a public debate based on the interpretation of sacred texts, the written word assumed greater importance. This common textual focus rendered the debates exercises in competitive scriptural exegesis, and as such they could be conducted on terms of parity, without any invocation of hierarchical authority or threats of compulsion.[91]

Dionysius was unable to attend the Council of Antioch in 264, convened to examine the teachings of Paul of Samosata, an influential

89. Eusebius, *Hist. eccl.* 7.24.9 (Oulton, ed., 2:194–97). On the significance of deference in a traditional society, see J. G. A. Pocock, "The Classical Theory of Deference," *AHR* 81 (1976), 516–23.

90. Eusebius, *Hist. eccl.* 7.24.5 (Oulton, ed., 2:192–93).

91. On the sovereignty of early Christian congregations, see, e.g., C. Vogel, "Primalialité et synodalité dans l'église locale durant la periode anténicéenne," in M. Simon, ed., *Aspects de l'orthodoxie: Structure et spiritualité* (Paris, 1982), 53–66.

Christian and relative of Zenobia of Palmyra.[92] According to Eusebius, Paul's theological position proposing the unity of God and the humanity of Christ had become cause for controversy.[93] Prominent Christians, led by Firmilian of Caesarea, Gregory Thaumaturgus, Maximus of Bostra (an interlocutor in Origen's discussion with Heracleides), and others, set out in separate interviews to ascertain Paul's views and to persuade him of his error.[94] The absent Dionysius articulated his own opinions in a writing that was read aloud in public, a practice foreshadowing subsequent Christian conciliar procedures (see ch. 7).

Yet despite the combined strength of the opposition, Paul was able to hold his own in the debates until Malchion, a priest and head of the *paideutērion*, the civic school of rhetoric, of Antioch, intervened and succeeded in formally securing Paul's defeat.[95] It is not easy to discover from Eusebius' very abbreviated account how Malchion was able to accomplish what numerous prominent bishops had failed to do. The explanation for Malchion's success has traditionally been sought in the genitive absolute phrase *episēmeioumenōn tachugraphōn*, which suggests that Malchion effected Paul's upset with the help of the stenographers he brought in to record the debate. This reading of the passage has recently been disputed by Marcel Richard, whose arguments remain inconclusive.[96] He points out that the traditional supposition leaves unaddressed the question of how the incorporation of stenographers into the debate turned the table in Malchion's favor, and he further argues that *notarii* in the third century scarcely enjoyed the prominence they were to have in later centuries.[97] Yet, at a minimum, a staff of shorthand writers implied ecclesiastical wealth, rich private patronage, or the interested support of secular elites. I suggest that the very introduction of stenographers was itself decisive, for they kept verbatim records with which debaters were able to point out their opponents' inconsistencies, and without which an effective *elenchos* or refutation would have been much more difficult to secure. In a fragment from an eleventh-century manu-

92. See F. G. B. Millar, "Paul of Samosata, Zenobia and Aurelian: The Church, Local Culture and Political Allegiance in Third-century Syria," *JRS* 61 (1971), 1–17.

93. Eusebius, *Hist. eccl.* 7.27.1.

94. Eusebius, *Hist. eccl.* 7.28.1–2. Compare this procedure with the informal interviews of Christian leaders with Bishop Beryllus in Eusebius, *Hist. eccl.* 6.33.2.

95. Eusebius, *Hist. eccl.* 7.29.2. See also Theodoret, *Haereticarum fabularum compendium* 2.8 (*PG* 83:396B).

96. The traditional interpretation has been challenged by M. Richard, "Malchion et Paul de Samosate: Le témoignage d'Eusèbe de Césarée," *Ephemerides Theologicae Lovanienses* 35 (1959): 325–38; he offers a different reading of the passage based on a close study of the key terms used by Eusebius.

97. Richard, "Malchion et Paul de Samosate," 328–29.

script that purports to refer to the exchanges between Paul and Malchion, Malchion recalled a previous statement by Paul in building his
own argument, a tactic most effective when used in concert with "un-
deniable" records of the debate.[98]

IN SEARCH OF CONSENSUS IN LATE ANTIQUITY

Most scholars agree that the third-century anarchy was a turning point
in Graeco-Roman society and culture. The crises, at once military, economic, and political—perhaps even spiritual—demonstrated the fragil-
ity of order and of its guarantor, secure political authority. They ushered
in new adaptive responses, particularly in terms of the ideological formulations and representations of power, as the classical Mediterranean
model of competitive parity yielded to a more overtly pyramidal and au-
thoritarian pattern of social relationship.[99] Understandably, established
modes of social interaction and competition between and within groups
were also altered to reflect this broader realignment. Thus, a growing
reliance on textual authority in debates was unexceptional at a time
when traditional authority held fast, especially in religious and philosophical circles.[100]

One concrete outcome of these changes was the increasingly negative reception of public debate as a form of social competition and dispute settlement. The focus of my study is to analyze this phenomenon
historically and critically, without reference to a spirit of irrationalism
that is at once unhelpfully tautological and mystifying. In this respect,
my approach is informed by works of anthropologists and sociologists,
notably Mary Douglas, whose labors to create understanding from observed social forms continually remind us that the ways in which communities adjudicate disputes correspond to their notions of authority and
cultural preferences. Social conflicts, of which public debate is but one
possible manifestation, and how people construe and approach them,
lay bare implicit assumptions about power and social structures.[101] By

98. See H. de Riedmatten, *Les actes du procès de Paul de Samosate: Étude sur la christologie
du III⁰ au IV⁰ siècle* (Fribourg, 1952), 157.
99. See P. R. L. Brown, *The Making of Late Antiquity* (Cambridge, Mass., 1978), 27–53.
100. See, e.g., A. H. Armstrong, "Pagan and Christian Traditionalism in the First
Three Centuries, A.D.," *SP* 15 (1984), 414–31.
101. Because it concerns the question of why certain people or groups perceived
danger in particular settings when others did not, a theoretical analysis of the selective
openness to risk is relevant here. For an anthropological approach to group culture and
risk, see the provocative studies in M. Douglas and A. Wildavsky, eds., *Risk and Cul-*

investigating late antique constructions of and responses to public debate, we stand to gain a richer understanding of the concrete dynamics involved in what modern scholars characterize as a phenomenon of growing traditionalism.

Many communities had found that their liminal social status guaranteed them freedom from intervention by outsiders, especially those on high, while the nature of some groups had disinclined the authorities to expect concord. These two considerations ensured that the social spaces occupied by philosophical and religious groups in the Roman world remained pockets of relative freedom, where disputes were allowed to unfold and resolve themselves in accordance with unsupervised local initiatives. Philosophers, especially those from different schools, were expected to dispute among themselves; thus little effort had been made to bring an end to philosophical dissension.[102] While they at times embarrassed the educated and inspired the satirist's wit, the philosophers' disagreements had no bearing on the status of the rulers, who could therefore acquiesce to their disarray.

When not subject to episodic local persecutions, Christians initially also benefited from the autonomy guaranteed by the rulers' neglect. Their disputes with Jews excited little external concern until they became riotous and violent. Although Christian communities were beset with factional disputes from the beginning, no Roman emperor intervened in their affairs in a meaningful way before Constantine. Earlier, the pagan Aurelian was said to have arbitrated a dispute between Christians in Antioch (c. 272–75), but he did so only in a rescript to a petition and because the question concerned the rightful possession of property. Even the imperious Aurelian acted more in the role of *iudex* than of *autokrator*.[103]

Constantine's engagement with Christians and their affairs shifted the delicate balance in significant ways. Christians were no longer marginal: much more property and wealth were at stake once Constantine bestowed his munificence on his new brethren; much more hinged on

ture: An Essay on the Selection of Technical and Environmental Dangers (Berkeley, 1982); and M. Douglas, *Risk Acceptability according to the Social Sciences* (New York, 1985).

102. A notable counterexample is the unsuccessful attempt of a Roman magistrate to bring together the different philosophical schools in Athens. The episode is narrated in Cicero, *De legibus* 1.20.53: "Cum pro consule ex praetura in Graeciam venisset essetque Athenis, philosophos, qui tum erant, in locum unum convocasse ipsisque magno opere auctorem fuisse, ut aliquando controversiarum aliquem facerent modum; quodsi essent eo animo, ut nollent aetatem in litibus conterere, posse rem convenire; et simul operam suam illis esse pollicitum, si posset inter eos aliquid convenire."

103. Eusebius, *Hist. eccl.* 7.30.18–19.

the rightful possession of the *nomen Christianum*, now that the name conferred privileges and status. Who would be entitled to priestly exemption from civic liturgies? Which factions would be endowed with imperial basilicas? These became pressing questions. There were also the beginnings of a demographic shift as Christians became more numerous and more socially prominent, swelling the imperial service and the new Constantinopolitan senate. In the post-Constantinian age, Christians picked up the pace of their march from social marginality toward the center of social and political power; as a result, rulers who earlier granted Christians freedom from intervention could no longer remain so indulgently detached.

The crises of the third century, the many decades of fratricidal wars for the imperial purple that brought on economic collapse and barbarian inroads, had reinforced in the minds of late Roman elites the supreme importance of consensus among themselves and with others.[104] The rhetoric of concord assumed greater weight as social reality became increasingly characterized by fragmentation, conflict, and anarchy. Disagreements among their subjects that had been tolerable, even amusing, when the burdens of empire were lighter became thorns in the side of soldier-emperors who were not (though some tried to be) the *civiles principes* of the early empire. Order was bound to become an obsessive goal for those attempting to tame a disorderly world, whether the pagan Diocletian or the Christian Constantine. In a law that would have been unthinkable during the principate, Constantine exhorted jurists, known for and distinguished by their professional disagreements, to end their interminable squabbles over the interpretation of legal minutiae so as not to undermine the authority of Roman law.[105]

A pronounced and energetic imperial advocacy for consensus in society could not fail to generate ripples that would reach, with varying strength and effect, the other strata of society. Such advocacy certainly had an impact on the development of imperial Christianity, including some immediate consequences that were not intended. The direct imposition of imperial demands for consensus was perhaps less important than the anticipation of imperial preferences, which often caused local leaders to impose unity on "their" people in the hope of courting imperial favor with greater success. This consideration was all the more

104. On the public representations of this imperial ideology, see H.-P. L'Orange, *Art Forms and Civic Life in the Late Roman Empire* (Princeton, N.J., 1965), 69–125.

105. *Codex Theod.* 1.4.1. On juristic rivalries during the principate, see R. A. Bauman, *Lawyers and Politics in the Early Roman Empire: A Study of Relations between the Roman Jurists and the Emperors from Augustus to Hadrian* (Munich, 1989), esp. 44–49.

crucial at a time of change, uncertainty, and experimentation. At an unsettling time when untraditional channels of patronage and power were thrown open to competing groups, the pressing question became: To which of the competing voices, to which hierarchizing principles, and to what types of personages should the *celsae potestates* pay heed? Out of the din generated by this intense competition for recognition and scarce resources, the voice that represented the unanimous concord of a *populus* was the one most likely to be heard.[106] Even the elder Symmachus, a powerful senator, thought that the opinion of the Roman curia would gain a fairer hearing from an imperial court not always sympathetic to Roman senatorial sentiments if it was offered as a consensual decision of the entire body.[107] The powerful force of unanimous advice was also recognized by nearly contemporary Chinese emperors, who heeded the axiom, "A hereditary ruler does not neglect precedents and the unanimous recommendations of officials."[108]

The collective voice of a people came to be regarded as an expression of authoritative opinion, even of truth, in late antiquity.[109] The corollary to this positive reception of vocal consensus was that demands made with discordant voices were likely to be passed over. According to the *Petitiones Arianorum*, Constantine's arrival at Alexandria (a visit I do not find attested elsewhere) was greeted by the customary official delegation followed by a crowd bearing requests and petitions. Among the petition-bearers were Arian Christians wishing to bring before the emperor accusations against Athanasius of Alexandria. They proceeded to shout their demands, apparently without prior coordination, and Constantine dismissed their request, convinced that "justice will not proceed from a multitudinous mob and from a Babel of sounds."[110]

Constantine's reaction is not surprising, for the emperor was accustomed to chants by choruses of trained voices—no babel would emanate

106. See P. R. L. Brown, "Poverty and Power," in his *Power and Persuasion in Late Antiquity: Towards a Christian Empire* (Madison, Wisc., 1992), 71–117.

107. See Symmachus, *Relatio* 3.2 (R. H. Barrow, ed., *Prefect and Emperor: The Relationes of Symmachus, A.D. 384* [Oxford, 1973], 34–35): "No disagreement of purpose is involved in this matter; for men no longer believe that they gain greater support among court officials if there is a difference of opinion about the matter of a petition (nulla est hic dissensio voluntatum, quia iam credere homines desierunt, aulicorum se studio praestare, si discrepent)."

108. A Han dynasty court memorial of 31 c.e., quoted in Hans Bielenstein, *The Bureaucracy of Han Times* (Cambridge, 1980), 144.

109. K. Oehler, "Der Consensus Omnium als Kriterium der Wahrheit in der antiken Philosophie und der Patristik: Eine Studie zur Geschichte des Begriffs der allgemeinen Meinung," *Antike und Abendland* 10 (1961): 103–30.

110. Athanasius, *Petitiones Arianorum* (*PG* 26:820).

from a self-respecting late Roman theater. The *voces* of assembled citizens rising up from the theaters and hippodromes long remained one of the most compelling forces countervailing the authority of late Roman emperors. The effect of this "popular" expression was enhanced when organized into metrical chants, which enabled many voices to coalesce into a single vox populi.[111] It was their control over this singular voice that entitled local notables to demand consideration from emperors. Yet this socio-political formula, featuring civic unity as a currency of negotiations between imperial and local elites, required that notables for their part vouchsafe in their cities a semblance of social order and deference to authority.[112]

Before long, the role of consensus became important to Christians who wished their voices heard. The establishment of Christian culture within the context of a supportive secular empire was a complex transformation that entailed forging new bonds between the imperial center and the local city, at the head of which now stood the bishop.[113] Late antique bishops, increasingly drawn from the decurionate and curial classes, became what Edward Shils calls macrosocial elites: people who by virtue of their grooming, training in politics, and relation to power possessed a keen awareness of the systemic ramifications of consensus and dissensus.[114] They well understood that the viability of the alliance between center and periphery rested precariously on the stability of two main fronts: the strength of local support for the bishop, and the reliability of imperial patronage.

To cement such a relationship, it was first necessary to forge local consensus, which in turn entailed the quelling of dissensus.[115] Diffused discussions and disputing, with individuals applying their powers of persuasion in a freewheeling way, were potentially dire threats to the shaky bond between center and periphery. The fluid manner in which

111. On the important theme of civic acclamations, see A. T. Klausner, "Akklamation," *RAC* 1:216–33, and C. Roueché, "Acclamations in the Later Roman Empire: New Evidence from Aphrodisias," *JRS* 74 (1984): 181–99.
112. See A. R. R. Sheppard, "*Homonoia* in the Greek Cities of the Roman Empire," *Ancient Society* 15/17 (1984/86), 229–52, and J. Colin, *Les villes libres de l'orient gréco-romain et l'envoi au supplice par acclamations populaires*, Collection Latomus 82 (Brussels, 1965), esp. 109–52.
113. See H. Chadwick, "The Role of the Christian Bishop in Ancient Society," in *Protocol of the 35th Colloquy*, Center for Hermeneutical Studies (Berkeley, Calif., 1980), 1–14, and the subsequent comments and discussions; G. W. Bowersock, "From Emperor to Bishop: The Self-Conscious Transformation of Political Power in the Fourth Century A.D.," *CPhil* 81 (1986): 298–307; and P. Brown, *Power and Persuasion*, 71–117.
114. E. Shils, *Center and Periphery: Essays in Macrosociology* (Chicago, 1975), 169–70.
115. Shils, *Center and Periphery*, 164–81.

pagans, Jews, and Christians debated "in the council-chambers of Greek cities, in the market-places of North African villages, and in thousands of humble homes" [116] became less desirable with the rise of new interest groups who preferred a *via media*—characterized by hierarchical order and firm group boundaries—to a more amorphous and unruly *via universalis.*

Though religious disputing was central to a proselytizing faith such as Christianity in the period of its early diffusion, in late antiquity the missionary religion par excellence was Manichaeism. The fear that local Christians might be lured into dispute by Manichaeans and then persuaded to "defect" long remained in certain regions of the empire.

The fear of influence through persuasion greatly increased at the highest end of the social scale, as when the imperial court itself became a cockpit for ecclesiastical struggles. Emperors and other imperial personages might be swayed by sophistic arguments to forsake one ecclesiastical party for another, with dire consequences for the spurned suitors. Sozomen alleged a direct appeal by Eunomius of Cappadocia, of whom more will be said in Chapter 4, to Theodosius I that was thwarted by Empress Flacilla only at the last moment. Mid–fifth century Constantinopolitans remembered this incident with a shudder: it was most unsettling to ponder how much still hung on a thread in the late fourth century, during the reign of that champion of orthodoxy, Theodosius I. [117]

The political alliance between center and periphery thus sported two Achilles' heels. These vulnerabilities threatened both aspiring and established Christian leaders of favored status while presenting opportunities for their challengers to exploit. The practice of disputing among Christians was an obvious concern for those who prized hierarchical authority and their position at the apex of a stable community. No amount of wishful thinking could make good the embarrassment engendered by open Christian controversies, which became, to the chagrin of many Christians, prime satirical fodder. On the comic stage, publicly brawling Christian prelates became stock figures, joining a cast of disreputable characters that included prostitutes. [118] A modern scholar of early Byzantine theater goes so far as to name this new subgenre "*der christologischer Mimus.*" [119]

116. Dodds, *Pagan and Christian*, 103.
117. Sozomen, *Hist. eccl.* 4.18.
118. See Gregory of Nazianzus, *Or.* 2 (*PG* 35:489B).
119. See G. J. Theocharidis, *Beiträge zur Geschichte des byzantinischen Profantheaters im IV. und V. Jahrhundert, hauptsächlich auf Grund der Predigten des Johannes Chrysostomos Patriarchen von Konstantinopel* (Thessaloniki, 1940), 93–102.

The public perception of widespread disputing, along with Christian rioting that at times turned murderous, rendered the myth of Christian solidarity meaningless. Worse, this situation arose in a veritable market economy of opinions, in which the notion of deference—that is, the willingness of the *humiliores* to give their assent to the guidance of the *honestiores*, who supposedly possessed better moral judgment—was irretrievably lost. Once deference, long considered a "voluntary" and "natural" state of affairs, had vanished among proliferating claims to knowledge and authority, it usually could not be regained by compulsion, which resulted only in a state of enslavement.[120] The "superior" Christian ethos of simplicity was mobilized, I suggest, as a means of counterbalancing this eroded sense of deference. Though both deference and simplicity contribute to a successful hierarchical ordering of society, the difference between them is great: deference is an unspoken rule of conduct enmeshed in a complex system of social exchange, whereas simplicity is a vocal ideology promoted by interested parties to mimic the former. The distinction is not trivial. Origen saw simplicity as a quality natural to some Christians, but later Christians would plead that other Christians, even if they did not consider themselves to be such, should nevertheless become *simplices*.

An intensified advocacy for apophatic simplicity as a paradigmatic virtue was but one of many results of this confluence of competing interests. Many individuals and groups sought to domesticate the perceived threat of dissensus in public disputing, choosing from various ideological strategies and cultural values to mobilize hierarchical forms of authority against a culture that validated individualistic claims and rational argumentation. This complex web, within which the classical heritage was slowly transformed into a Byzantine matrix during late antiquity, is one I propose to unravel, one strand at a time, in the remaining chapters of this book.

120. "Deference is expected to be spontaneously exhibited rather than enforced," according to Pocock, "The Classical Theory of Deference," 516.

TWO

DISPUTATION, DIALECTIC, AND COMPETITION AMONG PLATONIST PHILOSOPHERS

Late antique frescoes and marble busts portray philosophers as serene, dignified, detached figures.[1] In reality, many were deeply implicated in the rich texture of mundane social interactions and the spirit of competitive strife, or agon, that permeated Graeco-Roman culture. The recently published contents of an Oxyrhynchus papyrus fragment (second to third century C.E.) dismissively suggest that, in their quarrels, "far louder noises emanate from philosophers than from raving lunatics."[2]

Indeed, public competition between philosophers belonging to different *haireseis*, or sects, was engrained in popular expectations. When Lycinus, an interlocutor in Lucian of Samosata's satiric dialogue *Eunuchus*, reported that he had just witnessed two philosophers "wrangling (ἐρίζειν)" in the agora, his friend Pamphilius immediately inquired if the disputants were *heterodoxoi*, people from different schools of philosophy.[3] It came as something of a surprise to Pamphilius that the contenders, Diocles the Eristic philosopher and Bagoas the alleged castrato,

---

1. For stylistic developments in late antique philosophical portraiture, see H. von Heintze, "*Vir sanctus et gravis:* Bildniskopf eines spätantiken Philosophen," *JAC* 6 (1963): 35–53, and plates 1–9, and the publications by R. R. R. Smith cited in nn. 142ff.

2. *P. Oxy.* 52.3659.i.22–24 (pp. 59–62, at 61): "πολὺ μείζους κραυγὰς ἐκ τῶν φιλοσόφων ἢ τῶν μα]ινομένων."

3. Lucian, *Eunuchus* 2. Lucian's disapproval of the rivalry of the philosophical schools shows through clearly in his *Hermotimus*.

were in fact both Aristotelians.[4] Why then were they at odds with each other in public?

The bone of contention, it turned out, was a recently vacated chair of philosophy in Athens.[5] The stakes were high—great social honor and a stipend of ten thousand drachmas—and a tribunal ($\dot{\eta}$ $\delta i\kappa\eta$) of the city's wisest had gathered in the agora to judge the contest.[6] In the dialogue, the finalists tested each other's knowledge of Aristotle's *dogmata*, and when this failed to yield a clear winner, proceeded to compare each other's *ēthos*, or way of life.

Although Lucian made light of the incident, such a debate would have constituted high drama, not in the least because it was an infrequent occurrence. Such an open contest between philosophers of the same school ($\sigma\chi o\lambda\dot{\eta}$, $\delta\iota\alpha\tau\rho\iota\beta\dot{\eta}$) before a panel of external judges was rarely recorded during the empire, except when, as in this case, a coveted philosophical chair was at stake. Just as conflict had riddled the professional lives of Greek sophists, for whom an unforgiving rivalry appeared natural and expected, agon, competitive strife, wove deep into the institutional fabric of Graeco-Roman philosophical culture.[7]

In his recent study of the roles played by philosophers in Roman society, Johannes Hahn rightly characterizes a culture of competitive disputation as the constitutive component of ancient philosophical identity: "For the organization of the different philosophical teachings into schools essentially established traditional debate and exposition as the fundamental aspects of philosophical self-understandings."[8] It is to this important theme that I turn in this chapter by examining the nature of competition within the Platonist circles of late antiquity, especially in the groups surrounding Plotinus, Iamblichus, and Aedesius.[9] My aim is to elucidate the philosophers' social interactions rather than to shed further light on their teachings, which have until now claimed the lion's

4. Lucian, *Eunuchus* 3.

5. These endowed chairs of philosophy had been established by Marcus Aurelius in 176. For this institution, see J. P. Lynch, *Aristotle's School: A Study of a Greek Educational Institution* (Berkeley, Calif., 1972), 185–89.

6. The incumbents had been chosen by Herodes Atticus, who was commissioned by Marcus Aurelius to perform this task; see Philostratus, *VS* 566.

7. For the nature and form of professional rivalry among the sophists, see G. W. Bowersock, *Greek Sophists in the Roman Empire* (Oxford, 1969), 89–100.

8. J. Hahn, *Der Philosoph und die Gesellschaft: Selbstverständnis, öffentliches Auftreten und populäre Erwartungen in der hohen Kaiserzeit* (Stuttgart, 1989), 109.

9. See G. Fowden, "The Platonist Philosopher and His Circle in Late Antiquity," $\Phi\iota\lambda o\sigma o\phi i\alpha$ 7 (Athens, 1977): 359–83, esp. 362. The earliest attested mentions of "Platonist" (as opposed to Academic) philosophers appear on first-century inscriptions from Ephesus, see D. Runia, "Philosophical Heresiography: Evidence in Two Ephesian Inscriptions," *ZPE* 72 (1988), 241–43.

share of erudite attention.[10] This chapter will illustrate how various rituals of conflict, ranging from public disputation to subtler and less verbal forms, served the functions of social integration and hierarchical differentiation among Platonists.

Further, I propose to connect the attested growth of philosophical traditionalism in late antiquity to the devaluation of dialectical disputation as a technique of social competition.[11] As the philosopher-teacher evolved into a privileged figure of authority seated above those less established, philosophical disputation became an exercise in futility: if truth resided not in the dialectic of inquiry but in the very person of the philosopher (now appearing as a pagan holy man), dialectic was robbed of its ultimate legitimacy as a method for arriving at truth.[12] This shift in emphasis, epitomized by the Platonist philosophers' documented self-withdrawal from society, had a range of social implications, among which was a decrease in the importance of competitive disputations to the philosophical life. The tendency to ascribe innate authority to philosopher-teachers allowed the construction of stable philosophical authority and identity, even in environments of intense social competition brought about by a lack of firm boundaries between philosophical institutions, a lack of consensus in defining the philosophical virtues, and the rise of Christianity with its claim to represent the true philosophy.

DIALECTIC AND PUBLIC DISPUTATION IN CLASSICAL ANTIQUITY

Ever since Zeno of Elea (b. 490 B.C.E.?) was credited by Aristotle as the inventor of both the philosophical dialectic and the genre of the dialogue,[13] the relationship between the two forms has remained an

10. Previous works on the social history of the Platonists tend to focus more on instruction than competition. The works of Garth Fowden now supplement K. Praetcher, "Richtungen und Schulen im Neuplatonismus," *Genethliakon: Carl Robert zum 8 Marz 1910* (Berlin, 1910): 105–56; reprinted in H. Dörrie, ed., *Kleine Schriften* (Hildesheim, 1973).

11. See Armstrong, "Pagan and Christian Traditionalism," 414–31.

12. See G. Fowden, "The Pagan Holy Man in Late Antique Society," *JHS* 102 (1982): 33–59.

13. Aristotle, *Fragmenta* 65 (Rose, ed., 74–75); cf. Diogenes Laertius, *VP* 8.57, 9.25. In the post-classical period, Plato was increasingly regarded as the inventor of the dialogue; see, e.g., the anonymous *Prolegomena philosophiae platonicae* 5.44–46 (L. G. Westerink, ed., *The Anonymous Prolegomena to Platonic Philosophy* [Amsterdam, 1962], 12–13): "He [Plato] invented a new literary form, the dialogue (εὗρεν δὲ καὶ εἶδος συγγραφῆς τὸ διαλογικόν). For if anyone should object that Zeno and Parmenides wrote dialogues before him, we can answer that it was Plato more than anyone else who used this medium."

intimate one.[14] Ancient doxography identifies the old Parmenides of Elea (Zeno's teacher) as the man who instructed Socrates in the art of give-and-take, conversational dialectic. Socrates subsequently adapted this method for daily use in his interrogations of fellow Athenians. Employing his peculiar brand of cross-examination, Socrates succeeded in publicly demonstrating, in the cases of virtually all his interlocutors, the embarrassing fact that they had no bases for their ideas and beliefs, that they lacked *sophia*.[15]

Within the context of a democratizing aristocratic society in which the ruling elites needed more than ever to justify their positions by claims to virtue, especially to *sophia* and the virtue of knowledge, Socrates' rapid-fire questioning showed that these *aristoi*, supposedly the cream of the citizenry, did not in fact have *epistēmē*, or certain knowledge. The philosopher's eristic style tore through the composure of politicians trained to render continuous public discourses when questions were put to them, but unused to close examination by one who denied them refuge behind platitudes.[16] In this regard, his dialectical method, in addition to its philosophical utility, was also a tool of social critique, regardless of Socrates' avowed goals. Seen in this light, the unmitigated enmity of Socrates' accusers and his eventual conviction by a jury of Athenian dicasts become readily understandable.

Plato used Socrates' method of investigation as a vehicle for his own philosophical expression after the death of his teacher in 399.[17] The dialectical principle plays a prominent role in his early dia-

---

14. The fundamental tie between dialectic and the dialogue genre is explained by Diogenes Laertius in *VP* 3.48. See also McKeon, "Greek Dialectics," 1–25.

15. See M. Meyer, "Dialectic and Questioning: Socrates and Plato," *American Philosophical Quarterly* 17 (1980): 281–89. He convincingly associates Socrates' dialectical questioning of prominent Athenians with the questioning of authority (at 282): "Under the fire of Socrates' questions, the leading citizens must respond, and by their answers, justify themselves. But authority, by definition, makes it hard for those who have long since disposed of it to answer and justify themselves. The pretence of knowledge then reveals itself during the dialectical debate for what it is: a social pretence. Would Socrates, who is poor, be more knowledgeable than the richest and most reputed [i.e., the notables] for their wisdom [i.e., those who have σοφία]?" For the argument that sophists posed as challengers to the Athenian oligarchic establishment, see R. Mueller, "La sofistica e la democrazia," *Discorsi* 6 (1986): 7–23. In the Roman period, however, sophists themselves hailed from local aristocratic families; see E. L. Bowie, "The Importance of Sophists," *Yale Classical Studies* 27 (1982), 29–59.

16. The distinction between these two forms of verbal contest is discussed by H. L. Hudson William, "Conventional Forms of Debate and the Melian Dialogue," *AJP* 71 (1950): 156–69, esp. 168–69.

17. See Plato, *Alcibiades* 1.113a, where the Socratic method is characterized as involving ἐρώτησίς τε καὶ ἀπόκρισις. For Plato's criticism of reliance on untested philosophical axioms, see *Republic* 533–34.

logues.[18] The methodological emphasis in these dialogues may incline one to suppose that a Socratic style of elenchic disputation was taught in the Academy that Plato established, and that both disputation and the art of dialectic were included in its curriculum.[19] Gilbert Ryle questions this assumption by calling to attention Plato's reservations about philosophical disputation in *Republic* 537–39.[20] There, Plato's Socrates remarked on the potential of dialectic and disputation for corrupting the young—precisely one of the two formal charges brought against Socrates at his trial. Dialectical argumentation, a powerful tool for separating *epistēmē*, certain knowledge, from *doxa*, human opinion,[21] was thought unsuitable for those who saw it only as a competitive sport or a means for gaining advantage. Socrates explained his reservation by appealing to common experience:

> I suppose that it has not escaped you that young lads (οἱ μειρακίσκοι), whenever they taste their first disputation, treat it as a kind of game (ὡς παιδιᾷ), always using it for contention, and having imitated the refuters they themselves are refuted. They rejoice always—as puppies do (ὥσπερ σκυλάκια)—in pulling apart and tearing with words those near to them.[22]

Men in their twenties (οἱ μειρακίσκοι) were not to be trusted with the art of posing and answering questions: providing untempered young males with the opportunity to debate competitively could only bring harm and distress to themselves and to others (including the more advanced members of the Academy) by giving rein to the crueler instincts of youth. This caution was justified by the fear that they would become "infected with lawlessness (παρανομία)."[23] Furthermore, as no truth was held sacred in dialectical disputations, these youths also ran the risk of becoming demoralized and disoriented by their own relentless, icono-

18. See Meyer, "Dialectic and Questioning"; R. Diertele, *Platons Laches und Charmides: Untersuchungen zur elenktisch-aporetischen Struktur der platonischen Frühdialoge* (Freiburg, 1966), esp. 5, on the less didactic nature of Plato's earlier dialogues; V. Goldschmidt, *Les dialogues de Platon: Structure et méthode dialectique*, 2d ed. (Paris, 1963).

19. See *Republic* 534 and W. Müri, "Das Wort Dialektik bei Platon," *Museum Helveticum* 1 (1944): 152–68, esp. 160: the διαλεκτικὸς ἀνήρ was one who mastered ἡ τέχνη διαλεκτική.

20. G. Ryle, "Dialectic in the Academy," in G. E. L. Owen, ed., *Aristotle on Dialectic: The Topics* (Oxford, 1968), 68–79, esp. 71.

21. Plato, *Republic* 537d.

22. Plato, *Republic* 539b; my translation. On Attic ephebic training in general, see C. Pélékides, *Histoire de l'éphébie attique des origines à 31 avant J.-C.* (Paris, 1962) and Lynch, *Aristotle's School*, 36–37 n. 9. On the philosophical training of Athenian ephebes in particular, see M. N. Tod, "Sidelights on Greek Philosophers," *JHS* 77 (1957): 132–41, esp. 137ff.

23. Plato, *Republic* 537e. See also *Phaedo* 90c–d.

clastic debunking of hitherto unquestioned social norms. They would, as a consequence of such exercises, cease to respect their elders and the social values treasured by their society.

Because such an outcome was deemed undesirable, Plato's Socrates stipulated that only men over thirty (that is, the age of eligibility for Athenian magistracies) could practice philosophical disputation in the Academy.[24] His ratiocination relied on the belief that a direct, causal connection existed between age and good sense: "An older man would not wish to partake of this madness ($\mu\alpha\nu\iota\alpha$)."[25] By this and other restrictive qualifications, Socrates also contrived to prevent dialectical disputation from being trivialized as all a game for the young.[26]

Through Socrates, Plato clearly expressed his own convictions and educational ideals. His nuanced reservation about the dialectical art was reflected in his other writings: contrast the debate scenes involving Gorgias in the first book of the *Republic* with the less dialectical, almost monologic, style of the later books. In Plato's later dialogues, one detects his outright abandonment of dialectical inquiry. The dialogues become monologues, with discussion partners relegated to the role of obliging "nodders."

From these observations, one may surmise that Plato neither taught dialectic nor installed dialectical disputation in the curriculum of the Academy. This may explain why Aristotle claimed that he had to learn the art of dialectic by himself, in the process discovering the figure of the syllogism.[27] Yet even if Plato continued to entertain doubts about the value of dialectical disputation, he did not object to Aristotle's teaching of the topics in the Academy.

In the dialectic of questioning in Aristotle's works, the de[con]structive or critical dialectic of Socrates assumed a more domesticated form. Tradition holds that Aristotle originated and Theophrastus popularized the question-and-answer dialogue ($\zeta\eta\tau\eta\mu\alpha$ $\kappa\alpha\iota$ $\lambda\upsilon\sigma\iota\varsigma$), which preserved the central dialectical element of the philosophical dialogue while stripping it of its narrative trapping.[28] This Aristotelian form was to become one of the enduring vehicles of philosophical and scientific instruction in the ancient world.[29] The division of labor between the protagonists in

24. See R. Develin, "Age Qualifications for Athenian Magistrates," *ZPE* 61 (1985): 149–59.

25. Plato, *Republic* 539c. See Ryle, "Dialectic in the Academy," 73.

26. Plato, *Republic* 539c.

27. See Aristotle, *De sophisticis elenchis* 34.183a–b (Forster and Furley, eds., 148–49).

28. See Lloyd, *Revolutions of Wisdom* 155–58.

29. On the importance of the question-and-answer dialogue to the teaching of ancient medicine, see F. Kudlien, "Dialektik und Medizin in der Antike," *Medizinhistorisches Journal* 9 (1974): 187–200; J. Kollesch, *Untersuchungen zu den ps.galenischen Definitiones*

a question-and-answer dialogue was strictly observed: there were those who posed questions and those to whom questions were posed. The competitive parity among the protagonists in dialogues was sacrificed; so too the importance of mutual, dialectical inquiry for establishing truth.[30] Instead, the dialectical principle of philosophical disputation was harnessed into forms that served the functions of protreptic introduction and the socialization of the less advanced members of the philosophical circle.[31]

In the post-classical period, philosophical groups such as the Megarian *dialektikoi* pursued the specialized study and practice of dialectic.[32] Dialectical disputation remained an important component of Academic training, but we may deduce from certain literary philosophical texts—such as Cicero's *De finibus* and *Tusculan Disputations*, assuming that the school-debate setting of the Ciceronian treatises did not merely reflect literary topos but rather echoed ongoing social practice[33]—that the tone of the proceedings was hardly agonistic. The later manuscripts of the *Tusculan Disputations* place the exchanges firmly within the context of a teaching session by labeling the protagonists A. and M. for *auditor* and *magister*, pupil and teacher.

PLOTINUS AND PORPHYRY

What we know of Platonist philosophers and philosophical circles in the post-classical period is characteristically fragmentary, or anecdotal, or

---

Medicae (Berlin, 1973); L. G. Westerink, "Philosophy and Medicine in Late Antiquity," *Janus* 51 (1964): 169–77.

30. Meyer, "Dialectic and Questioning," 283, argues that the alternation of roles in dialectic serves as a basis for structural equality. The implied corollary is that the lack of meaningful alternation connotes a tendency toward authoritarianism.

31. Aristotle, *De sophisticis elenchis* 16.175a (Forster and Furley, eds., 88–89).

32. "The Dialecticians" (οἱ διαλεκτικοί) was a label that had been applied to several philosophical sects, said by Diogenes Laertius to be founded variously by Clitomachus of Carthage (*VP* 1.17: they were those who employed verbal trickery) and by Euclides of Megara (*VP* 2.106: they were those who rejected arguments from analogy). The latter were supposedly called διαλεκτικοί because they used the question-and-answer literary form to frame their arguments. In *VP* 10.8, Epicurus reportedly denounced these Megarian διαλεκτικοί as "destroyers (πολυφθόρους) of Hellas."

33. Cicero, *Tusculanae disputationes* 1.4.8: "Itaque dierum quinque scholas, ut Graeci apellant, in totidem libros contuli. Fiebat autem ita, ut, cum is, qui audire vellet, dixisset quid sibi videretur, tum ego contra dicerem. Haec est enim, ut scis, vetus et Socratica ratio contra alterius opinionem disserendi. Nam ita facillime quid veri simillimum esset inveniri posse Socrates arbitrabatur." See also Cicero, *De finibus* 2 *passim* on the question-and-answer method.

both.[34] One of the few philosophers about whose life and social circle it is possible to say something substantive is Plotinus of Lycopolis (205–70), a student of Ammonius Saccas[35] who began to give philosophical lectures in Rome in 244.[36] We owe this relative abundance of information to the biography composed thirty years after Plotinus' death by his disciple Porphyry of Tyre.

Although posterity would identify Plotinus' circle as a *schola*,[37] a term suggesting a high degree of institutional organization, scholars today describe those around Plotinus as a loose confederation comprising two main groups: the *akroatai* or interested listeners,[38] and the *zēlōtai* or serious students.[39] This two-fold division was characteristic of late antique philosophical and religious groups generally, and Platonist groups in particular.[40] Amelius Gentilianus, Porphyry, and a few others belonged to the intimate cadre of Plotinus' disciples that constituted his inner circle; a larger following of those who attended Plotinus' lectures, including many aristocratic Romans, formed the outer circle.[41]

34. See J. Dillon, *The Middle Platonists: A Study in Platonism 80 B.C. to A.D. 220* (Ithaca, N.Y., 1977), xiii–xiv.

35. On Ammonius Saccas, see H. Langerbeck, "The Philosophy of Ammonius Saccas," *JHS* 77 (1957): 67–74; E. R. Dodds, "Numenius and Ammonius," in *Les sources de Plotin*, Entretiens sur l'antiquité classique 5 (Vandoeuvres-Genève, 1957), 3–32; H. Crouzel, "Origène et Plotin élèves d'Ammonios Saccas," *Bulletin de Littérature Ecclésiastique* 57 (1956): 193–214.

36. On Plotinus' earlier career, see Porphyry, *Vita Plotini* 3.1–27; on the chronology of his life and career, see T. D. Barnes, "The Chronology of Plotinus' Life," *GRBS* 17 (1976): 65–70.

37. It was thus described, for example, by Augustine in *Ep.* 118.33 (*PL* 33:448): "Tunc Plotini schola Romae floruit, habuitque condiscipulos, multos acutissimos et solertissimos viros." J. Bidez's statement in *Vie de Porphyre: Le philosophe néo-platonicien* (Gand/Leipzig, 1913), 41, that "Plotin avait organisé toute une école, avec plusieurs degrés d'initiation; une sorte d'institut qui tenait à la fois des mystères païens et d'un couvent de contemplatifs chrétiens" is a conjecture not well supported by the sources.

38. *Vita Plotini* 1.14–15 (Armstrong, ed., 2–3): "ἐξῆν γὰρ τῷ βουλομένῳ φοιτᾶν εἰς τὰς συνουσίας." On the presence of senatorial figures in Plotinus' circles, see *Vita Plotini* 7. The Roman senator Rogatianus, who renounced his exalted station to embrace a philosophical life, was an exceptional, and therefore noteworthy, example.

39. See *Vita Plotini* 7.29–47 (Armstrong, ed., 26–29). We have no reason to assume that these people were fully committed to a life of philosophy or desired to become philosophers themselves; see M.-O. Goulet-Cazé, "L'école de Plotin," in Brisson et al., eds., *Porphyre: La vie de Plotin* 1:231–57.

40. Marinus, *Vita Procli* 38, highlights the distinction between the two classes of people who surrounded Proclus: those who merely wished to hear him speak and those who wished to become serious philosophers.

41. The individuals named in the *Vita Plotini* who can be securely identified with either group are listed accordingly in the prosopography compiled by Goulet-Cazé in Brisson et al., *Porphyre: La vie de Plotin* 1:61–140. The tally comes to three ἀκροαταί and eleven ζηλωταί.

The social cohesion of this layered group was provided by Plotinus himself and by a shared devotion to Plato: the group was consciously construed as a Platonist philosophical group, even though it bore no relation to the reconstituted Platonic succession in Athens.[42] The anniversaries of the founders' birthdays[43] were celebrated by Plotinus and company with sacrifices, banquets, and epideictic speeches.[44] Yet such occasions were not the high feasts of a "sect," narrowly defined,[45] nor were they restricted to Plotinus' regular listeners or disciples; he also invited other close friends (οἱ ἑταῖροι, here more encompassing than ζηλωταί) who were not professional philosophers.

During one such celebration of Plato's birthday, a rhetor named Diophanes recited an apologia of Alcibiades, the Athenian enfant terrible and disciple of Socrates. He argued, citing the famous association between the two men, that a philosopher's pupil should be willing to go as far as to have intercourse (εἰς συνουσίαν: the double entendre works in Greek as in English) with his teacher in order to advance in wisdom. The moral implications of this speech disturbed Plotinus who, according to Porphyry, wanted to leave the akoustērion a number of times in the course of Diophanes' delivery; he stayed and did not interrupt the speaker, but subsequently commissioned Porphyry to refute Diophanes' scandalous thesis in writing.

On more mundane occasions, the philosopher and his students met inside a private *domus* in regular *sunousiai*, from which no interested person was in theory excluded.[46] His immediate listeners were his only audience, except when one among them took notes for later transcrip-

---

42. Eubulus, the Platonic διάδοχος in Athens, sent Plotinus a number of *aporiae* concerning the writings of Plato; see *Vita Plotini* 15.18–22 (Armstrong, ed., 42–43). On the Platonic succession in Athens, see J. Dillon, *The Middle Platonists*, 231–33.

43. That is, those of Socrates and Plato. Traditionally, their birthdays fell on 6 and 7 Thargelion; see *Prolegomena philosophiae platonicae* 1 (Westerink, ed., 2–3).

44. See *Vita Plotini* 2.43–45 (Armstrong, ed., 6–7): "ὅτε καὶ λόγον ἔδει τῶν ἑταίρων τοὺς δυνατοὺς ἐπὶ τῶν συνελθόντων ἀναγνῶναι." At the feast of Plato, Porphyry recited "The Sacred Marriage," a discourse expressed in veiled, difficult language (*Vita Plotini* 15.1–6). Censured for this exhibition by some present, he was praised by Plotinus for proving himself at once poet, philosopher, and hierophant.

45. On the importance of these celebrations in later Platonist circles, see Marinus, *Vita Procli* 23. The Epicureans also celebrated the anniversary of their eponymous founder; see Diogenes Laertius, *VP* 10.18, and D. Clay, "The Cults of Epicurus," *Cron Ercol* 16 (1986): 11–28.

46. See *Vita Plotini* 1.14–15 for the open and public character of these meetings. Goulet-Cazé, "L'école de Plotin," 244–45, esp. 245n. 2, argues compellingly that the phrase "δημοσιεύοντες Πλωτῖνος καὶ Γεντιλιανὸς Ἀμέλιος" refers not to the fact that Plotinus and Amelius received public funds but to the fact that their philosophical lectures were open to the general public.

tion.[47] Oral exegesis of written texts was a cornerstone of Plotinian instruction. Plotinus frequently had others read aloud from the Middle-
Platonic and Pythagorean commentaries (τὰ ὑπομνήματα) on Plato: this
was the *lexis;* afterward, he expounded (ὁμιλοῦντα ἐοικέναι) his own
interpretations of the texts: this was the *theōria*.[48]

Plotinus was far from being a dogmatic lecturer. In fact, his two
most advanced students, Amelius and Porphyry, considered his style
meandering and incoherent, a deficiency often rendered more pronounced by his habit of interrupting his discourse to entertain questions from the audience.[49] The presence of this give-and-take element
does not, however, necessarily mean that Socratic dialectical questioning was practiced in the Plotinian lecture room, as one scholar has suggested.[50] The questions posed fell within the context of instruction, and
as such served as points of departure for continuous discourses on given
themes. This dynamic of the Plotinian lecture room can also be seen in
the reactions of Gregory Thaumaturgus (c. 213–70), a contemporary of
Plotinus, to the *aporia* raised by a certain Theopompus. Far from engaging the questioner in a Socratic exchange, Gregory at first flatly ignored
the query. When he finally addressed the question after Theopompus
revisited with an improved formulation, Gregory used the occasion as
the pretext for a monologue which became the *Dialogue with Theopompus
on the Impassibility and Passibility of God*, now extant only in Syriac.[51]

When Gregory Thaumaturgus and Plotinus entertained questions
from their audiences, they did so as purveyors of wisdom rather than as
equal partners in a Socratic exchange. The dominant ethos of the Plotinian circle, as far as our sources allow us to see, was one of deep respect
for the authoritative teacher. Yet this respect did not stop the *zēlōtai* from
interrupting with difficult questions. Porphyry confessed that, on at

47. See *Vita Plotini* 20 on philosophers' varied commitment to having their teachings
written down.

48. *Vita Plotini* 14.10–18. On how lectures might be followed by question-and-answer
periods, see A. C. Lloyd, *The Anatomy of Neo-Platonism* (Oxford, 1990), 6–8.

49. See *Vita Plotini* 18.6–8.

50. C. Evangeliou, *Aristotle's Categories and Porphyry* (Leiden, 1988), 2n. 10.

51. See de Lagarde, ed., *Analecta Syriaca*, 46–64, and Hoffmann, *Dialog*, 62 (see also
63–65 on Gregory): "Seine Methode ist dabei nicht die gemeinsame Wahrheitsfindung im
Gespräch, oder die Überführung des Gegners durch ihn zu Eingeständnissen zwingende
Fragen, sondern ausdrücklich der reine Lehrvortrag." On this genre among Christians,
see G. Bardy, "La littérature patristique des '*quaestiones et responsiones*' sur l'écriture
sainte," *Revue Biblique* 41 (1932): 210–36, 340–69, 515–37; 42 (1933): 14–30, 211–29, 328–
52; C. F. G. Heinrici, "Zur patristischen Aporienliteratur," *Abhandlungen der königlich
sächsischen Gesellschaft der Wissenschaften*, Phil.-Hist. Klasse 27 (1909): 843–60 and idem,
"Griechisch-byzantinische Gesprächsbücher und Verwandtes aus Sammelhandschriften,"
ibid. 28 (1911): 3–97.

least one occasion, he persistently asked difficult questions in such a way as to require Plotinus to break off from the train of his discourse to address them.[52] He recalled that

> once I kept on asking Plotinus over three days about the connection between the soul with the body, and he continued demonstrating (ἀποδεικνύς) to me. . . . A certain person named Thaumasius (who was studying universal propositions) had come into the lecture-room and said that he wished to hear Plotinus lecture with reference to written [philosophical] texts, but that he could not stand Porphyry's answers and questions (ἀποκρινουμένου καὶ ἐρωτῶντος).[53]

Although the connection between the soul and the body was long a central philosophical question,[54] for our purposes it is more instructive to read this and other passages bearing on the dynamics of the Plotinian lecture room in conjunction with Plutarch's little pamphlet De recte ratione audiendi, "How to Listen to a Philosophical Lecture."[55]

For Plutarch, who was concerned with the maintenance of an ideal philosophical lecture room in which eutaxia or good order reigned, the issue of proposing questions during a lecture was a delicate one. On the one hand, he pronounced listeners who insistently interjected uninvited questions (ἐρωτήματα), causing the speaker to digress, to be tiresome company at best.[56] On the other hand, he allowed that, should the speaker himself solicit questions, the audience must rise to the occasion by asking questions that were useful (χρήσιμον) and of pressing necessity (ἀναγκαῖον). This code of etiquette was vital: knowing when to speak up and when to remain silent was, according to Apuleius of Madaura, who sojourned in Athens in the mid–second century in search of philosophical wisdom, a virtue required of any aspiring follower of Plato.[57]

It is quite likely that Porphyry's particular interjections were not

---

52. Porphyry himself later composed a philosophical dialogue, Συμμικτὰ προβλήματα, perhaps based partly on his reminiscences of similar exchanges in the classroom. See Proclus, In Platonis Rempublicam (Kroll, ed., 1:223–34).

53. Vita Plotini 13.1–15 (Armstrong, ed., 38–39). See R. Lim, "The Auditor Thaumasius in the Vita Plotini," JHS 113 (1993), 157–60, at 160.

54. See K. Corrigan, "Body's Approach to Soul: An Examination of a Recurrent Theme in the Enneads," Dionysius 9 (1985): 37–52.

55. I quote from F. C. Babbitt, ed., Plutarch's Moralia (London/New York, 1927), LCL 1:201–59. This small treatise, addressed to Nicander, was originally delivered as a lecture. The title is given as Περὶ τοῦ ἀκούειν τῶν φιλοσόφων, or "On Listening to the Lectures of Philosophers" in Lamprias' catalog of Plutarch's works, as cited in the Teubner Moralia (Bernardakis, ed. [Leipzig, 1888–96], 7:473–77).

56. Plutarch, De recta ratione audiendi 10 (Babbitt, ed., 230–31).

57. Apuleius, Florida 15 (Helm, ed. [Leipzig, 1905], I.2:23.11–14): "Aeque et ipse in nomen eius [i.e., Plato's] a magistris meis adoptarer, utrumque meditationibus academicis didici, et, cum dicto opus est, inpigre dicere, et, cum tacito opus est, libenter tacere."

solicited by Plotinus, but they were encouraged by his customary openness to students who posed questions (ζητεῖν) during the *sunousiai*.[58] He
never browbeat student challengers—foremost among whom we must
count Porphyry—into assuming a more quiescent role.[59] According to
Porphyry, such exchanges became occasions for Plotinus to demonstrate
"his benevolence to the questioner and his intellectual vigour."[60] Moreover, Plotinus regarded this process as an indispensable component of
the philosophical enterprise. A number of Plotinus' objections to Aristotle's categories not found in the *Enneads* might have originated from
just such an oral setting.[61]

A similar indulgence toward questioning, even in contexts where
the dialectical element was severely restricted, was likely to be shared
by the *zēlōtai*. For Porphyry and others engaged in earnest pursuit
of wisdom, it was essential that intellectual difficulties be dealt with
squarely and in detail; those in the inner circle aimed to learn the means
by which they, too, might become wise philosophers. For that reason,
they naturally wished to participate in philosophical discussions as contributing partners.[62] Many among the *akroatai* and the masses (τὸ πολὺ
πλῆθος), however, might have been impressed by Plotinus' conclusions
even without knowing how he arrived at them, since their interest in
the precise methods of philosophical reasoning was not as great as that
of the *zēlōtai*.[63] In all historical periods, one readily finds people capable
of consuming philosophical axioms without requiring a logical demonstration of their validity,[64] including the undiscriminating listeners in
Plutarch's *De recta ratione audiendi*.[65]

From information gleaned from anecdotal asides, we know that rivalry was rife within the Plotinian circle, always bubbling just beneath

58. *Vita Plotini* 3.36–37 (Armstrong, ed., 10). See Goulet-Cazé, "L'école de Plotin," 251.
59. A word of rebuke from a philosopher could easily devastate a student; see Plutarch, *De recta ratione audiendi* 16 (Babbitt, ed., 248–51).
60. *Vita Plotini* 13.9–11 (Armstrong, ed., 38–39).
61. On the disagreement between Plotinus and Porphyry over the categories, see
P. Henry, "Trois apories orales de Plotin sur les Categories d'Aristote," in *Zētēsis: Album
Amicorum* (Antwerp/Utrecht, 1973), 234–67; and idem, "The Oral Teaching of Plotinus,"
Dionysius 6 (1982): 4–12.
62. See Eunapius, *VS* 456, on Porphyry's agony over this issue.
63. See Iamblichus, *De vita pythagorica* 18.88. Philosophers often gave protreptic lectures on the ideal way of life and on morality. Diogenes Laertius, *VP* 4.16, cited the example of the conversion of Polemon, later a Platonic successor, to a philosophical life. He
had lived a life of debauchery until he once stumbled drunk into Xenocrates' lecture on
temperance. The discourse he heard effectively restored him to the right path.
64. See Iamblichus, *De vita pythagorica* 18.82, 18.87–88.
65. See Plutarch, *De recta ratione audiendi* 7, 13 (Babbitt, ed., 220–25, 238–39).

the surface, especially wherever hierarchical distinctions were weak or nonexistent. Being a *zēlōtēs* automatically set one off from the barely initiated hearers, but among the *zēlōtai* themselves there existed a great drive to compete and excel. Internal stratification could be furthered by defining an innermost circle: Porphyry was doing precisely that when he boasted of his status as one among the most intimate companions (ὄντα ἐν τοῖς μάλιστα ἑταῖρον).[66] Indeed, we may surmise that this innermost circle was the arena in which the most intense jockeying for position took place.

Plotinus' circle was neither the Academy nor the Lyceum. It provided its members with little or no institutional mechanisms, such as regular intramural philosophical disputations, by which they might test themselves in public against each other, or the teacher. We can discern, however, more subtle techniques of rivalry through which members of the circle mutually competed and established an informal hierarchy. Plutarch astutely noted that even the classroom setting could provide the opportunity for ambitious individuals to show off by asking the teacher sharp questions designed to make an impression. Still, Plutarch thought it unwise to overindulge in this practice, counseling that one should avoid seeming to be "proposing many problems or proposing them often himself. For this is, in a way, the mark of a man who is taking occasion to show himself off."[67] Porphyry unwittingly confirmed the justice of Plutarch's remark when he claimed superiority over fellow disciples by virtue of the fact that he served as Plotinus' chief interlocutor in the *sunousiai*.

The student who tried to build his own reputation by asking the teacher clever questions was tied to him in a complex relationship that was at once antagonistic and intimate. Porphyry attached great weight to the signs of personal devotion Plotinus showed him. He proudly pointed out that Plotinus chose to entrust him (even more than Amelius) with the task of editing his lectures.[68] He boasted also that he was the one disciple asked by his teacher to prepare notes for the reply to the Platonic questions of Eubulus, the Platonic successor in Athens, and to furnish a rebuttal to Diophanes' controversial speech.

In a competitive culture lacking a formal set of criteria for assessing a student's worth and therefore dependent on subtler hierarchizing principles, tokens of intimacy with the teacher were a crucial means of creating a pecking order among the students. (It may be worthwhile to

66. See Porphyry, *Vita Plotini* 7.50 (Armstrong, ed., 28–29).
67. Plutarch, *De recta ratione audiendi* 12 (Babbitt, ed., 232–35).
68. *Vita Plotini* 7.50–52.

pursue this connection between the tendency to revere the teacher as a divine figure and the weak institutional framework of Platonist circles, where diffused social competition flourished.)[69] In such situations, philosophical authority was an asset amplified and passed down through networks of loyalties, rather than acquired by individuals through institutional accreditation or by open display of one's abilities in contests.

Junior philosophers sometimes did reach beyond the narrow inner group to seek external affirmation of their worth by demonstrating their abilities in public discourses, but the tendency toward such exhibitions was customarily considered a fault.[70] Eunapius told how Porphyry, returning to Rome from Lilybaeum in Sicily, continued the study of *logoi* and began to discourse before a general audience in an epideictic manner.[71] The *epideixis* was a rhetorical set piece intended to demonstrate a speaker's skill before large audiences. In Eunapius' view, Porphyry's ability to make his philosophy understandable and appealing to the general public compared favorably with Plotinus' austere and difficult style,[72] but the success of Porphyry's display was credited by the audience to Plotinus himself.[73]

Diffused rivalry existed not only between students in a philosophical group but also between teachers and students. This aspect of late antique philosophical circles may initially elude us, given the devotion of students to their teachers. But both Amelius and Porphyry had come to Plotinus as advanced students, having studied respectively in the philosophical school of Lysimachus and with the famous Longinus. Porphyry remained skeptical of the teachings of Plotinus because the latter disagreed with certain precepts of Longinus, whom he disparaged as a *philologos*.[74] Plotinus' contempt was reciprocated by Longinus, who at

69. The significance of subtle gestures in the construction of social boundaries and identities has been studied to good effect by S. R. Weitman, "Intimacies: Notes towards a Theory of Social Inclusion and Exclusion," *Archives Européennes de Sociologie* 11 (1970): 348–67.

70. Such a display was considered a cocky and ambitious gesture. When some junior Epicureans made the same mistake, they were criticized. See Philodemus' Περὶ Παρρησίας 4.3–8 (= *P. Herc.* 1471, in A. Olivieri, ed., [Leipzig, 1914]).

71. Eunapius, *VS* 456 (Wright, ed., 356–57): "καὶ τῆς περὶ λόγους εἴχετο σπουδῆς, ὥστε παρῄει καὶ εἰς τὸ δημόσιον κατ᾽ ἐπίδειξιν." Treatments of this episode include: R. Goulet, "Variations romanesques sur la mélancolie de Porphyre," *Hermes* 110 (1982): 443–57; F. Cumont, "Comment Plotin détourna Porphyre du suicide," *REG* 32 (1919): 113–20.

72. Lloyd, in *Revolutions of Wisdom*, 96, makes this colorful comparison: "The occasion of the sophistic *epideixeis* has some of the razzmatazz of the fairground sideshow."

73. Bidez's characterization of Porphyry as "né vulgarisateur" is not entirely fair. *Vie de Porphyre*, iii, 60.

74. See Porphyry, *Vita Plotini* 14.19–20.

first claimed not to understand the prose of his rival's works—here we see philosophical competition taking the form of stylistic criticism, illustrating the close connection between philosophy and culture.[75]

Porphyry's own disagreement with Plotinus went beyond matters of style and conflicting loyalties. His trip to Sicily, for which Eunapius gave a medical reason, probably had to do with his dispute with Plotinus over the latter's interpretation of the Aristotelian categories. This reading has been suggested by Evangeliou and merits serious consideration.[76] Plotinus had taken issue with the categories, reducing them from ten to five, and proposed to apply them to noetic reality. Porphyry, who had studied Aristotle's works under Longinus, could not bring himself to assent to Plotinus' innovation and even wrote against his teacher to show how he had mistakenly transferred the *skopos* of the categories from the sensible realm to the intelligible realm, to which they were never designed to apply.[77]

In the half decade Porphyry spent with Plotinus, he challenged his teacher both implicitly and explicitly by posing questions during lectures, and by drawing on his own expertise in Aristotle's works. Porphyry further observed that Plotinus' philosophical abilities declined steadily with old age. For all this, Porphyry could not have usurped his teacher's standing had he tried because the ethos of the group dictated that the highest philosophical excellence rested in the personal experience of the philosopher, not in his grasp of dialectic or other branches of philosophical learning.[78] Porphyry described, with a touch of envy, how during his student days Plotinus achieved mystical union with the divine some four times.[79] In contrast to such exalted experiences, dialectic was an accomplishment suited to beginners in the philosophical life.

75. *Vita Plotini* 20.1–14.

76. Evangeliou, *Aristotle's Categories and Porphyry*, 3–5. Porphyry was probably not, as has been suggested, paralyzed by melancholy during that very productive time in his career, which saw the composition of his famous introduction to Aristotle's *Categories* and his work against the Christians.

77. See C. Evangeliou, "The Plotinian Reduction of Aristotle's Categories," *Ancient Philosophy* 7 (1987), 147–62; A. H. Armstrong, "The Background of the Doctrine 'That the Intelligibles are not Outside the Intellect,'" in *Les sources de Plotin*, Entretiens sur l'antiquité classique 5 (Vandoeuvres-Genève, 1957), 393–413. The sharp antithesis between the two philosophers' attitudes toward the Aristotelian categories has recently been brought into question; see S. K. Strange, "Plotinus, Porphyry, and the Neoplatonic Interpretation of the 'Categories,'" *ANRW* 2.36.2 (Berlin, 1987): 955–74.

78. See E. R. Dodds, "Tradition and Personal Achievement in the Philosophy of Plotinus," *JRS* 50 (1960): 1–7, esp. 7.

79. *Vita Plotini* 23.15–17. See Dodds, "Tradition and Personal Achievement"; Armstrong, "Elements in the Thought of Plotinus at Variance with Classical Intellectualism," *JHS* 93 (1973): 13–22.

Yet, while a philosopher must first be trained in dialectic, to the point of becoming a complete dialectician (ὅλως διαλεκτικόν), he was expected to progress beyond syllogisms and logic as a child advances from basic letters to grammar and rhetoric.[80]

Given these beliefs, Plotinus in effect established himself on an unshakable platform above Porphyry and the other zēlōtai.[81] Even should Porphyry prove himself more steeped in Aristotelian teachings than Plotinus and more gifted at analytical philosophy—debatable points both— such accomplishments could still carry him only halfway. Truly superior knowledge could come only through divine possession or inspiration; it could not result from training in logic and dialectic, however advanced. An Egyptian priest, who upon arrival in Rome exhibited his powers by summoning Plotinus' daimon, causing a godlike spirit to appear, effectively confirmed Plotinus' innate philosophical superiority.[82]

As the source of philosophical authority shifted away from rational discourse to divine revelation, social competition between philosophers assumed a less verbal, more indirect form. Thus when Olympius of Alexandria, who had studied under Ammonius Saccas with Plotinus,[83] decided to compete with his fellow student "out of the desire to be top dog (διὰ φιλοπρωτίαν)," he tried to undermine his competitor by resorting to *ars magica* instead of challenging him to a debate.[84] Olympius' oblique attempt to contest Plotinus' supremacy in Rome was of no avail, according to Porphyry, because Plotinus' more powerful daimon averted the spell.

When the philosopher, who cultivated an ascetic way of life and practiced philosophical discourse, came to be regarded as a holy person and a fount of wisdom, philosophical authority left dialectic and alighted on the person of the philosopher-teacher himself. Because philosophical holiness was a quality that eluded precise measurement and frustrated attempts at direct comparison with others, the philosopher effectively withdrew himself from overt challenges. This personal authority at times manifested itself physiognomically: Plotinus' "intel-

---

80. Plotinus, *Ennead* 1.3.3–4.

81. See Bidez, *Vie de Porphyre*, 60.

82. See *Vita Plotini* 10.1–14. On this episode, see Dodds, *The Greeks and the Irrational* (Berkeley, Calif., 1951), 289–91, app. 3, iii; M. J. Edwards, "Two Episodes in Porphyry's *Life of Plotinus,*" *Historia* 40 (1991): 456–64.

83. See Dodds, "Numenius and Ammonius," 29; Fowden, "Platonist Philosopher and his Circle," 368.

84. *Vita Plotini* 10.1–14 (Armstrong, ed., 1:32–33). The Greek reads: "ἀστροβολῆσαι αὐτὸν μαγεύσας ἐπεχείρησεν." This is the only active usage of ἀστροβολέομαι cited in *LSJ*. The verb connotes the withering of plants in the sun; see Theophrastus, *Historia plantarum* 4.14.2.

lect visibly lit up his face."[85] As we turn to examine the circles around Iamblichus and Aedesius, we find these themes resurfacing with noted emphasis.

PLATONISTS OF THE FOURTH CENTURY

Interspersed throughout the *Vitae philosophorum et sophistarum* (c. 399)[86] of Eunapius of Sardis are anecdotal observations about the public self-representations of philosophers and the role of competition, verbal and otherwise, in fourth-century philosophical circles. Because Eunapius' work is frequently our only source for figures and events, questions of source dependency and redaction are difficult to address.[87] Though Eunapius' *Vitae sophistarum* partly derived from eyewitness and second- and thirdhand accounts, his stories—when checked against other evidence, as with the descriptions of Iamblichus—can sometimes be shown to provide an idiosyncratic, even an inaccurate, picture.

Iamblichus and His Circle

When Iamblichus of Chalcis (c. 242–325) came to study with Porphyry, he was already an advanced student of philosophy.[88] Earlier, Plotinus and Porphyry had differed over their reception of the Aristotelian categories; Iamblichus found himself disagreeing with Porphyry at the same intersection of logic and metaphysics. Like Porphyry, Iamblichus commented on Aristotle's *Categories*, but his interpretations tended to devalue the philosopher's system as a whole. He wrongly supposed that Aristotle had derived his ideas from the work of a Pythagorean named Archytas; that where their ideas coincided, Aristotle borrowed from the Pythagorean; and that where they differed, Aristotle corrupted the an-

85. *Vita Plotini* 13.6–8 (Armstrong, ed., 1:39).

86. See T. M. Bauchich, "The Date of Eunapius' *Vitae sophistarum*," GRBS 25 (1984): 183–92; R. Goulet, "Sur la chronologie de la vie et des oeuvres d'Eunape de Sardes," JHS 100 (1980): 60–72, at 60–64. Though I also consulted J. Giangrande's edition of *Eunapii Vitae Sophistarum* (Rome, 1956), I will cite from Wright's more widely accessible Loeb edition throughout, modifying for clarity when necessary.

87. See now R. J. Penella, *Greek Philosophers and Sophists in the Fourth Century, A.D.: Studies in Eunapius of Sardis*, ARCA. Classical and Medieval Texts, Papers and Monographs 28 (Leeds, 1990).

88. See J. Bidez, "Le philosophe Jamblique et son école," REG 32 (1919), 29–40; PLRE 1:450–51, s.v. "Iamblichus I"; J. Dillon, "Iamblichus of Chalcis (c. 240–325 A.D.)," ANRW 2.36.2 (Berlin, 1987), 862–909, who gives an excellent treatment of the philosopher's life and works.

cient tradition.[89] Iamblichus thus subordinated the Aristotelian logical enterprise to a more venerable and ancient Pythagorean science. This approach harmonized well with Iamblichus' noted pythagoreanizing tendencies and with his theory of the progressive decline of divine wisdom in a passage about astronomy: "This is true for all forms of knowledge that passed from the gods to men. With the inevitable passage of time, they, having commingled with much that is mortal, began to lose the divine character of knowledge."[90]

In his *Protrepticus*, a general exhortation to the philosophical life based on the traditional genre of the *protreptikos logos*, Iamblichus blended Platonic, Aristotelian, and Neopythagorean teachings to form a new synthesis. In line with traditional philosophical thought, he began with an introductory philosophical manual that stressed the need for the exercise of reason (τὸ λογίζεσθαι) in the purification of the soul.[91] But, although his system accommodated elements from the full range of philosophical and scientific knowledge, Iamblichus placed the personal judgment of the wise holy man (ὁ φρόνιμος) at the apex of philosophical attainments.[92] Interestingly, it was precisely as a wise holy man that Iamblichus himself appeared in Eunapius' *Vitae sophistarum*.[93]

"Of Iamblichus' circle of disciples we know nothing save what Eunapius tells us, and most of that is anecdotal."[94] Eunapius represented Iamblichus' relationship with his student-companions (οἱ ἑταῖροι) as a rather peculiar one: a skeptical group of students always putting their teacher to the test. Once, after Iamblichus directed his group to detour from a road on which a dead body had been carried to avoid ritual pollution, some of his more testy companions (φιλονεικότεροι τῶν ἑταίρων) resolved to take the original route.[95] Eunapius likened these Thomases to dogs going after the proof (ὥσπερ κύνες τὸν ἔλεγχον ἀνιχνεύοντες).[96]

89. Iamblichus has been credited with giving a decisive theurgic impetus to the Neoplatonic tradition. One of his major contributions was to formally establish the centrality of a Pythagorean way of life for Platonist philosophers. Of course, Porphyry had already written a *vita* of Pythagoras, but Iamblichus' *De vita pythagorica* was not so much a personal biography as an exposition of a Pythagorean way of life. See the discussion in D. J. O'Meara, *Pythagoras Revived: Mathematics and Philosophy in Late Antiquity* (Oxford, 1989), 96–97.
90. Iamblichus, *De mysteriis* 9.4, 277.1–18 (Des Places, ed., 204–5); my translation.
91. See Iamblichus, *Protrepticus* 13.
92. See Iamblichus, *Protrepticus* 8 (Des Places, ed., 69–70): "ἔτι δὲ τίς ἡμῖν κανὼν ἢ τίς ὅρος ἀκριβέστερος τῶν ἀγαθῶν πλὴν ὁ φρόνιμος;"
93. This is just how Iamblichus portrayed Pythagoras in his *De vita pythagorica*; see esp. 28.142.
94. Fowden, "Platonist Philosopher and his Circle," 373.
95. Eunapius, *VS* 459.
96. Eunapius repeated the usage in his description of how, after Aedesius retired to a country estate, he was hounded by people who desired to learn from him (*VS* 465;

They should not have wasted their effort by doubting Iamblichus' premonition, as they soon encountered the mourners returning from the funeral.

Eunapius' use of the language of philosophical demonstration in the context of "miraculous" proof is highly suggestive and to the point. These competitive and skeptical students continued to put their master to the test after this episode until Iamblichus acceded to their wish, saying: "It is irreverent to the gods to give you this demonstration (ταῦτα ἐπιδείκνυσθαι), but for your sakes it shall be done."[97] Iamblichus then demonstrated how spirits from the springs could be summoned, a deed vividly narrated by Eunapius, who admitted he learned it as hearsay. After this incident, the disciples desisted from seeking proof of Iamblichus' power; instead, convinced by the revealing demonstrations (ἀπὸ τῶν φανέντων δειγμάτων), they began to believe him in all matters.[98]

Like the Jesus of the synoptic gospels, the traditional Iamblichus was repeatedly tested by others. His contemporary Alypius of Alexandria, a renowned philosopher and "consummate dialectician" (ὁ διαλεκτικώτατος),[99] was usually attended by a large entourage of disciples. The paths of the two men and their students often crossed, and one such chance meeting, compared by Eunapius to the intersection of orbiting luminaries, became an occasion for a public contest.[100] A gathering crowd looked on as the spectacle (θεάτρον) unfolded before them:

> Iamblichus was waiting to have questions put to him rather than to ask them, but Alypius, contrary to all expectations, postponed all questioning about philosophy since an audience had gathered and asked: "Tell me, philosopher, is a rich man either unjust or the heir of the unjust, yes or no? For there is no middle course."[101]

Wright, ed., 392–93): "Τοὺς δὲ λόγων δεομένους ἢ παιδείας διὰ τὸ προκατακεχυμένον κλέος οὐκ ἐλάνθανεν, ἀλλ᾽ **ἀνιχνεύοντες** αὐτὸν περιεστήκεσαν, **ὥσπερ κύνες** ὠρυόμενοι περὶ τὰ πρόθυρα, καὶ διασπάσασθαι ἀπειλοῦντες"; emphasis mine.

97. Eunapius, VS 459 (Wright, ed., 368–69).

98. Eunapius, VS 459 (Wright, ed., 370–71): "οὐδὲν μετὰ τοῦτο ἐζήτησεν ἡ τῶν ὁμιλητῶν πληθύς, ἀλλὰ ἀπὸ τῶν φανέντων δειγμάτων, ὥσπερ ὑπ᾽ ἀρρήκτου ῥυτῆρος εἵλκοντο, καὶ πᾶσιν ἐπίστευον."

99. This is precisely the epithet the historian Sozomen chose to apply to Arius of Alexandria in Hist. eccl. 1.15.

100. See J. C. Faris, "'Occasions' and 'Non-Occasions,'" in M. Douglas, ed., Rules and Meanings (New York, 1973), 45–49; idem, "Validations in Ethnographical Description: the Lexicon of 'Occasions' in Cat Harbour," Man n.s. 3 (1968): 112–24.

101. Eunapius VS 460 (Wright, ed., 372–73): "'Ιαμβλίχου δὲ τὸ ἐπερωτηθῆναι μᾶλλον ὑπομείναντος ἢ τὸ ἐπερωτᾶν, ὁ 'Αλύπιος παρὰ πᾶσαν ὑπόνοιαν ἀφεὶς ἅπασαν φιλόσοφον ἐρώτησιν, τοῦ δὲ θεάτρου γενόμενος, 'Εἰπέ μοι, φιλόσοφε,' πρὸς αὐτὸν ἔφη 'ὁ

In his preference to receive rather than pose a philosophical question, Iamblichus resembled the legendary Apollonius of Tyana.[102] Presumably he planned to use the question as a springboard for a continuous, epideictic discourse on a given philosophical theme. But because their meeting had turned into a public spectacle, Alypius decided against the customary practice of proposing a philosophical theme (ἐρωτᾶν); instead, he asked Iamblichus to solve a logical dilemma.[103] Eunapius' stress on the fact that Alypius' action was contrary to accustomed usage (παρὰ πᾶσαν ὑπόνοιαν) tells us, by inversion, the cultural norms of philosophical interactions.

As described in the narrative, Alypius confronted Iamblichus with a request for a dialectical premiss. His further invocation of the phrase τούτων γὰρ μέσον οὐδέν, expressing the logical principle of the excluded middle, left Iamblichus no room to modify the limited choices presented to him.[104] Iamblichus was asked to give an answer of yes or no (ναὶ ἤ οὔ;) to a cunningly fashioned proposition: in neither case could he avoid offending the well-to-do among the audience. Once a particular proposition had been chosen by Iamblichus, it would become a thesis for Alypius to contradict or render meaningless. It is significant that the "consummate dialectician" Alypius allegedly refused to apply his dialectical skills to a discussion of metaphysics but instead aimed to impress his audience by sophistically posing an ethical dilemma.

Iamblichus so resented the limitation of the two admissible premisses in Alypius' *petitio principii* that he declined to respond. But after departing from the scene, Iamblichus reflected on the encounter and came to be impressed by Alypius' astuteness. He later cultivated a friendship with Alypius and held him in such high regard that, when the latter died without committing any of his teachings to writing, he composed a biography in commemoration.

Aedesius and His Circle

Following Iamblichus' death and the trial and execution of his prize student Sopater for treason, Aedesius of Cappadocia (d. 352–55) took over

---

πλούσιος ἢ ἄδικος ἢ ἀδίκου κληρονόμος, ναὶ ἢ οὔ; τούτων γὰρ μέσον οὐδέν.'" The translation offered by Wright—"giving himself up to making an effect with his audience" (373), for the genitive absolute in the Greek—is overwrought and misleading; I have replaced his phrase with my own in the text.

102. Philostratus, *Vita Apollonii* 1.17.
103. See Dillon, "Iamblichus of Chalcis," 873.
104. See Hadot, "Philosophie, dialectique, rhétorique dans l'antiquité," 143.

the master's *diatribē* and circle of student-companions.[105] Aedesius established himself in Pergamum, where his students engaged in competitive
disputations (ἆθλοι ὅσοι περὶ λόγους ἦσαν) either philosophical or rhetorical in nature.[106] He observed with dissatisfaction his students' arrogance, and strongly discouraged the putting on of airs[107]—interesting
advice from a man whom Eunapius described as one of the more contentious of Iamblichus' pupils.[108]

Regarded as part of the Iamblichan *diadochē*, Aedesius was courted
by the young prince Julian, who desired to study with him.[109] An incident that arose from Julian's attempt to become Aedesius' student is
highly instructive about the diffused rivalry among Aedesius' disciples.

Because Maximus of Ephesus and Priscus, Aedesius' foremost pupils, were not in Asia Minor at the time, the old philosopher entrusted
the education of the prince to Eusebius of Myndus and Chrysanthius.
Eusebius was a younger pupil of Aedesius who excelled in the dialectical art and who—according to Eunapius, who no doubt heard the story
from Chrysanthius, his erstwhile teacher and informant—regarded Maximus' emphasis on theurgy to be mere theatricality unworthy of a true
philosopher. Eusebius privately scorned Maximus' conjurer's tricks, yet
in deference to a more advanced fellow student, he never revealed his
profound reservations while Maximus was present (παρόντος μέν). At
those times, according to Eunapius, Eusebius

> used to avoid precise and exact divisions of a disputation and dialectical
> devices and subtleties (τὴν ἀκρίβειαν τὴν ἐν τοῖς μέρεσι τοῦ λόγου καὶ
> τὰς διαλεκτικὰς μηχανὰς καὶ πλοκὰς ὑπέφευγεν); though when Maxi-
> mus was not there (ἀπόντος δέ) he would shine out like a bright star.[110]

105. Eunapius, *VS* 461 (Wright, ed., 376–77): "ἐκδέχεται δὲ τὴν Ἰαμβλίχου δια-
τριβὴν καὶ ὁμιλίαν ἐς τοὺς ἑταίρους Αἰδέσιος ὁ ἐκ Καππαδοκίας." Sopater, Iamblichus'
famous pupil and heir presumptive, was condemned to death by imperial order. See discussion of Eunapius' account and the role of Sopater in Fowden, "Platonist Philosopher
and his Circle," 375–76.

106. Eunapius, *VS* 481.

107. Eunapius, *VS* 481–82.

108. Eunapius, *VS* 458–59.

109. For Julian's own ideas about what the Platonist succession meant, see his *Oratio*
7.222B (Wright, ed., 2:116–17).

110. *VS* 474 (Wright, ed., 432–33). The way Wright translates the next sentence ("ὅ
τε Ἰουλιανὸς τὸν ἄνδρα ἐσεβάζετο") suggests that Julian first revered Eusebius of Myndus
but turned against him after finding out about Maximus of Ephesus. It is more reasonable
to construe that the person (τὸν ἄνδρα) whom Julian worshipped was Chrysanthius, not
Eusebius, because of the absence of an adversative conjunction. In this view, Julian was
never very taken with Eusebius' strictly logical approach to philosophy. Furthermore, Julian's deep respect for Chrysanthius is a common theme throughout Eunapius' work; see,
e.g., *VS* 475 (Wright, ed., 432–33): "θεόν τινα νομίσας τὸν Χρυσάνθιον ἐπὶ τῷ λόγῳ."

When Eusebius disagreed with Maximus' theurgic practices, he was, knowingly or unknowingly, also competing with this elder student of Aedesius for legitimacy and authority within the philosophical circle. Thus he invariably concluded his discourses by advising his hearers to shun the deceptions of magic, sorcery, and wonder workers and to instead pursue the study of dialectic, which alone enabled one to grasp true reality (τὰ ὄντως ὄντα).

Asked by Julian to clarify his veiled polemic, Eusebius openly aired his differences with Maximus. He referred to the latter as an elder and more variously accomplished (πολλὰ ἐκπεπαιδευμένων) prodigy who had somehow "gone off the deep end." Maximus was someone who, during a spell of political favor, was said to have impressed the ordinary people of Constantinople as a walking oracle who bedecked himself in rich silken robes instead of the philosopher's humble garb.[111] The philosopher manqué had lost more than his outward seemliness; he had abandoned the security of rational philosophical demonstration (αἱ ἀπόδειξεις) in favor of what Eusebius described as madness (ἡ μανία).[112] Once, Eusebius explained, Maximus even invited his younger fellow students to a seance at the temple of Hecate, where he offered proof of his superior power by summoning the presence of divine spirits. For Eusebius, Maximus' theatrical exhibition was precisely the sort of sham that philosophical demonstration should unmask. He passed on the following advice to Julian: "You must not marvel at any of these things [Maximus' miracles], even as I marvel not, but rather believe that the thing of the highest importance is that purification of the soul which is attained by reason (διὰ τοῦ λόγου)."[113]

His words fell on deaf ears. Learning of Maximus' reputation, Julian judged Eusebius not to be the "true philosopher" he had been seeking and turned to the theurgist with a Parthian shot: "πρόσεχε τοῖς βι-

111. Eunapius, VS 477.
112. Maximus of Ephesus had composed a commentary on Aristotle's *Categories*, known to us from Simplicius, *In Categorias* 1.15.
113. VS 475 (Wright, ed., 434–35). One may argue that this episode signals Julian's rejection of the Platonic tradition represented by Plotinus and Porphyry in favor of the theurgical tradition represented by Iamblichus and Maximus. Such a preference would also explain why the future emperor refused to accept the tutelage of Aetius, an accomplished Christian "dialectician-philosopher" (see Chapter 4) whom his brother Gallus Caesar admired. According to Philostorgius, *Hist. eccl.* 3.27, and the disputed *Ep.* 82 from Gallus to Julian (Wright, ed., 3:288–91), Gallus sent Aetius to Julian's side in 351 in the hope that Aetius would steer the prince away from his interest in traditional polytheism. In this view, Julian's refusal to be influenced by Aetius was triggered as much by the latter's Christian views as by his emphasis on syllogisms: for Julian, Aetius had no more access to the true, elevated knowledge of the divine than had Eusebius of Myndus.

βλίοις." [114] By commenting that he was leaving Eusebius to his learned tomes, Julian tapped into an ancient reservoir of ambivalence toward book knowledge. Julian preferred to receive his knowledge through a personal intermediary. Though he had read Aristotle's logical treatises, he preferred to style himself the pupil of Priscus, who had sent him the works and who thereby, in Julian's view, initiated him into that branch of knowledge. [115]

Julian confessed to Priscus that he found Aristotle's logic easier to grasp than Plato's. [116] In general, philosophical dialectic had the dubious advantage of being easily learned. Even the proverbial old woman was supposed to command a rudimentary knowledge of logic. [117] In some measure, philosophers' objection to sophists and their art derived from the fact that rhetoric was thought to be a *technē* that could be mastered by dint of hard work (φιλοπονία). Iamblichus believed that a student could rapidly master the art of discourse (ἡ τέχνη κατὰ λόγους) to become a rival to his teacher; [118] such mastery was a cheap virtue that could be appropriated by repetition and practice: "ἀρετὴ δὲ ἥτις ἐξ ἔργων πολλῶν συνίσταται." [119] This sentiment revealed a deep-seated prejudice against achievement through hard work that persists today in written evaluations of student performance; the adjective "diligent," now as then, euphemistically hints at a slight deficiency in intellectual or philosophical capacity. [120] For instance, Porphyry may well have been putting down his fellow student Amelius when he commented on the latter's diligence in compiling voluminous lecture notes.

The Testing of Philosophers and Retreat from Competition

Sometimes the ability to answer questions meant the difference between life and death: charged with having fomented insurrection, Indian gym-

---

114. Eunapius, *VS* 475. See a similar usage in *P. Oxy.* 3:264: "ἀλλὰ τοῖς βιβλίοις σου αὐτὸ μόνον πρόσεχε φιλολογῶν καὶ ἀπ᾽ αὐτῶν ὄνησιν ἕξεις."

115. See Julian, *Ep.* 2 (Wright, ed., 3:2–7); the numbering of Julian's letters in this work follows that used by Wright in his LCL volumes.

116. Julian, *Ep.* 2 (Wright, ed., 3:4–5): "For while Maximus of Tyre in six books was able to initiate me to some extent into Plato's logic (τῆς Πλατωνικῆς λογικῆς), you, with one book, have made me, perhaps I may even say, a complete initiate (βάκχον) in the philosophy of Aristotle, but at any rate a thyrsus-bearer."

117. See Damascius, *Fragmenta* 356 (Zintzen, ed., 289).

118. *Protrepticus* 20 (Des Places, ed., 123ff).

119. *Protrepticus* 20 (Des Places, ed., 124).

120. See P. Bourdieu, *Homo Academicus*, trans. P. Collier (Stanford, Calif., 1984), 208–10.

nosophists were interrogated by Alexander the Great, who threatened to execute them if they failed to answer satisfactorily his supposedly insoluble questions (ἐρωτήματα ἄπορα).[121] But more often the stakes were not so high, or the matter was purely of antiquarian interest, as when the Christian Theodosius II (408–50) asked seven pagan philosophers, in a folkloric variant of the riddle test, to explain the significance of the statuary on the *spina* of the hippodrome in Constantinople.[122]

Testing philosophers in this manner was a popular sport. Witness Eustathius, the philosopher who in 358 conducted an embassy to Shāpūr and impressed, though finally failed to convince, the king of kings with his eloquence.[123] He triumphed in the face of such tests because, according to Eunapius, he was "most gifted with eloquence when put to the test (εἰς πεῖραν λόγων ἐλθεῖν δεινότατον)."[124] At these times, his words seemed "nothing less than witchcraft (οὐκ ἔξω γοητείας)."[125] But not all philosophers responded to questions in the expected fashion. After the deaths of Sosipatra and Eustathius, their son Antoninus lived and worshiped at the native Egyptian shrines at the Canobic mouth of the Nile by Alexandria.[126] According to Eunapius, people came from all over (πανταχόθεν) to converse with him, at which time,

> on being granted an interview with him, some would propound a logical problem, and were forthwith abundantly fed with the philosophy of Plato; but others, who raised questions as to things divine, encountered a statue. For he would utter not a word to any one of them, but fixing his eyes and gazing up at the sky he would lie there speechless and unrelenting, nor did anyone ever see him lightly enter into converse with any man on such themes as these.[127]

121. Plutarch, *Vita Alexandri* 64.

122. *Parastaseis syntomai chronikai* 64, in Averil Cameron and J. Herrin, eds., *Constantinople in the Early Eighth Century: The Parastaseis Syntomai Chronikai* (Leiden, 1984), 140–47.

123. Ammianus Marcellinus, *Res gestae* 17.5.15, 17.14.1.

124. It is likely that this Eustathius was the author of a commentary on Aristotle's *Categories* referred to by Elias, *In Aristotelis categorias* 243ʳ (A. Busse, ed., *Eliae in Porphyrii isagogen et Aristotelis categorias commentaria* CAG 18.1 [Berlin, 1900], 156).

125. Eunapius, *VS* 465 (Wright, ed., 392–95). On the intimate ties between elocutionary speech and spells from early times, see J. de Romilly, *Magic and Rhetoric in Ancient Greece* (Cambridge, Mass., 1975), 3–22.

126. See Eunapius, *VS* 471. For a review of the history of native Egyptian cults at Canobus, see F. Thélamon, *Païens et chrétiens au IVe siècle: L'apport de l' "Histoire ecclésiastique" de Rufin d'Aquilée* (Paris, 1981), 207–34.

127. Eunapius, *VS* 471–72 (Wright, ed., 420–21): "συνουσίας δὲ ἀξιωθέντες, οἱ μὲν λογικὸν πρόβλημα προθέμενοι, ἀφθόνως καὶ αὐθωρὸν τῆς Πλατωνικῆς ἐνεφοροῦντο σοφίας, οἱ δὲ τῶν θειοτέρων τι προβάλλοντες, ἀνδριάντι συνετύγχανον· οὐκοῦν ἐφθέγγετο πρὸς αὐτῶν οὐδένα, ἀλλὰ τὰ ὄμματα στήσας καὶ διαθρήσας εἰς τὸν οὐρανόν, ἄναυδος ἔκειτο καὶ ἄτεγκτος, οὐδέ τις εἶδεν αὐτὸν περὶ τῶν τοιούτων ῥαδίως εἰς ὁμιλίαν ἐλθόντα ἀνθρώπων."

When Antoninus chose not to accept all public challenges, he became a silent oracle. This is understandable, for the wisdom that Antoninus cultivated was, according to Eunapius, inaccessible to the masses: "σοφίαν τε ἄγνωστον τοῖς πολλοῖς." What remains unexplained is the selectivity of Antoninus' show of reserve: Why should he refuse to answer questions asked by people deemed qualified to converse with him (συνουσίας δὲ ἀξιωθέντες)? Perhaps he remained silent when asked about divine matters for the same reason that he shunned theurgy and similar practices: he feared accusations of sorcery, which was condemned under imperial law and frequently punished with execution.[128] But what is interesting in this scenario is the implicit division of philosophical knowledge into two distinct categories, logic and theology—the former being suitable for open discussion, the latter clearly out of bounds.

Though philosophers frequently found themselves tested in late antiquity, some chose to remove themselves from this relentless public scrutiny either by some perspicuous demonstration of power or by arguing the negative effects of cutthroat competition in public disputations. Two of Eunapius' philosophers, Priscus and Chrysanthius, deliberately refrained from philosophical disputation while furnishing quite incisive reasons for their choices.

Aedesius' pupil Priscus, praised by Julian as a true philosopher, taught at Athens, where he became a prominent figure.[129] Eunapius was especially interested in Priscus' *ethos*, to which he devoted a lengthy, though not entirely flattering, description.[130] He portrayed the philosopher as exceedingly secretive (κρυψίνους τε ἦν ἄγαν), with a stuffy, antiquarian attitude toward learning, and extreme in the caution with which he communicated his views to broader audiences. His reluctance to engage in public debates cast a faint shadow over his reputation, for

he might have been thought uneducated (ἀπαίδευτος), because it was hard to induce him to engage in disputation (διὰ τὸ μόλις χωρεῖν ἐς

128. Eunapius, VS 471 (Wright, ed., 418–19): "ἐπεδείκνυτο μὲν γὰρ οὐδὲν θεουργὸν καὶ παράλογον ἐς τὴν φαινομένην αἴσθησιν, τὰς βασιλικὰς ἴσως ὁρμὰς ὑφορώμενος ἑτέρωσε φερούσας." Fowden assumes that imperial attacks on pagan cults inspired Antoninus' reticence; see "Pagan Holy Man," 58. Penella, in Greek Philosophers and Sophists, 59, takes Eunapius' comment as a hint that Antoninus possessed theurgic powers. It is true that during a time of magic trials the practice of theurgy could entail serious dangers for the unwary practitioner, yet the passage in Eunapius explaining why Antoninus shunned theurgy is not connected with the later statement that Antoninus refused to enter into a discussion concerning "something more divine." Still, according to Iamblichus, in De vita pythagorica 32.215–18, his speaking out about divine matters nearly cost Pythagoras his life at the hands of the tyrant Phalaris of Acragas.

129. See Julian, Ep. 1 (Wright, ed., 3:2–3). See also Libanius, Oratio 14.32, 14.34.

130. See Eunapius, VS 481 (Wright, ed., 460–61).

διάλεξιν), and he kept his own convictions hidden as though he were guarding a treasure, and used to term prodigals those who too lightly gave out their views on these matters.[131]

This aloofness was disapprovingly regarded as eccentric by his contemporaries. Eunapius, realizing the need for an explanation of this apparently unphilosophical avoidance of disputation, had Priscus couch his reluctance in terms of the adverse effects of agonistic disputation (διάλεξις) on philosophers:

> For he used to say that one who is beaten (νικώμενον) in philosophical argument (ἐν ταῖς διαλέξεσιν) does not thereby become milder, but rather, as he fights against the might of truth and suffers the pains of thwarted ambition (φιλότιμον), he becomes more savage, and ends by hating both letters and philosophy equally, and by being thoroughly confused in his mind. For this reason, therefore, he usually maintained his reserve.[132]

Thus, Priscus attributed his reticence to his concern for adversaries whom he might better in debate. Yet this philanthropic motive does not square with Eunapius' own description of the philosopher as a proud and self-centered man. Priscus valued his inner calm much more than the rewards of a successful debate. He may even have feared that he might himself experience the anguish of the vanquished. Regardless of the authenticity of the motive attributed to Priscus, Eunapius' account makes explicit an ancient awareness of the pitfalls of agonistic disputation.

The views here ascribed to Priscus were later repeated in a similar story about Chrysanthius. By contrast with the haughty Priscus, Chrysanthius was a mild-mannered man, yet he shared with Priscus a deep ambivalence toward public disputations. Like Priscus, he held back from open contests because he believed the potential harm of public debate to outweigh its benefit: "It was not easy to rouse him to philosophical discussions or competitions (περὶ τὰς διαλέξεις καὶ φιλονεικίας), because he perceived that it is especially in such contests that men become embittered."[133] Here, too, the philosopher's avoidance of public competition was ascribed to his concern for others. Yet we can accept this reason at face value only if we are prepared to grant that neither Priscus nor Chrysanthius ever lost or anticipated losing a debate.

Chrysanthius shied away from public confrontations and contrived

131. Eunapius, VS 481 (Wright, ed., 460–61).
132. Eunapius, VS 481 (Wright, ed., 460–63).
133. Eunapius, VS 502 (Wright, ed., 548–49).

not to become the object of others' envy by studiously cultivating a conciliatory style, to the extent of commending the worthless statements
of others and applauding their "incorrect conclusions (τὰ δοξαζόμενα
κακῶς)."[134] As with Priscus, Chrysanthius' reluctance to dispute was
generally perceived as a sign of weak intellect and deficiency in learning.[135] The philosopher thus enjoyed a reputation for mildness (τὴν
πρᾳότητα) rather than for philosophical virtuosity. Given that Eunapius
reported but did not share this appraisal, it appears to accurately reflect
the contemporary reputations of the two philosophers.

Chrysanthius' reluctance to enter in a dialectical disputation before
an audience might not have been due entirely to his professed altruism.
Even philosophers could not be expected to excel in all forms of public
display. It may be that Chrysanthius shunned the *epideixis*, the declama-
tory showpiece by which Porphyry and other philosophers established
reputations for themselves, because he was not equipped to succeed in
that genre.[136] His gift was evident when he discoursed on philosophy
(διαλεγόμενος), and in this area he enjoyed an impressive reputation
among fellow philosophers:

> If in an assembly of those most distinguished for learning any dissen-
> sion arose, and he thought fit to take part in the discussion, the place
> became hushed in silence as though no one were there. So unwilling
> were they to face his questions (ἐρωτήσεις) and definitions (διορι-
> σμούς) [of philosophical terms] and powers of quoting from memory,
> but they would retire into the background and carefully refrain from
> discussion or contradiction (ἔξω λόγου καὶ ἀντιρρήσεως), lest their fail-
> ure should be too evident.[137]

According to Eunapius, it was Chrysanthius' superiority that caused
others to refrain from responding to his words. But this interpretation
of the silences that greeted Chrysanthius' discourses may well be Eunapius' own. Much less flattering reasons may be adduced. No matter, the
effect was the same: Chrysanthius, when he saw fit to take part or to
speak, could lecture on without fear of interruption from the audience.

134. Eunapius, *VS* 502 (Wright, ed., 548–49). One cannot help wondering whether
this comment is a clue to the meaning of Chrysanthius' public applause for the dialectical
prowess of Eusebius of Myndus.
135. Eunapius, *VS* 502 (Wright, ed., 548–51): "Many of those who knew him only
slightly, and therefore had not sounded the depth of his soul, accused him of lack of
intelligence." Compare Jerome, *Ep.* 52.8: "si solus tacueris, solus ab omnibus stultitiae
condemnaberis."
136. See Eunapius, *VS* 480. This point is quite confused in the *VS*, because elsewhere
(e.g., *VS* 502) Chrysanthius' skill in oratory is underscored.
137. Eunapius, *VS* 502 (Wright, ed., 548–49).

Physiognomy and the Anatomy of Visible Holiness

Vulnerability to public discomfiture, whether their own or others', was of great concern to philosophers of late antiquity, who, with the notable exception of the Cynics,[138] were careful to cultivate an image of unperturbed serenity. This aspiration to dignified styling assumed a high degree of self-consciousness in the fourth century, when it was correlated with a strong interest in physiognomy.[139]

Eunapius' portrait of Chrysanthius accorded well with the concern of philosophers for their public image and the sensibilities revealed in physiognomic works. People used to think (ἐνόμισαν) that Chrysanthius underwent a physical transformation as he engaged in dialectical disputations (ἐν ταῖς λογικαῖς κινήσεσιν):[140] his hairs stood on end (τῆς τε τριχὸς ὑποφριττούσης αὐτῷ), his eyes suggested that his inner soul (ἔνδον τὴν ψυχήν) was set in motion around his teachings (περὶ τὰ δόγματα),[141] and he appeared altogether transformed; he had become another (ἕτερόν τινα τοῦτον). The tense poignancy of logical disputations did not cause Chrysanthius to lose his classical composure, but allowed him to transcend it.

The Eunapian Maximus of Ephesus also had "winged eyes." An intense interest in the eyes can be found in the physiognomic texts and in imperial and philosophical biographies, and is richly documented by late antique material representations. The recently published group of philosophers' portraits from Aphrodisias in Caria includes a late antique tondo of Pindar that iconographically adapted a fifth-century portrait style.[142] The classical Greek style of a tight-lipped, reserved figure re-

138. For the exhibitionist antics of Cynic philosophers, see Dio Chrysostom, *Oratio* 32.8.

139. Physical description—that is, the comparison of a person's features to set classical ideals—became an instrument for assigning praise and blame in late antiquity. Julian, who styled himself a philosopher, was attacked by Gregory of Nazianzus with unflattering observations about his physiognomy. In contrast, Ammianus Marcellinus, Julian's supporter, praised the emperor according to the same conventions. On this ancient science, see E. C. Evans, "Physiognomics in the Ancient World," *Transactions of the American Philosophical Society* n.s. 59 (1969): 5–97. A supposed revival in physiognomics in the fourth century among people associated with Julian is explored on 74–83. Among the figures cited is Oribasius of Pergamum (b. 325?), a student of Zeno and private physician to Julian, who wrote a medical treatise on physiognomy.

140. Eunapius, *VS* 502.

141. This was a literary and hagiographical topos; see Marinus, *Vita Procli* 23.

142. R. R. R. Smith, "Late Roman Philosopher Portraits from Aphrodisias," *JRS* 80 (1990), 127–55; and idem, "Late Roman Philosophers," in R. R. R. Smith and K. T. Erim, eds., *Aphrodisias Papers 2: The Theatre, A Sculptor's Workshop, Philosophers, and Coin-Types,* Journal of Roman Archaeology Supplementary Series 2 (Ann Arbor, Mich., 1991), 144–58. See also Von Heintze, *"Vir sanctus et gravis."*

flected the mores of the traditional aristocracy. In the late antique adaptation, the mouth was drilled open and the eyes and eyebrows received greater detailing to make them appear more intense. According to Smith, this modification in effect transformed the archaic poet Pindar "from a cool, aloof aristocrat into a committed, energetic exponent of the spiritual hellenism of Late Antiquity."[143] The "Old Philosopher" portrait from the same group suggests a similar emphasis:

> It combines echoes from hellenistic philosopher images, with an expression of wide-eyed fervour that are very much of its own age. The knitted brows were a familiar sign for concentration and vigour of mind, for intellectual power, but the expression of the whole portrait is rather of an overriding intense, beatific spirituality.[144]

These developments in literary and material representations broadly parallel shifts in emphasis in philosophical ideology. Increasingly, a true philosopher was someone whose primary claim to consideration was divine inspiration.

In Eunapius' account, Sosipatra's inspired teaching compared favorably to the precision of Aedesius' philosophical statements ($\dot{\epsilon}\nu$ $\lambda\dot{o}\gamma o\iota\varsigma$ $\dot{\alpha}\kappa\rho\dot{\iota}\beta\epsilon\iota\alpha\nu$); she was likened to an omniscient goddess, or an oracle who alternated between bacchic frenzy and mystical silence.[145] This quality of hers could not be quantified or measured, unlike the gift of precise *logoi*, and hence could not be used as a basis for direct competition between philosophers.[146] Instead, competition rested in the degree of public recognition. A philosopher who desired the high estimation of others acquired it by claiming privileged access to the divine world. He achieved this access not so much through the methods of rational inquiry as through the mediation of a divine companion—though of course these two elements were not necessarily incompatible, as Socrates himself boasted of his daimon.[147] Thus, the true worth of a philosopher depended not on his skill in philosophical discourse but on the nature and power of his daimon.

143. Smith, "Late Roman Philosopher Portraits," 134.

144. Smith, "Late Roman Philosopher Portraits," 145. What is lacking in Smith's account is a clear statement of the art hermeneutical principles by which such interpretive meanings can be attached to the portraits. It would be interesting to determine the nature of the common ground between portraiture and literary representations. A contextualized theory on the relationship of patronage to artisanal production may furnish this missing link.

145. See Eunapius, *VS* 469–70 and Dodds, "Numenius and Ammonius," 30n. 1.

146. On the relation of precision to measurement, see D. Kurz, AKPIBEIA: *Das Ideal der Exaktheit bei den Griechen bis Aristoteles* (Göttingen, 1970) and Lloyd, *Revolutions of Wisdom*, 215–84.

147. See Plutarch, *De genio Socratis* 580F–81D, and Hirzel, *Dialog*, 2:148–63.

IN SEARCH OF TRUE PHILOSOPHERS
The Formation of Philosophical Identity

Like Julian, many people in the fourth century were constantly on the lookout for "true philosophers," [148] but the means used to find them varied with the seeker. At a time when *haireseis* had declined in importance and coherence and when *diadochai* or philosophical successions were not yet firmly established, there were no easy institutional markers or credentials that could set off "true" philosophers from pretenders to the title. Broad public recognition was of uncertain value. Ammonius Saccas, for example, who later enjoyed an enormous reputation as a philosopher (gained in part through the accomplishments of his students), was not known to Plotinus as one of the "approved" philosophers (οἱ εὐδοκιμοῦντες: individuals normally honored with statues and other civic privileges) in Alexandria when Plotinus was searching for a more fulfilling preceptor.

The problem of philosophical identity gradually resolved itself. By the fifth century, the notion of a Platonic *diadochē* as a holy race had become firmly entrenched in the work of Hierocles, who attempted to harmonize the entire philosophical tradition. [149] Later, Marinus traced a "Golden Chain" all the way back to Solon. [150] Even Eunapius tried to create a "true" *diadochē* of philosophers who could trace their lineage through Iamblichus to Plotinus and beyond to Plato. The crop of philosophers after the reign of Septimius Severus (d. 211) constituted for Eunapius the fourth and most current generation of philosophers. [151] Establishing this purified genealogy was not an easy task because the philosophers Eunapius wished to include did not always have a fixed abode and thus could not be classified according to locality. Iamblichus taught that, though the philosopher's body dwelled in one city, his *dianoia* traveled everywhere (πανταχῆ). [152] The geographical specificity of philosophical holiness underscored by Garth Fowden in his admirable study of late Platonists was a later fifth-century development that be-

---

148. See Julian, *Ep.* 1 (Wright, ed., 3:2–3), a letter to Priscus. See also Dio Cassius 52.36.4.

149. Hierocles, in Photius, *Bibliotheca* 214 [173a] (Henry, ed., 3:129–30). See Lynch, *Aristotle's School*, 184–89, and Fowden, "Pagan Holy Man," 33.

150. Marinus, *Vita Procli* 26.

151. R. Goulet, "Eunape et ses devanciers: À propos de *Vitae sophistarum*, p. 5.4–17, Giangrande" *GRBS* 20 (1979): 161–72; G. Nencei, "Eunapio, *Vitae sophistarum* II, 2, 6–8 e la periodizzazione della φιλόσοφος ἱστορία," *Annali della Scuola Normale Superiore di Pisa, Classe di Lettere e Filosofia* 3 (1973): 95–102.

152. See *Protrepticus* 14 (Des Places, ed., 104).

speaks the desirability of formal signs of recognition and authority derived from association with places that could boast a distinguished philosophical past.[153]

Before most popular audiences, whoever wore the *tribōnion*, the philosopher's cloak, and carried *sakkia* crammed with books could lay claim to being a philosopher. Even Christians began to appropriate the name in earnest. But Eunapius took pains to distinguish his philosophers from the common lot by mentioning in passing, for example, that certain people who professed to be philosophers exploited the fame of the philosophical couple Eustathius and Sosipatra by repeatedly quoting their sayings.[154] Eunapius' decision to censure by silence has effectively denied us knowledge of those whom he considered unworthy to be named philosophers.

Philosophers and Sophists: Dynamics of Categorization

An even more pressing difficulty in the formation of a distinctive philosophical identity was the well-documented confusion of professional boundaries between philosophers and sophists in late antiquity.[155] Isidore of Pelusium did not help matters when he called his correspondent Harpocras a sophist in name but a philosopher in his way of life.[156] The boundaries were transgressed not only in the attribution of professional labels but also in the professional practices themselves. Nymphidianus of Smyrna, the brother of Maximus of Ephesus and a trained sophist who achieved great renown under Julian,[157] naturally practiced the composition of rhetorical themes and the handling of problems ($\mu\varepsilon\lambda\acute{\varepsilon}\tau\alpha\varsigma$ καὶ τὰ ζητήματα), but also engaged in, though with less facility, the preliminary statements of proofs and philosophical disputation (τὰ δὲ ἐν προάγωσι καὶ τῷ διαλεχθῆναι).[158]

Eunapius' *Vitae sophistarum*, like the work of his predecessor Philostratus, included the *bioi* of individuals judged by various criteria to be-

153. Fowden, "Pagan Holy Man," 38–48.

154. Eunapius, *VS* 471.

155. See G. R. Stanton, "Sophists and Philosophers: Problems of Classification," *AJP* 94 (1973): 350–64, esp. 350; J. L. Moles, "The Career and Conversion of Dio Chrysostom," *JHS* 98 (1978): 79–100, esp. 88–93 on Dio Chrysostom; Hahn, *Der Philosoph und die Gesellschaft*, 46–53, on Philostratus.

156. Isidore of Pelusium, *Ep.* 5.458 (*PG* 78:1592C).

157. Nymphidianus served as Julian's *magister epistularum graecarum* in 361/363; see *PLRE* 1:636.

158. Eunapius, *VS* 497.

long to the categories of philosophers and sophists. Although Eunapius himself was trained as a sophist and considered *ho sophistēs* as an appellation of praise, it is far from clear that the philosophers he eulogized shared his view.

On the whole, Eunapius' philosophical heroes did not seek approbation from the general public. Given that this common trait was a topos favored by Eunapius, still we detect a number of reasons for the philosophers' avoidance of the limelight. The first was the growing importance of an imperial Christianity that claimed a monopoly on wisdom and the pressures this competition placed on pagan philosophers.[159] Another was the traditional philosophical suspicion of high office, noticeable ever since Diogenes asked Alexander of Macedon to move so as not to spoil his sunbathing. Chrysanthius was commended by Eunapius for his lack of experience with real authority; the abject fate of Maximus of Ephesus, whose involvement in high imperial politics resulted in his execution, served as a lesson discouraging philosophers from entering the maelstroms of high political life.[160] Indeed, the theurgist would have done well to heed the advice of Iamblichus, who, in his *Protrepticus*, urged his readers to shun the civic life of late antique society.[161] A third, less obvious consideration was the need for philosophers to distinguish themselves from sophists.

In the perennial battle of professional categories, the fundamental difference between philosophers and sophists rested in their valuation of the ends of verbal skill. The one camp, according to this analysis, entered into public debates to advance philosophical knowledge and to establish the truth through a dialectical process of discovery, whereas the other mobilized rhetorical techniques to achieve victory in law courts and political debates. The philosophers could be construed as engaging in a contest between ideas, not persons; the sophists, as fighting with others for supremacy and material advantage.

Persuasion, not objective truth, was the professed goal of sophistic argumentation. Eristics, as taught by Protagoras and popularized by treatises such as the *Dissoi Logoi* (Contrasting arguments, c. 400 B.C.E), aimed at winning over an audience, not at establishing *epistēmē*. The value of a sophistic argument could be judged only by its efficacy in securing victory, which was in turn measured by the extent of public acclaim.

159. See Brown, *Power and Persuasion*, 126ff., on the competition, both implicit and explicit, between Christian monks and pagan philosophers.

160. See Ammianus Marcellinus, *Res gestae* 29.1.42.

161. Iamblichus, *Protrepticus* 13.

The status of sophists thus depended almost exclusively on external affirmation, manifested in cheers and applause. According to Eunapius, when a "town and gown" dispute broke out in Athens[162] and the sophists were afraid to declaim in public (δημοσίᾳ) for fear of violence, the famous sophist Julian of Cappadocia built in his house a private auditorium that imitated the architectural style of the public theater, complete with marble facing and busts of his favorite students. Within this "private" public arena, the sophists of Athens, safe from the angry townspeople, continued to compete (ἀγωνιζόμενοι) among themselves in winning applause and fame.[163]

The judgment of the audience at hand was the central concern of sophists. They took great pains to solicit the audience's goodwill, and sometimes planted cheering squads made up of students or paid supporters.[164] Partisans commonly turned against their champion's opposition by stirring up a *thorubos*, a disruptive uproar—that is, by heckling—in the hope of ruining the competitor's delivery or at least adversely affecting its reception.[165] Even someone as skilled in rhetoric as the famed Prohaeresius, a student of Julian of Cappadocia, found his enthusiasm considerably dampened one day when he found his audience packed with rival partisans. His response is highly instructive: he asked them not to clap during his delivery. This imaginative request turned out to be a successful tactic, for Prohaeresius' rhetorical genius was given time to work its charm on the initially hostile audience.[166] A less bold sophist forthrightly demanded that the partisans of his rival—in this case, Libanius—be sent away before he commenced his declamation.[167]

A good reputation was essential to a professional sophist, who relied heavily for income on student fees; a successful public debate brought not just renown and honor but also new students and increased revenues and contacts.[168] After Libanius triumphed over Eubulus in

162. On the often violent prowlings of students, see Libanius, *Oratio* 1.19ff. and A. F. Norman, "Note on Eunapius P. 485B, *Vitae sophistarum* 10.1.5, Prohaeresius," *Liverpool Classical Monthly* 4 (1979): 135–36.

163. Eunapius, *VS* 483.

164. On the partisans who backed rival sophist teachers, see P. Wolf, *Vom Schulwesen der Spätantike: Studien zu Libanius* (Baden-Baden, 1952), 50.

165. There had been a long tradition of such proceedings, even in the more formal settings of dicastic trials in classical Athens; see V. Bers, "Dikastic *thorubos*," in P. A. Cartledge and F. D. Harvey, eds., *Crux: Essays in Greek History Presented to G. E. M. de Ste Croix on His 75th Birthday* (Exeter, 1985), 1–15.

166. Eunapius, *VS* 488.

167. Libanius, *Or.* 1.71.

168. Wolf, *Vom Schulwesen der Spätantike*, 52. See Bowersock, *Greek Sophists*, 84–100, for a consideration of fundamental historical reasons why certain sophists competed with others during the High Empire.

a series of debates in the winter of 354–55, the roster of his students jumped from seventeen to fifty.[169]

In this key respect, public debate was integral to the institutional life of Greek sophists in the Roman Empire,[170] as was the need to posit fine distinctions.[171] The demand for a high degree of accuracy and precision (ἀκρίβεια) in one's discourse derived from the need to surpass one's rivals in the estimation of others. This culture of cutthroat competition arose not from an irrational "love of rivalry" but from the very real needs of sophists to distinguish themselves in the eyes of prospective students and exalted patrons. As Philostratus aptly remarked with regard to Favorinus the sophist, echoing the *Works and Days* of Hesiod, that ambition or love of competition (τὸ φιλότιμον) is invariably aimed at one's rival in the same trade (τοὺς ἀντιτέχνους).[172]

In contrast, many of those who considered themselves philosophers shunned public competition and refused to have their status as philosophers determined by the uninitiated masses. Philosophical wisdom was not to be evaluated strictly by the applause it brought forth. The philosophical circle encompassed an enclosed institutional culture in which praise and blame were ideally accorded by members within the group, by the true cognoscenti.[173] This avoidance of public rivalry strengthened the boundary between philosophers and sophists. In any case, the philosophers had fewer material reasons to contend in public, as theirs was supposedly an ascetic vocation: "They ought above all to claim to avoid mercenary activity."[174]

Platonist philosophers increasingly stayed away from public places and the civic life of late Roman cities. They also tended to hail from

169. See Libanius, *Ep.* 405.4–5, and P. Petit, *Les étudiants de Libanius* (Paris, 1956), 948–49.

170. Wolf, *Vom Schulwesen der Spätantike*, 49: "Für Libanius sind die andern Rhetoriklehrer teils Kollegen, teils Rivalen. Rivalität ist zwischen Sophisten das normale Verhältnis."

171. See Eunapius, *VS* 491, on the experiences of Anatolius, the praetorian prefect of Illyricum, who summoned a congress of sophists circa 357–60 to declaim on a πρόβλημα which he had provided them beforehand. The high imperial official made fun of the sophists' emphasis on ἀκρίβεια and the extent of their mutual disagreement. This episode should be interpreted as a clash between institutional cultures and normative expectations. Significantly, Anatolius had received Latin legal training in which a consensual ideology was favored and preferred to sophistic rivalry; see *PLRE* 1:59–60, s.v. "Anatolius 3."

172. Philostratus, *VS* 481.

173. See Themistius, *Oratio* 28.343b–c (Dindorf, ed., 414).

174. Ulpian, *De omnibus tribunalibus* 8: "An et philosophi professorum numero sint? et non putem, non quia non religiosa res est, sed quia hoc primum profiteri eos oportet mercenariam operam spernere."

wealthy aristocratic families and to marry exclusively within their narrow circles.[175] The possession of wealth was after all the only thing that
could distinguish theurgists from quacks, *goētai,* who plied their craft
for profit, *kerdos.*[176] Because philosophers were not to be concerned with
material possessions, much less perform before large audiences for their
livelihood, they needed to be fairly prosperous to start with.[177] This ri-
gidification of boundaries lessened both social mobility and social competition in philosophical circles.

The philosophical enterprise of the late Platonists possessed internally consistent rules and objectives that have yet to be examined historically. The reception of dialectic and the practice of philosophical
disputation are instructive in this regard. Philosophers who wished to
acquire or magnify a reputation for excellence used public debate as a
means for upward advancement within the philosophical circle. Thus
the junior members were usually the ones associated with the ardent
application of dialectic; they were also often criticized for it. Dialectic
constituted a powerful tool which, in theory at least, allowed a junior
member such as Eusebius of Myndus to show that he was as good as, or
superior to, older students (or even the teacher).

Yet, employed as a personal claim to consideration, dialectic made
an unsatisfactory hierarchizing principle on which to build stable communities, if such was the goal, because of its intrinsically agonistic and
egalitarian character. To establish such groups, philosophers needed to
attach the greatest value to the attainments of those contributing the
most to the common good, and not to the dialectical excellence of philosophers who pursued their own advancement.

The Socratic prohibition of philosophical disputation for those under thirty years of age, if ever heeded, was most likely observed in late
antiquity in the breach. In theory at least, this measure helped to insu-
late the more advanced members of the philosophical circle from the
recurring public challenges of ambitious and gifted students in their
teens or twenties. But no such boundary, whether practical or ideological, shielded the teacher from the testings and competitive challenges
of the *zēlōtai.* The struggle between older and younger generations for

175. See a useful discussion of the clannish character of such coteries in Fowden,
"Pagan Holy Man," 55–56.
176. Eunapius, *VS* 474.
177. Iamblichus, *Protrepticus* 6 (Des Places, ed., 70): "τὸ γὰρ μήτε μισθοῦ παρὰ τῶν
ἀνθρώπων γινομένου τοῖς φιλοσοφοῦσι." See R. Goulet, "Les intellectuels païens dans
l'empire chrétien selon Eunape de Sardes," *Annuaire: École Pratique des Hautes Études,* Section de Sciences Religieuses 87 (1978–79): 289–93, esp. 289–90.

power and even survival was a central element of Greek culture, as evidenced in many cosmogonic stories and heroic myths. In the culture of the philosophers, an underlying agonistic ideology continued to exist in the absence of clear hierarchical markers. Unlike their counterparts who opted for the *cursus honorum* of a civic career, those who joined a Platonist circle did not necessarily advance through carefully graduated stages even after the advent of a Pythagorean discipline. The ways in which philosophical groups managed to survive with no explicit mechanism for harnessing competition among members merits closer scrutiny.

Numenius of Apamea meditated on the institutional fragmentation of philosophical groups in *On the Divergence of the Academics from Plato*, a treatise which itself survives only in fragments. The Platonic Academy split up, he thought, because ambition caused later members to challenge the teachings of their predecessors, including those of Plato himself.[178] Stoics were worse yet, for they fought over inconsequential differences; their rivalry continued into Numenius' own time.[179] Only the Epicureans were able to maintain group coherence by strictly forbidding challenges to Epicurus' teachings and the introduction of novel ideas.[180] The Epicureans also possessed a more hierarchical group structure, clearly delineating grades within the philosophical life beyond the distinction between *zēlōtai* and *akroatai*.[181] They further employed the ideology of *philia* or friendship to bind members to each other.[182] These measures may have contributed to the Epicureans' success in avoiding the almost complete institutional factionalization noted in the other schools.[183] Though present in the Platonist philosophical circles of late antiquity, the influence of Pythagorean friendship, the outright avoid-

178. Numenius, *Fragmenta* 24.12–14 (Des Places, ed., 62–63).

179. Numenius, *Fragmenta* 24.37–48 (Des Places, ed., 63–64).

180. Numenius, *Fragmenta* 24.26–36 (Des Places, ed., 63). Fowden notes that he has been unable to find any reference to Epicurean philosophers in the third and fourth centuries C.E. ("Pagan Philosopher in Late Antique Society: With Special Reference to Iamblichus and His Followers," Ph.D. diss., University of Oxford, 1979, 69n. 2), but this does not suggest that the Epicureans no longer existed as distinct groups because there is not necessarily a correlation between the longevity of a group and the prominence of individual members.

181. See D. K. O'Connor, "The Invulnerable Pleasures of Epicurean Friendship," *GRBS* 30 (1989), 165–86; P. Mitsis, "Epicurus on Friendship and Altruism," *Oxford Studies in Ancient Philosophy* 5 (1987): 126–53.

182. The six grades were: σοφός, φιλόσοφοι, φιλόλογοι, καθηγηταί, συνήθεις, and κατασκευαζόμενοι; see N. W. de Witt, "Organization and Procedure in Epicurean Groups," *CPhil* 31 (1936): 205–11 at 211.

183. See Numenius, *Fragmenta* 24.33–38 (Des Places, ed., 63) and Lynch, *Aristotle's School*, 144.

ance of conflict,[184] and the common ascetic life were less pervasive there than among Epicureans.[185]

If pronouncing the master's teachings indisputable, as the Epicureans appear to have done, seems somewhat drastic and contrary to the spirit of dialectical inquiry shared by Platonists and Aristotelians (even at a time when philosophical dogmatism was on the rise), certainly the underlying principle is clear. One may argue that it was unnecessary to put rivalry out of bounds in such a forthright manner, that containing it within tolerable limits would have sufficed. Rampant public competition could have been stemmed by undercutting the very principles that conferred legitimacy on such proceedings. This goal was sometimes achieved by transferring ascribed value from dialectic, a competitive skill, to other forms of philosophical attainment; other times it was reached by hierarchizing the philosophical virtues so that mastery of dialectic alone became a relatively minor accomplishment, a humbler philosophical *aretē*.[186]

Tacitus observed: "Dabunt Academici pugnacitatem, Plato altitudinem."[187] How could one reconcile the two? The increasing reverence accorded to Plato and his writings within the context of an Aristotelianizing movement among the later Platonists contributed to a process of establishing a hierarchy of philosophical authorities and, by implication, cultural virtues.

For Marinus' Proclus, Aristotle's intellectual system represented the lesser mysteries:[188] the greater mysteries were rooted in the teachings of Plato. Proclus himself possessed a kind of divine knowledge or *epistēmē* that he arrived at, it was said, "neither methodically, nor demonstratively nor by means of syllogisms."[189] In the subsequent Neoplatonist tradition, this manifest subordination of Aristotle to Plato showed itself more and more explicitly. Notice the specific terms of valuation employed by Damascius in his *Vita Isidori:*

> Those people, however, who labor on perishable and human things, or those who would understand or wish to become knowledgeable quickly, accomplish nothing great with respect to the wisdom that is

184. See Iamblichus, *De vita pythagorica* 22.101, 33.229–33.

185. Caracalla banned the common mess of the Aristotelians in Alexandria; see Dio Cassius 78.7.3.

186. See the ranking of the philosophical virtues in Marinus, *Vita Procli* 3. The theurgic virtues were the highest ones Proclus dared name. See also *Vita Procli* 27.

187. Tacitus, *Dialogus de oratoribus* 31.6.

188. Marinus, *Vita Procli* 13. This appears to reflect the anti-Alexandrian prejudices of the Late Platonists of Athens.

189. Marinus, *Vita Procli* 22.

divine and great. For Aristotle and Chrysippus were the most clever (εὐφυεστάτους) of the ancient philosophers, but they became most diligent for learning (φιλομαθεστάτους) and, moreover, most given to meticulous scholarship (φιλοπόνους). Still they did not complete the entire ascent. Hierocles, and others like him among the more recent philosophers, while they lacked nothing with regard to human culture, were in many ways very deficient in the realm of divine concepts.[190]

The hierarchization and harmonization of the philosophical traditions envisioned by Damascius were a response to the threat posed by increasingly dominant Christians, who saw fragmentation as lack of truth, but these processes were not accomplished until the fifth century, when a Platonist *diadochē* was reestablished in Athens with Plutarch, Syrianus, and Proclus.[191] Meanwhile, the strength of charismatic authority, such as that attributed to Neopythagorean sages, carried the philosophical groups through the transitional period of the late fourth century. The pages of Eunapius' *Vitae sophistarum* brim with an array of marvelous philosophical figures whose lives and deeds loomed large on a horizon increasingly usurped by Christians.[192] The contest between polytheists and Christians could proceed only on common ground, and trials of power provided one such field of battle in a way that public debates could not. Thus the words *thauma, thaumazein,* and cognates appear some fifty times in Eunapius' *Vitae sophistarum,* a fact indicative of the work's tone.[193] Just as the Eunapian Iamblichus, shouting *pausasthe thaumazontes,* dispelled the wonder of onlookers by dismissing an apparition as a gladiator's phantom (εἴδωλον), so too Eunapius wished his readers to see that it was the polytheists, and not the Christians, who possessed the truly great daimons.[194]

In the pagan circles described by Eunapius, the philosopher was fast becoming a holy figure. This is not to say that the decline of competitive disputation and the concomitant rise of the philosopher-teacher may be explained by a rise in the spirit of irrationalism or a "failure of nerve."

190. Damascius, *Vita Isidori* 36 [337b], in Photius, *Bibliotheca* 242.36 (Henry, ed., 6:15).

191. See H. I. Marrou, "Synesius of Cyrene and Alexandrian Neoplatonism," in A. Momigliano, ed., *The Conflict between Paganism and Christianity in the Fourth Century* (Oxford, 1963), 128–56, esp. 150.

192. See G. J. M. Bartelink, "Eunape et le vocabulaire chrétien," *VChr* 23 (1969), 293–303; D. F. Buch, "Eunapius of Sardis and Theodosius the Great," *Byzantion* 58 (1988): 36–53.

193. See I. and M. M. Avotins, *Index in Eunapii vitas sophistarum* (Hildesheim, 1983), 110.

194. Eunapius, *VS* 473. It is tempting to see this remark as veiled anti-Christian polemic insofar as it attacks the martyrs' cult of the Christians.

Instead these shifts can be seen as institutional responses to the pressures brought about by otherwise unchecked social competition. The appreciation in value of personal authority and spiritual power allowed the polytheist philosophers to placidly traverse a competitive social landscape that, more and more under a Christian empire, replaced the charmed intellectual worlds in which they had lived.

THREE

MANICHAEANS AND PUBLIC DISPUTATION IN LATE ANTIQUITY

According to both its apologists and its detractors, as the inexorable tide of Manichaean religion swept out of its Mesopotamian home, its impact and diffusion met with local resistance, sometimes in the form of public debates.[1] In the later Roman Empire, the Manichaeans were especially feared and loathed as formidable public debaters.[2]

In this chapter,[3] I focus on the verbal prowess of the Manichaeans as it elucidates their social interactions with other groups. For this purpose, I postulate two analytically distinct activities often subsumed under the rubric of public debate. First is the more familiar form of disputation, in which two or more protagonists engage in a formal verbal contest for the benefit of an audience. Second is the Manichaean practice of posing aporetic questions as a means of securing their listeners' attention and preparing the way for their preaching.

We have no basis for assuming that the Manichaeans engaged others

---

1. On the spread of Manichaeism, see E. de Stoop, *Essai sur la diffusion du manichéisme dans l'empire romain* (Ghent, 1909); F. Cumont, "La propagation du manichéisme dans l'Empire romain," *RHLR* n.s. 1 (1910): 31–43; P. R. L. Brown, "The Diffusion of Manichaeism in the Roman Empire," *JRS* 59 (1969): 92–103; S. N. C. Lieu, *Manichaeism in the Later Roman Empire and Medieval China: A Historical Survey* (Manchester, 1985).

2. See P. R. L. Brown, *Augustine of Hippo: A Biography* (Berkeley, 1969), 43, 48, 141n. 5; idem, "St. Augustine's Attitude to Religious Coercion," *JRS* 65 (1964), 107–16, reprinted in idem, *Religion and Society in the Age of St. Augustine* (London, 1977), esp. 265n. 1.

3. An earlier version of this chapter appears in *RecAug* 24 (1992), 233–72.

in public debate in the usual sense as a regular part of their missionary activity. They tended to employ more intimate forms of suasion, often posing questions to individuals or small circles. Prominent set-piece debates with Manichaeans were initiated by their opponents, who sought through such high-profile encounters to stop the success of the Manichaeans' proselytizing efforts.

The shape of the evidence at hand—formal public debates recorded in either shorthand transcription or descriptive narrative form—suggests a deliberate strategy in which written accounts were used to displace actual events. This much is certain: the increasing prominence of written documentation in the environment of public debate was neither a neutral nor a negligible factor. By tracing the developing role of writing in public debates, we can follow the rise and fall of the Manichaean public debater.

DISPUTATION AND THE MANICHAEAN KERYGMA

Disputation was central to Manichaean religious identity from the inception of the movement. More by means of radical reinterpretation than direct negation, Mani's kerygma brought into question the very legitimacy of the religious self-understanding of Jews, Christians, Zoroastrians, and Buddhists.[4] Manichaeans could not convey the cogency and compelling nature of their message without undercutting the fundamental religious claims of others.[5]

According to the so-called *Cologne Mani-Codex*,[6] which contains the Manichaean work "Concerning the Birth of His Own Body," an agonistic exchange of words marked the beginning of the rift between Mani and the other Jewish-Christian baptists in Babylonia. The narrative presents a dichotomy between speech (public disputing) and silence (lack of pub-

4. See F. C. Andreas and W. B. Henning, "Mitteliranische Manichaica aus Chinesisch-Turkestan II," *SPAW*, Phil.-hist. Klasse 5 (1933): T.2.D126.IR, 295.

5. H. J. Drijvers, "Conflict and Alliance in Manichaeism," in H. G. Kippenberg, ed., *Struggles of the Gods* (Berlin/New York/Amsterdam, 1984), 99–124; see esp. 105, on the imagery of war.

6. *Codex Manichaicus Coloniensis* (hereafter *CMC*), in A. Henrichs and L. Koenen, eds., "Der Kölner Mani-Codex (P. Colon. inv. nr. 4780) ΠΕΡΙ ΤΗΣ ΓΕΝΝΗΣ ΤΟΥ ΣΩΜΑΤΟΣ ΑΥΤΟΥ, Edition der Seiten," *ZPE* 19 (1975): 1–85; 32 (1978): 87–199; 44 (1981): 201–318; 48 (1982): 1–59. Critical edition by L. Koenen and C. Römer, eds., *Der Kölner Mani-Kodex: Über das Werden seines Leibes*, Papyrologica Coloniensia 14 (Wiesbaden, 1989). The early dating of the text to the fourth and fifth centuries has recently been challenged on paleographical grounds; see B. L. Fonkič and F. B. Poljakov, "Paläographische Grundlagen der Datierung des Kölner Mani-Kodex," *BZ* 83 (1990): 22–29.

lic disputing) that is fraught with significance. The hagiographic text emphasizes that young Mani initially refrained from disputing with his fellow sectarians even while receiving revelations of errors in the baptists' religious practices and beliefs.[7] At twenty-four or twenty-five years of age, he finally began to make public his doubts: he openly disputed the two central pillars of the sect's self-understanding, the tradition of Elchasaius and the value of ablution, by putting forth questions in a public setting. This act understandably failed to endear Mani to the other members of the sect, who are described as becoming especially furious because they were incapable of responding to his questions, and thus were made to look foolish.

In the *Mani-Codex*, this lopsided debate very nearly ended in mob violence. The shamed and enraged baptists proceeded to threaten Mani with physical harm, an outcome averted thanks to the timely intervention of Patticius, Mani's father and spiritual patron. Afterward, an assembly was convoked to discuss the situation, and the baptists decided to expel Mani. Here we see that, in a sect with no graduated scheme of discipline, expulsion was the only means of dealing with a member who defied the group's central ethos.

After his expulsion, Mani commenced his missionary career by traveling as far east as India.[8] In broken lines of Greek, the *Mani-Codex* discloses the only attested formal public debate involving the charismatic figure. Mani was already far advanced in his public career, having been favorably received at the royal court in Ctesiphon by Shāpūr *shāhānshāh* by the time he arrived at a local village to preach his customary message. His unsolicited attempt to proclaim his kerygma before an assembled religious congregation publicly challenged the authority of local leaders. Accordingly, the leader of the religious sect in question invited Mani to a public debate: "He [the leader of the religious sect] conducted a debate

7. *CMC* 5:7–11. Such claims made ex post facto can of course constitute a veiled apologetic attempt to show that Mani's break with the baptists had long been prepared for and was no accident. See A. Henrichs, "Mani and the Babylonian Baptists: A Historical Confrontation," *HSCP* 77 (1973): 23–59, esp. 43–59; J. J. Buckley, "Mani's Opposition to the Elchasaites: A Question of Ritual," in P. Slater, D. Wiebe, M. Boutin, and H. Coward, eds., *Traditions in Contact and Change* (Waterloo, 1983), 323–36; idem, "Tools and Tasks: Elchasaite and Manichaean Purification Rituals," *Journal of Religion* 66 (1986): 399–411.

8. The Middle Persian account of Mani's encounter with an Indian wise man named Gwndyš seems to describe a private discussion rather than a public debate. See text and German translation in W. Sundermann, ed., *Mitteliranische manichäische Texte kirchengeschichtlichen Inhalts*, Berliner Turfantexte 11 (Berlin, 1981), 4b.1:M6040, 4b.2:M6041 (pp. 86–89). Mani eventually asked Gwndyš whether he could explain the origins of the world and the latter was not able to respond: "Er ko[nnte] ihm keine Antwort geben. Und er handelte wie ein Unwissender, der nichts begreift" (4b.2:M6041, R18[1377]–V5[1395]; pp. 88–89).

(διάλογος) with me before men of his faith (δόγμα).⁹ On all points he was worsted and incurred laughter with the result that he was filled with both envy and malice."¹⁰

The vanquished leader tried to avenge his public disgrace and temporary exclusion from his social group by uttering incantations (ἐπωδάς) against the stranger. The fragmentary nature of the *Mani-Codex* does not allow us to learn more about the nature of the incantations and their intended purpose, though they may be construed as a maledictory curse to inflict harm on Mani or as attempts to constrain his ability to speak in public. In either case, the efforts of the debater-turned-magus were in vain; Mani's guardian spirit or *suzugos* deflected the spells and he suffered no harm.¹¹ Here we see, as we will elsewhere, that formal public debate was only one of several possible forms of social and religious conflict. The threat of physical violence and the use of illocutionary acts such as the casting of spells clearly retained their viability within the broader spectrum of such contests.¹²

Mani proclaimed his kerygma openly, emulating his favorite apostle, Paul, but I know of no extant evidence that Mani resorted to public debate as a *modus operandi*. The noun *dialogos* and the verb *dialegomai* are used in the *Mani-Codex* mainly to describe the act of preaching, not the act of debating.¹³ Proclamation of the kerygma and the performance of miracles characterized Mani's missionary activities as well as those of his disciples.¹⁴ In this respect, a document such as the *Doctrina Addai*, which may after all contain Christian anti-Manichaean polemic, can help

9. This word reflects the standard terminology used to describe religious sectarian groups in the Codex; see, e.g., *CMC* 102.12.

10. *CMC* 138.2–9; text and German translation in Henrichs and Koenen, "Kölner Mani-Codex," *ZPE* 48 (1982): 30–31 [348–49]: "[διά]λογον ἐ[ποίησεν π]ρὸς με ἐμ[προ-σθεν] ἀνδρῶν τοῦ αὐ[τοῦ δόγ]ματος. ἐν πᾶσι [δὲ ἡττ]ήθη καὶ γέλω[τα ὤφλ]ησεν ὡς καὶ [φθόνου] καὶ κακίας πλη[σθῆναι]. καὶ κατὰ τὴν . . . καθεσθεὶς ἐπε[λάλησεν] ἐπωδὰς τῶν . . . [αὐ]τοῦ." On the role of laughter in defining and revising social boundaries, see E. Dupréel, "Le problème sociologique du rire," *Revue Philosophique* 106 (1928), 228–60.

11. *CMC* 139.11–13.

12. See P. L. Ravenhil, "Religious Utterances and the Theory of Speech Acts," in W. J. Samarin, ed., *Languages in Religious Practice* (Rowley, Mass., 1976), 26–39; see esp. 28–31 on spells and "magical" speech as illocutionary acts.

13. The case discussed above is the only occurrence of διάλογος being used to connote a public debate. Elsewhere in the *Mani-Codex*, διάλογος refers to preaching; see, for example, *CMC* 118.11, where διάλογος and διδασκαλία are used interchangeably. On δι-αλέγομαι as the act of preaching, see *CMC* 64.9 and L. Cirillo, A. Concolino Mancini, and A. Roselli, eds., *Codex Manichaicus Coloniensis "Concordanze"* (Cosenza, 1985), 53–54.

14. On Manichaean missionary activities and the working of miracles, see the excellent comprehensive account in Lieu, *History of Manichaeism*, e.g., 54–90. On the Manichaeans and public preaching, see Middle Persian fragment M219, in Andreas and Henning, "Mitteliranische Manichaica aus Chinesisch-Turkestan II," 311–12.

us comprehend the historical milieu and expectations governing the interactions between charismatic missionaries and local communities in late antiquity.[15]

For the advancement of his missionary career, Mani possessed the double gift of special revelation and the aid of a *suzugos*. His disciples and followers, however, required assistance to ensure the success of their own missionary efforts. The reputed success of the early Manichaeans in public debates may be attributed to the fact that they were equipped with writings specifically intended for use in situations of controversy. When Mani sent his disciples abroad to spread his kerygma, he instructed them to carry his own writings and to study them with care.[16]

Addas, a disciple who ventured as far as Alexandria, is traditionally thought to have brought with him three of Mani's writings, including the *Living Gospel*. In a city in which various religious and philosophical groups competed with each other on a constant basis, Addas could expect to become involved in public debates,[17] and he needed to be prepared to respond to criticisms.[18] Many would wish to subject a novel message to public testing, the more so since its bearer was a stranger without recognized credentials.[19]

A hagiographic Middle Persian source describes Addas as emerging triumphant from these early encounters, thanks to his use of Mani's writings.[20] It further asserts that Addas' fundamental imperative was to

15. See H. J. Drijvers, "Addai und Mani: Christentum und Manichäismus im dritten Jahrhundert in Syrien," *OCA* 221 (1983): 173–85.

16. On Manichaean scriptures, see P. Alfaric, *Les écritures manichéennes*, vols. 1, 2 (Paris, 1918–19).

17. See M2 RI 1–37 in Andreas and Henning, "Mitteliranische Manichaica aus Chinesisch-Turkestan II," 301. Addas is said to have "opposed the 'dogmas' with these [writings], [and] in everything he acquitted himself well. He subdued and enchained the 'dogmas,'" English translation from J. P. Asmussen, *Manichaean Literature: Representative Texts Chiefly from Middle Persian and Parthian Writings*, Persian Heritage Series 22 (Delmar, N.Y., 1975), 21. The text does not specify whether these events took place in Alexandria or while Addas was on his way there. See also L. J. R. Ort, *Mani: A Religio-historical Description of His Personality* (Leiden, 1967), 63.

18. Thus the importance of Stoic dialectic to Christians like Clement of Alexandria, who invited pagans to embrace Christianity. See J. Pépin, "La vraie dialectique selon Clément d'Alexandrie," in *Epektasis: Mélanges offerts à Jean Daniélou* (Paris, 1972), 375–83.

19. See J. Pitt-Rivers, "The Stranger, the Guest and the Hostile Host: Introduction to the Study of the Laws of Hospitality," in J.-G. Peristiany, ed., *Contributions to Mediterranean Sociology: Mediterranean Rural Communities and Social Change* (Paris, 1968), 13–30.

20. See M1750, in Sundermann, ed., *Mitteliranische manichäische Texte kirchengeschichtlichen Inhalts*, 183–85:2.5, p. 26; Andreas and Henning, "Mitteliranische Manichaica aus Chinesisch-Turkestan II," M216c V9–11. See M. Tardieu, "Gnose et manichéisme," in *Annuaire: École Pratique des Hautes Études*, Section de Sciences Religieuses 96 (1987–88): 296–301, esp. 299.

establish communities of the faithful; there was no hint that he deliberately debated in public to gain adherents. Addas did debate with others, according to the source, but because he had to, not because he wanted to. We may surmise that debating in public was an unavoidable aspect of his missionary career rather than his means of carrying out his mandate.

Arising from a biblical tradition, the Manichaeans cherished a specific body of authoritative writings, some of which were at least readily adaptable to, and perhaps specifically designed for, the task of addressing religious controversy. In geographical areas where Christian communities abounded, particularly on the Roman Empire's extensive eastern frontier, Manichaean missionaries quickly discovered that many whom they encountered were especially interested in the status of the Hebrew bible as divine revelation. By initially focusing on this issue, Manichaeans positioned themselves to preach their own distinctive message of the principles of light and darkness to their engrossed listeners.

To exploit this opening, the Manichaeans (like most other religious groups) were not averse to using texts from other traditions. In particular, the *Antitheses* of Marcion of Sinope (mid–second century), whose teachings were very popular in eastern Syria, were quickly seized upon because they refuted the claim that the Hebrew bible was the work of a benign deity.[21] Such documents were sometimes reworked and incorporated into the Manichaean tradition, as was the case with *Modios* (meaning "small basket" or "dry-measure"), which adapted arguments from the *Antitheses* and was attributed to the disciple Addas. In an effort to make their writings widely available in local languages, the Manichaeans later translated the *Modios* into Latin. Considering the cost and labor involved in copying texts, let alone translating them, we may surmise that the arguments contained in the *Modios* were useful in disputing with Latin Christians.[22]

MESOPOTAMIA

The apparent ease with which the Manichaeans extended their influence in the Roman Empire caused general alarm among Christians and pagans (such as the philosopher Alexander of Lycopolis), who regarded

21. See Lieu, *History of Manichaeism,* 38–40.
22. It was for this reason that Augustine composed a refutation of this work of Adimantus, as Addas was known to Latin speakers; see *Contra Adimantum* in CSEL 25:115–90; *Retractationes* 1.21.1, CSEL 36:100; F. Châtillon, "Adimantus Manichaei discipulus," *Revue de Moyen Age Latin* 10 (1954): 191–203; Lieu, *History of Manichaeism,* 64–65.

with apprehension the new sect's success in a zero-sum competition for the scarce commodity of popular allegiance. Christians also perceived the spread of Manichaean beliefs and practices as a series of acts of seduction in which loyal believers were infected by the contagious disease of heresy. Confused and helpless, local groups searched for an antidote, but at first there was no consensus as to the means of combating the disease. Even makeshift treatments were difficult to devise for so elusive an enemy. The virus of Manichaeism was all the more threatening in that it was disseminated within intimate circles in a manner easily overlooked.

When no scientific cure can be found, communal ritual must serve. A collective act of catharsis was needed, one similar to the *apopompē* or communal expulsion of scapegoats, in order to bring the crisis to the forefront of people's attention and to allay the fear of the unknown.[23] Historically, such an act might showcase a dramatic public confrontation with a representative of the Other. If no such representative could be found to take the stand for this purpose, or if the catharsis was meant to extend to several locales, then a written account could be substituted, complete with crisis, confrontation, and resolution. In the case of Manichaeism, local heroes such as Christian bishops and prominent Christian notables were pitted against the heresiarch Mani himself in public debate.

Such was the strategy adopted by the author of the *Acta Archelai*, a work composed before circa 350 in either Greek or Syriac,[24] and surviving only in a Latin translation from 392.[25] Incidental details in the fictive account shed much light on Christian perceptions of Manichaean-Christian relations in a sensitive border region of the empire.

According to the *Acta*, Mani once attempted to extend his influence to a Mesopotamian city called Carchar.[26] His plan was to convert one of

23. See J. Bremmer, "Scapegoat Rituals in Ancient Greece," *HSCP* 87 (1983): 299–320.

24. See the convincing arguments advanced to support the thesis of a Greek original of the *Acta Archelai* in S. N. C. Lieu, "Fact and Fiction in the *Acta Archelai*," in Peter Bryder, ed., *Manichaean Studies I* (Lund, 1988), 74–76.

25. Text in C. H. Beeson, ed., *Hegemonius: Acta Archelai*, GCS 16 (Leipzig, 1906). See Hoffmann, *Dialog*, 91. The *terminus ante quem* is provided by a reference in Cyril of Jerusalem, *Catecheses* 6:30–35. See Lieu, "Fact and Fiction in the *Acta Archelai*," 69–89. Lieu argues (73), *e silentio* and not entirely convincingly, that the lack of mention of the *Acta Archelai* in Eusebius of Caesarea's account of Manichaeism in his *Hist. eccl.* (written, according to Lieu, in 326–30) provides a *terminus post quem*.

26. On the identity of the place, see Lieu, "Fact and Fiction in the *Acta Archelai*," 76–82. He presents a number of strong arguments against identifying Carchar with Carrhae but proposes (80) to locate the city "somewhere along the Syrian and Mesopotamian *limes*." See M. Scopello, in *Annuaire: École Pratique des Hautes Études*, Section de Sciences Religieuses 96 (1987–88): 301.

the city's preeminent citizens, a man called Marcellus, whose influence would then convert the entire city and the surrounding region: "[Mani] praesumebat enim universam se posse occupare provinciam, si prius talem virum sibimet suadere potuisset."[27]

Mani wrote personally to Marcellus, recalling the legendary correspondence that King Abgar of Edessa initiated directly with Jesus. The letter, delivered by Mani's disciple Turbo, urged Marcellus to follow his teachings, but instead the notable secured the aid of Archelaus, the local bishop. By directing the spotlight to the local bishop as the primary arbiter in such matters, the author of the *Acta* may well have been suggesting to his (Christian?) readers that they do likewise were they to come into contact with Manichaeans: rather than take the matter into their own hands, they were to seek the advice of the local ecclesiastical leader. After consultation with Archelaus, Marcellus resolved to entice Mani to Carchar so that he could be defeated by the bishop in a public debate. Marcellus set the trap by inviting Mani to explicate his teachings in person.

Mani crossed the border into the Roman Empire with a retinue of twenty-two *electi* described as young men and virgins.[28] He is portrayed as an utter foreigner, exotically garbed in a manner befitting a doctor from the East. Significantly, he arrived carrying Babylonian books under his left arm. This orientalist image cast Mani as a subversive (non-Roman) *barbaros* from Persia, a power frequently at war with Rome.[29]

The debate, although held at the private *domus* of Marcellus, was nonetheless a town event, as was indicated by the much-trumpeted prominence of the local notables in attendance.[30] Four distinguished and learned men were selected to sit as the *iudices* of the forthcoming debate: Manippus, an expert in grammar and rhetoric; Aegialeus, an *archiatros*[31] and a *nobilissimus vir* learned in letters; and Claudius and Cleobulus, both rhetors. That pagans presided in this public debate between two

27. *Acta Archelai* 4.1–2 (Beeson, ed., 4–5).

28. *Acta Archelai* 14.1–3 (Beeson, ed., 22).

29. Christian teaching was considered *paterna* while Manichaean dogma was *aliena*. On the portrayals of the Manichaeans as unattractive foreigners and strangers, see L. J. Van der Lof, "Mani as the Danger from Persia in the Roman Empire," *Augustiniana* 24 (1974): 74–84, esp. 80–81. There was also an attempt to deflate Mani's social status from that of *artifex morbi* (physician) to that of *artifex* (craftsman); see Van der Lof, "Mani as the Danger," 84.

30. *Acta Archelai* 14.5–6 (Beeson, ed., 23). These pagan *iudices* had to be advised to rely on the Torah and the Hebrew prophets for their judgment of the debate.

31. On the Roman archiatrate in late antiquity, see *Cod. Theod.* 13.3.2; T. Meyer, *Geschichte des römischen Ärztestandes* (Kiel, 1907), 54–65; V. Nutton, "*Archiatri* and the Medical Profession in Antiquity," *PBSR* 32 (1977): 191–226.

who were emphatically not pagan, and that these *iudices* rendered their opinion in a communal voice throughout the dialogue, are particularly noteworthy aspects of this narrative.

The debate held significance for at least three parties: Christians, Manichaeans, and polytheists. In the account, Christians and Manichaeans were competing for the hearts and minds of the pagan elites of the city. This sensibility, expressed through the incidental though instructive detail of pagan participation, may reflect the concern of the Christian writer of the *Acta*; it may also be a realistic appraisal of the balance of power in a border town in fourth-century Mesopotamia.

In the ensuing debate, according to the *Acta Archelai*, Mani was soundly defeated by Archelaus. Having lost the verbal contest, the foreigner was further disgraced by being driven out of town by the assembled *turba*, which "concitavit se ad effugandum Manen." [32] Here we glimpse one possible role of a partisan audience, namely, to impose firm closure on a debate. Mani fled from Carchar but settled in a nearby city to resume his missionary activities. There his influence was soon felt and the local Christians sent for help from their brethren in Carchar, especially from the victorious Archelaus. Interestingly, Archelaus first dispatched the records of the Carchar debate as a means of opposing his rival, and only later went to confront Mani in person for a second time. Predictably, the *Acta* credits Archelaus with another success.

The role of stenography was critical in helping to render the defeat of Mani by Archelaus more permanent and more widely known. In the *Acta*, Marcellus made sure that stenographers were present to record the event: "Quoniam vero placuit Marcello disputationem hanc excipi atque describi, contradicere non potui [Hegemonius]." [33] Once the notations were transcribed into legible longhand, the records of the debate could be perused by others long after the original audience had dispersed: "Finita ergo disputatione ista, Archelaus turbas cum pace dimisit ad propria, ego Egemonius, scripsi disputationem istam exceptam ad describendum volentibus." [34] The translocal and transtemporal character of written texts was especially important in view of Manichaean mobility: through networks similar to those facilitating the Manichaeans' peripatetic travels, Christians could disseminate writings to distant communities, thus shadowing their opponents' missionary efforts.

32. *Acta Archelai* 43.1 (Beeson, ed., 63).
33. *Acta Archelai* 43.3 (Beeson, ed., 63).
34. *Acta Archelai* 68.5 (Beeson, ed., 98). See M. Tardieu, "Les manichéens en Égypte," *Bulletin de la Société Française d'Égyptologie* 94 (1982): 5–19.

EGYPT

Located just beyond the Mesopotamian frontier, Egypt seems to have been the major destination of the first Manichaean efforts to penetrate the Roman Empire. The movement met with great success there, as the plentiful Coptic Manichaean texts attest.[35] Manichaean influence extended beyond Alexandria and the Nile Delta to Upper Egypt far into the oasis towns of the western desert, as the recent find of a Coptic-Aramaic Manichaean book at Ismant El-Kharab illustrates.[36]

The Christian bishops of the Hermopolite nome were important landowners in the fourth century, but their privileged socioeconomic status did not necessarily bring with it a facility for argumentation.[37] In an area where the Manichaeans had been so successful, rosy optimism of the kind found in the *Acta Archelai*, with its hero's easy victories over Mani himself, may well have struck Christians contending with actual Manichaeans as unhelpfully simplistic, even incredible. One may even surmise that Manichaeans were not uncommonly favored to carry the day in such debates, as is clear from reports of an incident set in the city of Hermopolis Magna.

Copres, an Egyptian ascetic and leader of a small monastic community of fifty, arrived in Hermopolis one day to find that a Manichaean had been successful in persuading the local people to join his cause.[38] From Copres' perspective, the unnamed Manichaean engaged in the deception of the inhabitants: "κατελθὼν γάρ ποτε ἐν τῇ πόλει εὗρον ἄνδρον τινὰ Μανιχαῖον τοὺς δήμους ἀποπλανήσαντα." The wording in the Greek text of *Historia monachorum in Aegypto*, our oldest source for this encounter, does not lend support to Lieu's assumption that Copres happened across the Manichaean while the latter engaged a large crowd in

35. E.g., C. Schmidt and H. J. Polotsky, "Ein Mani-Fund in Ägypten: Originalschriften des Mani und seiner Schüler," *SPAW*, Phil.-hist. Klasse 1 (1933): 4–90. More generally, see W. Seston, "L'Égypte manichéene," *Chronique d'Égypte* 14 (1939): 362–72; G. Stroumsa, "Manichéisme et marranisme chez les manichéens d'Égypte," *Numen* 29 (1983): 184–201; idem, "The Manichaean Challenge to Egyptian Christianity," in B. A. Pearson and J. E. Goehring, eds., *The Roots of Egyptian Christianity* (Philadelphia, 1986), 307–19.

36. On the site in general, see C. A. Hope, "Three Seasons of Excavations at Ismant el-Kharab in Dakhleh Oasis, Egypt," *Mediterranean Archaeology* 1 (1988): 160–78. Notices of the find appear in J. Leclaut and G. Clerc, "Fouilles et travaux en Égypte et au Soudan, 1987–1988," *Orientalia* 58 (1989): 404–5; eaedem, "Fouilles et travaux en Égypte et au Soudan, 1988–1989," *Orientalia* 59 (1990): 410–11.

37. A. K. Bowman, "Landholding in the Hermopolite Nome in the Fourth Century, A.D.," *JRS* 75 (1985): 137–63.

38. See *Historia monachorum in Aegypto* 10.30–35 [190–225] (A.-J. Festugière, ed., *Historia monachorum in Aegypto*, Subsidia Hagiographica 53 [Brussels, 1971], 87–89); and see Rufinus, *Historia monachorum* 9 (*PL* 21:426C–427B).

debate.[39] The phrase "$τοὺς$ $δήμους$ $ἀποπλανήσαντα$" should be interpreted simply to mean that the Manichaean had been finding support
among the inhabitants of the town, probably through appeals to small
groups and individuals. The aorist participle in the Greek text (though
not the present participle in the Latin) certainly suggests that the deception took place prior to Copres' arrival. The references to actual crowds
of people ($τὸ$ $πλῆθος$, $οἱ$ $ὄχλοι$) appear some lines later, after the point
where Copres engages the Manichaean in debate before the public
($δημοσίᾳ$). Thus we may assume that these references are to the people,
perhaps including both pagans and Christians, who would have gathered for a debate unfolding in an open area of the town.

In this contest, Copres did not enjoy the good fortune that attended
Archelaus in his debate with Mani. Even Copres admitted that he utterly
failed to convince his opponent, a euphemistic circumlocution implying
that he lost the debate. Unperturbed, Copres resorted to a more unsa-
vory means of demonstrating the truth of his faith:

> Since ($ὡς$) I was unable to persuade him in public, I turned and said to
> the crowds of listeners: "Light a great fire on the open road ($εἰς$ $τὴν$
> $πλατεῖαν$) and we are both going into the fire, and whichever one of us
> remains unhurt shall be the one who has the noble faith ($καλὴν$ $πί-$
> $στιν$)." When this had been done and the crowd zealously lit up the
> fire, I carried him with me into the flame.[40]

At this point, the Manichaean blurted out what any clever youngster
in a similar bind would say: "Let each of us go in by himself and you
should go first since *you* suggested it." Undaunted, Copres crossed himself in the name of Christ,[41] leapt into the fire, and remained there un-

39. See Lieu, "Fact and Fiction in the *Acta Archelai*," 83–84. See Tardieu, "Les manichéens en Égypte," 13–14.
40. *Historia monachorum* 10.30–31 (Festugière, ed., 87–88). See also the version in
Rufinus, *Historia monachorum* 9 (*PL* 21:426C–427A):

> Once I came down to the city and found there a man, a certain doctor of the
> Manichaeans, who was seducing the people. I had a debate with him, but be-
> cause he was very cunning I was unable to shut him up with words. *Fearing lest
> the crowds of listeners should be harmed if he were to depart with the appearance of being
> the victor in debate (veritus ne auditorum turbae laederentur, si ille quasi superior ab-
> scessisset in verbis),* I said before the crowds of listeners: 'Light a fire in the middle
> of the street and we will both go into the flame. You should believe that which-
> ever one of us is not scorched by it, his is the true faith.' After I said this, the
> people were mightily pleased and a great fire was lit without delay.

Note the interesting expository expansion in Rufinus' version, italicized here.
41. On the invocation of the name and titles of Christ as a form of protection against
harm and sickness, see C. H. Roberts, *Manuscript, Society and Belief in Early Christian Egypt*
(London, 1979), 82–84; R. W. Daniel and F. Maltomini, *Supplementum Magicum I*, Papyrologica Coloniensia 16.1 (Wiesbaden, 1989), nos. 22, 23, and esp. 35, pp. 61–66, 102–3.

scathed for half an hour, after which the crowd shouted an acclamation (ἀνεβόησαν) before the deed of wonder (τὸ θαῦμα).[42] It was the Manichaean's turn to do the same, and the poor man was pushed against his will into the flames, where he suffered like any mortal lacking divine protection. After this clear demonstration of who had the upper hand, the assembled Hermopolite citizenry lifted up the victorious Copres and carried him in procession toward the church while praising God.[43]

No doubt elaborated according to hagiographic conventions, this story nevertheless has a peculiar aspect of verisimilitude. If the story were invented out of whole cloth, the author would most likely not have wished to bring attention to the fact that the final victory was achieved only after an initial setback.[44] In any case, the observation that the Manichaean could hold his own in a public debate with a Christian holy man is instructive about ancient expectations. The plot's further development reminds us that Christians, failing to compete with Manichaeans in public debates for which the latter were normally well-prepared, sometimes altered the nature of the conflict or public demonstration to suit their own particular strengths. Needless to say, the ordeal, as a test of the extent of one's control over his own physical body, was a form of demonstration that clearly favored an ascetic who had made self-mortification his daily practice.[45]

The easy shift from public debate to ordeal recounted above reminds us of the limitations of the cultural realm within which formal public disputations were appreciated. Illiterate and unlearned audiences found demonstrations of power by deeds more convincing than the ability to spin arguments.[46] In encounters between religious rivals, deeds of wonder were commonly, though not necessarily, interpreted as signs of divine favor, whereas skill in argument was viewed as being of human, or even diabolical, origin.[47] The report of a miracle of power possessed

42. *Historia monachorum* 10.32 (Festugière, ed., 88); see J. Colin, *Les villes libres de l'orient gréco-romain,* 109–52.

43. See Lieu, *History of Manichaeism,* 157, citing a later Syriac version of this story in the writings of Anan-Isho.

44. I also accept Scott Bradbury's suggestion that this setback may reflect a hagiographical plot device to prepare the audience for a demonstration of power.

45. This is not to say that Manichaeans were not respected ascetics in late antiquity; in fact, the opposite is true.

46. For example, the success of the apostle Addai in Edessa was due to his deeds of wonder: "There was no one who stood against him, for the deeds which he did permitted no one to rise against him." See *Doctrina Addai* f.21b; English translation from G. Howard, ed., *The Teaching of Addai* (Ann Arbor, Mich., 1981), 67. On the low level of literacy in the ancient world, see W. V. Harris, "Literacy and Epigraphy I," *ZPE* 52 (1983): 87–111.

47. On this issue see, for example, Julian the Apostate and Eusebius of Rome in the Julian legend, in H. Gollancz, *Julian the Apostate* (Oxford, 1928), 58–59.

wider and more direct appeal as a readily accessible icon for those who could not, or would not, embrace the bewildering complexities of verbal disputation. The ordeal can thus be read as the functional equivalent— a kind of *sermo humilis*—of the public debate.

GAZA

A story similar to that of Copres and the Manichaean can be found in Pseudo-Mark the Deacon's *Vita Porphyrii*.[48] Porphyry, the bishop of Gaza, was a staunch promoter of Christianity in Palestine and a resolute destroyer of pagan temples.[49] In 392, his friend John, bishop of Jerusalem (387–417), had designated him guardian of the relics of the true cross (ὁ σταυροφύλαξ).[50] When he assumed the episcopal seat of Gaza in 395, Porphyry continued in his self-appointed task of sanctifying the holy land, a project he had shared with his associates in Jerusalem. Arriving in the city as an aristocrat from distant Thessalonica, the new bishop faced the daunting challenge of installing himself as a major player in the politics of Gaza, where the reigning pagan aristocracy resisted him as both foreigner and Christian. He painstakingly cultivated ties with the imperial court, competing with the native aristocrats for acceptance as Constantinople's man in Gaza.[51]

Much of a Christian bishop's credibility as a local defender of imperial interests rested on his claim to a solid constituency in his city. Thus it was vital for Porphyry to maintain a sure grip on the allegiance of his own congregation, after which he could expand his power by attracting the support of the court at Constantinople. For this reason, Porphyry dealt swiftly and decisively with any perceived threat to Christian solidarity in Gaza, including the missionary efforts of a Manichaean named Julia circa 402:

> At that time a certain Antiochene woman called Julia, who belonged to the abominable heresy of those called Manichaeans, arrived in the city. Upon realizing that there were certain neophytes who were not yet

48. See Lieu, *History of Manichaeism*, 155–56; F. C. Burkitt, *The Religion of the Manichees* (Cambridge, 1925), 7–11.

49. See *Vita Porphyrii* 85–91 (H. Grégoire and M.-A. Kugener, eds., *Marc le diacre: Vie de Porphyre évêque de Gaza* [Paris, 1930], 66–71). See also G. Fowden, "Bishops and Temples in the Eastern Roman Empire," *JTS* n.s. 29 (1978): 53–78.

50. See M. Van Esbroeck, "Jean II de Jérusalem et les cultes de saint Étienne de la sainte-Sion et de la Croix," *AB* 102 (1984): 99–134.

51. See discussion of these issues in R. Van Dam, "From Paganism to Christianity in Late Antique Gaza," *Viator* 16 (1985): 1–20.

confirmed in the holy faith, she, having gone among them, corrupted them through her fradulent teaching (διδασκαλία γοητική), and even more through the gift of money. For he who founded the aforementioned godless heresy [i.e., Mani] could not ensnare so many people if not by the furnishing of money.[52]

The charge of using monetary gifts to seduce the young is intriguing though not unattested in the history of polemical accusations.[53] Here we see the charge extended back to Mani, the eponymous founder of the heresy. Such allegations allowed Christians to rationalize the appeal of Manichaean teachings, which Christian polemicists consistently characterized as filled with madness and utterly absurd to those possessing intellect (τοῖς γε νοῦν ἔχουσιν).

Julia's success soon drew the unwanted attention of wary local Christians, who promptly informed Porphyry of the stranger's actions. As a prominent member of the establishment in Gaza, Porphyry was able to have strangers brought before him for public interrogation: "Porphyry, counted among the holy, sent after her and asked her who she was, where did she belong and what manner of philosophical and/or religious view (δόξα) did she bring."[54] This line of questioning may suggest that the information Porphyry received from his congregation was vague, in which case it implies that, when Christians noticed a stranger becoming influential in their city, they expressed their diffused concern by rallying behind the local bishop and demanding to know more about the subversive individual.

Pseudo-Mark recounts that Julia readily professed that she was Antiochene and a Manichaean, which frank and unguarded declarations provoked barely restrained hostility from the audience. This detail suggests that those present were not generally aware of Julia's religious affiliation. Porphyry calmed down the locals and urged them to exhort Julia to revise her position rather than to attack her. He himself approached Julia and said,

> "Sister, cut yourself off from this evil belief (κακοδοξία) for it is satanic." But she replied: "Speak and listen, and either persuade or be persuaded." The blessed one said: "Get ready till the dawn and appear here." And she, having been ordered, departed.[55]

52. *Vita Porphyrii* 85 (Grégoire and Kugener, eds., 66–67). English translation mine.
53. Since Manichaean *electi* could not reproduce themselves, there was a need to recruit others, especially from among the young; see, for example, Mani in *CMC* 121.11 through 123.13 in *ZPE* 48 (1982): 13–15.
54. *Vita Porphyrii* 87 (Grégoire and Kugener, eds., 68).
55. *Vita Porphyrii* 87 (Grégoire and Kugener, eds., 68).

The historical Porphyry of Gaza was more a man of action than an intellectual powerhouse; even the literary Porphyry knew that Julia was likely to outperform him in a public debate. However, as the *Vita* informs us, the bishop felt he was entering the fray not so much with a human being as with the devil himself. He prepared for the next day by fasting and praying that he might confound the devil, the superhuman adversary behind Julia. Yet Porphyry also readied himself in a more practical manner: he summoned certain Christians, both laity and clergy, to attend the debate, mobilizing a sizeable retinue of partisan supporters. By contrast, Julia arrived the next morning with only four companions:

> Two men and as many women. They were young and beautiful, but they were all pale, while Julia was well-advanced in age. All of them steeped in the λόγοι of worldly παιδεία, though Julia was more advanced than they were. Their countenance was humble and their manner meek. . . .[56]

After Julia and Porphyry were seated, they began the debate (τὴν ζήτησιν ἐποιοῦντο). Porphyry brought along the gospels and, as befitted a guardian of the relics of the true cross, "made the sign of the cross in his own mouth" before requiring Julia to explain her *doxa*.[57] Like Copres, Porphyry crossed himself in preparation for a contest with an enemy of the faith, but whereas Copres made the gesture before jumping into flames, Porphyry did so to anoint his mouth before plunging into a verbal contest. The purpose of making the sign of the cross in such situations must have varied from person to person; Cyril of Jerusalem considered the act potent in rendering speechless one's opponents in debate.[58]

The debate was a solemn occasion with the airs of an official judicial inquiry, and the words spoken by the seated protagonists were carefully recorded. Among the local Christians was a certain Cornelius, skilled in brachygraphy and capable of writing down with a few strokes (πρὸ βραχέος) the statements made by both sides.[59] He was made a deacon

56. *Vita Porphyrii* 88 (Grégoire and Kugener, eds., 68–69). The youths were no doubt ascetics. On the *electi* who allegedly accompanied Mani to his debate, see the discussion of *Acta Archelai* above.

57. *Vita Porphyrii* 88 (Grégoire and Kugener, eds., 69).

58. See Cyril of Jerusalem, *Catecheses* 13.22 (PG 33:799–800): "Whenever you are about to debate with unbelievers concerning the cross of Christ, first make the sign of the cross of Christ with your hand, and the questioner will be silenced (φιμοῦται ὁ ἀντιλέγων)."

59. On Greek shorthand, see A. Mentz, "Die hellenistische Tachygraphie," *Archiv für Papyrusforschung* 8 (1927): 34–59; H. J. M. Milne, *Greek Shorthand Manuals: Syllabary and Commentary edited from Papyri and Waxed Tablets in the British Museum and from the Antinoë Papyri in the Possession of the Egypt Exploration Society* (London, 1934). In the *Vita*, Cornelius

of the church of Gaza forthwith so that he could serve as church notary, in which capacity he sat next to Porphyry during the debate.[60] Supplementing the efforts of Cornelius, Baruch and Mark the deacon drew up the minutes of the meetings.[61] According to the author, the records of this encounter were still extant when he composed the *Vita*.[62]

After many hours of debate, Julia remained obdurately and embarrassingly undefeated. As he witnessed Julia, who was inspired by the devil,[63] continuing in her utterance of blasphemous statements, Porphyry was moved by divine zeal (like the biblical Phineas) to call upon the Christian god to shut Julia up, ἵνα μὴ λαλῇ δύσφημα.[64] The *ira Dei* manifested itself and

> the punishment (ἡ θεία δίκη) followed the statement straightaway. For Julia began to tremble and to change her appearance, and remained outside her body for almost an hour. She did not speak (οὐκ ἐλάλει),

is said to know τὰ Ἐννόμου σημεῖα. Unfortunately, nowhere else is a person called Ennomos associated with a system of Greek shorthand symbols (τὰ σημεῖα). Thus the editors of the Budé volume, after summarizing the debate over the interpretation of this phrase, seem inclined to consider it a corruption of ἐκ νόμου, making τὰ ἐκ νόμου σημεῖα the Greek equivalent of *juris notae;* see Grégoire and Kugener, eds., lxxxviin. 1, 136. It is interesting to note that L. Parmentier, the editor of Theodoret's *Hist. eccl.*, has conjectured the alternative reading of Εὐνομίου, a reference to the Eunomius of Cappadocia who was involved in the christological controversy of the late fourth century (see Theodoret, *Hist. eccl.* 4.18, on Protogenes of Edessa, who taught in Antinoë: "Τὰ Εὐνομίου γράμματα πεπαιδευμένος καὶ γράφειν εἰς τάχος ἠσκημένος"). Eunomius had learned stenography as a young man and was Aetius the Syrian's personal secretary; see L. Parmentier, "Eunomius tachygraphe," *Revue de Philologie* 33 (1909): 238–46.

60. It is not clear whether Cornelius was required to become a deacon before serving officially as the *tachugraphus,* but this combination of duties was not uncommon; see Epiphanius, *Panarion* 71.1.8, on Anysius, the *tachugraphus* and deacon present at the debate between Basil of Caesarea and Photinus. On the increasingly elaborate ranking of *notarii* in the Christian ecclesiastical hierarchy from the fourth century on, see the study by H. C. Teitler, *Notarii and Exceptores: An Inquiry into Role and Significance of Shorthand Writers in the Imperial and Ecclesiastical Bureaucracy of the Roman Empire (from the Early Principate to c. 450 A.D.)* (Amsterdam, 1985), esp. 89–92.

61. The meaning of the genitive absolute phrase ἐμοῦ καὶ τοῦ ἀδελφοῦ Βάρυχα ὑπομνησκόντων is not entirely clear as Cornelius was presumably already present to record the debate. Perhaps Baruch and Mark were there to make a set of minutes or τὸ ὑπόμνημα in which would be set down the general nature of what was said, while Cornelius was there to record verbatim the *ipsissima verba.*

62. *Vita Porphyrii* 88 (Grégoire and Kugener, eds., 69): "I did not include the dialogue in this book because it was long, wishing to include it in the present writing in brief. But I placed in another book the dialogue for those who wish to learn the wisdom given by God to the most holy Porphyry and the old wives' tales which Julia, the fraud and poisoner whom divine justice quickly went after, uttered."

63. *Vita Porphyrii* 89 (Grégoire and Kugener, eds., 69–70): "γυναικὸς ἐνεργουμένης ὑπὸ τοῦ διαβόλου."

64. *Vita Porphyrii* 89 (Grégoire and Kugener, eds., 70).

but she was voiceless (ἄφωνος) and motionless (ἀκίνητος), having eyes which were open and fixated on the most holy bishop. Those who were with her, seeing what happened, were very afraid.[65]

No amount of first aid from her companions could revive Julia, who had lost all speech and the ability to move. Still speechless (ἄφωνος) almost an hour later, she died.[66] Reducing someone to a state of literal *aphōnia* was a complete refutation and triumph in a public debate. To an undiscriminating audience, it did not much matter whether success came from one's own arguments or from divine intervention.

This reported miracle was a powerful demonstration that could be ignored by neither firsthand witnesses nor those who subsequently learned of it. Julia's four youthful companions, and "as many as were corrupted by her," threw themselves at Porphyry's feet crying, "We have erred, we seek repentance."[67] Porphyry exploited this reaction by ordering the Manichaean sympathizers to anathematize Mani, which they promptly did. They received catechism, were later baptized, and thus were incorporated (or reincorporated) into the structure of the church of Gaza.

In this as in earlier episodes, the Manichaeans did not conduct public debates as part of their missionary activity. A historical Julia would probably have much preferred to go about her business peacefully and far from the attention of the local bishop. In general, Manichaean teachers stood to gain little from high-profile debates, because they fared splendidly in more intimate settings. However, though Manichaeans did not generally initiate public debates as part of a grand missionary strategy, they rarely avoided public contests with opponents less ready for such encounters. A Manichaean missionary-teacher could not afford to be seen backing down from a contest, however contrived and fraught with peril. Julia did not shrink from Porphyry's challenge even though he packed the audience with his clergy and laity. The proceedings at Porphyry's church resembled a public trial, an image enhanced by the stenographer sitting at his side.[68]

---

65. *Vita Porphyrii* 90 (Grégoire and Kugener, eds., 70).

66. *Vita Porphyrii* 90 (Grégoire and Kugener, eds., 70). Julia passed into the Dark Realm (σκότος). Here Mark was making a joke at the expense of the deceased by emphasizing the fact that the Manichaeans, unlike Christians, regarded darkness (σκότος) as an ever-existing principle of the cosmos. By extension he could thus claim, though rather unjustifiably, that Julia in fact worshiped σκότος.

67. *Vita Porphyrii* 91 (Grégoire and Kugener, eds., 70–71).

68. See Prudentius, *Peristephanon* 9.23 (*PL* 60:435A); the famous fourth-century diptych of Rufius Probianus flanked by two *exceptores*, in A. Venturi, *Storia dell'arte italiana* (Milan, 1901), 2:356; *Dictionnaire d'archéologie chrétienne et de liturgie* (Paris, 1935), 12:1625.

As in the *Acta Archelai*, the pagans in the *Vita* constituted the silent partner in this confrontation between a Christian and a Manichaean. Our author even claims that Manichaeans were in the habit of acknowledging many gods so as to find favor with pagans.[69] This alleged alliance of Manichaeans with polytheists, or at least the ambiguous separation of the two, made it possible for Julia to be identified as a Manichaean in the Greek text of the *Vita Porphyrii* and a pagan philosopher in the Georgian recension.[70] Regardless of whether Julia was a Manichaean missionary or a philosopher, her final experience had, according to the *Vita*, a broad impact: many polytheists allegedly converted to Christianity after this showing of the bishop's might.[71]

ALEXANDRIA

In the mid–fourth century, a certain Aphthonius, identified by our source Philostorgius as a leader (ὁ προεστώς) of the Manichaeans, arrived in Alexandria, where he soon acquired an impressive reputation "among many on account of his wisdom and his skill in words (δεινότητι λόγων)."[72] Aphthonius' fame reached the ambitious Christian Aetius the Syrian (see ch. 4), who earlier had been defeated by a member of a gnostic sect, the Borboriani, in a debate in Cilicia. Wishing to restore his confidence in reaffirming his verbal powers,[73] and drawn by Aphthonius' reputation, Aetius made the journey south to Alexandria.[74] This connection between fame and ensuing challenges to debate harked back to an earlier time when Origen's fame "was noised abroad everywhere," and learned men as well as so-called heretics "came to him to make trial of the man's sufficiency in the sacred λόγοι" (see ch. 1).[75]

69. *Vita Porphyrii* 87 (Grégoire and Kugener, eds., 68).
70. See H. Peeters, "La vie géorgienne de saint Porphyre de Gaza," *AB* 59 (1941): 65–216, esp. 196 (§§85–86). References to Manichaeans are lacking in this recension.
71. Though today Manichaeans are sometimes confused with pagans, philosophers of the day found Manichaeism particularly objectionable as an intellectual system. One of the most celebrated instances of anti-Manichaean polemic is found in the Neoplatonist Egyptian philosopher Alexander of Lycopolis' *Dialogue against the Doctrines of Mani*: see PG 18:411–48 (A. Brinkmann, ed., *Alexandri Lycopolitani contra Manichaei opiniones disputatio* [Leipzig, 1895]; A. Villey, ed., *Alexandre de Lycopolis: contre la doctrine de Mani* [Paris, 1985]).
72. Philostorgius, *Hist. eccl.* 3.15 (J. Bidez and F. Winkelmann, eds., *Philostorgius Kirchengeschichte* [Berlin, 1972], 46–47).
73. See Philostorgius, *Hist. eccl.* 3.15 (Bidez and Winkelmann, eds., 46): "καί τις τῶν Βορβοριανῶν, λόγοις αὐτῷ ὑπὲρ τῆς ἰδίας δόξης συμπλακείς, εἰς ἐσχάτην κατέστησεν ἥτταν." (See p. 115 for translation.)
74. Philostorgius, *Hist. eccl.* 3.15.
75. Eusebius, *Hist. eccl.* 6.18.2–4.

After Aetius located his intended victim in Alexandria, the two men went at each other "as if in a contest for supremacy (ὡς ἐς ἅμιλλαν)." Soon Aetius, "having forced Aphthonius into a state of speechlessness (ἀφωνία), brought the latter from great fame to great shame." Unused to such reverses, Aphthonius fell sick and died a week later. The difference between this account and earlier reports of public disputations between Christians and Manichaeans is significant: Aetius actually defeated a Manichaean by arguments without resorting to other means.[76] There was no intervention of supranatural power; Aetius triumphed by emerging as the superior debater. The Manichaean was no stranger confronted by a local Christian leader; Aetius expressly sought Aphthonius out in Alexandria. In many ways, the two had more in common with each other than with a local Christian bishop: both were peripatetic, and neither had a firm constituency locally. Theirs was a world of fluid movement, chance encounters, and public debates with others who possessed reputations for wisdom. Such debates took place on terms of parity, for neither party had the actual power to impose inequality. Aetius could not bring to bear on Aphthonius the "psychological pressures" that Porphyry heaped on Julia in the *Vita Porphyrii*.[77]

ROMAN NORTH AFRICA

Manichaeism as "Dialectical" Christianity

West of Alexandria, in the cities of Roman North Africa, people gathered around *scholae doctorum hominum* and debating formed part of the institutional culture.[78] It was within this context of intellectual curiosity and exchange that the most famous Manichaean convert took to the precepts of Mani. The searching Augustine discovered that the Manichaeans offered what he and many others regarded as a more rigorously rational form of Christianity.

Such an outlook had great appeal, particularly among young catholic Christians from the middling rungs of society. These ambitious and inquisitive youths, later to rise to positions of considerable authority within the catholic ecclesiastical hierarchy, were attracted by the Manichaeans' disavowal of that unquestioning acceptance of "superstitious" beliefs found in the Hebrew bible which exposed Christians to charges of

76. See Philostorgius, *Hist. eccl.* 4.12.
77. See Lieu, *History of Manichaeism*, 156.
78. See Augustine, *De utilitate credendi* 2 (CSEL 25:4).

idol worship. Using such well-tried *topoi* as those contained in Marcion's *Antitheses*, Manichaeans led the way in attacking the common catholic Christians' uncritical acceptance of the Hebrew bible.[79] Thus one Manichaean proudly proclaimed, "Non credo prophetis Hebraeis."[80] In a manner arguably more critical than constructive (and hence existing in a close dialectical relationship with that which they sought to criticize), the Manichaeans offered a religious alternative that many found more philosophically and logically cogent than what their catholic counterparts professed.

Given the centrality of disputation to the legitimacy and appeal of the Manichaeans, it is not surprising that they often invited discussion by posing challenging questions in public.[81] One of their famous opening lines was "Whence evil (*unde malum*)?"[82] This loaded question confronted catholic Christians with the difficult theological task of reconciling evil, free will, divine omnipotence, and providence.[83] But the Manichaeans did not throw out such questions casually; they were trained to deal with the likely responses of their interlocutors.[84] By anticipating probable responses and counter-responses, Manichaean debaters, like experienced chess players, could comfortably and predictably disarm the opposition. This aspect of the Manichaean movement in North Africa has been aptly described as a cult of "knockabout rationalism."[85] It was in this cult that Augustine discovered his spiritual home during his youth in Carthage.

In antiquity, ambitious and educated youths warmed naturally to the dialectical art.[86] It not only afforded one who was *cupidus veri* a straight path toward truth but also provided a set of intellectual weap-

79. See *De utilitate credendi* 2 (CSEL 25:4). The treatise, composed in 391 just after Augustine became a priest, is addressed to Honoratus, a Manichaean friend whom he hoped to convert to catholic Christianity; see Brown, *Augustine of Hippo*, 43; Decret, *L'Afrique manichéenne (IVᵉ–Vᵉ siècles): Étude historique et doctrinale* (Paris, 1978), 1:72–78.

80. C. *Faustum* 13.8 (CSEL 25:389).

81. See C. *Faustum* 23.1 (CSEL 25:707).

82. See Augustine, *Confessiones* 3.7: "Nesciebam enim aliud, vere quod est, et quasi acutule movebar, ut suffragarer stultis deceptoribus, cum a me quaereretur, unde malum est?"

83. See Augustine's recollection of a question he used to pose before catholic Christians while he was a Manichaean: "Et dicebam parvulis fidelibus tuis, civibus meis, a quibus nesciens exulabam, dicebam illis garrulus et ineptus: 'cur ergo errant anima, quam fecit deus?'" (*Confessiones* 7.15).

84. See *De duabus animabus* 10 (CSEL 25:63): "Hic fortasse quis dicat: 'unde ipsa peccata et omnino unde malum? si ab homine, unde homo? si ab angelo, unde angelus?'"

85. See W. H. C. Frend, "The Gnostic-Manichaean Tradition in Roman North Africa," *Journal of Ecclesiastical History* 4 (1953): 13–26, esp. 21.

86. See *De utilitate credendi* 2 (CSEL 25:4): "adulescentis animus cupidus ueri."

ons with which to demonstrate his superiority over others, to be *superbus et garrulus:*[87] as training in the asking and answering of questions, dialectic furnished both weapon and armor. It was especially suited to the young and impetuous because it was freely accessible to those who possessed talent and ambition but lacked institutional authority. Handbooks outlining the system could be acquired and read. Enterprising individuals could teach themselves the art in a relatively short time, as did Augustine when he mastered Aristotle's *Categories* with little or no help from preceptors.[88] An autodidact could thus avoid a long, socializing apprenticeship to a master.

In late antiquity the practice of dialectic was closely associated with clever and hotheaded youth, among whom were Aetius, Eunomius, and Augustine. Augustine recalled that the two bonds tethering him to the Manichaeans were social familiarity and the dizzying success he experienced when debating others with Manichaean arguments:

> I used to almost always enjoy a certain harmful victory (*noxia victoria*) in debates while discoursing with inexperienced Christians who nevertheless eagerly endeavored to defend their own faith, each as he could. . . . Thus from their [Manichaeans'] arguments (*sermones*) a burning zeal for disputations (*certamina*) was daily renewed; from the outcome of the disputations (*ex certaminum proventu*) love for them was daily renewed.[89]

The association of dialectic with the arousal of an unsuitable "ardor of youth" was recognized as a difficulty in philosophical circles as early as Plato's time.[90] Later, Diogenes Laertius related a relevant story about Zeno of Citium. When the Stoic philosopher heard a young boy posing a certain philosophical question (ζήτημά τι) with rather more reckless

---

87. *De utilitate credendi* 2 (CSEL 25:4). See Decret's discussion in *Aspects du manichéisme dans l'Afrique romaine: Les controverses de Fortunatus, Faustus et Felix avec saint Augustin* (Paris, 1970), 31.

88. *Confessiones* 4.16. See L. Minio-Paluello, "The Text of the 'Categoriae': the Latin Tradition," *CQ* 39 (1945): 63–74. Aetius, too, was a self-taught person; see Socrates, *Hist. eccl.* 2.35. Augustine was called the African Aristotle by Julian of Eclanum, in Augustine, *Opus imperfectum contra Iulianum* 3.199 (*PL* 45:1333); and *dialecticus Augustinus* by Sidonius Apollinaris (*Ep.* 9.2). See in general J. Pépin, *Saint Augustin et la dialectique*, The Saint Augustine Lecture 1972 (Villanova, 1976).

89. *De duabus animabus* 11 (CSEL 25:65–66): "Quod quaedam noxia uictoria paene mihi semper in disputationibus proueniebat disserenti cum inperitis, sed tamen fidem suam certatim, ut quisque posset, defendere molientibus christianis . . . ita ex illorum sermonibus ardor in certamina, ex certaminum prouentu amor in illos cotidie nouabatur." On the selective bias of Augustine's retrospective summary, see Brown, *Augustine of Hippo*, 50; J. O'Donnell, *Augustine: Confessions* (Oxford, 1992), 2:184–85.

90. See Plato, *Republic* 537–39; and also M. Meyer, "Dialectic and Questioning," 281–89.

zeal (περιεργότερον) than seemed proper, he was troubled. He stood the young boy before a mirror and asked, "Is it seemly for someone who looks like this to ask these sorts of questions (ζητήματα)?"[91]

This intimate vignette captures the ambivalence surrounding the posing of questions in antiquity. Excessive ambition, as culturally defined, was frowned upon, especially when manifested by the young. Dialectic was not a tool for showing off one's superiority but rather a science for the mature, to be cultivated as a part of one's progress in a philosophical life of virtue. But the ideal of a soul freed from passion was not necessarily shared by all, especially the young and others who stood to gain from open competition.

Augustine's reconversion from "super-rational" Manichaeism to the catholic Christianity of his boyhood coincided with the shedding of his youth. Or so he said. In later years, the Manichaeans who previously had been so dear to him became "false and deceitful men."[92] The mature Augustine decisively reconstructed and renounced his youth as a champion dialectician, commenting on the puerile nature of the Manichaean competitive ethos he had once loved:

> They consider that they reign supreme (*regnare se putant*) in this question, as if to ask were to know. Would that this were so! Then no one more knowledgeable than I would be found. But somehow the propounder of a great question in a controversial situation (*in altercando*) always puts on the appearance (*personam ostentat*) of a great teacher while for the most part he himself is more unlearned in the issue concerning which he would overawe another than the person whom he would overawe.[93]

Philostratus' Apollonius of Tyana and the Syrian Bardaisan were among those who expressed the view that posing questions was a typical preoccupation of youth, whereas answering them was the duty of the mature who had acquired a measure of wisdom.[94] Augustine likewise considered himself much more serious than in his heady days as

91. Diogenes Laertius, *VP* 7.19.

92. *De duabus animabus* 1 (CSEL 25:51).

93. *De duabus animabus* 10 (CSEL 25:63–64): "hac in quaestione illi regnare se putant, quasi uero interrogare sit scire. utinam id esset; nemo me scientior reperiretur. sed nescio quomodo saepe in altercando magnae quaestionis propositor personam magni doctoris ostentat plerumque ipse ipso. quem terret, in eo, de quo terret, indoctior." See Frend, "The Gnostic-Manichaean Tradition," 17–20, on the common pursuit by Manichaeans and gnostics of the answer to the question, "Whence evil?"

94. Philostratus, *Vita Apollonii* 1.17: "μειράκιον ὢν ἐζήτησα, νῦν δὲ οὐ χρὴ ζητεῖν, ἀλλὰ διδάσκειν ἃ εὕρηκα." Bardaisan also affirmed that masters were to be asked questions while disciples were to pose them so as to gain understanding; see Bardaisan, *Book of the Laws of the Countries* 11 (F. Nau, ed., *Le livres des lois des pays* [Paris, 1899], 28).

a brash Manichaean auditor. He did not reject the gravity and relevance of the "great question" that the Manichaeans were in the habit of bandying about; instead, he insisted that this question was "one that needs much calm discussion among those who are the most learned (*doctissimos*)."[95]

This emphasis on learning derived partly from the reflections of a more mature person.[96] Still, there is an element of "credentialism" in Augustine's approach to Christian theological speculation. One's ability to speak persuasively depended, he argued, on the mastery of a large body of complicated knowledge, a vast and deep *scientia* requiring years of immersion in learned tomes. In contrast, the mastery of dialectic alone was a "short-cut" to knowledge. There is no doubt that Augustine's interests in a more philosophically sophisticated anthropology and epistemology reflected the changed interests of an inquiring intellect. Nevertheless, his insistence that Christians pay attention to what he conceded were "obscure and recondite things (*rebus obscuris abditisque*)" deflected questions from certain common topoi of theological discussion that Manichaeans were accustomed to exploiting.[97] Most important, Augustine could argue a fortiori that since most Christians were unable to master even the knowledge of things terrestrial, they had no business trying their hands at the knowledge of things divine.[98]

Yet Augustine's caveat about public debate applied only to what he characterized as recklessly critical dialectical disputations. It did not prevent him from engaging the Manichaeans in a series of staged disputations that have come down to us in versions recorded by the winners, the catholic Christians. These debates between Augustine and various Manichaeans provide valuable insights into the nature of religious contact and conflict in proconsular Africa.[99] This body of well-known material includes the *Contra Fortunatum* (392), the *Contra Felicem* (404), and the long treatise *Contra Faustum* (397–98).

95. *De duabus animabus* 2 (CSEL 25:52): "multum serenae disputationis inter doctissimos indigens."
96. See Brown, *Augustine of Hippo*, 59.
97. See *De duabus animabus* 13 (CSEL 25:68). Basil of Caesarea also used scientific knowledge about the physical world to combat Manichaeans, among others, though there were none in his immediate vicinity; see *Hexaemeron* 2.4 and bk. 4 (S. Giet, ed., 26 bis [Paris, 1968], 158–62, 358). On the absence of Manichaeans in Asia Minor, see F. Decret, "Basile le grand et la polémique antimanichéenne en Asie Mineure au IVe siècle," *SP* 17 (1983): 1060–64.
98. See Pseudo-Basil, *Ep.* 16 (Deferrari, ed., 1:114–17).
99. See the important treatment of this corpus by Decret, *Aspects du manichéisme*.

Augustine and Fortunatus

Eodem tempore presbyteri mei, contra Fortunatum, quemdam Manichaeorum presbyterum disputavi.[100]

On 28 and 29 August 392, a young presbyter of the catholic church of Hippo Regius debated in public with the presbyter of a different *ecclesia*, the Manichaean Fortunatus.[101] Like Pseudo-Mark's Julia, Fortunatus was singled out for attention by the local catholic Christians because of his success in attracting support within the local community.[102] According to Possidius' *Vita Augustini*, a body of *cives* and *peregrini* of Hippo, comprising both catholics and Donatists, turned to the young Augustine for aid and comfort.[103] Their choice was a natural one, for Augustine was trained in dialectic and familiar with Manichaean teachings. Troubled by the influence Fortunatus had gained among the *cives* and *peregrini* of Hippo and its environs,[104] Augustine responded, like Pseudo-Mark's Porphyry, by challenging the Manichaean leader to a high-profile contest aimed at the edification of the community. The strategy was intended to ensure that Manichaeans, who relied for their success on the intimacy of teacher-disciple relationships,[105] could no longer present their arguments unchallenged before Christians who, in Augustine's view, were

100. *Retractationes* 1.15 (CSEL 36:82). See A. Mandouze, ed., *Prosopographie de l'Afrique chrétienne*, vol. 1 of *Prosopographie chrétienne du Bas-Empire* (Paris, 1982), s.v. "Fortunatus 2," 490–93.

101. See *C. Fortunatum,* preface (CSEL 25:83): "Sexto et quinto Kalendas Septembris Arcadio Augusto bis et Quinto Rufino uiris clarissmis consulibus actis habita disputatio aduersum Fortunatum Manichaeorum presbyterum in urbe Hipponensium regionum in balneis Sossii sub praesentia populi."

102. *Retractationes* 1.15 (CSEL 36:82). Fortunatus had been successful as a teacher and community organizer in Hippo, a fact Augustine admits: "Qui [Fortunatus] plurimum temporis apud Hipponem uixerat, seduxeratque tam multos ut propter illos ibi eum delectaret habitare." Note here the recurrence of the language condemning seduction. This fear of seduction on the part of anti-Manichaean polemicists on the one hand reflects the Manichaean propensity to attract the young (see above discussion), who were seen as lacking in discrimination, and on the other hand reveals the paternal ideology at work: those in authority were seen as responsible for the *imperiti* under their care, and any threat to that relationship was construed as seduction. Agency and initiative were not granted to the *imperiti* under this scheme.

103. Possidius, *Vita Augustini* 6 (*PL* 32:38).

104. See Decret, *Aspects du manichéisme*, 40. Were the *peregrini* merchants, *negotiatores* like Firmus who were responsible for much of the spread of the Manichaean movement outside of the main towns, or were they displaced Roman aristocrats? In any case, they were an important group over which a local Christian leader had little direct social control; they therefore needed to be impressed by other means.

105. See the importance of the teacher-disciple relationship in the *Fragmenta Tebestina;* P. Alfaric, "Un manuscrit manichéen," *RHLR* n.s. 6 (1920): 62–94.

inexperienced and unable to judge for themselves ("diu multumque de inperitorum erroribus latissime ac uehementissime disputabant").[106]

Though Augustine chose to view his response as protecting the *imperiti*, it can also be seen as a reaction against the seemingly uncheckable movement of community members—particularly the intelligentsia—across sectarian boundaries. The influence of charismatic teachers like Fortunatus threatened the tolerable *modus vivendi* of mutual boycott.[107] Yet lest we think that the Manichaeans were taking over the Christian community in great numbers, we should remember that Augustine later joked about Fortunatus' small base of support compared with his own much stronger catholic Christian community: "your very small number" (*tanta vestra paucitate*).[108]

Augustine's staged *disputatio* with Fortunatus was held in the Baths of Sossius in Hippo Regius, *sub praesentia populi*.[109] The audience of the debate, at least on the second day, was made up mostly of catholic Christians, according to Augustine himself in *Contra Fortunatum*.[110] It was a solemn affair. Stenographers, most likely *notarii* affiliated with the catholic church, recorded the event. The contest itself was preceded by a series of preliminary negotiations concerning the topic of the debate and the mode of demonstration to be used.[111]

It is almost certain that Augustine and the catholic Christians of Hippo applied tremendous pressure to force the Manichaeans to make an appearance at this debate by spreading rumors, perhaps even *libelli famiosi*, which echoed charges of immorality not infrequently brought against Manichaeans.[112] The Manichaeans were put on the spot: if they forfeited the chance to clear their name, they tacitly confessed to the accusations leveled at them; otherwise, they had to descend for battle onto a field carefully selected and prepared by their opponents.

The proceedings resembled a trial by judge and jury rather than a fair debate.[113] The Manichaean argued that both he and Augustine

106. *De utilitate credendi* 2 (CSEL 25:5).

107. See Augustine, *Sermones* 182.2, 302.19; Brown, "Religious Coercion in the Later Roman Empire: The Case of North Africa," *History* 48 (1963): 283–305.

108. See Decret, *Aspects du manichéisme*, 40n. 1; idem, *L'Afrique manichéenne*, 1: 189–90.

109. *C. Fortunatum*, prologue (CSEL 25:83).

110. *C. Fortunatum* 37 (CSEL 25:112): "fideles sunt."

111. See *C. Fortunatum* 1–3 (CSEL 25:83–86).

112. On such traditional charges, see A. Henrichs, "Pagan Ritual and the Alleged Crimes of the Early Christians: A Reconsideration," in P. Granfield and J. A. Jungmann, eds., *Kyriakon: Festschrift Johannes Quasten* (Münster, 1970), 1:18–35.

113. See Decret, *Aspects du manichéisme*, 45: "Avec . . . la déférence d'un accusé devant un jury."

should confine themselves to discussing the morals of the Manichaeans, his primary concern:

> The issue to be considered is our way of life, concerning the false criminal accusations by which we have been assaulted. Therefore let the respectable men present hear from you whether the charges upon which we are accused and sought out are true, or false.[114]

Like earlier Christian apologists faced with charges of gruesome crimes and misdeeds, Fortunatus wanted to make his defense by appealing to the moral and ascetic virtues of the elect. Augustine quickly responded that faith and morals were separate matters and ought to be discussed independently of each other. For the moment, he wanted to limit the discussion to doctrine alone, and he justified this choice by shrewdly claiming that only the *electi* alone could know their mode of life.[115]

Fortunatus complied with Augustine's restriction; he probably had no choice in the matter. He made a declaration of his *professio* by pronouncing the attributes of God: incorruptible, perspicuous, unapproachable, ungraspable, impassible, and so on. Augustine, trained in dialectical disputation and particularly versed in Aristotle's predicate logic, could now methodically dismantle the proposed theses using well-tried tools.

Augustine moved gingerly, reluctant to let Fortunatus raise counter-questions[116] or to shift to different lines of argument that were probably part of Manichaean training. When Fortunatus tried to turn the debate back to scriptures, Augustine's reference to the "men of note" present (who presumably were able to follow rational arguments) was enough to bring the discussion back to the latter's proposed topic.

114. *C. Fortunatum* 1 (CSEL 25:84). See, for example, the charges Augustine assembled circa 405 in his *De natura boni contra Manichaeos* 47 (CSEL 25:886–87).

115. *C. Fortunatum* 3 (CSEL 25:84–85): "Ad aliud uocas, cum ego de fide proposuerim, de moribus autem uestris plene scire possunt, qui electi uestri sunt. nostis autem me non electum uestrum, sed auditorem fuisse . . . quaestionem de moribus, ut inter electos uestros discutiatis, si discuti potest. mihi fides data est a uobis, quam hodie inprobo. de ipse proposui. ad propositum meum mihi respondeatur."

116. See Augustine's reply to Fortunatus' request for a dialectical premiss from him (whether the Word of God "anima dei est, an non?") in *C. Fortunatum* 10 (CSEL 25:89): "Si iustum est, ut non interrogatis meis respondeatur et ego interroger, respondeo." Though Augustine finally granted Fortunatus' request, he was careful to score a tactical point by noting that Fortunatus was not willing to respond to his questions in *C. Fortunatum* 11 (CSEL 25:89): "Tantum illud memineris te noluisse respondere interrogatis meis, me autem tui respondere." Later in *C. Fortunatum* 13 (CSEL 25:90), he stated for the record that though he was willing to entertain Fortunatus' questions, the latter was not willing to answer some of his. This kind of argument was only possible because the debate was being recorded by stenographers.

Later in the debate, Augustine again appealed to the nature of the audience when Fortunatus resorted to the proven Manichaean tactic of appealing to accepted scriptural texts for dialectical premisses.[117] The audience itself responded:

> At this point an uproar came from the audience who wished the debate to be held rather with rational arguments (*rationibus*) because they saw that Fortunatus was not willing to accept the things written in the apostolic book. Then here and there a discussion began to be held by everyone. . . .[118]

On the following day, Fortunatus, handicapped by many constraints, found himself in extremis after a series of exchanges. He helplessly exclaimed, "What then am I to say?"[119] Augustine, sensing his opponent's despair, did not press on; he had reduced his adversary to silence and had therefore won the debate. He concluded the proceedings by expounding the catholic faith to all present.[120] Though Fortunatus went away ignominiously to confer with his superiors (*meis maioribus*),[121] there was no actual capitulation, nor did Augustine try to bring one about. That the closure of this debate was not as dramatic or as firm as, for example, the end of the encounter between Augustine and Felix suggests that in 392 the goals of the young priest were limited. It sufficed to humble Fortunatus, a man of established reputation for whom Augustine no doubt had some regard. But this gentility of the early 390s would succumb to the requirements of maintaining episcopal authority once Augustine succeeded Valerius to the see of Hippo in 395.

Augustine and His *Contra Faustum*

The Numidian Faustus, referred to as an *episcopus manichaeorum*, was a much more formidable opponent for Augustine than Fortunatus.[122] Of

117. *C. Fortunatum* 19 (CSEL 25:96): "Rationibus ut discuteremus duarum naturarum fidem, interpositum est ab his, quis nos audiunt. sed quoniam ad scripturas iterum confugisti. . . ."

118. *C. Fortunatum* 19 (CSEL 25:97). On an ancient speaker's deliberate attempt to incite the audience to make an uproar against his rival in a verbal contest, see V. Bers, "Dikastic *thorubos*," 1–15, esp. 9.

119. *C. Fortunatum* 36 (CSEL 25:112): "Quid ergo dicturus sum?"

120. *C. Fortunatum* 37 (CSEL 25:112): "Sed si confiteris te non habere quod respondeas, omnibus audientibus et recognoscentibus quoniam fideles sunt, catholicam fidem, si permittunt ut uolunt exponam."

121. The debate ended on an almost amicable note; see *C. Fortunatum* 37 (CSEL 25:112).

122. *C. Faustum* 1.1 (CSEL 25:251). See Decret, *Aspects du manichéisme*, 51–70; Mandouze, ed., *Prosopographie de l'Afrique chrétienne*, 390–97, s.v. "Faustus 2."

humble origins, he achieved a widely known reputation for eloquence, and was already a distinguished figure when the young Augustine first met him.[123] In those earlier years, Faustus had come to Carthage and there daily displayed his skill in words;[124] he commanded immense presence and greatly impressed those around him with the panache of his discourse.[125] It was to Faustus that Augustine presented his own doubts while a Manichaean auditor, probably in the manner of disciples who proposed *aporiae* for their teachers to solve. Only years later and after a serious change of heart did Augustine judge the man unlearned.[126] Three years after Augustine departed for Italy in 383, Faustus was brought before the *proconsularis Africae* by catholic Christians and sent into exile until 387.[127]

Yet even while physically removed from Roman North Africa, Faustus was able to strike back at his persecutors by composing the *Capitula de christiana fide et veritate*, in which he set forth thirty-three *disputationes* debunking beliefs held by catholic Christians.[128] The work began to have influence in catholic Christian circles and soon reached the attention of Augustine,[129] who reacted to it in the same way that he was to react to the Donatist bishop Petilian's *Ad presbyteros* circa 400.[130]

To rebut Faustus' arguments in the *Capitula*, Augustine composed a lengthy work which he called his grand opus.[131] Augustine wrote his *Contra Faustum* as if he were refuting Faustus in person. Like Irenaeus[132]

123. See *Confessiones* 5.6.
124. *Confessiones* 5.6.
125. *Confessiones* 5.13.
126. *Confessiones* 5.36. On the prejudice that the learned directed against the "semi-learned," see R. Reitzenstein, "Alexander von Lykopolis," *Philologus* 86 (1930–31): 185–98. Reitzenstein argues (197) that the pagan philosopher Alexander's objections to Manichaeans stemmed from traditional educated elite prejudice against the pretensions to knowledge of "upstarts."
127. See *C. Faustum* 5.8 (CSEL 25:280). See P. D. Garnsey, "The Criminal Jurisdiction of Governors," *JRS* 58 (1968): 51–59.
128. See P. Monceaux, *Le manichéen Faustus de Milève: Restitution de ses Capitula*, Mémoires de l'Institut National de France, Académie des Inscriptions et Belles-Lettres 43 (Paris, 1933), esp. 14–43; A. Bruckner, *Faustus von Mileve: Ein Beitrag zur Geschichte des abendländischen Manichäismus* (Basel, 1901). Decret views as speculation the supposition that this work was designed as a compendium for the Manichaean polemicist for use in local settings; see *Aspects du manichéisme*, 61.
129. See Decret, *Aspects du manichéisme*, 62, 62n. 2.
130. See Frend, "Manichaeism in the Struggle between Saint Augustine and Petilian of Constantine," *Augustinus Magister* (Paris, 1954): 859–66, esp. 861. Compare *C. Faustum* 1.1 in regard to how the religious rivals' controversial writings came into Augustine's hands.
131. *Retractationes* 2.33 (CSEL 36:139).
132. See Decret, *Aspects du manichéisme*, 15n. 2.

or Origen, Augustine began his fictive debate by stating, "I judge it convenient to put his words under his name and to place my response under mine."[133] This dialogic convention enabled Augustine to render a detailed refutation of the favorite arguments of Faustus, and of the Manichaeans in general. He deliberately contrasted his own slow and lowly style with Faustus' sharpness and eloquence,[134] but explained that "a sharp mind and a polished tongue are of no value unless the steps of the person are guided by his Master."[135]

Augustine's work was aimed at a broad audience, though perhaps especially at those who harbored Manichaean sympathies. It provided counterarguments to Faustus' pointed questions and anticipated the situation of face-to-face debates: "Et hoc quidem nunc a nobis ita responsum sit, quia uobis placet argumentari et arma temptatis aliena dialectice disputare uolentes."[136] Even so, Augustine was well aware that he did not furnish his readers with arguments that could pass as philosophical demonstrations. His goal was rhetorical persuasion and not *demonstratio*. In fact, Augustine cautioned his audience that it was not proper for them to expect philosophical proof in such contexts, for "you should consider first who you are (even as if you are moved by reason) and how very unfit you are for understanding the nature of your own soul, not to mention the soul of God."[137]

Augustine was willing to provide others with ready-made arguments against Manichaeans, but these arguments were not invitations to further investigation, because this regressive curiosity led to such doubt as attracted Christians to Manichaean teachings in the first place. Augustine confounded Faustus' arguments by the sheer weight of the encyclopaedic learning that he mobilized against them. The same stratagem of underscoring the complexity of human anthropology and cognition was later used to discourage Christians from "undue curiosity" about supramundane issues.[138]

133. *C. Faustum* 1.1 (CSEL 25:251): "Commodum autem arbitror sub eius nomine uerba eius ponere et sub meo responsionem meam." Yet later traditions relished portraying Augustine engaged in a *disputatio* with Faustus; see J. and P. Courcelle, "Quelques illustrations du 'contra Faustum' de saint Augustin," in *Oikoumene* (Catinae, 1964), 1–21, esp. plates 1–4. The illuminated manuscripts date from the twelfth to the fifteenth centuries.

134. *C. Faustum* 1.1 (CSEL 25:251).

135. *C. Faustum* 1.1 (CSEL 25:251): "Nihil sit acutum ingenium et lingua expolita, nisi a domino gressus hominis dirigantur."

136. *C. Faustum* 26.2 (CSEL 25:730).

137. *C. Faustum* 33.9 (CSEL 25:796–97): "Si autem quasi ratione mouemini, primum cogitetis, quinam sitis, quam minus idonei ad conprehendendam naturam, non dicam Dei, sed animae uestrae, conprehendendam sane."

138. See, e.g., Gregory of Nazianzus, *Oratio* 27.9–10.

Augustine and Felix

By 404, the year of Augustine's debate with the Manichaean Felix, the hold of the catholic church on North Africa and elsewhere had already been considerably strengthened by the Theodosian settlement. Imperial support brought new confidence and a radical shift in the catholic bishops' strategies for coping with religious rivals. In particular, this affected their relationship with the Donatists, the other Christian church in North Africa.

Before 404, catholic Christians had approached the schism as a matter to be resolved in traditional ecclesiastical fashion, through collegial discussion, exhortation, and public debate. The Donatists had wisely turned down invitations to such debates. With no compromise in sight, the catholic bishops began in 404 to petition the imperial government for rescripts authorizing them to take repressive actions against the Donatists.[139] Once these laws had been obtained, they were not enforced immediately but were used instead as psychological weapons to induce noncatholics to voluntarily abandon their "error." Force was eventually used and later rationalized. It was at this juncture, with the balance about to shift dramatically in the favor of the catholic bishops, that Augustine debated Felix in Hippo: "Contra Manichaeum quemdam nomine Felicem, praesente populo, in ecclesia biduo disputavi."[140]

Since the last recorded disputation between a Christian and a Manichaean, the venue had moved from the public Baths of Sossius to the bishops' cathedral—purportedly to protect Felix from an angry Christian mob. Much else had changed. In these proceedings, the Manichaean debater was extremely respectful, addressing Augustine the catholic bishop as *sanctitas tua*.[141] At one point, Felix referred to his handicaps in the debate:

> Non tantum ego possum contra tuam uirtutem, quia mira uirtus est gradus episcopalis, deinde contra leges imperatoris. et superius petiui compendiue, ut doceas me, quid est ueritas; et si docueris me, quid est ueritas, parebit quod teneo mendacium esse.[142]

The two negotiated the grounds for debate before proceeding. Felix wanted to use Manichaean texts that had already been confiscated, but Augustine agreed to discuss only one of them, the *Epistula Fundamenti*,

139. See Brown, "Religious Coercion," 283–306.
140. *Retractationes* 2.34 (CSEL 36:141). See Mandouze, ed., *Prosopographie de l'Afrique chrétienne*, 417–18, s.v. "Felix 20."
141. *C. Felicem* 1.2, 1.6 (CSEL 25:802, 807).
142. *C. Felicem* 1.12 (CSEL 25:813). MSS. P, R, S, and b have the plural *imperatorum;* only T (twelfth century) has *imperatoris*. See below on the *leges imperatoris.*

which he had already refuted in 396.[143] In this debate, Augustine was
nothing if not well prepared and the outcome understandably did not
favor the Manichaean.

Events at the end of this debate remain mysterious. Though earlier
exchanges between Felix and Augustine had been noted with care, and
presumably with accuracy, their final words were quickly glossed over:
"After many words had been exchanged between them, Felix said" (Post
haec cum multis uerbis inter se agerent, Felix dixit.)[144] It would be interesting to know whether these *verba* were exchanged in the hearing of
all, or whether the words "inter se" refer to a private conversation. The
surprising silence of the stenographic record, along with what transpired later, suggests a private exchange. Perhaps Felix was even nego-
tiating with Augustine the terms of his surrender, for he then asked
Augustine: "What do you want me to do?" (Quid uis faciam?)[145]

Why did not Felix simply concede defeat and walk away, as did Fortunatus by pleading that he would seek advice from his *maiores*? Why
did he ask Augustine what the latter would have him do? For one thing,
Felix was in a much weaker position than Fortunatus had been. His
opponent was no longer a presbyter but a powerful *episcopus* to whom
much respect was due. *Tua uirtus* and *tua sanctitas* were ever on Felix's
lips, and his demeanor must also have expressed studious deference to
Augustine and the *gradus episcopalis*.

Though Felix had vowed to burn with the confiscated Manichaean
codices if Augustine succeeded in finding evil in them, this was not a
commitment to unconditional surrender in the case of defeat. Instead,
he dramatically anathematized Mani and his teachings. It is difficult to
know whether Felix did so out of fear that the bishop would invoke the
anti-Manichaean legislations against him. Augustine himself had reas-
sured Felix that "no one will force you against your will" (nemo enim te
cogit inuitum).[146] In any case, the scenario surrounding the anathema
seems contrived, and quite possibly prearranged.[147]

143. *Contra Epistulam quam vocant Fundamenti* (CSEL 15:193–248); fragments in A.
Adam, *Texte zum Manichäismus* (Berlin, 1969), 27–30. See the recent attempt to reconstruct
the letter from Augustine's corpus in E. Feldmann, *Die "Epistula Fundamenti" der nordafrikanischen Manichäer: Versuch einer Rekonstruktion* (Altenberge, 1987).

144. *C. Felicem* 2.22 (CSEL 25:851).

145. *C. Felicem* 2.22 (CSEL 25:852).

146. *C. Felicem* 2.22 (CSEL 25:852).

147. The text of the anathema in *C. Felicem* 2.22 (CSEL 25:852): "Ego Felix, qui Ma-
nichaeo credideram, nunc anathemo eum et doctrinam ipsius et spiritum seductorem, qui
in illo fuit, qui dixit deum partem suam genti tenebrarum miscuisse et eam tam turpiter
liberare, ut uirtutes suas transfiguraret in feminas contra masculina et ipsas iterum in
masculos contra feminea daemonia, ita ut postea reliquias ipsius suae partis configat in

For prominent figures like the African rhetor Marius Victorinus, a staged exhibition of a realignment in one's religious affiliation was an act preceded by serious, private negotiations with those in authority.[148] The act of conversion itself was a highly stylized ritual. It is very likely that Augustine had pressured Felix to debate with him on very unequal terms and that the latter, sensing the hopelessness of his situation from the outset, had decided to appear conciliatory and deferential and had already privately negotiated the terms of his capitulation.[149]

After anathematizing Mani, Felix urged Augustine to do the same: "Ut confirmes me?" We may suppose that Felix wanted a public affirmation that his Manichaean past would not mar his future career as a catholic Christian by reminding all present that Augustine, too, had once been a Manichaean.[150] More puzzling is the question of why Augustine agreed to do so.

Perhaps Augustine invited Felix to make this request of him. Disturbing rumors that Augustine remained a crypto-Manichaean were rampant during this period, suspicions disseminated by Petilian and others such as Julian of Eclanum (in his reply to Augustine's response to his *Ad presbyteros*).[151] This debate, in addition to signaling the triumph of catholic Christianity over Manichaeism, also served as the most public of proofs that Augustine was no longer a Manichaean, a fact that the new bishop's *Confessions*, published circa 397, also aimed to demonstrate.[152] Thus both debaters wrote and signed with their own hands, "in the church before the people" (in ecclesia coram populo), their re-

---

aeternum globo tenebrarum. has omnes et ceteras blasphemias Manichaei anathemo." For the attribution of another anathema, formerly believed to refer to Felix's conversion, to Cresconius, see S. N. C. and J. Lieu, " 'Felix conversus ex Manichaeis': A Case of Mistaken Identity," *JTS* n.s. 32 (1981): 173–76. Their interesting suggestion is rejected by Decret in "Du bon usage du mensonge et du parjure: Manichéens et Priscillianistes face à la persécution dans l'empire chrétien (IVe–Ve siècles)," in *Mélanges P. Lévêque* (Paris, 1990), 4:144n. 21.

148. See P. Hadot, *Marius Victorinus: Recherches sur sa vie et ses oeuvres* (Paris, 1971); O'Donnell, *Confessions*, 3:12–13. On Marius' conversion, see Augustine, *Confessiones* 8.2.

149. See D. Newman, "Pleading Guilty for Considerations: A Study of Bargain Justice," *Journal of Criminal Law, Criminology and Police Science* 46 (1956): 780–90, at 780.

150. On the practical need for public recognition of such a change in one's religious allegiance, see Brown, "Religious Coercion," 327, on the *tesserae* issued by catholic bishops to converted Manichaeans referred to in the *Commonitorium Sancti Augustini* (*PL* 42:1153–56).

151. See Augustine, *Contra Litteras Petiliani* 3.6, 19 (CSEL 52:177); *Contra Cresconium* 3.80.92.

152. See A. Vecchi, "L'antimanicheismo nelle 'confessioni' di sant'Agostino," *Giornale di metafisica* 20 (1965): 91–121.

spective renunciations of Manichaeism.[153] The staging could not have been more effective.

Augustine had succeeded in his later dealings with Manichaeans because of his enviable advantage of having been an insider. He knew how to maneuver Fortunatus. At the end of their second day's debate, when Fortunatus confessed that he was at a loss, Augustine replied: "I know that you don't have anything to say. Even I could never find anything to say on this question when I was an auditor among you."[154]

Few other Christians possessed Augustine's fortuitous mixture of gifts and his imposing authority as a catholic bishop, and were therefore not so well equipped to defeat Manichaeans in a debate. Yet Augustine could help these *imperiti* in two significant ways.

First of all, as we have seen, he could furnish written refutations of Manichaean arguments and beliefs for circulation among catholics. Even Christians unable to recall the details of Augustine's convoluted arguments could wield his books as an authority or a talisman. The contest between catholic Christians and Manichaeans could then be raised from the local level of face-to-face encounters to the realm of proxy debate through treatises.

Second, Augustine could defeat select Manichaean leaders in highly publicized debates. Narratives of these carefully choreographed events could then circulate as edifying *exempla* for other Christians. In either case, individual Christians did not need to argue afresh all the familiar points of contention, so common as to be *topoi;* they needed to know only that it had already been done for them. Through this process, catholic Christians gained advantages originally held by the Manichaeans, namely, the possession of a body of useful controversial texts and a resulting tradition of success in debates.[155]

---

153. *C. Felicem* 2.22 (CSEL 25:852): "Augustinus ecclesiae catholicae episcopus iam anathemaui Manichaeum et doctrinam eius et spiritum, qui per eum tam execrabiles blasphemias locutus est, quia spiritus seductor erat non ueritatis, sed nefandi erroris ipsius."

154. *C. Fortunatum* 37 (CSEL 25:112).

155. The relationship between elenchic disputation and question chains has been noted by Ryle, "Dialectic in the Academy," 75: "Written minutes or abstracts of the argument-sequences deployed are kept and consulted. . . . Like chess-players' 'combinations,' lines of argumentation are public property, and a tactical improvement made by myself becomes henceforth a part of anyone else's stock of arguments for or against the same thesis." The only known fourth-century Latin anti-Manichaean treatise written for catholic Christians is an anonymous work attributed to Marius Victorinus; see Pseudo-Victorinus, *Liber ad Justinum Manichaeum contra duo principia Manichaeorum et de vero carne Christi,* in *PL* 8:999–1010. Augustine's anti-Manichaean writings therefore provided useful refutations of certain central Manichaean claims that Latin Christians had hitherto been unable to challenge successfully. By the fifth century, Latin catholic Christians would have access to a number of *florilegia* or prooftexts designed for arguing against positions deemed heretical; see the collected texts in *Florilegia Biblica Africana saec. V* CCSL 90 (Turnhout,

THE NARROWING OF THE HORIZONS

When the first Manichaean missionaries arrived in the Roman Empire, they brought with them written texts designed to aid them in sectarian religious controversy. Their ability to convince, as our sources inform us, depended on their grounding in these writings. Manichaeans developed a repertoire of topics certain to interest Christians, and from such opening gambits they moved on to the Manichaean gospel of the two principles.

The use of formal public disputation as part of the Manichaean missionary effort is almost unattested. Instead we find an emphasis on aporetic disputation using such questions as "Whence evil?" Their purpose was not to draw listeners into debate, though this sometimes happened, but to allow them to appreciate the Manichaean kerygma as the solution to real theological problems.[156] In the fictive *Acta Archelai*, we recall, Mani singled out the local notable Marcellus for conversion through the private suasion of an exchange of letters. It appears that neither Mani nor his disciples wanted to come into town to engage in formal disputation. The debate in the *Acta Archelai* was thrust upon Mani by his opponents, just as most staged public debates involving Manichaeans were initiated by local catholic and other Christians as a means of countering the missionaries' local influence. Although Manichaeans were notoriously mobile, subsequent records of the debates followed the Manichaeans, shadowing them with the effects of one decisive loss.

The early history of Manichaeism and the stories about debates between Manichaeans and other religious figures depict a world of relative religious diversity and fluid frontiers. From the late fourth century onward this picture was turned on its head. "To study Manichaeism is to study the fate of a missionary religion in a world of shrinking horizons."[157] With increasingly powerful local bishops acting as religious police to enforce their own interests, and a hostile imperial legislation to back the bishops up, Manichaeans, like many other religious groups,

---

1961), especially Pseudo-Augustine, *Solutiones diversarum quaestionum ab haereticis obiectarum* (B. Swank, ed., 149–223).

156. On the Manichaeans and their propensity for asking "Whence evil?" see Titus of Bostra, *Adversus Manichaeos* A.4 (Paul de Lagarde, ed., *Titi Bostreni, quae ex opere contra Manichaeos edito in codice Hamburgensi servata sunt* [1859; reprint, Wiesbaden, 1967], pp. 3 [Greek], 5 [Syriac]). In general, see P.-H. Poirier, "Le *contra Manichaeos* de Titus de Bostra," *Annuaire: École Pratique des Hautes Études*, Section de Sciences Religieuses 98 (1989–90): 366–68, esp. 368; H. Puech, *Le manichéisme, son fondateur, sa doctrine* (Paris, 1949), 152.

157. Brown, "Diffusion of Manichaeism," 98.

could no longer compete as equals in the religious market of late antiquity. One stunning change was that Christians no longer had to debate Manichaeans on equal terms; they could demand a written abjuration from suspected sectarians.[158]

Writing played a central role in this new world of rising religious authoritarianism. The career of Augustine attested to the developing use of stenography and its relationship to power.[159] In November of 386, Augustine had engaged stenographers to take down his dictation at Cassiciacum when he was composing his Skeptical *Contra Academicos* as part of the stock exercise of late antique intellectuals to defend their views against competing models of truth.[160] In 392, the young priest made good use of stenography in his debate with Fortunatus in Hippo, and in 404 he again used stenography, this time to secure the binding, written anathema of Felix. Finally, in 411, he used stenography to its best advantage at the celebrated anti-Donatist Council of Carthage, which he dominated. Augustine of Hippo had learned over the years that stenography, a friend to the Roman imperial government for centuries, could be an equally loyal and useful friend to a Christian bishop.

In addition, the Christian bishop increasingly resembled an imperial official in terms of the coercive power he possessed. The gist of the ominous anti-Manichaean *leges* referred to by Felix in 404 can be discerned by reading the *Theodosian Code*.[161] Knowing that the local catholic bishop

158. For abjuration formulae for deconversion from Manichaeism in general, see *PG* 1:1461–74; M. Richard, ed., *Ioannes Caesariensis Presbyteri et Grammatici Opera* CCSG 1 (Turnhout, 1977), xxxiii–xxxix (long formula); *PG* 100:1217–25 (short formula). See text, translation, and commentary in S. N. C. Lieu, "An Early Byzantine Formula for the Renunciation of Manichaeism: the *capita VII contra Manichaeos* of ⟨*Zacharias of Mytilene*⟩," *JAC* 26 (1983): 152–218; this is reviewed by M. Tardieu in *Studia Iranica* 7:139. See H. Garfinkel, "Conditions of Successful Degradation Ceremonies," *American Journal of Sociology* 61 (1956): 420–24.

159. In general, see D. Ohlmann, "Die Stenographie im Leben des heiligen Augustin," *Archiv für Stenographie* 56 (1905): 273–79, 312–19.

160. See Hoffmann, *Dialog*, 135–43. See now the discussion by T. Fuhrer, "Das Kriterium der Wahrheit in Augustins *contra Academicos*," *VChr* 46 (1992): 257–75, esp. 258.

161. See *Cod. Theod.* 16.5.35 (Krueger and Mommsen, eds., 866), issued by Arcadius and Honorius from Milan and addressed to the vicar of Africa:

> Noxios Manichaeos execrabilesque eorum conventus, dudum iusta animadversione damnatos, etiam speciali praeceptione cohiberi decernimus. Quapropter quaesiti adducantur in publicum ac detestati criminosi congrua et severissima emendatione resecentur. In eos etiam auctoritatis aculei dirigantur, qui eos domibus suis damnanda provisione defendent.

See also E. H. Kaden, "Die Edikte gegen die Manichäer von Diokletian bis Justinian," in *Festschrift für Hans Lewald* (Basel, 1953), 55–68; P. Beskow, "The Theodosian Laws against Manichaeism," in P. Bryder, ed., *Manichaean Studies*, 1, 1–11. On imperial persecutions against the Manichaeans in general, see Lieu, *History of Manichaeism*, 154–77.

could invoke such laws made the Manichaeans more timid, at least in public.[162] Yet Felix's plight was not quite the unhappiest predicament in which a Manichaean would find himself in the Christian empire. That distinction must be reserved for the Manichaeans involved in two incidents during the reign of the emperor Justinian.

John of Ephesus related one of the incidents, the date of which is unknown, though the account precedes a story dated to the nineteenth year of Justinian's reign, or 546.[163] According to John, Justinian called before him the Manichaeans that had been arrested in pogroms initiated by the emperor himself, and then proceeded to personally attempt their conversion by means of debate.[164] His prisoners, many of them noble women and senators, refused "with satanic obstinacy" to alter their religious allegiance, even at the cost of martyrdom. The emperor obliged them, taking the unusual (though perhaps prudent) step of burning their corpses at sea so that the waves might take their remains.

The other incident concerns a disputation sponsored by the emperors Justin and Justinian. Not long after the enactment of the anti-Manichaean law of 527, which saw the public execution of prominent individuals known to be Manichaeans, a staged disputation (ἡ διά-λεκτος) was held by imperial command.[165] The principals were a champion of the Manichaean faith (ὁ μὲν τῆς Μανιχαϊκῆς δόξης προϊστά-μενος), a teacher (διδάσκαλος) called Photinus, and Paul the Persian, a Christian.[166]

The debate lasted four days. The arguments relied heavily on Aristotelian dialectic; the Manichaean also attempted the familiar attacks on the Hebrew bible. Finally, after Paul successfully answered a baiting question from Photinus about whether Christ upheld or destroyed the Mosaic commandments, the Manichaean grew silent: "σιωπήσας οὐδὲν ἀπεκρίνατο."

Throughout this disputation, Photinus was hardly on an equal foot-

162. See Brown, "St. Augustine's Attitude to Religious Coercion."

163. See F. Nau, "Analyse de la seconde partie inédite de l'Histoire Ecclésiastique de Jean d'Asie, patriarche jacobite de Constantinople (d. 585)," Revue de l'Orient Chrétien 2 (1897): 455–93, esp. 478–79 (Syriac) and 481 (French).

164. On the moral duty felt by judges in witchcraft trials in early modern Europe and their sermonizing exhortations, see E. Delcambre, "Les procès de sorcellerie en Lorraine: psychologie des juges," Revue d'Histoire du Droit 21 (1953): 408–15.

165. Disputationes Photini Manichaei cum Paulo Christiano, in PG 88:529A–551C. See discussion in Lieu, History of Manichaeism, 172–73. See the valuable study of this episode and discussion of the Vatican and Sinai MSS by G. Mercati, "Per la vita e gli scritti di 'Paolo il Persiano': Appunti de una disputa di religione sotto Giustino e Giustiniano," in Note di letteratura biblica e cristiana antica, Studi e Testi 5 (Rome, 1901): 180–206.

166. Disputationes Photini cum Paulo (PG 88:529A).

ing with Paul: he was in chains and probably under guard. Lieu is justified in characterizing Paul as less a partner in debate than an "inquisi-
tor."[167] Photinus was relegated to the role of a disciple posing questions
to his teacher.[168] Furthermore, in accordance with standard procedure,
the emperors chose Theodore Teganistes, "the Frier," as the secular dignitary assigned to supervise the religious debate. Theodore had already
been prefect of Constantinople four times by 527.[169] Bearing the court
title of *ho endoxotatos*, he was one whose presence at the debate guaranteed the carrying out of imperial wishes.[170]

The ideological shift brought about by the outlawing of Manichaeism was decisive. With the rise of catholic and orthodox Christianities
to a central position in the Roman Empire, increased social closure was
needed to reflect the new imperial identity. In Max Weber's view, such
social closure was achieved by increasing rigidity in group boundaries,
curbing freewheeling competition, and preventing individual movement
across boundaries. Public debates became no more than showcases exhibiting, for the edification of all Christian subjects as well as the marginalized Other, the wide gulf between sanctioned and illegitimate religious self-identifications.

Gradually, the division between things Manichaean and things
Christian became less murky, and the polemical literature contributed
to this process of differentiation. In John of Damascus' *Dialogus contra
Manichaeos*, we find what might be called a template debate.[171] The genre
was that of Leontius of Neapolis' *Apologia contra Judaeos* (surviving in
quotations by John of Damascus), which was assembled out of adaptable
florilegia of prooftexts.[172] The two interlocutors in this dialogue were
referred to as "the Orthodox" and "the Manichaean." This clear-cut
juxtaposition of their differences was reassuring to those ideologically
committed to maintaining a definition of the Christian church based on

167. *Disputationes Photini cum Paulo* (PG 88:533D–535B); Lieu, *History of Manichaeism*, 173.

168. See Mercati, "Per la vita e gli scritti di 'Paolo il Persiano,'" 196–98.

169. See *PLRE* 2:1006, s.v. "Theodorus *qui et* Teganistes 57." His nickname suggests
either that he rose from the humble origins of "a frier" to an exalted status, or that he
possessed a stern reputation as a magistrate who meted out exceedingly harsh punish-
ments. His theological views, if any, were unknown.

170. See *PG* 88:529. This important dignitary sponsored Christian buildings in the
capital when he was the *praefectus urbis* of Constantinople for the third time in 520; see
PLRE 2:1006.

171. Text in *PG* 94:1505–84. This text is different from the dialogue between a certain
"John the Orthodox" and a Manichaean; text in *PG* 96:1320–36, and *Iohannis Caesariensis
Presbyteri et Grammatici Opera* (Richard, ed., 109–28).

172. See V. Déroche, "L'authenticité de l' 'apologie contre les juifs,'" *BCH* 110 (1986):
655–69. On the *adversus Judaeos* genre as a whole, see Williams, *Adversus Judaeos*.

doctrinal purity and communal solidarity. After definitions of truth and falsehood had been established using dialectical arguments, the discussion opened with a variation of a Manichaean classic: "Do you say that there is one first principle (ἀρχή), or two?" the Manichaean asked John.[173] Like Paul the Persian, John was trained in philosophical dialectic and would have been a formidable foe to any historical opponent, let alone the imaginary Manichaean of the dialogue.[174] The Manichaean was not always able to respond and consequently the dialogic principle in this writing gradually deteriorated. Soon John began to lecture in a monologic style, using *kai palin* and other rather artless devices to connect disparate arguments presented sequentially.

The conflict between orthodox Christianity and Manichaeism was now conducted more and more through anonymous pamphleteering.[175] The Manichaean debater had by the sixth century become a shadowy figure in the Roman Empire, with no life of his own.[176] Yet this process was only the flip side of the crystallization of an orthodox tradition, for the Christian refutations of Manichaeism also assumed a nameless and timeless quality: the short anonymous pamphlet *Syllogismi sanctorum patrum* lists thirteen useful anti-Manichaean arguments in the form of pithy syllogisms culled from the works of Didymus the Blind and Gregory of Nyssa.[177]

Further afield, in the less structured and more welcoming environment of Central Asia, Manichaeans retained their traditional skill in arguing from set texts. In the Chinese Manichaean *Compendium* from Tunhuang, being "well versed in the seven scriptures and eminently skilled in debate" normally entitled one to respect within the Manichaean monastic community.[178] Yet even here, new social pressures had overtaken the glamorous Manichaean debater. The *Compendium* makes clear that the monastic virtue of obeying Manichaean precepts was considered

173. *Dialogus contra Manichaeos* 2 (*PG* 94:1508B).

174. See G. Richter, *Die Dialektik des Johannes von Damaskos: Eine Untersuchung des Textes nach seinen Quellen und seiner Bedeutung* (Ettal, 1964), esp. 262–80.

175. See Zacharias of Mytilene, *Disputatio* (*PG* 85:1143–44), on the refutation of a writing advancing the two Manichaean principles during the reign of Justinian. The writing was simply left on the streets, perhaps as a challenge.

176. See I. Rochow, "Zum Fortleben des Manichäismus im byzantinischen Reich nach Justinian I," *Byzantinoslavica* 40 (1979): 13–21.

177. See Richard, ed., 131–33. On the use of dialectic as an "anti-heretical" weapon, see, e.g., Gregory of Nazianzus, *Oratio* 29.

178. *Taishō shinshū daizōkyō* 2141A, LIV 1280c8; English translation from G. Haloun and W. B. Henning, "The Compendium of the Doctrines and Styles of the Teaching of Mani, The Buddha of Light," *Asia Major* n.s. 3 (1952): 196. See new edition in N. Tajadod, *Mani: Le Bouddha de Lumière: catéchisme manichéen chinois*, Sources gnostiques et manichéenes 3 (Paris, 1990).

much more important than charismatic authority stemming from eloquence and learning:

> If a *mu-shē* [one of the twelve teachers] be violating the commandments, no one shall accept his instructions. Even though he is well-versed in the seven scriptures and eminently skilled in debate, if he has faults and vices, the five grades will not respect him.[179]

The routinization of charisma took place among the Manichaeans wherever their communities assumed the form of hierarchical monastic institutions. A similar process was at work in the later Roman Empire within Christian communities, which increasingly gravitated toward their local bishops. As a result of this growing monopoly over authority, groups such as the Anomoeans and the Manichaeans, once existing in symbiotic dialectical relationship with orthodox and catholic Christians, were dramatically and forcibly redefined as the alien Other. Within this new context, in which unsupervised debate between individual Manichaeans and Christians manifested an undesirable lack of closure, emphasis was placed instead on the authority of written documents—many of which were closely connected with controversy, such as the *acta* and *catenae* of prooftexts—and on carefully controlled public disputations conducted by Christian authorities.

Like the classical Greeks, Christians in the later empire discovered that the written word fettered the dynamic *logos* and the dialectical element of speech.[180] Yet while the Greeks viewed such a constraint negatively, Christians, with their belief in revealed truth and their need to achieve social closure, found in the written word a god-sent gift.

179. *Taishō shinshū daizōkyō,* 2141A, LIV 1280c7–9. English translation from Haloun and Henning, "Compendium," 195–96.

180. Even in law courts, Athenians preferred spoken testimony to written documentation; see T. M. Lentz, "Spoken versus Written Inartistic Proof in Athenian Courts," *Philosophy and Rhetoric* 16 (1983): 242–61, esp. 247–48.

FOUR

DIALECTIC, QUESTIONING, AND COMMUNITY IN THE ANOMOEAN CONTROVERSY

Self-appointed Christian apologists were often quick to compare the monolithic universalism of their religion with the plurality of divergent philosophical views and religious practices found among their polytheist competitors.[1] The force and validity of this contrast required that common consensus be seen as a self-evident marker of truth:

> The Greeks at any rate do not acknowledge (οὐχ ὁμολογοῦντες) the same views, but because they argue (ἀμφισβητοῦντες) with each other, they do not have the true teaching. But the holy fathers who are the heralds indeed of the truth both agree (συμφωνοῦσι) with each other and also are not at odds (οὐ διαφέρονται) with their own people.[2]

This self-congratulatory comment by Athanasius of Alexandria must stand for many like it. For most Christians, this juxtaposition of Chris-

---

1. See J. Daniélou, "ΜΙΑ ΕΚΚΛΗΣΙΑ chez les pères grecs des premiers siècles," in *l'Église et les églises: Études et travaux offerts à Dom Lambert Beauduin* (Chevetogne, 1954), 1:129–39; idem, "Les pères de l'église et l'unité des chrétiens," *SP* 7 (1966): 23–32. This claim of universalism was also used to distinguish between "good" and "bad" Christians, as in Irenaeus' treatment of the gnostics; see G. Levesque, "Consonance chrétienne et dissonance gnostique dans Irénée 'Adversus haereses' IV, 18, 4 à 19, 3," *SP* 16 (1985): 193–96; and L. H. Grondys, "La diversità delle sette Manichee," in *Silloge Bizantina in onore di Silvio Giuseppe Mercati* (Rome, 1957): 177–87, esp. 183–87.

2. Athanasius, *De decretis nicaenae synodi* 4.4 (H.-G. Opitz, ed., *Athanasius Werke II* [Berlin/Leipzig 1935–41], 4). See also his *Homilia de semente* (PG 28:149–50): "Τί τὸ ὄφελος . . . Εἰ μὲν γὰρ σοφιστοῦ διδασκαλεῖον ἦν ὁ Ἐκκλησία, εὐγλωττίας ἦν ὁ καιρός."

tian unity with pagan disarray was a compelling demonstration of their monopoly over truth. Adapting a familiar argument proving the existence of the Deity by the intelligent arrangement of the cosmos, Athanasius attributed good social order (εὐταξία) to the influence of a ruling principle.[3]

But such a robust claim was strangely fragile and easy to discredit from within. One of the most damaging effects of the Arian controversy in the Greek east was that it further uncovered the open secret of rampant feuding among Christians.[4] To many thoughtful Christians, the increasingly prominent and protracted displays of their own institutional fragmentation before nonbelievers compromised their cause incontrovertibly. Ramsay MacMullen muses that "by far the most frequent item of news, and the steadiest influence on the course of historical development, must certainly be the cities' excitement, angry divisions, even bloodshed, and broad involvement in disputes about due worship."[5] The triumphalist arguments used by Christians against polytheists were turned back against them at a time when their new prominent status exposed their internal feuds to public scrutiny, so that pagans began to comment on the strife, discord, and confusion among them. Socrates Scholasticus attributed to Constantine the statement that, while pagan philosophers disagreed with each other, they were at least—unlike the Christians of the time—socially cohesive within each *secta*.[6] This comment is especially ironic given the ancient philosophers' reputation for being quarrelsome.[7]

To modern scholars, Christian disarray may readily be explained by diverse factors, including considerations of institutional culture and the difficulties inherent in maintaining group solidarity over a long period. To certain late antique Christian minds, however, this fissiparous ten-

3. See Athanasius, *Contra gentes* 38.
4. According to Sozomen, *Hist. eccl.* 6.36, the philosopher and senator Themistius gave an oration before Valens in which he pointed out that, while Christians were split in their views, polytheist philosophers were locked in endless disputes. On the impact of the Arian controversy on the solidarity of Christian communities, see S. L. Greenslade, "Heresy and Schism in the Later Roman Empire," in D. Baker, ed., *Schism, Heresy and Religious Protest* (Cambridge, 1972), 1–20. Generally, see now R. Williams, *Arius: Heresy and Tradition* (London, 1987).
5. R. MacMullen, "The Historical Role of the Masses in Late Antiquity," in *Changes in the Roman Empire: Essays in the Ordinary* (Princeton, 1990), 250–76, 385–93, at 266, focuses on the actual body counts as an indicator of the severity of the problem. His grim characterization is now challenged by Neil McLynn, who examines the peculiar historical conditions leading to the most dramatic outbursts of Christian violence; see McLynn, "Christian Controversy and Violence in the Fourth Century," *Kodai* 3 (1992): 15–44.
6. Socrates, *Hist. eccl.* 1.7 (*PG* 67:57A).
7. See Chapter 1 on philosophical rivalry.

dency was caused by the subtle machinations of the devil himself.[8] One prevalent explanation held that because the universal church was on the verge of overwhelming its external enemies under the patronage of Constantine, the archslanderer implanted ambition and jealousy among Christians, goading them to contend among themselves for supremacy instead of cooperating for the common good. This paradigm, which placed blame squarely on the shoulders of select individuals, offered a much-needed explanation for the fact of disunity and at the same time deflected criticism from the institutional weaknesses of the church.

To this latter end, the wily poser of sophistic questions, often conflated with the figure of the dialectician, served as a useful foil,[9] recurring in numerous guises, sometimes even in connection with the devil. Gregory of Nyssa, in an encomium of his brother Basil, painted a literary gallery of infamous "heresiarchs"—Arius, Eudoxius, Aetius, and Eunomius—by means of this associative principle.[10] Much of this polemical categorization came into the foreground during the so-called Anomoean controversy, a doctrinal debate of great moment in the Greek east during the late fourth century.[11]

Modern scholars have scrutinized the Anomoean controversy mainly in terms of the competing theological ideas it generated. I wish to argue that the differences and conflicts expressed were social (in a broad sense) as well as theological, for also at issue were the definition and validation of competing *habitus* among late antique Christians.[12] To anatomize

8. See Evagrius Scholasticus, *Hist. eccl.* 1.1.

9. See, e.g., Socrates, *Hist. eccl.* 1.36 on Asterius the sophist; also W. Kinzig, *In Search of Asterius: Studies on the Authorship of the Homilies on the Psalms* (Göttingen, 1990), 14–21. See the excellent and provocative study of earlier occurrences of these characterizations by A. le Boulluec, *La notion d'hérésie dans la littérature grecque* (Paris, 1989), esp. 1:136–54 and 2:281–88.

10. Gregory of Nyssa, *Encomium of Basil* 9–10; see J. A. Stein, *Encomium of Saint Gregory Bishop of Nyssa, on his brother Saint Basil Archbishop of Cappadocian Caesarea* (Washington, D.C., 1928), 15–17.

11. For more comprehensive treatment of the controversy, see E. Cavalcanti, "Studi Eunomiani," *OCA* 202 (1976), 1–147; T. A. Kopecek, *History of Neo-Arianism* (Philadelphia, 1979); R. P. C. Hanson, *The Search for the Christian Doctrine of God: The Arian Controversy, 318–381* (Edinburgh, 1988), 594–636. Although terms such as "Anomoeans," "Eunomians," and "Neo-Arians" (the appellation preferred by Kopecek and Hanson) are not entirely satisfactory as labels for a *social* group, I have adopted the convention of using "Anomoeans" for the period before about 381 and "Eunomians" for thereafter. Although I may sometimes switch between the two, the meaning of the references should be readily perspicuous from the immediate contexts.

12. Pierre Bourdieu defines *habitus* as "a system of shared social dispositions and cognitive structures which generates perceptions, appreciations and actions"; *Homo Academicus*, 279n. 2. A more systematic exposition of the meaning and implications of *habitus* appears in his *Outline of a Theory of Practice* (Cambridge, 1977); originally published as *Esquisse d'une théorie de la pratique* (Geneva, 1972).

the process of "moral categorization" by which the figure of the dialectician was constructed and deprecated,[13] I will focus on the careers of
Aetius and Eunomius, both labeled by their opponents as disruptive
dialecticians, and delineate the cultural preferences clashing in the ostensibly dogmatic controversy. The prescribed roles of dialectic and public disputation among eastern Christians will become perspicuous in the
course of this discussion; other pertinent aspects will be addressed in
Chapter 5.

THE ANOMOEANS: THE SOCIAL CONSTRUCTION
OF TROUBLEMAKERS

Aetius the Syrian

Aetius was born in Antioch on the Orontes circa 313.[14] His colorful
career represents a classic study in upward social mobility in the later
Roman Empire.[15] His opponent Gregory of Nyssa asserted, maliciously
but not without some plausibility, that Aetius' involvement in dogmatic
controversy derived from his need to earn a living.[16] Indeed, talent, ambition, and opportunity together elevated this son of humble parents to
prominent ecclesiastical roles in the company of imperial princes.[17]

Aetius' career was made possible by his possession of the gift of
basic literacy.[18] As a boy, he acquired sufficient rudimentary skills to
conduct business and to draft contracts in his native city.[19] By 326, his

---

13. On the significant connections between the categorization of persons/actions and
the maintenance of the social order, see L. Jayyusi, *Categorization and the Moral Order* (Bos-
ton/London, 1984).

14. See G. Bardy, "L'héritage littéraire d'Aétius," *RHE* 24 (1928): 809–27; M. Jugie, in
Dictionnaire de Théologie Chrétienne, 667–79, s.v. "Aétius 3."

15. See the helpful account in Kopecek, *History of Neo-Arianism*, 1:61–75.

16. Gregory of Nyssa, *Contra Eun.* 1.36 (Jaeger, ed., 1:34–35): "ὅν μοι δοκεῖ μὴ το-
σοῦτον πρὸς τὴν τῶν δογμάτων ἀπάτην βλέπων ἐζηλωκέναι, πολὺ δὲ μᾶλλον πρὸς τὴν τοῦ
βίου παρασκευήν τε καὶ εὐπορίαν."

17. See Philostorgius, *Hist. eccl.* 3.15. Kopecek argues that Aetius' father belonged to
the poorer and humbler *curiales* of Antioch on the basis of Philostorgius' witness that he
worked in the office of the provincial governor; *History of Neo-Arianism*, 1:62–63.

18. See H. C. Youtie, "ΑΓΡΑΜΜΑΤΟΣ: an Aspect of Greek Society in Egypt," *HSCP*
75 (1971): 161–76. On literacy among Christians in Egypt, see E. Wipszycka, "Le degré
d'alphabétisation en Égypte byzantine," *REAug* 30 (1984): 279–96, esp. 288–91.

19. On the importance of such a mediating role in a society characterized by low literacy, see H. C. Youtie, "ΥΠΟΓΡΑΦΕΥΣ: The Social Impact of Illiteracy in Graeco-Roman
Egypt," *ZPE* 17 (1975): 201–21. If such indeed was Aetius' background, he continued in
his later career to operate in the capacity of a mediator of knowledge to others: see discussion of his *Syntagmation* below.

natural aptitude for learning had turned him from his trade to the study of logical argumentation under the bishop Paulinus of Antioch.[20] After his mother's death had freed him from having to work as a craftsman to support the family (his father died when he was very young), Aetius devoted himself wholeheartedly to the "logical studies" in which he soon came to excel.[21]

The young Aetius distinguished himself in public contests of words (αἱ ἁμίλλαι περὶ λόγων), successfully becoming the darling of the masses while a stripling of thirteen years.[22] The Suidas tells us that these public debates were conducted on specific questions or *zēteseis* and that Aetius performed so well that he won the general audience (οἱ πολλοί) to his side.[23] Kopecek interprets the *zēteseis* as exegetical questions about scriptures based on the entry in Lampe's *Patristic Greek Lexicon*.[24] However, the word *zētēsis* enjoyed a much broader semantic range in antiquity, including proposed questions and dialectical premises (whether based on scriptures or not) in public disputations.[25] The latter interpretation accords much better with the train of Philostorgius' narrative, which by this point has already established Aetius' facility with logic, but has yet to mention him engaging in scriptural studies.

Aetius' youthful triumphs were so resounding and achieved so rapidly that he aroused the jealousy or *phthonos* of others. According to the Suidas, the resentment of his competitors was amplified by the fact that they were beaten by a young lad (νέος) and erstwhile craftsman (δημιουργός).[26] Philostorgius repeatedly employs a topos depicting Aetius as pursued by *phthonos* wherever he went—itself a gentle echo of Philostratus' dictum that *phthonos* ever assailed a wise man[27]—and for all its glibness such a characterization is consistent with Aetius' likely impact on others. The implacable Aetius was not one to spare others' feelings

20. Philostorgius, *Hist. eccl.* 3.15 (Bidez and Winkelmann, eds., 45): "διὰ ῥώμην φύσεως ἐπὶ τὰς λογικὰς ἐπιστραφῆναι μαθήσεις." See 3.15b (45) in Suidas, *Lexicon*, s.v. Ἀέτιος: "ἐπεὶ δὲ ἡ φύσις αὐτῷ μειζόνων ὠρέγετο μαθημάτων πρὸς λογικὰς θεωρίας ἐτράπετο." See also Sozomen, *Hist. eccl.* 3.15.
21. Gregory of Nyssa, *Contra Eun.* 1.37–46.
22. This is not an impossibly young age for an accomplished prodigy; see the examples collected by M. Kleijwegt, in *Ancient Youth: The Ambiguity of Youth and the Absence of Adolescence in Greco-Roman Society* (Amsterdam, 1991): 118–31.
23. Philostorgius, *Hist. eccl.* 3.15b.
24. Kopecek, *History of Neo-Arianism*, 1:65.
25. See, e.g., H. Tarrant, *Scepticism or Platonism?: The Philosophy of the Fourth Academy* (Cambridge, 1985), 69–71.
26. Philostorgius, *Hist. eccl.* 3.15b (Bidez and Winkelmann, eds., 46).
27. Philostratus, *Vita Apollonii* 1.34. See A. Louth, "Envy as the Chief Sin in Athanasius and Gregory of Nyssa," *SP* 15 (1984): 458–60.

even as an adult; as a brash young man, he could easily have made numerous enemies.

Aetius' position remained secure so long as his patron and teacher Paulinus offered him protection. After Paulinus died, Aetius' enemies prevailed on the new bishop Eulalius to expel his predecessor's protégé. In the words of Philostorgius, "Jealousy (φθόνος) moves Eulalius to drive Aetius from Antioch."[28] Compelled to leave his native home in 327, Aetius traveled up to the city of Anazarbus in Cilicia Secunda to seek his fortunes.

There Aetius studied briefly with a local Christian grammarian, who took him in and taught him basic literary skills in exchange for domestic help.[29] When Aetius refuted (καταστὰς εἰς ἔλεγχον) and rebuked his patron in public (δημοσίᾳ) for what he perceived to be a fallacious interpretation of scriptures, the grammarian threw him out. Fortunately for Aetius, who in one stroke was expelled (ἐλαθείς)[30] from classroom and home, the local Arian bishop Athanasius, a student of Lucian of Antioch, saw fit to take him in and even taught him how to read the gospels.[31] Aetius' subsequent study with two other Lucianist teachers—Antoninus in Tarsus and Leontius in Antioch—completed his training in biblical studies.[32] In emphasizing the scriptural focus of Aetius' education, the partisan Philostorgius was probably responding indirectly to the charges advanced by critics such as Socrates, who accused Aetius of being unschooled in scriptural learning (τῶν ἱερῶν Γραμμάτων ἀμύητος) and expert solely in the art of refutative argumentation (τὸ ἐριστικὸν μόνον).[33]

According to Philostorgius, Aetius, once again the target of jealousy, was forced to leave Antioch a second time. He again undertook a journey to Cilicia, and there met a purported member of the gnostic Borboriani sect, who engaged him in a (presumably public) contest of words. Philostorgius described the dramatic humbling of his hero with but a

28. Philostorgius, *Hist. eccl.* 3.15 (Bidez and Winkelmann, eds., 45).

29. Philostorgius, *Hist. eccl.* 3.15; on this episode, see Kaster, *Guardians of Language*, 3–7.

30. Kopecek, *History of Neo-Arianism*, 1:68, wrongly translates this participle as "without being observed."

31. Gregory of Nyssa, *Contra Eun.* 1.37 (Jaeger, ed., 1:35). Kopecek argues that Athanasius of Anazarbus also taught Aetius the exegesis of scriptures using syllogisms; *History of Neo-Arianism*, 1:69–70.

32. See Philostorgius, *Hist. eccl.* 3.15 (Bidez and Winkelmann, eds., 46). On the Lucianists, see Philostorgius, *Hist. eccl.* 2.14 (Bidez and Winkelmann, eds., 25); G. Bardy, *Recherches sur saint Lucien d'Antioche et son école* (Paris, 1936).

33. Socrates, *Hist. eccl.* 2.35.

few words: "A certain member of the Borboriani, having agreed on debates with him in defense of his own opinion, brought about an ultimate defeat."[34] Aetius the proud Christian dialectician-philosopher was soundly beaten by his gnostic opponent and, unaccustomed to such reversals of fortune, fell into a mood of deep despair (ἀθυμία) over what he considered the victory of falsehood over truth.

Not long after his upset, Aetius received word from Alexandria that Aphthonius, a Manichaean leader, was acquiring a formidable reputation in that city by his debating skill. The Syrian resolved to secure a contest with the Manichaean to reestablish his own adequacy. "Drawn by his [Aphthonius'] fame," Aetius descended on Alexandria, challenged the Manichaean to a debate,[35] and definitively refuted his opponent by reducing him to virtual speechlessness (see ch. 3).

Late Roman Alexandria was a teeming cosmopolis of competing religious and philosophical groups.[36] Its cultural diversity gave rise to struggles for place, and its abundant stores of intellectual resources offered the tools for responding to such competitive situations.[37] Aetius' own career path intersected with those of Christian, gnostic, and pagan intellectuals, as had the paths of Origen and Plotinus before him. Inhabiting the interstices between these competing groups, he articulated a set of Christian beliefs that could hold its own against anticipated challenges from religious and philosophical rivals.[38]

Both Philostorgius and Gregory of Nyssa identified Aetius as a student of medicine who learned the traditional specialty of Alexandria from a certain Sopolis, a physician.[39] Aetius himself was known to Sozomen as a physician.[40] Aetius' studies in Alexandria probably did in-

34. Philostorgius, *Hist. eccl.* 3.15 (Bidez and Winkelmann, eds., 46): "καί τις τῶν Βορβοριανῶν, λόγοις αὐτῷ ὑπὲρ τῆς ἰδίας δόξης συμπλακείς, εἰς ἐσχάτην κατέστησεν ἧτταν."

35. Philostorgius, *Hist. eccl.* 3.15.

36. On Alexandrian Jewish and pagan communities, see C. J. Haas, "Late Roman Alexandria: Social Structure and Intercommunal Conflict in the Entrepôt of the East" (Ph.D. diss., University of Michigan, 1988), chs. 4, 5.

37. See Gregory of Nazianzus, *Or.* 7.6–7; Ammianus Marcellinus, *Res gestae* 22.16.16–17; Sozomen, *Hist. eccl.* 3.15 (Bidez, ed., 125): "Ἐν τούτῳ δὲ καὶ παντοδαπὴ σοφία ᾤκει."

38. See R. A. Mortley, *From Word to Silence* (Bonn, 1986), 2:131–32, on Aetius' need to defend himself against Neoplatonist philosophers. On the possible impact of a similar concern on Arius, see R. Lyman, "Arians and Manichees on Christ," *JTS* n.s. 40 (1989): 493–503, at 503: "Arius was not responding to abstract exegetical or philosophical problems alone, but rather . . . to the competitive teachers in the agora . . ."

39. Philostorgius, *Hist. eccl.* 3.15; Gregory of Nyssa, *Contra Eun.* 1.42–46 (Jaeger, ed., 1:36–38).

40. Sozomen, *Hist. eccl.* 3.15 (Bidez, ed., 126).

clude both medicine and Aristotelian learning, for the two branches of knowledge were commonly combined.[41] Certainly his familiarity with the use of Aristotelian dialectic and syllogisms was later a common charge against him. He may even have visited with the city's various Aristotelian *didaskaloi*, though the tradition is divided on this point.[42] This association was perhaps a natural one for ancient authors to make because the city maintained throughout late antiquity a reputation for logical training and dialectical disputation.[43]

Ancient physicians were known to have broad intellectual interests. Gregory of Nyssa reported that, in the mid–fourth century, the medical schools of Alexandria served as hotbeds of philosophical and theological discussion, often involving dialectic.[44] When Aetius posed his astounding thesis of the "dissimilarity" of divine *ousiai*, he exploited the love of innovation among members of the Alexandrian medical *scholai*.[45] In a similar vein, Epiphanius noted that Aetius practiced daily the dialectical skill with which he discoursed about God.[46]

The art of posing philosophical questions was a powerful and useful tool for establishing someone's reputation in the city's preeminent medical circles.[47] Magnus of Nisibis, a student of the iatrosophist Zeno of Cyprus, established a school of instruction (διδασκαλεῖον) in Alexan-

41. On the iatrosophists in Alexandria, see Eunapius, *VS* 494–500. On earlier dialectical medicine in the same city, see the interesting description of the physician Thessalus of Tralles (first century), in H.-V. Friedrich, *Thessalos von Tralles* (Meisenheim am Glan, 1968). He was probably also Thessalus the "magician"; see J. Z. Smith, "The Temple and the Magician," in J. Z. Smith, ed., *Map is Not Territory: Studies in the History of Religions* (Leiden, 1978); G. Fowden, *The Egyptian Hermes: A Historical Approach to the Late Pagan Mind* (Cambridge, 1986), 161–65.

42. This was reported as hearsay; see Sozomen, *Hist. eccl.* 3.15 (Bidez, ed., 127): "ἐλέγετο γὰρ καὶ διὰ τῶν Ἀριστοτέλους μαθημάτων ἐλθεῖν καὶ ἐν Ἀλεξανδρείᾳ φοιτῆσαι τοῖς τούτων διδασκάλοις." Socrates, *Hist. eccl.* 2.35, asserted the contrary, that is, that Aetius was an autodidact.

43. For the city's intellectual circles, see also F. Schemmel, "Die Hochschule von Alexandria im IV. und V. Jahrhundert p. Ch. n.," *Neue Jahrbücher für das klassische Altertum* 24 (1909): 438–57, esp. 439.

44. Gregory of Nyssa, *Contra Eun.* 1.45–46 (Jaeger, ed., 1:37); see also Philostorgius, *Hist. eccl.* 3.15. Sozomen, *Hist. eccl.* 3.15 (Bidez, ed., 127), described Aetius as visiting the schools in Alexandria where Aristotle's works were taught, thus contradicting Socrates' statement (*Hist. eccl.* 2.35) that Aetius learned his Aristotle by reading the *Categories* without help from an Academic preceptor.

45. Gregory of Nyssa, *Contra Eun.* 1.45–47 (Jaeger, ed., 37–38).

46. See Epiphanius, *Panarion* 76.2.2: "[Aetius] ὑποβὰς καὶ σχολάσας ἐν Ἀλεξανδρείᾳ Ἀριστοτελικῷ φιλοσόφῳ καὶ σοφιστῇ καὶ τὰ τῆς διαλεκτικῆς δῆθεν ἐκείνων μαθών, οὐδὲν ἕτερον πλὴν σχηματοποεῖν τὴν περὶ θεοῦ λόγου ἀπόδοσιν."

47. See Ammianus, *Res gestae* 22.16.18; V. Nutton, "Ammianus and Alexandria," *Clio Medica* 7 (1972): 165–76.

dria.[48] When he held discussions with physicians who excelled at healing the sick, he turned to his philosophical knowledge to gain a competitive edge:

> In order to lend force to his words (ἐς τὸ δύνασθαι λέγειν), he dragged in Aristotle in connexion with the nature of bodies . . . and so compelled the doctors to keep silent in the matter of rhetoric, but he was thought to be less able in healing than in speaking (σιωπᾶν μὲν ἐν τῷ λέγειν τοὺς ἰατροὺς ἠνάγκαζε, θεραπεύειν δὲ οὐκ ἐδόκει δυνατὸς εἶναι καθάπερ λέγειν).[49]

Elsewhere, Magnus was described as "a physician in regards to words, yet an inexperienced practitioner in regards to deeds."[50] By introducing what Aristotle would have considered false figures from a general to a specific field,[51] he managed to maintain professional credibility, even to acquire a considerable reputation, despite his supposed deficiency in therapeutic praxis. By carefully emphasizing his Aristotelian learning, he "still got the better of the doctors in the matter of talking and putting questions (ἐρωτήσεις),"[52] and became a celebrated figure enjoying sufficient prominence to be mentioned years later by Libanius, Eunapius, and Philostorgius.[53] Such a deliberate professional strategy could only succeed if the other physicians conceded a greater value to the art of posing questions than to the craft of healing. This concession may be explained by the longstanding intimate relationship between ancient medicine and dialectic; medical training had long been transmitted through a dialectical procedure of questions and answers.[54]

After his Alexandrian sojourn, Aetius returned to his native Antioch, where he began to teach circa 350. He made an immediate and decisive impact on that city:

> Straightaway he began to shock those whom he met with the strangeness of his expressions (εὐθὺς οὖν ἐξενοφώνει τοὺς ἐντυγχάνοντας).

48. Eunapius, VS 497–98. See discussion in Penella, *Greek Philosophers and Sophists,* 111–12, 115–16.

49. Eunapius, VS 497–98 (Wright, ed., 530–31). I have adapted Wright's translation. See Penella, *Greek Philosophers and Sophists,* 115–16.

50. Theophilus Protospatharius, *De urinis* preface (Ideler, ed., 261); quoted in Penella, *Greek Philosophers and Sophists,* 111–12.

51. See Aristotle, *De sophisticis elenchis* 11.172a (Forster and Furley, eds., 64–65).

52. Eunapius, VS 497–98.

53. Libanius, *Ep.* 843, 1208; Philostorgius, *Hist. eccl.* 8.10.

54. On the use of dialectical argumentation and question-and-answer dialogues for ancient medical instruction, see Kudlien, "Dialektik und Medizin," 187–200; Kollesch, *Untersuchungen zu den ps.galenischen Definitiones Medicae* (Berlin, 1973). See also Westerink, "Philosophy and Medicine," 169–77.

And this he did trusting in the Aristotelian categories; indeed Aristotle had a book written on the subject. Aetius was engaged in disputation by drawing upon the categories (ἐξ αὐτῶν τε διαλεγόμενος) and did not realize that he was fashioning sophistic reasoning for himself. Nor did he learn the *skopos* of Aristotle['s ideas] from wise men.[55]

I shall explore such characterizations of the Syrian's dialectical genius later. By this time Aetius had already established himself as a valuable player in the intricate game of ecclesiastical politics favored by eastern prelates. He became a valued client of the Cappadocian George, the forceful and ill-starred bishop of Alexandria, who appointed him a deacon circa 348 in that city.[56] It was there that Eunomius, Aetius' famous disciple, came to join him.

Eunomius

Eunomius' life story is not unlike that of Aetius.[57] The subsequently much-feared *technologos* was born circa 335 to farmers[58] in the small town of Oltiseris on the border between Cappadocia and Galatia, a fact supplied by the snide remark of a later opponent.[59] Command of basic literacy first allowed Eunomius to acquire the training of a shorthand writer, a *tachygraphos*.[60] Aspiring to greater opportunities, the youth followed his dreams to Constantinople on a journey that was to take him far.[61]

After Constantinople, Eunomius made the rounds of the other cultural centers of the late Roman world. Not surprisingly, he first traveled

---

55. Socrates, *Hist. eccl.* 2.35 (*PG* 67:297B–C):

εὐθὺς οὖν ἐξενοφώνει τοὺς ἐντυγχάνοντας. Τοῦτο δὲ ἐποίει, ταῖς κατηγορίαις Ἀριστοτέλους πιστεύων· βιβλίον δὲ οὕτως ἐστὶν ἐπιγεγραμμένον αὐτῷ· ἐξ αὐτῶν τε διαλεγόμενος, καὶ ἑαυτῷ σόφισμα ποιῶν οὐκ ᾔσθετο, οὐδὲ παρὰ τῶν ἐπιστημόνων ἔμαθε τὸν Ἀριστοτέλους σκοπόν.

On the verb *xenophonein*, used to mean employing strange expressions, see Dexippus, *In Categorias* 7.1–2 (A. Busse, ed., CAG 4, 6).

56. Epiphanius, *Panarion* 76.11.

57. The main sources on Eunomius include: F. Loofs, *RE*, 3d ed., s.v. "Eunomius," 597–601; F. Diekamp, "Literaturgeschichtliches zu der eunomianischen Kontroverse," *BZ* 18 (1909): 1–13; X. le Bachelet, in *Dictionnaire de Théologie Chrétienne*, 1501–14, s.v. "Eunomius"; L. Abramowski, in *RAC* 6:936–47, s.v. "Eunomios"; A. M. Ritter, in *Theologische Realenzyklopaedie* (Berlin and New York, 1980) 10:525–28, s.v. "Eunomius"; R. P. Vaggione, *Eunomius: The Extant Works* (Oxford, 1987).

58. See Gregory of Nyssa, *Contra Eun.* 1.49 (Jaeger, ed., 1:39).

59. Gregory of Nyssa, *Contra Eun.* 1.34 (Jaeger, ed., 1:33).

Gregory of Nyssa, *Contra Eun.* 1.50 (Jaeger, ed., 1:39). See L. Parmentier, "Euchygraphe," 238–46. Kaster cites the close association between the *notarius* and lact in *Guardians of Language*, 48.

gory of Nyssa, *Contra Eun.* 1.50 (Jaeger, ed., 1:39).

to Antioch, then continued his quest to Alexandria, where he became the secretary and disciple of Aetius. Like his admired teacher, Eunomius was a quick study: it was during his stay in Alexandria that he allegedly learned the art of eristic disputation and the Aristotelian technical vocabulary.[62] The two men, sealing an alliance built first on their teacher-disciple relationship, eventually succeeded in establishing for themselves an enduring, though not universally positive, reputation.

The Anomoeans' Reputation as Dialecticians

Returning to Antioch from Alexandria, Aetius and Eunomius were instrumental in the victory of the Arian party at the Council of Antioch in 358. Their powers of speech again found expression at a council held in Constantinople in 360, a meeting called by Constantius after a 359 council at Seleucia had failed to resolve the outstanding disputes in the Christian east. Constantius was known as an active mover in the world of ecclesiastical politics; Ammianus Marcellinus faulted the emperor for multiplying councils and thus adding to, rather than ameliorating, ecclesiastical tensions.[63]

The meeting in Constantinople was convoked so that bishops who favored a homoiousian creed (κατ' οὐσίαν ὅμοιον) could settle their differences with those endorsing an Anomoean definition.[64] Aided by Constantius' offer of the use of the *cursus publicus,* a stream of bishops, mostly from the eastern cities, began to rush into the capital. Among them were Basil of Ancyra and Eustathius of Sebaste, leaders of those who favored the homoiousion. On the journey to Constantinople, Eustathius recruited a promising young reader, Basil of Caesarea, to assist at the council's formal debates; he duly arrived in the capital with his bishop, Dianius. In the opposing corner stood Aetius, whose "shield-mate" (τοῦ συνασπίζοντος) was Eunomius.[65]

Philostorgius, whose *History* stands as our main source for this encounter, placed Basil and Eunomius in the auxiliary role (ὁ συνασπίζων) attributed to Athanasius at the earlier Council of Nicaea.[66] Yet for reasons that may have involved a preliminary assessment of his adversar-

---

62. Socrates, *Hist. eccl.* 2.35 (*PG* 67:300A).

63. Ammianus Marcellinus, *Res gestae* 21.16.18. On the participatory role of Constantius in ecclesiastical affairs, see R. Klein, *Constantius II und die christliche Kirche* (Darmstadt, 1977); G. Gigli, *L'ortodossia l'arianesimo e la politica di Constanzo II (337–361)* (Rome, 1949).

64. See Kopecek, *History of Neo-Arianism,* 2:299–303.

65. Philostorgius, *Hist. eccl.* 4.12 (Bidez and Winkelmann, eds., 64).

66. Philostorgius, *Hist. eccl.* 4.12. On a later perception of Athanasius' role at Nicaea, see Socrates, *Hist. eccl.* 1.15.

ies' support in the council, Basil chose to retire from the impending fray and to repair to his native Cappadocia.⁶⁷ As it was widely believed that the help of professionals skilled in the art of elenchic disputation—those who possessed δύναμις τοῦ λέγειν—was essential to open theological debate, the departure of Basil foreshadowed the imminent defeat of the homoiousian cause.⁶⁸

Left to their own devices, the homoiousian bishops became especially apprehensive of Aetius' "power in words." They tried to neutralize his advantage by proposing that bishops had no need to discuss dogma with mere deacons. But this evasive tactic was overruled by the council majority, who expressed the view that considerations of ecclesiastical rank were of no concern in an impartial quest for the truth:

> Since they feared his power in words (τὴν δύναμιν τῶν λόγων), they said that, being bishops, it was not necessary for them to be set against a deacon in disputations (εἰς λόγους). But after those who dissent from this view replied that the occasion was not a trial of ecclesiastical rank, but a quest for the truth, the party of Basil [of Ancyra] unwillingly accepted the contest (τὸν ἀγῶνα).⁶⁹

The homoiousian prelates, thus forced into the doctrinal contest (ἄμιλλα δογμάτων), were soundly beaten, vanquished above all "by the power in Aetius' tongue (κατὰ κράτος τῇ τοῦ Ἀετίου γλώσσῃ)." To complete their disgrace, they were compelled to confess in writing (χειρὶ οἰκείᾳ) an Anomoean dogmatic formulation.

The outcome of this council was partially overturned by Constantius after a private audience with Aetius, whom he exiled to Pepuza in Phrygia.⁷⁰ But the dialectical prowess of Aetius and Eunomius left an indelible impression on their contemporaries. Aetius' fame as a public debater was such that a story of his defeat of Basil of Ancyra and Eustathius of Sebaste appears in Philostorgius' *Historia ecclesiastica*. Yet this

---

67. See Basil, *Ep.* 94; Gregory of Nyssa, *Contra Eun.* 1.81 (Jaeger, ed., 1:50). Also S. Giet, "Saint Basile et le concile de Constantinople de 360," *JTS* n.s. 6 (1955): 94–99. Basil himself afterward criticized the council in his *Ep.* 244 (Deferrari, ed., 3:470–71) to Patrophilus of Aegae.

68. Philostorgius, *Hist. eccl.* 4.12 (Bidez and Winkelmann, eds., 64). The assistance of experts at disputations was common at least in the fifth century. Perhaps Socrates, in *Hist. eccl.* 1.15, accepted Rufinus' characterization because it harmonized with current practices known to him.

69. Philostorgius, *Hist. eccl.* 4.12 (Bidez and Winkelmann, eds., 64–65): "δείσαντες αὐτοῦ τὴν δύναμιν τῶν λόγων, οὐκ ἔφασαν δεῖν ἐπισκόπους ὄντας διακόνῳ περὶ δογμάτων εἰς λόγους καθίστασθαι. ἀντειπόντων δὲ τῶν διαφερομένων ὡς οὐκ ἀξίας νῦν ἐστι κρίσις, ἀλλ᾽ ἀληθείας ἐπιζήτησις, δέχονται μὲν καὶ ἄκοντες οἱ περὶ Βασίλειον τὸν ἀγῶνα."

70. Philostorgius, *Hist. eccl.* 4.12 (Bidez and Winkelmann, eds., 65).

tradition is probably a dim echo of the events at Constantinople in 360 rather than a unique reference to an encounter unattested in any other source.[71]

Those with the charismatic gift of eloquence were courted by ecclesiastical politicians, who were constantly in search of exceptional talent to support their own causes. Aetius was himself patronized by the powerful George of Cappadocia.[72] While Aetius was in exile from Constantinople after 360, Eunomius was made bishop of Cyzicus by Eudoxius of Constantinople, an appointment Basil of Caesarea considered a reward for impiety, that is, for contributing to the cause of Eudoxius.[73] Socrates Scholasticus attributed the decision more plausibly to Eunomius' impressive powers of persuasion. The two explanations are not mutually exclusive: Eunomius' argumentative skills would certainly be needed to win over a congregation still brooding over Eudoxius' deposition of their beloved Eleusius.

Both Aetius and Eunomius could count on the friendship and support of powerful bishops of established sees, among them George of Cappadocia, bishop of Alexandria, and Eudoxius, bishop of Antioch and later Constantinople.[74] But their circles extended beyond the boundaries of the increasingly significant ecclesiastical domain. The pair enjoyed a mobility not available to bishops after Nicaea, with opportunities for exerting influence in even the highest circles. Their ease of movement recalls the urbane world of the Greek sophists during the High Empire, when charismatic rhetors won renown in the metropolitan cities and collected coteries of like-minded admirers.[75]

Other Christians' fear of the Anomoeans' influence was due in no small measure to their access to court. Having endured the vicissitudes of the reigns of Constantius and Julian, orthodox Christians were only too keenly aware of the precariousness of their situation.[76] Privileges granted by imperial fiat could be withdrawn by the same means; imperial support, won by select individuals with access to court, could have dire consequences for the delicate balance of power in ecclesiastical poli-

---

71. Philostorgius, *Hist. eccl.* 3.16 (Bidez and Winkelmann, eds., 47): "Ὅτι Ἀέτιος, φησί, τοῖς περὶ Βασίλειον τὸν Ἀγκύρας καὶ Εὐστάθιον τὸν Σεβαστείας εἰς τοὺς περὶ τοῦ ὁμοουσίου λόγους καταστάς, καὶ πάντων ἀνθρώπων αὐτοὺς διελέγξας ἀφωνοτάτος, ὡς οὗτος τερατολογεῖ, εἰς μῖσος αὐτοῖς ἄσπονδον κατέστη."

72. See Gregory of Nyssa, *Contra Eun.* 1.38–39 (Jaeger, ed., 1:35–36).

73. Basil, *Contra Eunomium* 1:2.72–73.

74. See Kopecek, *History of Neo-Arianism,* 1:61.

75. See Bowersock, *Greek Sophists,* 89–100.

76. See S. L. Greenslade, *Church and State from Constantine to Theodosius* (Westport, Conn., 1954), 23–35.

tics.[77] Aetius wrote letters to Constantius in which, according to Socrates, he employed involved sophistic arguments.[78] He later made a favorable impression on Gallus, who sent him to his brother Julian in the hope that Aetius' influence might turn the future apostate emperor away from his emerging polytheistic inclinations.

The rivals of Eunomius feared his broad appeal and the possibility that he might succeed in captivating the imperial ear. Sozomen recounted how the orthodox shuddered at the thought that Eunomius might gain influence at court on account of his "skill in dialectical debates (τὴν ἐν ταῖς διαλέξεσιν Εὐνομίου δεινότητα)."[79] This fear was not groundless: Eunomius almost succeeded in obtaining an audience with Theodosius, who would no doubt (as Sozomen thought) have been swayed to the bishop's cause. A disastrous reversal of the recently rising fortunes of orthodox Christians was averted only at the last minute thanks to the offices of Empress Flacilla, a devotee of the orthodox cause.[80]

THE ANOMOEANS AND THE QUESTIONING OF AUTHORITY

Eunomius as *Technologos*

Il est un point sur lequel tous les contemporains et les historiens anciens sont d'accord, même s'ils l'apprécient différemment: Eunome était 'le technologue' par excellence.

It is a point on which all contemporaries and ancient historians agreed, but which they evaluated differently: Eunomius was the *technologos* par excellence.[81]

In the late fourth century, the Cappadocians charged Eunomius and his associates with being *technologoi*, opening a new chapter in the already complicated history of intra-Christian polemics. Theodoret of Cyrus said Eunomius "turned *theologia* into *technologia*."[82] Earlier, Basil

---

77. This peril might have been deliberately underscored in the tradition; see R. Snee, "Valens' Recall of the Nicene Exiles and Anti-Arian Propaganda," *GRBS* 25 (1985): 395–419.

78. Socrates, *Hist. eccl.* 2.35 (*PG* 67:300B).

79. Sozomen, *Hist. eccl.* 7.6 (Bidez, ed., 307).

80. Gregory of Nazianzus composed her funeral oration; see *Oratio funebris in Flacillam Imperaticem*. On her influence on ecclesiastical politics, see K. G. Hollum, *Theodosian Empresses: Women and Imperial Dominion in Late Antiquity* (Berkeley, Calif., 1982), 22–44.

81. Sesboüé, ed., *Contre Eunome*, 1:36 (translation mine). See Kopecek, *History of Neo-Arianism*, 1:75n. 3.

82. Theodoret of Cyrus, *Haeretiearum fabularum compendium* 4.3 (*PG* 83:420B): "οὗτος τὴν θεολογίαν τεχνολογίαν ἀπέφηνε."

cited *theologein* and *technologein* as the two activities dividing the Christian community: "τεχνολογοῦσι λοιπόν, οὐ θεολογοῦσιν οἱ ἄνθρωποι."[83]

In attempting to untangle the significance of this potent, clearly negative, but also very ambiguous characterization, scholars have followed ancient witnesses in associating *to technologein* and *hoi technologoi* with the Anomoeans' reliance on Aristotelian dialectic. In fact, the Stagirite was deeply implicated in the polemical literature against the Anomoeans and their enterprise:[84] Christian controversialists went so far as to pin the blame for the disturbances within the churches on the baneful influence of his *Categories* and syllogisms. Such a charge was to enjoy a long and fruitful life, especially although not exclusively in the Greek east.[85]

Aristotelian dialectic and syllogisms epitomized for some Christians an artful subtlety that was antithetical to their preference for plain speech. Gregory of Nazianzus insisted with thinly veiled ire that Christ came to save Christians through the simplicity of fishermen and not in an Aristotelian manner: "ἁλιευτικῶς ἀλλ᾽ οὐκ Ἀριστοτελικῶς."[86] Yet this charge was not as straightforward as it may seem at first glance because the Cappadocians themselves relied heavily on the works of Aristotle.[87] Eunomius himself once called Basil an Aristotelian.[88] In order to identify and clarify the issues more precisely, it is worthwhile to re-

83. Basil, *Ep.* 90 (Deferrari, ed., 2:124–25).

84. Chrysippus and Stoic logic were also cited in connection with Christian doctrinal disputes; see J. de Ghellinck, "Quelques mentions de la dialectique stoïcienne dans les conflits doctrinaux du IVᵉ siècle," *Abhandlungen über die Geschichte der Philosophie I: Philosophia Perennis* (Regensberg, 1930): 59–67.

85. Later the Monophysites were also accused of basing their error on Aristotle's works, especially his *Categories*. Anastasius of Sinai (seventh century) equated each of the ten horns of the dragon in Revelation with a heresiarch who based his error on one of Aristotle's ten categories; see L. S. B. MacCoull, "Anastasius of Sinai and the Ten-Horned Dragon," *Patristic and Byzantine Review* 9 (1990): 193–94. I wish to thank the author for bringing this reference to my attention.

86. Gregory of Nazianzus, *Or.* 23.12. Gregory was referring specifically to the use of Aristotelian dialectic and not to other aspects of Aristotle's work such as his ontological research or scientific inquiry. See also Gregory of Nazianzus, *Oratio* 27.10.

87. On Basil's use of syllogisms in *De spiritu sancto* 29–30, see J. Coman, "La démonstration dans le traité sur le saint Esprit de saint Basile le grand," *SP* 9 (1966): 172–209. In general, see D. Runia, "Festugière Revisited: Aristotle in the Greek Patres," *VChr* 43 (1989): 1–34. He points out that Festugière has ignored citations concerning dialectic and logic so that "not enough attention is paid . . . to the repeated association of Aristotelian dialectic with the origin and practice of heresy" (3). See K. Oehler, "Aristotle in Byzantium," *GRBS* 5 (1964): 133–46.

88. See Gregory of Nyssa, *Contra Eun.* 2.411 (Jaeger, ed., 1:346); A. Meredith, "Traditional Apologetic in the *Contra Eunomium* of Gregory of Nyssa," *SP* 14 (1976): 315–19, at 319; L. R. Wickham, "The *Syntagmation* of Aetius the Anomean," *JTS* n.s. 19 (1968): 532–69, at 561.

hearse the scholarly debate and shifting interpretations of these vague accusations.

In 1930, de Ghellinck argued in a pioneering article that the polemics against the Anomoeans and the negative evaluation of philosophical dialectic should be seen as a manifestation of the fundamental opposition between Christianity and Greek *paideia*.[89] Reservations about the Aristotelian heritage were thus part and parcel of the Christian rejection of polytheistic Graeco-Roman culture. Unfortunately, the a priori dichotomy between Christianity and Greek culture posited by this stance is not so easy to discern. Moreover, because both sides of the Anomoean dispute employed philosophical dialectic and rhetoric, one must ask why boundaries were drawn on either side of certain intellectual constructs and social practices at given moments.

Vandenbusschen's examination of the *technologos* charge against Eunomius turns the debate to a new direction.[90] To begin with, he correctly notes that the evaluations of Eunomius in Socrates Scholasticus, Sozomen, and Theodoret can be traced to initial treatments of the same figure by the Cappadocians—Basil, Gregory of Nazianzus, and Gregory of Nyssa. Thus the latter were primarily responsible for creating the influential image of their opponent as a disruptive, heretical *technologos*.

Vandenbusschen equates the term more or less with "dialectician"; in his view, calling Eunomius *ho technologos* was another way of focusing attention on Eunomius' reliance on the *ars dialectica*. Vandenbusschen skirts de Ghellinck's solution by rejecting the latter's attempt to characterize this debate as a sideshow of the fundamental opposition between Christianity and *paideia;* instead, he locates the reason for the conflict in the perennial opposition between philosophers and sophists.

Drawing on the works of students of literary style,[91] Vandenbusschen suggests that characterizing Eunomius as a *technologos* was tantamount to labeling him a sophist dabbler in philosophy.[92] But because the

89. J. de Ghellinck, "Quelques appréciations de la dialectique d'Aristote durant les conflits trinitaires du IVᵉ siècle," *RHE* 26 (1930): 5–42; see 7–8 on the association of the gnostics with dialectic in the works of Irenaeus, Tertullian, and Hippolytus.

90. E. Vandenbusschen, "La part de la dialectique dans la théologie d'Eunomius 'le technologue,'" *RHE* 40 (1944–45): 47–72.

91. See, e.g., E. Norden, *Die Antike Kunstprosa* (Leipzig, 1898), 2:558–62; L. Méridier, *L'influence de la second sophistique sur l'oeuvre de Grégoire de Nysse* (Paris, 1906).

92. Vandenbusschen, "La part de la dialectique," 51: "La technologie ne désigne pas une profession de ce genre; mais ce nom était plutôt réservé à l'orientation philosophique de la formation sophistique. Le technologue est le sophiste-philosophe. Il ne faut surtout pas le confondre avec le philosophe proprement dit." More recently Sesboüé (*Contra Eunome*, 36), though qualifying Vandenbusschen's claim somewhat, accepts the idea that Eunomius was a sophist-philosopher, both "par goût autant que par formation." It is

term "sophist" was mostly used as a slight devoid of specific content—and Vandenbusschen represents no exception here—we should proceed with caution. The conclusion that Eunomius was a sophist is based on observations of his literary and rhetorical style, which was heavily dependent on the Second Sophistic. This bizarre philological method of labeling as a sophist one who never so identified himself derives from good ancient authority: Philostratus used it to distinguish between sophists and philosophers in his *Vitae*.[93] Still, it is scarcely necessary to point out the methodological difficulties involved in deriving social categories from literary style. Even should this reading be adopted, it provides little insight into the fourth-century conflict; as a construct, the distinction between philosophers and sophists was as much an *explanandum* as that which it was supposed to elucidate.[94]

Daniélou resumes the discussion by proposing another course of inquiry.[95] In "Eunome l'arien et l'exégèse néo-platonicienne du Cratyle," he carefully cites the Neoplatonist elements of Eunomius' thought, thereby proposing to reject the theory that Aristotle was the only primary inspiration behind the *technologos*.[96] For him, Eunomius was above all an Iamblichan Neoplatonist.[97] This conclusion is based on an analysis of the Eunomian theory of naming, which proposed that linguistic labels were created according to the nature of the thing ($\kappa\alpha\tau\grave{\alpha}\ \phi\acute{\upsilon}\sigma\iota\nu$). In contrast, Basil and Gregory shared a more common syncretistic attitude of the period, which held that language was fashioned according to human convention ($\kappa\alpha\tau\grave{\alpha}\ \theta\acute{\epsilon}\sigma\iota\nu$), though not in complete disregard of the thing itself.[98] From this observation about Eunomius' strong nominalist

---

worth noting that no words bearing the root *technolog-* appear in Eunapius' *VS*, where we might indeed expect to find some such reference to sophist-philosophers.

93. See, e.g., Philostratus, *VS* 484, 486.

94. See Hahn, *Der Philosoph und die Gesellschaft*, 46–53. Hahn emphasizes the advantage of seeking the distinction between the two categories in social praxis rather than in stylistic approach or philosophical method.

95. Daniélou, "Eunome l'arien et l'exégèse néo-platonicienne du Cratyle," *REG* 69 (1956): 412–32.

96. H. A. Wolfson, "The Philosophical Implications of Arianism and Apollinarianism," *DOP* 12 (1958): 3–28, esp. 8. Independently of Vandenbusschen and Daniélou (and two years after the latter's article), Wolfson reasserts the claim that the epithet *technologos* owes nothing to an association with Aristotle.

97. Daniélou, "Eunome l'arien," 429: "La caractéristique d'Eunome est donc d'unir à platonisme mystique, influencé par la théurgie, une technique philosophique principalement aristotélicienne." Athens is the fertile ground for this syncretistic mix: "Le néoplatonisme aristotélisant sera le propre de cette école." The spiritual elitism that Daniélou implicitly ascribes to the teachings of Eunomius, and therefore also to his religious practice, by arguing that he should be seen as a mystagogue and hierophant challenges the previous characterization of Eunomius as a sophist; see 430.

98. Daniélou, "Eunome l'arien," 422.

position, Daniélou extrapolates an entire Neoplatonist philosophical program.[99]

Given the eclectic nature of individual allegiance to philosophical systems throughout late antiquity, this attribution of philosophical genealogy remains a highly questionable procedure. Moreover, Eunomius' theory of naming had been developed during a running debate with the Cappadocians as ad hoc support for his argument that human language was adequate to describe the divine.

Daniélou's thesis is all the more surprising in that twelve years earlier he has published a weighty tome contrasting Gregory of Nyssa's mysticism with Eunomius' extreme intellectualism.[100] In the more recent essay, he characterizes the opposition between Eunomius and the Cappadocians as the conflict between two parallel yet hostile traditions: Eunomius represented late Hellenism, noted for its lack of interest in scientific knowledge and the visible world in general (similar to the mystery religions), while Gregory of Nyssa championed a classical (read "pure") Greek philosophical tradition uncontaminated by the excesses and passions associated with Neoplatonist mysticism. The triumphalism of this analysis, hinting at a Christian monopoly over classical rationalism, ought to inspire skepticism toward a link between Eunomius and Iamblichus.[101]

It is time to pause and examine the fundamentals of this scholarly debate, which until now has focused on the meanings of labels that rivals used against each other. By making the exercise of the dialectic method a personal attribute—that is, in constructing a category of persons who have the attribute of using dialectic as part of their "nature"— the opponents of Eunomius were in fact playing a game of "moral categorization."[102] In this view, approved Christians employed dialectic as

99. See Daniélou, "Eunome l'arien," 417–18. He argues that Eunomius' sense of the word *epinoiai*, deriving from the works of Clement of Alexandria and Origen, would require that various aspects of Christ be the result of a real diversity in Christ's person. From this observation, Daniélou concludes that "le système d'Eunome est en fait un système néo-platonicien, une explication de la genèse du multiple à partir de l'Un" (428). Yet others have rightly located the Eunomian circle in a wider context using the evidence from Eunomius' own preface in his *Liber apologeticus;* see Diekamp, "Literargeschichtliches zu der eunomianischen Kontroverse," 2.

100. Daniélou, *Platonisme et théologie mystique: Essai sur la doctrine spirituelle de saint Grégoire de Nysse* (Paris, 1944), esp. 7.

101. Daniélou's association of Eunomius with Iamblichus is a thesis that has been examined and rejected by J. M. Rist, "Basil's 'Neoplatonism': Its Background and Nature," in Fedwick, ed., *Basil of Caesarea* 1:137–220, esp. 185–88.

102. To call one's opponent in a controversy a *technologos* appears to have been a novel practice in the late fourth century; see *Thesaurus Linguae Graecae* (Paris, 1848–54) 7, s.vv. τεχνολογέω, τεχνολογία, τεχνολός. The first cited usage of *technologos* comes from

a tool to wage war for a just cause, but their opponents did so out of single-minded ambition.[103]

This observation may explain why orthodox Christians such as the Cappadocians were not shy about claiming expertise in dialectic on occasion: they simply characterized their mastery, and that of their partisans, as one of numerous admirable qualities. Thus Jerome praised Didymus the Blind for the breadth of his learning, mentioning dialectic as one of a long list of accomplishments.[104] Gregory of Nazianzus eulogized his friend Basil in a similar manner.[105]

By contrast, the same parties portrayed the Anomoeans as narrowly focused specialists who knew nothing except the art of dialectical argumentation. In antiquity, a certain amount of opprobrium was attached to specialization and typecasting was a common technique used to undercut the legitimacy of one's rivals. In this case, Eunomius was cast in the type of dialectician, and the effectiveness of the strategy may have been much enhanced by the invocation of a novel (but vaguely disreputable) personal category.

In the past, the Anomoeans have been treated with scant sympathy by scholars who regarded them as hair-splitting rationalists lacking in true religious feeling. Their intellectualist approach to faith is cited as evidence for this deficiency. In line with a current movement to reinstate the Anomoeans, especially Eunomius, scholars such as Rousseau and Wiles argue that the celebrated controversy between Eunomius and Basil over epistemology should be read as a veiled debate over ecclesiology or even soteriology.[106] Eunomius was, in this view, as much a

---

Gregory of Nazianzus, *Or.* 29.21. By contrast, the use of *technologeō* and *technologia* was long established in the Greek tradition; see, e.g., Aristotle, *Ars rhetorica* 1354b.17, 27; 1355a.19.

103. Jayyusi, *Categorization and the Moral Order,* 28, spells out the relationship between categorization and the construction of a moral social order:

> In political debates or polemics between different parties the negatively implicative actions of the opponent are often deprived of explanation-by-grounds and transformed instead into a feature of the opponent's character (in the wide sense of the term), whilst an exactly similar action by one's own party is provided with an occasioned *reason.*

104. Jerome, *De virus illustribus* 109.

105. Gregory of Nazianzus, *Or.* 43.23. Both Basil and Gregory would be praised by Severus of Antioch as "all-rounders" in his *Homilia* 9.6–11; see F. Graffin, ed., *Les 'homiliae cathedrales' de Sévère d'Antioche PO* 38:2, no. 175 (Turnhout, 1976): 338–41.

106. P. Rousseau, "Basil of Caesarea, *Contra Eunomium:* the Main Preoccupations," *Prudentia* Supplementary Number (1988): 77–94; M. Wiles, "Eunomius: Hair-splitting Dialectician or Defender of the Accessibility of Salvation?" in Williams, ed., *The Making of Orthodoxy,* 157–72.

spokesman for a particular religious community as was Basil. Rousseau asserts that "Eunomius was a churchman as well as a theologian: he, too, had pastoral motives. He was a bishop, and he took his religion seriously." [107] We must note that Rousseau's various propositions are not necessarily interdependent and that much hinges on the definition of what is taken to constitute "religion." To support this construct, a number of arguments have been advanced that fail, on closer inspection, to bear the weight of the edifice.

The claim that Eunomius represented a functioning religious community because of his tenure as bishop of Cyzicus is not convincing. Eunomius' abortive tenure in Cyzicus was not sufficient occasion for him to develop a set of pastoral concerns that then influenced his stance on epistemology. Not only the brevity of his stay but also the hostility of local clergy and laity militate against this position. [108] It is difficult to imagine that the congregation in Cyzicus, which eventually brought accusations against him before Eudoxius and the emperor, was in fact the religious community whose values Eunomius rose to defend.

Likewise, it is unsatisfactory to argue from his *Expositio fidei* (Explanation of the creed) that Eunomius' overriding concern was for the coherence of a worshiping religious community. The credal statement was most likely composed as an apologetic and missionary document. [109] It may even have been part of the material Eunomius read aloud to the audience of friends and foes who sought him out at his private estate in Chalcedon following his exile.

There is no evidence that the *Expositio fidei* was ever used as the baptismal creed of the Christian community in Cyzicus. [110] According to Eunomius, the credal statement was not a group charter but a protreptic device for those, including the emperor Theodosius, "who wish to . . . acquire an easy and convenient knowledge of our opinion." [111] Eunomius knew that a credal statement alone could never safeguard orthodoxy, as he observed in connection with controversies associated with Sabellius, Marcellus, and Photinus. [112] Static dogmatic statements were

107. Rousseau, "Basil of Caesarea, *Contra Eunomium*," 86.

108. See Socrates, *Hist. eccl.* 4.7 (*PG* 67:473A–B).

109. See Vaggione, *Eunomius*, 132.

110. Kopecek's conjecture that Eunomius' *Liber apologeticus* 28 represents the altered Cyzican creed is highly speculative; see *History of Neo-Arianism*, 2:402–4; see also 2:398–99, esp. 399n. 1.

111. Eunomius, *Liber apologeticus* 4 (Vaggione, *Eunomius*, 36–37). Vaggione argues (12?· that the work was produced in connection with events following the Council of ntinople 381.

'. See Eunomius, *Liber apologeticus* 6 (Vaggione, *Eunomius*, 38–41).

susceptible to misinterpretation, whether deliberate or not. It was safer to anchor one's belief by employing one's trained reason to form personal judgments from basic principles.[113]

The revisionist readings of Eunomius clearly indicate a feeling among modern scholars that, in order to rehabilitate Eunomius as a credible Christian figure, they must whitewash his ultra-rationalist image and recast him as a latter-day Arius who has finally been "reinstated" through sympathetic studies that depict him as a charismatic ascetic grappling in earnest with questions about the relationship between christology and soteriology.[114]

The new emphasis on Eunomius as church leader is an improvement over the acceptance of orthodox polemics at face value, but completely inverting the orthodox characterization of Eunomius is not entirely satisfactory because the debate remains entirely within the parameters of the evaluative framework set up by Basil and others, who focused on the presence of so-called legitimate religious concerns (i.e., issues related to ecclesiology and soteriology) as a criterion for judging the legitimacy of religious leaders.[115] This stance derives from a preconceived notion of a "religious community" as being held together mainly by adherence to a credo and a defined set of religious practices.[116] To avoid the need to argue for the presence of a Eunomian worshiping community in the fourth century that was similar to the orthodox churches in almost every regard except in credal formulation and baptismal rite,[117] we must explore other plausible social models of the Anomoean movement that would adequately account for the prominence of debate in its midst.

Aetius' circle resembled a philosophical coterie. In the minds of contemporaries, the Anomoeans operated as a *diadochē*, along the same

113. See Eunomius, *Liber apologeticus* 2 (Vaggione, *Eunomius*, 36–37).

114. See R. C. Gregg and D. E. Groh, "The Centrality of Soteriology in Early Arianism," *Anglican Theological Review* 59 (1977): 260–78; idem, *Early Arianism: A View of Salvation* (Philadelphia, 1981), 50–70.

115. See M. Anastos, "Basil's KATA EYNOMIOY: A Critical Analysis," in Fedwick, ed., *Basil of Caesarea*, 1:67–136, esp. 126–27. Anastos shows that Basil's debate with Eunomius over the interpretation of the sharing of *ousia* by the Son and the Father was not concerned with soteriology.

116. See T. A. Kopecek, "Neo-Arian Religion: The Evidence of the *Apostolic Constitutions*," in R. C. Gregg, ed., *Arianism: Historical and Theological Reassessments* (Philadelphia, 1985), 153–55.

117. Sozomen, *Hist. eccl.* 6.26, stated that fifth-century Eunomians had one immersion into the death of Christ and not three immersions into the Father, Son, and Holy Spirit. The practice of the single immersion, however, is explicitly explained as beginning with Theophronius and Eutyches, Eunomius' disciples.

principles that characterized many late antique philosophical circles.[118] Aetius sometimes expressed his relationship with his readers as that between father and children.[119] The readers of his *Syntagmation*, disciples (μαθηταί) as well as colleagues, were also "heroes and heroines in the contest of true religion."[120] Although Eunomius later took steps to form a separate church hierarchy, that aspect of the movement was not a central preoccupation. More important was the dynamic relationship between the charismatic teacher and his *zēlōtai* and *akroatai*, recalling the Neoplatonist circles described by Porphyry and by Eunapius. After Eunomius departed from Cyzicus, he retired to an estate where "multitudes (πλῆθος) resorted to him; some also gathered from different quarters, a few with the design of testing his principles (ἀποπειρώμενοι), and others merely from the desire of listening to his discourse."[121]

For the most part, Aetius and Eunomius presided over a broad confederation of like-minded people rather than a discrete organization or community. Such a "movement" may be characterized as elitist, though not necessarily in a socioeconomic sense, but in terms of its exacting emphasis on the insoluble link between correct understanding and worship.[122] I suggest instead that the solidarity of such groups came from disputing and questioning rather than adherence to set beliefs. These groups could flourish only at the margins of more stable communities, with which they shared a symbiotic relationship.

The Popularization of the *Logos: Technologia* and *Technē*

Both Eunomius and Aetius insisted that theological discourse required a strict, systematic method that could be studied and mastered. In this sense, association of the *technologos* with Aristotelian philosophy and with sophistry need not be mutually exclusive. Sozomen called Eunomius a *technitēs logōn* who was contentious and who delighted in the use of crafty syllogisms.[123] Perhaps another reason why Eunomius was called *ho technologos* was because he made theological discourse a *technē*,

118. See Epiphanius, *Panarion* 76.54.32.
119. The parental imagery shows strongly in the Anomoean redaction of the *Apostolic Constitutions*; see C. H. Turner, "Notes on the *Apostolic Constitutions*," *JTS* 16 (1914–15): 54–61.
120. See Wickham, "*Syntagmation* of Aetius," 540 (Greek text), 544–45 (English).
121. Sozomen, *Hist. eccl.* 7.6 (NPNF, 379; Greek text in Bidez, ed., 307).
122. See Aetius, *Syntagmation* 37, in Wickham, "*Syntagmation* of Aetius," 544 (Greek text), 549 (English).
123. Sozomen, *Hist. eccl.* 6.26 (Bidez, ed., 272): "τεχνίτης λόγων καὶ ἐριστικὸς καὶ συλλογισμοῖς χαίρων."

an art that others could master through careful study of a manual—*hē technē* could connote both an art and the handbook explaining its workings to aspiring learners.[124]

Socrates Scholasticus charged Aetius with deriving his astounding theological views from teachings in Aristotle's *Categories*.[125] Gregory of Nyssa accused Eunomius with first relying on the *Categories* and then failing to interpret it correctly.[126] This association of the Anomoeans with the *Categories* was reiterated when Theophronius of Cappadocia, a disciple of Eunomius, was said by both Socrates and Sozomen to have based his own novel interpretation of the standard Eunomian line on his reading of Aristotle's *Categories* and *On Interpretation*.[127] From these he composed a work, now lost, called *Peri Gymnasias Nou* (On the exercise of the intellect).

Collectively, these claims are not a priori incredible. The rules of deduction in Aetius' *Syntagmation* do appear to have been based on Aristotelian and Stoic categories.[128] Eunomius' *Liber apologeticus* and *Apologia Apologiae* likewise reveal a reliance on concepts from the *Categories*, as Gregory of Nyssa pointed out. However, if we trust the testimony of Socrates and Sozomen, then it appears that the *Categories* was not commonly read in Anomoean circles, since the fact that Theophronius read and relied on it was considered a significant enough detail to emphasize.

Attempts to forge a direct connection between the Anomoeans and the *Categories* bespeak the tendency of those engaged in heresiological discourse to look for ultimate origins. Instead of reading Aristotle's works directly, many probably familiarized themselves with the written works of Aetius and Eunomius into which the philosophical insights had been integrated and adapted to the context of Christian theological discourse. These texts were eminently more useful and, to borrow a current idiom, more user-friendly.

The memorization of texts by rote as preparation for situations of

124. See Sextus Empiricus, *Pyrr. hypotyposes* 2.205, on the Dogmatics' use of *technologia*, the systematic treatment of logical definitions.

125. Socrates, *Hist. eccl.* 2.35 (*PG* 67:297B).

126. Gregory of Nyssa, *Contra Eun.* 1.181 (Jaeger, ed., 1:80).

127. Socrates, *Hist. eccl.* 5.24; Sozomen, *Hist. eccl.* 7.17 (Bidez, ed., 325).

128. See Wickham, "*Syntagmation* of Aetius," 561–62, 561n. 1. Note the judicious caveat against accepting the Aristotelian connection too readily because of its polemical usage. Wickham's argument that the propositions in Aetius' *Syntagmation* do not strictly qualify as syllogisms (534) may be due to an overly stringent application of technical criteria, a noted modern tendency; see Lee Tae-Soo, *Die griechische Tradition der aristotelischen Syllogistik in der Spätantike: Eine Untersuchung über die Kommentare zu den analytica priora von Alexander Aphrodisiensis, Ammonius und Philoponus*, Hypomnemata, Untersuchungen zur Antike und zu ihrem Nachleben 79 (Göttingen, 1984), 95.

verbal contest was long a common feature of the Greek system of learning and education. This was especially prevalent in rhetorical training. According to Aristotle, the teachers of eristics

> gave their pupils to learn by heart speeches which were either rhetorical or consisted of questions and answers, in which both sides thought that the rival arguments were for the most part included. Hence the teaching which they gave to their pupils was rapid but unsystematic; for they conceived that they could train their pupils by imparting to them not an art but the results of an art (οὐ γὰρ τέχνην ἀλλὰ τὰ ἀπὸ τῆς τέχνης).[129]

Aetius' *Syntagmation* was laid out in the form of alternating question (ἐπαπόρησις) and answer (λύσις) for explicit, pedagogical reasons: "On grounds of clarity and ease in grasping the points of the proofs, I have set them out in the form of alternating problems and solutions. . . ."[130] Aetius' readers could pick and choose what they needed from the *Syntagmation*, adapting deductive syllogisms for use in disputes both offensively and defensively. In fact, Aetius complained in the preface to the second edition that the work was tampered with earlier and that the order of the demonstrations had been altered. He did not say that this was done by enemies; perhaps certain well-meaning persons freely adapted his syllogisms and circulated the *Syntagmation* in a form that they found most useful.

The circle of the Anomoeans, as a social phenomenon, acquired its cogency through a common theological method disseminated by means of a body of written texts and some oral teaching. The *Syntagmation*, judging from the preface to the revised version, was widely circulated among those whom the author considered to be like-minded individuals and was not directed at any specific community.[131]

With the aid of the proofs in Aetius' *Syntagmation*, kindred spirits were encouraged to refrain from sustained argument against an opponent in a disputation. They had no need to invent their arguments *de novo*. Instead, they could simply reiterate one of the powerful proofs—of which Epiphanius claimed there were originally three hundred—which have been aptly described as

> withering retorts with which the student is to stop the mouth of his adversaries. For this purpose what could be better than short deductive proofs, especially if they echo, as they often appear to do, something an opponent might be presumed to say? The sarcastic tone which cer-

129. Aristotle, *De sophisticis elenchis* 34.183b–184a (Forster and Furley, eds., 154–55).
130. Wickham, "*Syntagmation* of Aetius," 540 (Greek text), 545 (English).
131. See Wickham, "*Syntagmation* of Aetius," 532–69.

tain of these arguments exhibit (e.g., § 12) reveals something of the contentious character of their author and of the movement he led.[132]

That this text, deliberately controversial in the most literal sense, commanded respect is underscored by the fact that Eunomius composed textual commentaries or scholia to it.[133] The perceived threat of the *Syntagmation* was so great that Epiphanius devoted to its refutation a lengthy and detailed treatise to which we owe the survival of the original text. Even more interesting are the dialogues by Pseudo-Athanasius in which an orthodox Christian interlocutor and various heretics, including Anomoeans, became engaged in theological debate when the claims of Aetius' *Syntagmation* were cited and refuted point by point.[134]

An Oppressive *Logos*?

Aetius and Eunomius appealed in their writings to people like themselves who were disposed to believe in an insoluble link between precise theological formulation and correct worship. Stated in general terms, this is not a controversial thesis: in order to pay proper tribute to God, one had to understand the nature of God and the true import of his attribute as the Unbegotten One (ὁ ἀγέννητος). To Aetius, the name could not be an arbitrary human attribution because

> if ingeneracy does not represent the substance of the Deity, but the incomparable name is of human imagining (ἐπινοίας ἀνθρωπίνης), the Deity is grateful to those who thought the name up, since through the concept of ingeneracy he has a transcendence of name which he does not bear in essence.[135]

This central point was also emphasized in Eunomius' definition of the Father as the Unbegotten One; he explained why this point was so significant to Christian worship:

> When we say "Unbegotten," then, we do not imagine that we ought to honour God only in name, in conformity with human invention (κατ' ἐπίνοιαν); rather, in conformity with reality (κατ' ἀλήθειαν), we ought

132. Wickham, "*Syntagmation* of Aetius," 535.
133. Mentioned in Pseudo-Athanasius, *Dialogus de sancta trinitate* 2.6 (*PG* 28:1165A–B); see Vaggione, *Eunomius*, 166–67. It is of course not certain that the *Syntagmation* is the specific text that Eunomius commented on.
134. *PG* 28:1115–1201; see A. Heron, "The Two Pseudo-Athanasian Dialogues against the Anomoeans," *JTS* n.s. 24 (1973): 101–22. Compare Theodoret's *Eranistes*, particularly the preface.
135. Aetius, *Syntagmation* 12, in Wickham, "*Syntagmation* of Aetius," 541–42 (Greek text), 546 (English).

to repay him the debt which above all others is most due God: the acknowledgement that he is what he is.[136]

Fallible human conceptions were of no use in finding a name that accurately and sufficiently described God as who he is: a sovereign philosophical method was needed to progress toward true knowledge of him. The Aristotelian categories provided an analytical terminology for nouns and adjectival predicates (e.g., Father, Son, Generate, Ingenerate); the syllogistic method served as a means to put these terms together into tightly built logical propositions. Favoring a dialectical method in one's discourse meant adopting the notion that it was always possible to argue from a given premiss to a set conclusion: "A partir du moment où l'on admet un certain point de départ, l'enchaînement nécessaire des syllogismes mènera inexorablement à la conclusion."[137] For certain Christians, this method enabled the development of a theological discourse rooted in divinely endowed reason.

Those who refused to be persuaded by the systematic application of such implacable reasoning could be accused of acting in a contentious manner (φιλονείκως).[138] Resting on the authority of the dialectical method, Eunomius even turned the language of his accusers against themselves in an appeal to his sympathizers:

> Don't be afraid of human censure; don't be deceived by their sophistries or led astray by their flatteries. Give a true and just verdict on the issues of which we've spoken; show that the better part has clearly won out among you all. Let right reason prevail over these troublemakers and flee all the traps and snares laid for us by the devil; he has made it his business either to terrify or entice the many who fail to put what is right before what is pleasurable.[139]

One person's belief in invincible reason is another's tyranny. Those who wished to resist the authority of the dialectical method were faced with an even more unsettling belief: that questioners need not know their subject, or the answer to their question. Culturally, this license was the prerogative of the young; not surprisingly, the Anomoeans were often thought to act like irresponsible youth (πρὸς μειρακιώδη τινὰ φιλοτιμίαν).[140]

The popularization of dialectical questioning placed great strain on those in authority, who frequently would have been called to account.

136. Eunomius, *Liber apologeticus* 8 (Vaggione, *Eunomius*, 40–43).
137. Hadot, "Philosophie, dialectique, rhétorique dans l'antiquité," 140.
138. See Eunomius, *Liber apologeticus* 24 (Vaggione, *Eunomius*, 66–67).
139. Eunomius, *Liber apologeticus* 27 (Vaggione, *Eunomius*, 72–73).
140. Gregory of Nyssa, *Contra Eun.* 1.11 (Jaeger, ed., 1:25).

When so challenged, those in authority could choose silence at the risk of being considered stupid or uneducated, or they could venture a response that might make matters worse. Aristotle allowed respondents to questions involving obscure and multivalent terms to say, "I don't understand,"[141] but doing so meant forfeiting one's claim to *gnōsis* and severely compromising one's social standing among the educated. This was equivalent to throwing off one's shield and running away in battle:

> To excuse oneself when combat is offered
> Has consigned valour to deep obscurity.[142]

One might also beg for a brief respite,[143] as Amphilochius of Iconium apparently did when faced with such questions.[144] The answers Amphilochius devised in this breathing space were evidently ineffectual. Finding himself hard-pressed, he sought advice from a learned friend experienced in such controversies. In a series of letters in 376, Amphilochius anxiously requested Basil of Caesarea's help in framing credible responses to a series of questions.[145] In one letter, the Caesarean wrote eloquently of the perceived threat of dialectical questions, citing the celebrated question Anomoean sympathizers were prone to ask: "Do you worship what you know or what you do not know?"[146] Basil wisely declined to answer this question in an ad hoc manner, as he often did elsewhere; instead, he objected to the sophistry of dialectical questioning *sui generis*.

The question is a fine specimen of the carefully crafted "yes or no"

141. Aristotle, *Topica* 160a18–34.

142. Lines of poetry (otherwise unknown) cited by Phaedimus when confronted by a challenge to debate by Aristotimus, in Plutarch, *De sollertia animalium* 23 (Cherniss and Helmbold, eds., LCL, *Moralia* 12:415).

143. See Plutarch, *De sollertia animalium* 23.

144. Interestingly, while the historical Amphilochius was hard-pressed by these questionings, in later tradition he appeared as the superior protagonist in a disputation with Eunomius himself. In an unpublished dialogue, Amphilochius made lengthy replies to the heresiarch's short questions. See Εὐνομίου αἱρετικοῦ ἐρώτησις πρὸς τὸν ἅγιον Ἀμφιλόχιον ἀπὸ τῶν εὐαγγελικῶν ῥημάτων (*Codex Oxoniensis Bodleianus Canon* 41, folios 83ʳ–84ʳ), cited in Vaggione, *Eunomius*, 187. On Amphilochius in general, see C. Datema, ed., *Amphilochii Iconiensis Opera* CCSG 3 (Turnhout, 1978), x–xi; K. Holl, *Amphilochius von Ikonium in seinem Verhältnis zu den grossen Kappadoziern* (Tübingen/Leipzig, 1904).

145. See Basil, *Ep.* 235 (Deferrari, ed., 3:376–85), to Amphilochius on faith and knowledge. Deferrari, editor of the LCL edition, believes this letter to be directed at gnostics because the word *gnōsis* is mentioned. However, from the context of this correspondence it seems quite clear that the letter concerns dialectical questioners.

146. Basil of Caesarea, *Ep.* 234 (Deferrari, ed., 3:370–71). See discussion in C. G. Bonis, "The Problem Concerning Faith and Knowledge, or Reason and Revelation, as Expounded in the Letters of Basil the Great to Amphilochius of Iconium," *Greek Orthodox Theological Review* 5 (1959): 27–44, esp. 37–41.

proposition. In ideal circumstances, either response would provide the other side with a dialectical premiss to refute. But the popularization of argumentative techniques and ready-made controversial texts ensured that Amphilochius would be confronted with a series of prepared retorts.

Basil regarded the question to be a baited sophism because its terms lacked precision. If Amphilochius had answered that he did not know what he worshiped, the concession would have rendered him an object of ridicule; if he had said that he *did* know, he could expect this retort (ταχεῖα παρ' αὐτῶν ἡ ἀπάντησις): "What is the substance (οὐσία) of that which is adored?" The implied assumption—which should have required demonstration but was accepted as a premiss—was that "to know" something meant to fully grasp its essence; yet it was precisely the articulation of the divine essence that constituted the crux of contemporary doctrinal disputes.

It was difficult to find satisfactory responses to such questions. Elsewhere, Basil coached other Christians with painstaking care in responding to syllogistic propositions posing as invitations to debate:

> Hold fast to the text, and you will suffer no harm from men of evil arts. Suppose your opponent argues, "If He was begotten, He was not"; you retort, "He was in the beginning." But, he will go on, "Before He was begotten, in what was He?" Do not give up the words "He was." Do not abandon the words "In the beginning." The highest beginning point is beyond comprehension; what is outside beginning is beyond discovery. Do not let any one deceive you by the fact that the phrase has more than one meaning. . . . Never give up the "was" and you will never give any room for vile blasphemy to slip in. Mariners laugh at the storm, when they are riding upon two anchors. So will you laugh to scorn this vile agitation which is being driven on the world by the blasts of wickedness, and tosses the faith of many to and fro, if only you will keep your soul moored safely in the security of these words.[147]

Isidore of Pelusium similarly aided a certain Synesius in framing a response to the questioning of others. In a letter cited in the *Patrologia Graeca* as a letter on Arians and Eunomians, he offered the following: "What you want to learn is brief but nonetheless secure. If God is always the same, if he never acquires anything, he is always the Father. And if he is always the Father, he always has the Son. Then the Son is ever coexisting with the Father."[148]

Neither the ecclesiastical position nor the elevated social status of Amphilochius, Basil, or Synesius shielded them from difficult ques-

147. Basil of Caesarea, *Homilia* 16.1 (*PG* 31:473B–76C; trans. from P. J. Fedwick, *The Church and the Charisma of Leadership in Basil of Caesarea* [Toronto, 1979], 58–59).
148. Isidore of Pelusium, *Ep.* 1.241 (*PG* 78:329–30C).

tions; dialectical questioning was no respecter of persons. The challenge that skill in debate posed to episcopal authority was not monopolized by those who opposed the Nicene position. Germinius of Sirmium, a bishop who espoused a homoian position and who enjoyed the favor of the Arian emperor Valens, debated a layperson who upheld the Nicene formulation on 13 January 366. The *Altercatio Heracliani,* derived from the stenographers' notes from the proceedings, depict an extraordinarily embarrassing scenario in which Germinius was reduced to speechlessness by Heraclian for more than an hour.[149] Even subscribers to Arian theology were vulnerable to pressures from those who were nominally on their side. Local Anomoeans (though not Aetius or Eunomius) used to harass Demophilus, the Arian bishop of Antioch, not because they disagreed with his dogma but because he had managed to arrive at their shared convictions without going through a process of dialectical reasoning.[150] Getting the intermediate steps right counted at least as much as having the proper answer at the end. Demophilus' inability to construct a logical theological discourse later received scathing comment from the Eunomian historian Philostorgius.[151]

The situation is further complicated by evidence that even Eunomians felt pressured by this stubbornly methodological exercise of dialectic. After the death of Eunomius, his disciple Eutyches made a bitter enemy of the new nominal head (ὁ προεστώς) of the Eunomian group in Constantinople[152] with dialectical questions. The new head even went so far as to refuse to commune with Eutyches because, according to Sozomen, the two clashed over the internal hierarchizing principle to be accorded most value within the group. The leader felt resentful "because he was not able to answer Eutyches' question (τῆς ζητήσεως), and found it impossible to solve his proposed difficulty (διαλύειν τὸ πρόβλημα)."[153] The episode hints at the principle of routinization already at work among the Eunomian followers after the first generation; it also

149. See M. Meslin, *Les ariens d'occident 335–430,* Patristica Sorbonensia 8 (Paris, 1967), 69–70, 294–99. Text of the *Altercatio Heracliani* in C. Caspari, ed., *Kirchengeschichte Anecdota nebst denen Ausgaben patristicher und kirchlichmittelalterlicher Schriften* (Christiania, 1883), 1:133–47. Germinius prevailed nonetheless thanks to his episcopal authority, an outcome that underscores a vital difference between eastern and western constructions of authority.

150. For a comprehensive discussion of this episode, see Kopecek, *History of Neo-Arianism,* 2:437: "It was not enough to agree with the Neo-Arians; one had to agree with them for the right reasons. The Neo-Arians were extremely precise about their doctrinal demands."

151. Philostorgius, *Hist. eccl.* 9.14.

152. See Sozomen, *Hist. eccl.* 7.17 (Bidez, ed., 325).

153. Sozomen, *Hist. eccl.* 7.17 (Bidez, ed., 325–26).

shows that the individualistic, competitive outlook behind the culture of questioning was not confined within particular sectarian boundaries.

It is important to emphasize that the threat posed by the popularization of dialectical questioning was felt especially by those in authority. The Anomoean promotion of theological discourse as a "precise science" or *akribologia*[154] through the dissemination of writings brought into being a generation of dialectical questioners, who in turn magnified the threat to established authorities by asking questions which, because they were based on a culturally established method, demanded a response.

Such challenges were understandably disagreeable to people who felt they alone were fit to wield ecclesiastical authority. Similar disorder in civic life would have been quickly labeled a *stasis*, an insurrection. On the one hand, few leaders, whether secular or ecclesiastical, would have actually enjoyed justifying their social positions on a daily basis through adversarial proceedings, especially with social inferiors.[155] On the other hand, as few would have been willing to forgo a pretense to knowledge. Forced to compete for consideration on a level playing field, the leaders became vulnerable to public disgrace in this "language game."

To resist this pressure and to place dialectical questioning back within tolerable limits, those most affected took evasive measures, including the elevation of an ascetic way of life as an exemplum of values antithetical to those of dialectical questioners. In the remainder of this chapter, I explore this tactic of turning the contest into one of rival *habitus* as a social construction involving the original connection between dialectic, upward social mobility, and notions of social order.

OPPOSING WAYS OF LIFE: THE DIALECTICIAN AND THE MONK

Paideia and Prejudice

The notion of *paideia*, allied with the strict moral code that traditionally accompanied inherited wealth and leisure, distinguished the well-born few from the common man.[156] The Graeco-Roman cultural ideal created a universal linguistic and moral code for the scions of late Roman elites from Spain to Syria, but few progressed beyond rudimentary *paideia* to

154. See Epiphanius, *Panarion* 76.3.7.
155. See Meyer, "Dialectic and Questioning," 281–89.
156. On the relationship between wealth, leisure, and intellectual pursuits in antiquity, see J.-M. André, *L'otium dans la vie morale et intellectuelle romaine, des origines à l'époque augustéenne* (Paris, 1966).

attain greater mastery and professionalism in chosen fields.[157] A formula tethering *paideia* to the mores of the landed aristocracy only served to reinforce social prejudices and boundaries at a time when a greater number of careers were in theory *ouvertes aux talents*.[158]

For many, *paideia* served as a means of exhibiting status, not a way to acquire it. The elder Iamblichus expressed a conventional view when he explained that *paideia* did not aim to prepare an individual for a specific goal in life.[159] To specialize prematurely in one field for the sake of professional advancement without first securing a firm grounding in all-round education or *egkuklios paideia* was likely to provoke scorn.

Prosopographical studies of the later empire have shown that, in the latter part of the fourth century, a solid core of middling elites, consisting mostly of *curiales* and local decurions, occupied the highest rungs of the ecclesiastical positions in eastern cities.[160] These Christians brought to their vocation the traditional social values of the upper classes and required little by way of christianization to become immediately acceptable.[161] It is thus not surprising that Christian writers should echo the known, established prejudices of the secular elites.

It was in people's descriptions of themselves and others that these underlying views were expressed. Gregory of Nazianzus, for example, compared himself to his rival Helladius of Caesarea (who was either a *curialis* or a *principalis*):

> Should certain people view us naked and judge between us two our suitability for the priestly office, what would one possess which is superior to what the other has? Birth (γένος)? Upbringing (παίδευσις)?

157. See I. Karayannopoulos, "St. Basil's Social Activity: Principles and Praxis," in Fedwick, ed., *Basil of Caesarea*, 1:375–91, at 381: "We must, therefore, draw a line between the classical *paideia* and education that the rich gave their children, and the study of rhetoric by those who learned it in order to become professional teachers." On the relationship of training to official positions, see F. S. Pedersen, "On Professional Qualifications for Public Posts in Late Antiquity," *Classica et Mediaevalia* 31 (1975): 161–213.

158. See K. Hopkins, "Social Mobility in the Later Roman Empire: The Evidence of Ausonius," *CQ* n.s. 11 (1961): 239–49; idem, "Elite Mobility in the Roman Empire," in M. Finley, ed., *Studies in Ancient Society* (London, 1974), 103–120; Ramsay MacMullen, "Social Mobility and the Theodosian Code," *JRS* 54 (1964): 49–53; Kaster, *Guardians of Language*, 32–95.

159. Iamblichus, *Protrepticus* 1 (Des Place, ed., 40) on *paideia*: "οὐ . . . πρὸς ἕν τι τῶν πάντων παρασκευσάξει τὸν ἄνθρωπον."

160. A. H. M. Jones, *The Later Roman Empire 284–602* (Oxford, 1964), 2:925–29. See the conclusions of the prosopographic studies of fourth-century bishops: F. D. Gilliard, "The Social Origins of Bishops in the Fourth Century" (Ph.D. diss., University of California at Berkeley, 1966); T. A. Kopecek, "The Social Class of the Cappadocian Fathers," *Church History* 42 (1973): 453–66, esp. 460–61; and A. Rousselle, "Aspects sociaux du recrutement ecclésiastique au IVᵉ siècle," *Mélanges d'Archéologie et d'Histoire de l'École Française de Rome* 89 (1977): 333–70.

161. See Van Dam, "Emperors, Bishops, and Friends."

> Free association with the mighty and the famous? Knowledge of theo-
> logical matters (γνῶσις)? All the qualities are found among us in more
> or less equal measure.[162]

This juxtaposition highlights the patches of common ground on
which were based the alliances of late antique ecclesiastical and secular
elites.[163] Birth to a prominent family, a proper upbringing, friends and
relations in high places, a modicum of learning, even gnōsis: these were
the qualities that entitled a man to the consideration of his peers and the
devotion of the less fortunate.

The creation of this common culture, of course, entailed acts of social exclusion. Even among pagan philosophers, the language of social
prejudice was frequently mobilized against a rival with devastating effect.[164] As is well known, using ēthos as both defense and offense was a
venerable part of Greek rhetorical tradition dating at least to the time of
the Attic orators.[165] Classically trained Christians like Basil of Caesarea
and Gregory of Nazianzus, both of whom had studied under the sophist
Prohaeresius in Athens, were no strangers to this tradition of ethical
invective.[166]

Gregory was thoroughly familiar with the polished rhetorical styles
of the Second Sophistic and knew well how to compose a psogos, a negative biographical characterization.[167] In a famous example, he methodically defamed a fellow countryman, George of Cappadocia, the Arian
bishop of Alexandria and erstwhile mentor of Aetius. George, later
lynched by an angry pagan mob in Alexandria for his attacks on temples,
was unkindly described by Gregory as having been born near the border
of Cappadocia (a slight to proud Cappadocians), the result of a half-
servile union (i.e., like a mule's mixed progenitors), and as having risen

162. Gregory of Nazianzus, Ep. 249.32. See M.-M. Hauser-Meury, Prosopographie zu
den Schriften Gregors von Nazianz, Theophaneia 13 (Bonn, 1960), 94–95, s.v. "Helladius I";
P. Devos, "S. Grégoire de Nazianze et Hellade de Césarée en Cappadoce," AB 79 (1961),
91–101; Kopecek, "Social Class of the Cappadocian Fathers," 453–66, esp. 455, 455n. 16.
In general, see E. F. Bruck, Kirchenväter und soziales Erbrecht (Berlin/Göttingen/Heidelberg,
1956), esp. 3, 17–18. On Gregory's family, see J. Bernardi, "Nouvelles perspectives sur la
famille de Grégoire de Nazianze," VChr 38 (1984): 352–59; P. Gallay, La vie de saint Grégoire
de Nazianze (Lyons/Paris, 1943), 250–51.
163. See R. Van Dam, "Emperors, Bishops, and Friends in Late Antique Cappadocia,"
JTS n.s. 37 (1986): 53–76.
164. See the delightful essay by G. E. L. Owen, "Philosophical Invective," Oxford
Studies in Ancient Philosophy 1 (1983): 1–25.
165. See W. Süss, Ethos (Leipzig, 1910), 247–54.
166. Socrates, Hist. eccl. 4.26; Sozomen, Hist. eccl. 6.17.1.
167. See R. R. Ruether, Gregory of Nazianzus: Rhetor and Philosopher (Oxford, 1969),
111. On the psogos, see Rhetores Graeci (C. Walz, ed., 9:402–3).

from menial labor without a liberal education.[168] Though these slights should not be accepted at face value, it is important to remember that ancient rhetors, to assassinate character most convincingly, preferred accentuating existing defects to inventing nonexistent ones.[169]

For people with reputations as *arrivistes*, avarice and ambition usually featured prominently in the catalogue of their vices. Gregory of Nazianzus related with relish a rumor that George embezzled funds destined for the relief of the poor in Alexandria and used them instead for bribery in high places.[170]

Similar ad hominem attacks were made against Aetius and Eunomius. Gregory of Nyssa coldly observed that Aetius had once been a hired manual laborer engaged in a degrading menial trade (βάναυσον τέχνην).[171] The Syrian was further upbraided by Epiphanius of Salamis for not having had the benefit of a proper education in his youth.[172] Characterization of someone as *apaideutos* had implications beyond the lack of formal education; it distinguished a successful barbarian general or nouveau riche merchant from the ranks of the established aristocracy. The charge thus suggested that Aetius lacked the moral formation that was normally nurtured through early association with a grammarian.[173]

Gregory of Nyssa stated that Eunomius was known to have once been a pedagogue, a position customarily staffed by slaves.[174] Interestingly, at times Eunomius seemed to accept his opponents' characterization of his lowly origins. Here we see the two sides engaged in a kind of ritual dance: as the Cappadocians resorted to a language of social condescension, Eunomius willingly became the social outsider, casting him-

168. Gregory of Nazianzus, *Or.* 21.16; see Kopecek, *History of Neo-Arianism,* 1:138–45.

169. Cicero, *De oratore* 2.43.182: "Valet igitur multum ad vincendum probari mores et instituta et facta et vitam eorum, qui agent causas, et eorum, pro quibus, et item improbari adversariorum, animosque eorum, apud quos agetur . . . conciliantur autem animi dignitate hominis, rebus gestis, existimatione vitae, *quae facilius ornari possunt, si modo sunt, quam fingi si nulla sunt.*" Emphasis mine.

170. On the wealth and power of the Alexandrian patriarchs, and the use of such resources as bribes at the imperial court, see P. Batiffol, "Les présents de saint Cyrille à la cour de Constantinople," in *Études de liturgie et d'archéologie chrétienne* (Paris, 1919), 154–79.

171. Gregory of Nyssa, *Contra Eun.* 1.38 (Jaeger, ed., 1:35). Gregory could not resist making Aetius a swindler as well; see *Contra Eun.* 1.40–41 (Jaeger, ed., 1:36).

172. Epiphanius, *Panarion* 76.2: "οὗτος ὁ Ἀέτιος καὶ κατὰ τὸν κοσμικὸν λόγον ἀπαίδευτος ἦν ἕως τῆς τελείας αὐτοῦ ἡλικίας, ὡς ὁ λόγος."

173. See Kaster, *Guardians of Language,* 11–14. Aetius' deficiency in breeding and comportment would become more exaggerated in later traditions; see R. Vaggione, "Some Neglected Fragments of Theodore of Mopsuestia's *Contra Eunomium,*" *JTS* n.s. 31 (1980): 403–70, esp. 408–19.

174. Gregory of Nyssa, *Contra Eun.* 1.49–50 (Jaeger, ed., 1:39).

self in the role of the humble champion of truth, whose opponents stood in error regardless of their worldly wealth and rank.[175]

It is arguable that this social gulf separated the Cappadocians and Eunomius more effectively and irreconcilably than any amount of theological and philosophical disagreement. In such matters, style was of supreme importance. Gregory of Nyssa, referring to his *Contra Eunomium*, requested that his readers devote special attention to the parts in which he demolished the arguments employed by Eunomius in his *Apologia Apologiae* to justify the trial imagery used in his *Liber apologeticus;* but here substance, while important, is somewhat eclipsed by the duel between the two over the issue of prose style.[176] Eloquence of language, an attainment emblematic of one's *paideia*, became part of the contest because even the educated person with little interest in theological learning appreciated the cadences of well-balanced phrases.

Although more accomplished than that of Aetius, Eunomius' prose revealed to trained eyes many belabored rhetorical devices and the tortuous style of the much-maligned Second Sophistic, though he was clearly able to compose in good Attic Greek. Eunomius' rhetorical ploy was attributed by his enemies to an excessive desire to impress his audience. His baroque presentation betrayed an obsession with scoring points (φιλονεικία) and the inability to admit defeat or show proper deference.

Using the language of a wrestling match—deliberately adopted to answer Eunomius' earlier interpretation of his appointment to the bishopric of Cyzicus as an *athlos*, a prize for victory—Gregory of Nyssa called Eunomius a "bad sport" for not admitting defeat in argument. An explicit analogy between athletic contest and verbal argumentation can be traced to ancient works, including Aristotle's *De sophisticis elenchis:*

> For just as unfairness in an athletic contest takes a definite form and is an unfair kind of fighting, so contentious reasoning is an unfair kind of fighting in argument; for in the former case those who are bent on victory at all costs stick at nothing, so too in the latter case do contentious arguers. Those, then, who behave like this merely to win a victory, are generally regarded as contentious and quarrelsome, while those who do so to win a reputation which will help them make money are regarded as sophistical. . . . Quarrelsome people and sophists use the same arguments, but not for the same reasons; and the same argument will be sophistical and contentious but not from the same point of view. If the semblance of victory is the motive, it is contentious; if the semblance of wisdom, it is sophistical: for sophistry is an appearance of wisdom without the reality.[177]

175. See Eunomius, *Liber apologeticus* 27 (Vaggione, *Eunomius*, 72–73).
176. Gregory of Nyssa, *Contra Eun.* 1.11ff. (Jaeger, ed., 1.25ff.).
177. Aristotle, *De sophisticis elenchis* 11.171b (Forster and Furley, eds., 62–63).

Viewed in this light, Eunomius and those like him were at once contentious and sophistic. To a well-born male in late antiquity, this kind of
unsporting behavior was to be expected only of someone who was not a
gentleman. A clever person who would violate the rules of a sport could
not be relied on to uphold social peace and the greater good, but instead
would most likely stir up trouble for the sake of self-aggrandizement.
All in all, it was far better to affect simplicity and detachment than to
become too clever and obsessed with victory.

Eunomius was, to be sure, sensitive to such criticisms. He maintained that he did not advance his self-consciously controversial theological views out of ambition (φιλοτιμία) or a love of rivalry (φιλονεικία). Using the rhetoric of outsiders, he pronounced that true judgment
transcended social considerations, even the powerful claims of kinship,
"which so often darken the soul's power of judgement." [178] Yet his radical
subordination of *philia* to personal philosophical judgment certainly un-
dermined the very basis of the authority of ecclesiastical elites, who depended on *philia* to knit together their privileged social worlds. [179]

What was outrageous about Aetius, Eunomius, and their sympathizers was not so much their theology as the manner in which they
sought to propagate it. According to Sozomen, Aetius was deposed from
the diaconate

> because he wrote in a combative manner (ἐριστικῶς) to demonstrate a
> philosophical position (σοφία) which diverged from the expressed ec-
> clesiastical position, and because he constructed arguments in a dis-
> honorable fashion (τὰς διαλέξεις δυσφήμως ποιούμενον), and because
> he was the cause of the uproar and factionalism in the churches (ταρα-
> χῆς τε καὶ στάσεων ταῖς ἐκκλησίαις αἴτιον). [180]

Thus Aetius was accused of recklessly bringing about with his dialectical art what elites in the ancient world feared most, confusion and
strife, *tarachē* and *stasis*. This he did because he was not properly formed
in *paideia*. The cultivation of *paideia* was a process of socialization that
ideally enabled a person to know how to act responsibly in public. [181]

---

178. Eunomius, *Liber apologeticus* 2 (Vaggione, *Eunomius*, 36–37).
179. See Van Dam, "Emperors, Bishops and Friends," 53–76.
180. Sozomen, *Hist. eccl.* 4.24 (Bidez, ed., 178).
181. An admirable description of the *mores* of *paideia* is given by Kaster in *Guardians
of Language*, 60–61, where he interprets the meaning of *verecundia* in Macrobius' *Saturnalia*:

> One of the cardinal virtues, *verecundia* can be translated as 'modesty'; more ac-
> curately (if more cumbersomely), it names the sense of propriety deriving from
> a regard for the opinion of other men and an awareness of one's own position
> (especially one's hierarchical position) relative to others in a given context. . . .
> *Verecundia* is the virtue of knowing one's place, the virtue *par excellence* of the
> *status quo*, an abundantly social virtue, regulating the behavior of men in groups.

These social virtues, the fruits of prescribed moral formation, were said to be lacking in the Anomoeans, who spoke with misplaced *parrhēsia*.[182] Gregory of Nyssa accused them of not knowing when to speak and when to remain silent.[183] By contrast, the philosopher Chrysanthius, who belonged to the senatorial rank, knew, according to Eunapius, what to say and what to leave unspoken (τὰ μὲν εἰπεῖν, τὰ δὲ σιωπῆσαι).[184] Synesius,[185] a leading citizen and later bishop of Cyrene, claimed that only properly educated persons knew how to act responsibly in public by adhering to the middle course; "the uneducated fellow, on the other hand, normally fell prey to one of two extremes: either to stay silent altogether or to speak aloud on matters that one customarily kept silent on (ἤτοι σιγᾷν, ἢ λέγειν ὅσα νόμος σιγᾶσθαι)."[186]

Paideia and Ascetic Virtues

Ancient *paideia* was not merely a program of education. Most of all, it was a process of moral formation and a way of life. In this respect, the marks of traditional *paideia*, including the cultivation of philanthropic and ascetic virtues, came to represent useful defenses against the demanding claims of the dialectical questioners. In stark contrast to the individualistic and confrontational tendencies of the latter *ēthos*, the ascetic way of life shunned dissension. Though an ascetic could periodically exercise his *parrhēsia* on behalf of the just,[187] or to correct those who had lapsed into error,[188] he was normally someone who stood above unseemly sectarian rivalry.[189] When Basil of Caesarea advised Chilo on the proper behavior for a Christian ascetic, he cautioned him especially about the need to shun controversy because someone who wished to find God must be "quiet of demeanour, not hasty in speech, nor contentious (μὴ ἐριστικός), quarrelsome (μὴ φιλόνεικος), vainglorious, nor given to interpreting of texts (μὴ ἐξηγητικός)."[190]

182. Sozomen, *Hist. eccl.* 6.26 (Bidez, ed., 275–76).
183. Gregory of Nyssa, *Contra Eun.* 1.54 (Jaeger, ed., 1:40): "εἴ τινι σχολὴ δι᾽ ἀκριβείας μαθεῖν, ἐκείνους διερωτάτω οἷς ἀνεύθυνον φέρειν τι τῶν ἀπρεπῶν διὰ στόματος· ἡμεῖς δὲ σιγήσομεν."
184. Eunapius, *VS* 500.
185. See E. Cavalcanti, "Y a-t-il des problèmes eunomiens dans la pensée trinitaire de Synésius?" *SP* 13 (1975): 138–44.
186. Synesius of Cyrene, *Dion* (PG 66:1128A). See C. H. Coster, "Synesius, a *curialis* of the Time of the Emperor Arcadius," *Byzantion* 15 (1940–41): 10–38.
187. See Sozomen, *Hist. eccl.* 7.6 (Bidez, ed., 307–8).
188. See Isidore of Pelusium, *Ep.* 5.171.
189. A wise person gives good, uninterested advice, whereas a clever person calculates for his own advantage; see Aristotle, *Nicomachean Ethics* 6.13.1144a.
190. Basil, *Ep.* 42 (Deferrari, ed., 1:248–49).

The strong opposition between the values of dialectician and ascetic was frequently invoked in the polemic against the former. In his *Contra Eunomium*, partly an apologia defending his brother Basil against Eunomius' accusations that the Caesarean prelate was lacking in intelligence, Gregory of Nyssa asked his readers to compare the characters of his brother and Eunomius and then to choose between them.[191] The manner in which the choice was presented left no doubt as to how his readers ought to make their selection: Basil, when not yet a priest, had distributed his inheritance to the poor, while Eunomius had disgraced himself by living a dissolute life in Constantinople;[192] Basil cultivated an austere and sober way of life, while Eunomius indulged his appetites.[193] Sozomen later pronounced his judgment that Eunomians in general did not practice philosophy in deed, for they

> were not in the habit of praising a good way of life (βίον ἀγαθόν) or manners or mercy toward those in need—unless they should extol the same deeds—as much as someone who would discourse in an eristic fashion and would appear to triumph in syllogistic reasoning. Such a person is considered pious (εὐσεβής) above all others.[194]

This portrayal unmistakably served the polemical purpose of deprecating the Anomoeans before an audience unsympathetic to their obsessive cleverness and lack of concern for Christian works.[195] It would, however, be rash simply to pass by this comment as an entirely unfounded accusation, for ancient polemic often contained a kernel, however small, of truth. Furthermore, I suggest that this alleged social attitude harmonizes with a particular cultural model that can adequately describe the Anomoean movement.

Even within fairly homogenous cultures, people seldom ascribe the same degree of worth to an identical set of cultural values. Thus we cannot assume that the vast majority of late antique Christians appreciated the kinds of "Christian works" cited by Sozomen to an equal extent,

191. Gregory of Nyssa, *Contra Eun.* 1.10 (Jaeger, ed., 1:25).

192. On Basil's activities as a benefactor, see S. Giet, *Les idées et l'action sociales de saint Basile* (Paris, 1941), esp. 419–23; B. Gain, *L'Église de Cappadoce au IVe siècle d'après la correspondance de Basile de Césarée 330–379*, OCA 225 (Rome, 1985), 277–87.

193. See Jerome, *De viris illustribus* 23. In the competition between Justin Martyr and Crescens, gluttony and the fear of death were two faults that discredited a philosopher from consideration.

194. Sozomen, *Hist. eccl.* 6.26 (Bidez, ed., 272–73).

195. See Gregory of Nyssa, *Contra Eun.* 3.1–2 (Jaeger, ed., 2:3–4) on people's natural suspicions toward those who were clever in speech. This was already a tired topos; see Socrates' claim not to be *deinos legein* in Plato's *Apologia* 1. See M. Girardi, "'Semplicità' e ortodossia nel dibatitto antiariano di Basilio di Cesarea: la raffigurazione dell'eretico," *Vetera Christianorum* 15 (1978): 51–74.

or that their definitions of a *eusebēs*, a pious person, necessarily agreed. The Anomoeans exemplified a culture of great upward social mobility, particularly in the persons of Aetius and Eunomius, whose status was achieved by the charismatic authority derived from their verbal skills. Their eristic abilities could only be validated in open contests with others: the agon was therefore a necessary part of their world.

The centrality of dialectical prowess to Anomoean culture could in theory find expression in venues less confrontational than out-and-out debates, but this redirection often did not occur during the pioneering generation. Subsequent generations usually took up the agenda of cultivating the aristocratic reserve and philanthropy expected of the upper classes. Further, it is likely that Eunomius and his associates did not sympathize with monastic ideals because the cenobitic form of Christian asceticism had been propagated in Asia Minor by their inveterate enemies, Eustathius of Sebaste and Basil of Caesarea.[196]

This convoluted conflict continued into the fifth century. In contrast to the orthodox responses in adversarial sources already discussed, the writings of Philostorgius present the Eunomian case.[197] Philostorgius' family, originally from Cappadocia, embraced the teachings of Eunomius when his father Carterius converted his mother, uncles, and grandfather from a Nicene theological position.[198] The family's self-conscious choice to depart from the stance of Basil of Caesarea, under whom Carterius' father-in-law served as priest, is a testament to the vital appeal of this sectarian alternative in fifth-century Cappadocia.

As a young man of about twenty, Philostorgius had been deeply impressed by Eunomius during a visit to his estate, to which he had retired from 387 to 390, and had eventually written a laudatory biography (now lost). Later the historian became a partisan in the losing battle against imperial orthodoxy. Indeed, his *Historia ecclesiastica*, characterized by Photius of Constantinople as an encomium of heretics,[199] omitted mention of many prominent figures who were unsympathetic to Eunomius' cause, including John Chrysostom, as if to impose on these figures the penalty of *damnatio memoriae*.

Refuting the charge that Eunomians harbored no love for good deeds or an ascetic way of life, Philostorgius expressed open admiration for certain ascetics who were not Eunomians. His glowing portrayal of

---

196. See D. Amand, *L'ascèse monastique de saint Basile* (Paris, 1949); M. Simonetti, *La crisi ariana nel IV secolo* (Rome, 1975), 411–18.

197. See G. Geutz, *RE* 20:119–22, s.v. "Philostorgius 3."

198. See Philostorgius, *Hist. eccl.* 9.8–9.

199. Photius, *Bibliotheca* 137–38.

Theophilus Indus, a monk supposed to have converted many inhabitants of India to Christianity, may be attributed to his appreciation for Theophilus as a seasoned traveler and as a successful missionary.[200]

Philostorgius followed this account by saying that Eunomians too were willing and able to convert others. He pointed to certain early fifth-century Eunomians who were known as rigorous ascetics and performers of miracles. Among his examples was Agapetus, a Eunomian who performed many *paradoxa erga*, miraculous wonders, causing witnesses to convert to Christianity.[201] We may reasonably surmise that this decidedly apologetic emphasis arose, at least partly, as a response to criticisms of Anomoeans reviewed earlier.

But Philostorgius' interest in asceticism did not extend to the institution of organized monasticism featured prominently in the accounts of Theodoret, Socrates, and Sozomen. The modern editors of Philostorgius' *Historia ecclesiastica*, comparing Theodoret's exaggerated reverence toward monks, propose convincingly that Philostorgius should not be expected to approve of an institution that received its impetus from Eunomius' enemies, Eustathius of Sebaste and Basil of Caesarea.[202]

Monks were drawn predominantly from the ranks of the *humiliores;* these unkempt souls found little favor with urban elites. Pagan disdain for illiterate black-robed monks was faintly echoed by the lay Christian Sozomen, an admirer of ascetics who nevertheless recognized their ignorance of civilized conduct, including the settling of differences. In his account of the Origenist controversy, Sozomen related that

> a certain terrible conflict ($\check{\epsilon}\rho\iota\varsigma$) reigned among the monks out of this. They did not think that they should persuade each other by conducting debates ($\tau\grave{\alpha}\varsigma$ $\delta\iota\alpha\lambda\acute{\epsilon}\xi\epsilon\iota\varsigma$) among themselves in an orderly fashion ($\grave{\epsilon}\nu$ $\kappa o\sigma\mu\tilde{\omega}$), but they turned to deeds of outrage ($\check{\upsilon}\beta\rho\epsilon\iota\varsigma$).[203]

The crude, barbaric "simplicity" of the desert monks did not commend itself to Philostorgius. Like Socrates and Sozomen after him, he was an educated layman who valued culture. Judging from his work, both his learning and his range of interests exceeded those of his anti-Eunomian counterparts. Philostorgius was conversant in biblical studies and was keenly interested in the intricacies of dogmatic controversies,

200. See Philostorgius, *Hist. eccl.* 2.6; 3.4–5.
201. See Philostorgius, *Hist. eccl.* 2.8.
202. Bidez and Winkelmann, eds., cxii–cxiii. See C. A. Frazee, "Anatolian Asceticism in the Fourth Century: Eustathios of Sebastea and Basil of Caesarea," *Catholic Historical Review* 66 (1980): 16–33; L. Lèbe, "Saint Basile et ses règles morales," *Revue Bénédictine* 75 (1965): 193–200.
203. Sozomen, *Hist. eccl.* 8.12 (Bidez, ed., 366).

which he described with a familiarity noticeably missing from Socrates' and Sozomen's narratives.[204]

Philostorgius possessed many other admirable qualities. Like Cosmas Indicopleustes, he was a sectarian layman well-traveled and well-informed about contemporary scientific theories regarding earthquakes, meteorites, astronomy, cosmography, and similar phenomena.[205] He also had some knowledge of medicine.[206] Allusions in the *Historia ecclesiastica* indicate a grasp of ancient learning comparable to that of the classicizing historians writing at around the same time.[207] Yet at heart Philostorgius was resolutely Christian, to the extent of composing refutations to Porphyry's attacks on Christianity.[208]

It is remarkable that the Eunomian interpretation of Christianity continued to attract strong devotion within the intellectual circles of an imperial state that had tried repeatedly to stamp it out through public humiliation[209] and stiff legal penalties, including the imposition of the *infamia* of an *intestabilis*, the deprivation of one's competence to make a legally binding testament.[210] Clearly, the intellectual rigor of Eunomian Christianity appealed to Philostorgius and many like him.

In Philostorgius the new wine had aged in the span of a generation. Skill in debate still figured significantly in his work, but the charisma of being *deinos legein* now stood as one among many virtues. The uncompromising sharpness of the first generation of dialectical questioners had mellowed into a culturally more established, and more rounded, form of *habitus*. It may not be too much to say that in Philostorgius a synthesis was achieved between the values of the Cappadocians and those of the early Anomoeans.

204. Philostorgius' *Hist. eccl.* 9.14, 9.14a; contrast Sozomen, *Hist. eccl.* 6.27, where the author explained that he neither understood well nor could easily explain the dogmatic controversies.

205. See Bidez and Winkelmann, eds., cix.

206. See Philostorgius, *Hist. eccl.* 3.15.

207. See R. C. Blockley, *The Fragmentary Classicising Historians of the Later Roman Empire: Eunapius, Olympiodorus, Priscus and Malchus*, ARCA. Classical and Medieval Texts, Papers and Monographs 6 (Liverpool, 1981), 86–94.

208. Philostorgius, *Hist. eccl.* 10.10.

209. According to *Parastaseis syntomai chronikai* 39, Theodosius II erected in the forum of Constantinople statues of Eunomius, Arius, Sabellius, and Macedonius, so that passersby could "shit, piss, and spit" on them. These were still visible in the eighth century.

210. E.g., *Codex Theod.* 16.5.17, 21–23, 25, 27, 31–32, 34, 36, 49, 58, 61, 65; 16.6.7. On the implications of the imposition of *infamia* on individuals, see A. H. J. Greenidge, *Infamia: Its Place in Roman Public and Private Law* (Oxford, 1894), 144–53, 186–99.

FIVE

MEDDLESOME CURIOSITY, MYSTIFICATION, AND SOCIAL ORDER IN LATE ANTIQUITY

Surveying the imperial city around the time of the Council of Constantinople in May 381, Gregory of Nyssa observed tense mutual testing throughout (κατά) the town. While conducting his daily business, he was forced to his deep dismay to brave a gauntlet of people openly challenging each other, and him as well, over precise theological beliefs. His classic response, recorded in *De deitate filii et spiritus sancti* (On the divinity of the Son and the Holy Spirit), deserves repetition here:

> Throughout the city everything is taken up by such discussions: the alleyways, the marketplaces, the broad avenues and city streets; the hawkers of clothing, the money-changers, those selling us food. If you ask about small change, someone would philosophize to you about the Begotten and Unbegotten. If you inquire about the price of bread, the reply comes: "The Father is greater and the Son is a dependent." If you should ask: "Is the bath prepared?" someone would reply, "The Son was created from not-being."[1]

This comic passage is customarily invoked to convey a sense of the widespread nature of theological debates in late antiquity,[2] but little note has been taken of the fact that the social categories referred to

---

1. Gregory of Nyssa, *De deitate filii et spiritus sancti oratorio* (PG 46:557).
2. See, e.g., T. E. Gregory, *Vox Populi: Popular Opinion and Violence in the Religious Controversies in the Fifth Century A.D.* (Columbus, Ohio, 1979), 3–4.

were from the Constantinopolitan "service industry." The *nummularii*,[3] among whom were the money changers, were avid participants in public theological discussions and enjoyed the dubious honor of being specifically cited in a 404 imperial edict forbidding such activities, in which the heads of the guilds and the owners of slaves were held responsible for their charges' trespasses.[4]

Aristocrats did not take kindly to a populus that failed to show the requisite deference.[5] In the charged environment of the 380s, "fighting words" were uttered not so much to declare one's membership in a particular doctrinal group as to convey a general challenge. The well-bred Gregory of Nyssa found such forward behavior on the part of the *humiliores* objectionable, even outrageous.[6] The popularized rivalry over theological matters manifested in public debates clearly upset the ancients' cherished ideal of social order (εὐταξία).[7]

In this chapter, I explore the relationship between certain late antique notions of social order and concern over the popularization of theological discussion. I argue that the phenomenon of curiosity expressed through debate, while disturbing to some, was a diffused social praxis that could not be effectively curtailed by the ad hominem appeals discussed in Chapter 4. Instead, interested parties mobilized various ideological pressures and strategies in attempts to curb rampant dis-

3. See *RE*, 17:1415–55 s.v. "*nummularius*"; R. Bogaert, "Changeurs et banquiers chez les Pères de l'Église," *Ancient Society* 4 (1973): 239–70; idem, "Les ΚΟΛΛΥΒΙΣΤΙΚΑΙ ΤΡΑΠΕΖΑΙ dans l'Égypte gréco-romaine," *Anagennesis* 3 (1983), 21–64.

4. *Codex Theod.* 16.4.5 (Krueger, Mommsen, and Meyer, eds., 1:2, 854):

> Si quis servos in hac sacratissima urbe possideat, eos a tumultuosis conventiculis faciat temperare, sciens se pro singulis servis, qui interesse conventibus interdictis fuerint conprehensi, trium librarum auri dispendio feriendum, servis videlicet puniendis. Quam formam in nummulariis ceterisque huius almae urbis corporibus volumus sub poena graviore servari, ut unumquodque corpus pro his, qui de suo numero conventus celebrare inlicitos detegentur, ad quinquaginta pondo auri solutionem multae nomine adstringatur.

In this context, it is not clear whether the *nummularii* mentioned were mint workers or money changers. See generally A. F. Norman, "Gradations in Later Municipal Society," *JRS* 48 (1958): 79–85.

5. See R. MacMullen, "Personal Power in the Roman Empire," *AJP* 107 (1986): 513–24; reprinted in *Changes in the Roman Empire* (Princeton, 1990), 190–97, 351–54. For a discussion of the notion of deference, see Pocock, "Classical Theory of Deference," 516–23.

6. Writing to the community in Nicomedia, Gregory (*Epistula* 17) asserted that the simple had no business meddling but should defer to their betters. See E. P. Thompson, "Patrician and Plebeian Society," *Journal of Social History* 7 (1974): 382–405, esp. 385, on the connection between the accusation of disorderly behavior and the nature of patron-client relationships. See also his *Customs in Common* (London, 1991), 16–96.

7. See Socrates, *Hist. eccl.* 2.2 (*PG* 67:185–88), on the alleged social disruptions caused by widespread disputing during the Arian controversy.

puting. Such efforts, I wish to suggest, included the mystification of the divine essence (οὐσία) and a concomitant insistence on communal prayer. To illustrate these connections, I will focus on two sets of public orations delivered in the 380s by men who felt besieged by excessive theological disputing: the Constantinopolitan "Theological Orations" of Gregory of Nazianzus, and the Antiochene sermons "On the Incomprehensible Nature of God" of John Chrysostom.

A DEBATE OVER THE *LOGOS*

The appreciation of the human *logos* (here meaning "discourse" or "rational principle") was a central issue for those concerned with rampant discussion. Before Constantine, many Christian apologists had taken pride in the fact that even uneducated and nearly illiterate Christians were able to discuss supramundane topics, hitherto the exclusive preserve of upper-class philosophers.[8] Now the *via universalis* had become problematic for many Christians. What shaped the acceptability of pervasive discussion was not so much the subject matter at hand but the outlook of those threatened by such activities. Whereas in earlier days those most affected had been outsiders such as the pagan Celsus, as Christianity encompassed a larger share of the population and a wider spectrum of society, many of those troubled became fellow Christians.

In a culture that gave privileged consideration to rational speech, human *logoi* furnished a basis for close mutual scrutiny through demands and counterdemands for statements of belief. Among Christians, the growing reliance on a precise technical theological vocabulary adapted from the Greek philosophical tradition meant that many were in a position to require from others a high degree of accuracy in the expression of their dogmatic views. To discrete terms and adjectives was imputed the greatest significance. In a language game that allowed for the clear articulation of nuances, people pressured each other to profess their beliefs in the middle of a controversial minefield, the features and contours of which were just beginning to be mapped.[9] With the devel-

8. See H. J. Carpenter, "Popular Christianity and the Theologians in the Early Centuries," *JTS* n.s. 14 (1963): 294–310.

9. An anxious concern to articulate the correct christological formulation figures prominently in the surviving writings of fourth-century Christians, who had to choose between the unpalatable extremes of outright dualism and complete identification of Christ with God the Father, while also harmonizing scriptures with certain tenets of philosophy. A full and useful treatment of these so-called Arian controversies and the Cappadocian contribution can be found in Hanson, *Search for a Christian Doctrine of God.*

oping sophistication of Christian theological speculation, there came to be less and less room for "fudging," because "the absence of ambiguity is a basic requirement for all scientific discourse."[10]

Even exalted late Roman emperors found themselves vulnerable to this exacting pressure. In an autocratic society with a state religion (after the Theodosian settlement had established an orthodox faith for the empire), it was important to assure his pious subjects that the emperor himself held the correct theological views. In the *Vita sancti Danielis*, the assembled citizenry demanded a clear profession of faith from Anastasius' predecessor, Zeno.[11] "Let us hear what your faith is, Emperor!" they shouted. The emperor's counselors advised him to yield, and he eventually did so for the sake of political expedience, signing a statement of orthodoxy in tradition.[12] Anastasius I (491–518) was probably the first emperor from whom a written profession of faith was demanded upon his accession.[13] This is not surprising, though, for he had been known as a Monophysite with rumored Eunomian leanings.[14]

Behind such demands for a profession of belief stood the potential threat of popular outrage and perhaps even violence, although the likelihood of high melodrama is often overemphasized in modern accounts. This aspect of late Roman social life rendered clear and forthright speech in doctrinal matters a risky proposition. In such a charged environment, guarded silence or deliberate obfuscation was often the safest course.

Basil of Caesarea was known to have deliberately refrained from publicly stating his theological position on the Holy Spirit for fear of needlessly antagonizing some and alienating others, not to mention running the risk of being driven out by detractors.[15] The prominent Meletius of Antioch at first held back from discoursing openly on doctrinal matters, preferring to devote his sermons to less problematic moral themes.[16] His tactic of theological abstinence appeared especially prudent in hindsight because, as soon as he broke silence and began to expound on issues of doctrine, he found himself in a "sticky situation," having alienated many of his listeners.

10. See Edlow, *Galen on Language and Ambiguity*, 8.

11. *Vita Danielis* 83, in E. Dawes and N. Baynes, *Three Byzantine Saints: Contemporary Biographies of St. Daniel the Stylite, St. Theodore of Sykeon and St. John the Almsgiver* (New York, 1977), 58. Greek text in H. Delehaye, ed., "Vita S. Danielis Stylitae," *AB* 32 (1913): 121–229, at 198.

12. *Vita Danielis* 84.

13. See J. B. Bury, *Constitution of the Later Roman Empire* (Cambridge, 1917), 28.

14. *PLRE* 2:78–80, s.v. "Anastasius 4"; and *Excerpta Valesiana, pars posterior* 78 (Moreau, ed., 22): "imperator volens . . . sectam Eunomianam sequi."

15. See Gregory of Nazianzus, *Ep.* 58.4–15 (Gallay, ed., 52.17–54.18).

16. See Socrates, *Hist. eccl.* 2.44 (*PG* 67:357A).

Even the most seemingly well-meaning audience could contain spies sent by one's rivals to exploit moments of weakness, or imperial inform- ers eager to challenge and to accuse. Gregory of Nazianzus summed up the anxiety of many late antique bishops when he exclaimed that, at a time when the entire cosmos had become a contested theological battle- ground, the dignity of the bishop's throne gave neither pleasure nor satisfaction.[17]

Though knowing one's audience was of supreme importance to would-be propounders of theological views, church leaders did not al- ways have this luxury, especially when newly appointed to a post in a strange city where the mood was uncertain or openly hostile. This was the case with Cyrus Panopolites, a famed Egyptian poet, high imperial dignitary, and appointee to the episcopal seat of the small Phrygian town of Cotyaion in the 440s.[18] When he arrived at his new see, he was greeted by a suspicious crowd, which compelled him to speak because they thought he was a Hellene, that is, a pagan. The audience immedi- ately demanded to know his theological views.[19] Cyrus reluctantly com- plied with their wish (which was probably expressed through acclama- tions), and allegedly declaimed as follows: "Brothers, let the birth of our God and Saviour Jesus Christ be honoured in silence (σιωπῇ), because by hearing alone he was conceived in the Holy Virgin; for he was the Word. Glory to Him through the ages. Amen!"[20]

17. Gregory of Nazianzus, *De se ipso et episcopis* 142–43 (*PG* 37:1176A): "τό τε θρόνου τοσούτου μὴ στέργειν κράτος, κόσμου ῥαγέντος ἐν μάχης μεταιχμίῳ."

18. See the biographical sketches by D. J. Constantelos, "Kyros Panopolites, Re- builder of Constantinople," *GRBS* 12 (1971): 451–64, and Al. Cameron, "Wandering Poets: A Literary Movement in Byzantine Egypt," *Historia* 14 (1965): 470–509. The alleged dis- patch of Cyrus to Cotyaion by Theodosius II was not so much a demotion as a potential death warrant: according to one tradition, the local populace had already lynched four previous bishops.

19. He was removed from office by Theodosius II because he was suspected of being a "Hellene," i.e., a polytheist; see Constantelos, "Kyros Panopolites," 454ff. See discus- sion on this point in M. and M. Whitby, eds., *Chronicon paschale 264–628 AD* (Liverpool, 1989), 78n. 261.

20. *Chronicon paschale* 450 (Whitby and Whitby, eds., 78). This "sermon" also appears in Malalas, *Chronographia* 14.16 (Niebuhr, ed., CSHB 17 [Bonn, 1831], 362); Theophanes, *Chronographia* 5937 (Niebuhr, ed., CSHB 41 [Bonn, 1839], 149); and John of Nikiu, *Chroni- con* ch. 84. Even if this report is not a verbatim record of Cyrus' speech, its illustrative value as the point of view of a redactor is significant. The speech became much more elaborate in John of Nikiu's *Chronicon* 84.56–57: "Know yet, my brethren, that this day is the day of the Nativity of our Lord and Saviour Jesus Christ. Let us honour him as is befitting, for it was of his own will alone that he was conceived in the womb of the holy Virgin Mary; for He is the primeval Word the Creator—praise be unto Him—together with His Father (supremely) good and the Holy Lifegiving Spirit, Consubstantial Trinity for evermore." Translation from the Ethiopic by R. H. Charles, in *The Chronicle of John, Bishop of Nikiu* (Oxford, 1916), 97.

Following this address, Cyrus was acclaimed by a delighted crowd and was given leave to live at peace in the city.[21] The difficult situation had called for a tactful solution, and Cyrus, by resorting to apophatic obfuscation, succeeded in extricating himself from a tight corner.

Timothy Gregory has argued that this pithy sermon was not "an expression of simple, uneducated Christianity" suggesting the futility of theological speculation[22] "but a clever—one might even say wily—statement of orthodox theology."[23] Yet Gregory's subsequent reasoning assumes that the Cotyaion locals were intimately familiar with sermons preached in Constantinople by the bishops Proclus and Atticus, by which they then understood Cyrus' own address.[24] This interpretation has merits, but is unnecessary. The significance of this widely reported story lies in the fact that Cyrus managed not to strike the wrong note with his audience. He succeeded in not offending his listeners by choosing to give a brief and seemingly orthodox statement, thereby avoiding the perils of a lengthy exposition. If his address had conveyed a deeper message, it would have eluded all but a very small handful of listeners or readers, then as now. His exhortation to honor Christ in silence ($\sigma\iota\omega\pi\hat{\eta}$) was Cyrus' response to the pressures of an endemic theological curiosity "among the quick witted and heterogeneous populations of the East"; it was perhaps the only way to break the cultural cycle of the agon, in which "opposition to a particular line of theological teaching could only be carried through by producing a rival system."[25]

As this vigorous verbal culture thrived in the cities of the Greek east, another development was gaining momentum and would eventually remold significant elements of the classical tradition to its Byzantine form. By the later fifth century, Byzantine mystical theology had reached maturity in the corpus of Pseudo-Dionysius the Areopagite.[26] These works

21. *Chronicon paschale* 450 and Malalas, *Chronographia* 14.16.

22. T. E. Gregory, "The Remarkable Christmas Homily of Kyros Panopolites," *GRBS* 16 (1975): 317–24. See also Constantelos, "Kyros Panopolites," 463.

23. Gregory, "Remarkable Christmas Homily," 323.

24. On his Marian, see *PG* 65:679–92; F. X. Bauer, *Proklos von Konstantinopel: Ein Beitrag zur Kirchen- und Dogmengeschichte des fünften Jahrhunderts* (Munich, 1919). On Atticus' sermons, see J. Lebon, "Discours d'Atticus de Constantinople 'sur la sainte Mère de Dieu,'" *Le Muséon* 46 (1933): 167–202; M. Brière, "Une homélie inédite d'Atticus, patriarche de Constantinople," *Revue de l'Orient Chrétien* 29 (1933–34): 160–80.

25. H. J. Carpenter, "Popular Christianity and the Theologians in the Early Centuries," *JTS* n.s. 14 (1963): 294–310, at 308.

26. Texts of the corpus: *De caelesti hierarchia* (*PG* 3:119–370; R. Roques, G. Heil, and M. de Gandillac, eds., *Denys L'Aréopagite: La Hiérarchie Céleste* SC 58 [Paris, 1958]); *De ecclesiastica hierarchia* (*PG* 3:369–584); *De mystica theologia* (*PG* 3:997–1064); *De divinis nominibus* (*PG* 3:585–736).

had intellectual roots reaching back to Proclus and Iamblichus[27] and perhaps to Philo of Alexandria,[28] or even to the Parmenides of Plato's dialogue.[29]

Pseudo-Dionysius' mystical construct was founded on a pyramidal hierarchy of divine and human beings not unlike the steep social order of the later empire. The *gradus* of this structure of beings was maintained by the clear differentiation of authority and power, including the capacity for knowledge. For instance, only a higher being could grasp the nature of reality sufficiently to correctly name a lower being.[30] The necessary corollary was that lower beings could only attain limited knowledge of those above them. Intermediary signs ($\sigma\eta\mu\varepsilon\hat{\iota}\alpha$) and sometimes even the agency of angelic mediators were deemed essential to securing knowledge of the divine world because the contemplation ($\theta\varepsilon\omega\rho\acute{\iota}\alpha$) of the higher order through human reason ($\lambda\acute{o}\gamma o\varsigma$) alone was a fundamentally impossible proposition.[31]

Though Pseudo-Dionysius is credited with the classic formulation of Byzantine mystical theology, it is important to scrutinize the historical and social circumstances that propelled this intellectual current to the forefront of attention.[32] To do so we must examine the function of apo-

27. The classic account is E. Norden's *Agnostos Theos* (Leipzig/Berlin, 1913); see discussion in E. R. Dodds, *Proclus: The Elements of Theology*, 2d ed. (Oxford, 1963), 310–13. See also S. E. Gersch, *From Iamblichus to Eriugena: An Investigation of the Prehistory and Evolution of the Pseudo-Dionysian Tradition* (Leiden, 1978). See now the impressively comprehensive work by Mortley, *From Word to Silence*, esp. 2:221–41.

28. See H. A. Wolfson, *Philo* (Cambridge, Mass., 1947), 2:113ff. Now see L. A. Montes-Peral, *Akataleptos Theos: Der unfassbare Gott* (Leiden, 1987).

29. See, e.g., Plato, *Parmenides* 142a, and discussion in Dodds, *Proclus*, 311. See also Mortley, *From Word to Silence*, 2:10–124, on the increasing importance of a discourse of silence; H. A. Wolfson, "The Knowability and Describability of God in Plato and Aristotle," *HSCP* 56/57 (1947): 233–49.

30. See R. Roques, *L'univers dionysien: Structure hiérarchique du monde selon le pseudo-Denys* (Paris, 1954), 154–67, 200–244; R. F. Hathaway, *Hierarchy and the Definition of Order in the Letters of Pseudo-Dionysius: A Study in the Form and Meaning of Pseudo-Dionysian Writings* (The Hague, 1969).

31. See, e.g., *De mystica theologia*.

32. In *Christianity and the Rhetoric of Empire: The Development of Christian Discourse*, Sather Classical Lectures 1986 (Berkeley, Calif., 1991), Av. Cameron refocuses scholarly attention on the relationship between mystical theology, the *via negativa*, and the emerging tradition of the veneration of iconic images. Some of the issues are also treated in her "New and Old in Christian Literature," in *Major Papers of the 17th International Byzantine Congress* (New York, 1986), 45–58. Cameron's insight into the connection between the rhetorical base of the cult of icons and the earlier Christian emphasis on the paradox of revelation shows a historical continuity between late antique and early Byzantine "thought worlds." She sees this development as an intrinsic *Tendenz* of Christian discourse, which she characterizes as relying heavily on paradox. Another historical dimension may be

phatic language in the formative period of the late fourth century, when
Basil of Caesarea, Gregory of Nazianzus, and Gregory of Nyssa gave
impetus to the crystallization of an ideological scheme effectively shield-
ing divine essence from human cognition.[33] Theirs was no mere passive
reception of earlier philosophical and theological traditions.[34] At the
time when these figures sought to formally delegitimize human *logoi* as
a means for achieving certain knowledge of the divine, they were involved in serious debates among Christians over the possibility of a
popular and rational theological discourse.[35] Gregory of Nyssa's "mysti-

---

added by examining how such a discourse was used in intra-Christian disputes. Cameron
herself has pointed out that this mystical theology failed to silence the *logos;* I argue that
the process of mystification should be seen not only in the area of *ekphrasis* or verbal
description but also in a dialectical relationship with the continued sway of rational
speech.

33. See Mortley, *From Word to Silence*, 2:169. Evagrius Ponticus served as one of the
conduits of the Cappadocians' mystical theology; see esp. N. Gendle, "Cappadocian Elements in the Mystical Theology of Evagrius Ponticus," *SP* 16 (1985): 374–84. Maximus
Confessor (580–682), the commentator of Pseudo-Dionysius, also drew heavily from Gregory of Nazianzus; see P. Gallay, ed., *Grégoire de Nazianze: Discours 27–31, Discours théologiques*, SC 250 (Paris, 1978): 345–46. On the influence of Chrysostom and Cyril of Jerusalem, see Roques, "Pierre l'Ibérien et le 'corpus' dionysien," *Revue de l'Histoire des Religions*
145 (1954): 69–98, esp. 90–96.

34. Daniélou states in J. Daniélou, A.-M. Malingrey et al., eds., *Jean Chrysostome: Sur
l'Incompréhensibilité de Dieu I: Homélies I–V*, 2d ed., SC 28 bis (Paris, 1970): 16: "En face de
cette erreur, les docteurs du IVᵉ siècle finissant vont être amenés à remettre l'accent sur le
caractère incompréhensible de l'essence divine, en précisant que, même, pour l'intelligence éclairée par la grâce, elle reste mysterieuse."

35. Thus we find that at the time when a mature mystical theology was articulated in
the works of Pseudo-Dionysius, there existed also widespread apprehension concerning
the adverse influence of "excessive" rational speech in theological matters. The contemporary biographer of Daniel Stylites (409–93), in his conventional hagiographical account,
explained the reasons he saw for disturbances in the Christian churches (*Vita Danielis* 90;
Dawes and Baynes, eds., 62–63; Delehaye, ed., 204–5):

> Through the Devil's working a tumult (τάραχός τις) once arose in the most holy
> churches, for tares had sprung up from vain disputations and questionings (ἐκ
> λογισμῶν καὶ συζητήσεων ματαίων). . . . These mischief-makers came to the
> holy man and tried to confound him with similar arguments, but he who kept
> the foundation of the holy faith unmovable and unshakable answered them
> saying, "If the question which you raise is concerning God, your inquiry (ἡ
> ζήτησις) is no simple or ordinary matter, for the Divinity is incomprehen-
> sible. . . . Let us abstain from vain and dangerous questionings and let us each
> consider that which concerns ourselves knowing that it is not without danger
> that we separate ourselves from our holy mother, the Church. . . . Therefore it
> suffices us to believe unquestioningly in the Father, Son and Holy Ghost. . . ."
> With this and similar counsel and warning he led their hearts away from soul-
> destroying questionings (τῶν ψυχοφθόρων ζητημάτων) and kept them unshaken
> in the faith.

cal" epistemology, for example, articulated in his *Contra Eunomium*, was specifically aimed at that bitter rival:

> For the simplicity of the teachings of the truth assumes that God is who He is, i.e., someone who can be grasped neither by any name nor by any thought nor any other conception, remaining loftier than the grasp of not only human beings, but even angelic and every supramundane being. He is indescribable, unutterable and higher than all signification through *logoi*.[36]

Gregory's opponents, especially Eunomius and his supporters, regarded human language as sufficient for divine contemplation and description. In their view, the names of things were created in reference to the nature of the things themselves (κατὰ φύσιν) and not just according to human convention (κατὰ θέσιν). This strong nominalist epistemology theoretically grounded a rational method for divine contemplation because one could move from relationships between names to relationships between essences. This epistemological scheme rendered even the essence of the Deity perspicuous to human intellect because knowledge of the divine conformed to a logical system of words, predicates, and propositions.[37] Thus, arguing on the premiss that the adjectival epithet *Agennētos* (Ingenerate) was the defining attribute of God the Father, Eunomius and others contended that the relation between the Father and the Son was deducible from the causal relation of their constitutive attributes in accordance with known rules of philosophical logic.

Given that the orthodox Christians sought to circumscribe human understanding of the divine in a controversial setting, their claims cannot be read as statements of detached reflection. A fuller understanding of the historical setting is particularly necessary because the mystical theological stance was championed not just by intellectual system builders but by preaching priests and bishops. To bring this argument into sharper focus, I will examine two sets of public sermons directed not just at the intelligentsia but at general audiences,[38] and which greatly influenced the development of mystical theology: Gregory of Nazianzus' *Orations* 27 through 31, and five of John Chrysostom's sermons on the incomprehensibility of God.

36. Gregory of Nyssa, *Contra Eun.* 1.683 (Jaeger, ed., 1:222).

37. Mortley, *From Word to Silence*, 2:157.

38. Daniélou, "L'incomprehensibilité de Dieu d'après saint Jean Chrysostome," *RSR* 37 (1950): 176–94, at 177, on Basil and Gregory of Nyssa: "Mais les deux Cappadociens s'adressaient à des théologiens. Chrysostome s'address au peuple chrétien. Il insiste donc moins sur l'argumentation savante et davantage sur l'attitude concrète."

GREGORY OF NAZIANZUS' "THEOLOGICAL ORATIONS" (CONSTANTINOPLE, 380)

Until the early 380s, the orthodox Christian community in New Rome had managed to survive, albeit in a precarious state, despite being eclipsed by other Christian groups. In 379, Gregory of Nazianzus, invited to lead this congregation, arrived to find a small and embattled group distinguished by its stubborn loyalty to the Nicene settlement[39] and living alongside more confident and impressive congregations, including those headed by rival Arian bishops. At the time, the Arians had established themselves in the main basilica of the capital and catholic Christians had to meet in a modest structure converted from a private house. A grander edifice was later built and dedicated on the site of the *domus* and named Anastasia to commemorate Gregory's tenure as the turning point for the rebirth of orthodox Christianity in Constantinople.[40] The process of "regeneration" did gain strength under Gregory, but we must not overestimate his immediate success. Although later traditions magnified the impact of his "patriarchate," Gregory's own feelings on the subject were mixed, and often colored by disillusionment and powerlessness.[41] To him, the bishop's throne represented not power or prestige but careworn anxiety.[42]

39. See Gregory of Nazianzus, *Carmen de vita sua* 585–94.

40. On the Anastasia church, see Socrates, *Hist. eccl.* 5.7, and Sozomen, *Hist. eccl.* 7.5. On the possible derivation of the name from Gregory's writings, see *Carmen de vita sua* 1125 (*PG* 37:1106). On the building and site, see R. Janin, *Le siège de Constantinople et le patriarchat oecuménique*, vol. 1 of *La géographie ecclésiastique de l'Empire byzantin* (Paris, 1953), 26–29.

41. For a characteristic Byzantine account (similar to those in Theodoret of Cyrus' *Hist. eccl.* and Evagrius' *Hist. eccl.*), see Nicetas' tenth-century *Encomium of Gregory of Nazianzus* 16; trans. J. J. Rizzo, *The Encomium of Gregory Nazianzen by Nicetas the Paphlagonian*, Subsidia Hagiographica 58 (Brussels, 1976), 49 (Greek text), 104 (English):

> Now because by Gregory's day pagan hair-splitting and error and their abominable rites and all impieties had been brought to an end through the work of divine apostles and the prize-winning heroism of martyrs, and because by that time the darkness of idolatry had been lifted and the true light of faith had shone on every righteous soul, the worst demons were no longer able to make war upon the orthodox by means of external foes, and so they set Christians themselves against each other (or rather they dragged off the more unsound and light-headed among us and by means of corrupt words caused them to dash against the orthodox) and ranged them opposite each other in bitter and hard-fought strife. The demons employed sophistry and insolence. Through the former they won over the less intelligent by specious argumentation ($\pi\iota\theta\alpha\nu o\lambda o\gamma\iota\alpha\iota\varsigma$); through the latter they attacked the weaker, terrified them with fear of their effrontery, and tried to make them submit to their heresies.

42. Gregory of Nazianzus, *De se ipso et episcopis* 142–43 (*PG* 37:1176A).

Yet this retiring man, who had assumed both priesthood and episcopate with ambivalence and who until recently had lived in the shadow
of his friend Basil of Caesarea, found renewed vigor in rallying his new
congregation.[43] He later reflected on these difficulties in his *Carmen de
vita sua.*

Gregory of Nazianzus eventually became known in the Byzantine
tradition as "the Theologian" (τὸν θεολόγον Γρηγόριον)—the fond epithet, firmly attached to his name from the mid–fifth century,[44] was a
singular honor in an age of accomplished Christian intellectuals and
theologians. Gregory's claim to this title was based on his so-called "Five
Theological Orations," composed in Constantinople and partly delivered there.[45]

In these sermons, the new leader forged with the fire of rhetoric a
set of dogmatic views about the Trinity, a subject he claimed had previously been neglected by his congregation. More importantly, he examined afresh the very notion of theology, articulating the qualifications of
a Christian *theologos* and defining the enterprise of philosophizing concerning God. He undertook these labors not out of a passion for philosophy but to develop a polemic against the Constantinopolitan enthusiasm for disputation over points of doctrine.

Thus from the outset his definitions of the theologian and theology
were restrictive and prescriptive. He began by proposing a strict limit
on the discussion of theology:

> Discussion of theology (τὸ περὶ θεοῦ φιλοσοφεῖν) is not for everyone, I
> tell you, not for everyone—it is no such inexpensive or effortless pur-

43. See Gregory of Nazianzus, *Ep.* 47–49. On the recent debate over the date of
Basil's death, see P. Maraval, "La date de la mort de Basile de Césarée," *REAug* 34 (1988):
25–38.

44. See Philostorgius, *Hist. eccl.* 8.11 (Bidez and Winkelmann, eds., 111–12); J. Plagnieux, *Saint Grégoire de Nazianze théologien* (Paris, 1951).

45. The Greek text I am relying on is Gallay, ed., *Grégoire de Nazianze*; English quotations from F. Norris, ed., *Faith Gives Fullness to Reasoning: The Five Theological Orations of
Gregory Nazianzen*, Supplements to Vigiliae Christianae 13 (Leiden, 1991). See also J. Bar-
bel, ed., *Gregor von Nazianz: Die Fünf Theologische Reden, Testimonia Band* III (Düsseldorf,
1963), and the still very useful text and commentary by A. J. Mason, ed., *The Five Theological Orations of Gregory of Nazianzus*, Cambridge Patristic Texts (Cambridge, 1899). Though
these orations are now collected as a set which coheres from a theological and dogmatic
point of view, it is important to note that they do not all belong to an original series of
delivered speeches. *Or.* 28 was included when the five were first published as a body; see
Gallay, ed., *Grégoire de Nazianze*, 7–9. *Or.* 31 is generally thought to have been composed
to refute supporters of Macedonius' position on the Holy Spirit, or perhaps the Anomoeans; see F. W. Norris, "Gregory Nazianzen's Opponents in Oration 31," in R. Gregg,
ed., *Arianism: Historical and Theological Reassessments* (Philadelphia, 1985), 321–26. On the
difficulty of dating the orations, see J.-M. Szymusiak, "Pour une chronologie des discours
de S. Grégoire de Nazianze," *VChr* 20 (1966): 183–89, esp. 186, 189.

suit. Nor, I would add, is it for every occasion, or every audience; neither are all its aspects open to inquiry (ἐν θεωρίᾳ). It must be reserved
for certain occasions, for certain audiences, and certain limits must be
observed. It is not for all men, but only for those who have been tested
and have found a sound footing in study, and, more importantly, have
undergone, or at the very least are undergoing, purification of body
and soul.[46]

The irritation evident throughout Gregory's orations is especially
noticeable here. With whom was Gregory conducting this indirect debate? Most scholars have assumed that Gregory's remarks were aimed at
the supporters of Aetius and Eunomius, that is, "heretics" and religious
outsiders. This is a fair and reasonable assumption in light of suggestive,
though inconclusive, ancient testimonia.[47] Also, the internal evidence of
a number of Gregory's theological arguments may suggest such an identification.[48] Finally, the well-attested presence in Constantinople of those
called Eunomians by their detractors is often noted in later histories and
in a number of imperial laws in the Theodosian Code.

However, I argue that the question of the putative audience to
whom Gregory addressed his admonition ought to remain an open

46. Or. 27.3 (Norris, ed., 218; Gallay, ed., 76).

47. At first sight, ancient testimonies appear to support this claim. Jerome, De viris
illustribus 117, referred to two otherwise unknown Adversus Eunomium libri written by
Gregory of Nazianzus. To Gallay (51–56), this suggests that orations 27–30 constitute the
"lost" works against Eunomius. In addition, Rufinus identified Or. 27 (his De Arrianis) as
directed against maxime Arrianos in his Latin translation of Gregory of Nazianzus' works.
But Jerome referred to Adversus Eunomium libri, as opposed to Adversus Eunomianos libri,
the proper way to characterize Gregory's orations, as in the later tituli of Or. 27. The Adversus Eunomium libri of Basil of Caesarea and Gregory of Nyssa specifically targeted Eunomius; this is not the case with Gregory's orations, which addressed neither Eunomius
nor his associates. An accompanying argument about the applicability of Jerome's testimony has been his citation of a De spiritu sancto by Gregory, which presumably refers to
Or. 31. Why then did Jerome not also mention a De filio, a De patre deo, and so on? Furthermore, while Jerome might actually have been present in Constantinople during Gregory's orations (see Jerome, Ep. 52; and also S. Rebenich, Hieronymus und sein Kreis: Proso-
pographische und sozialgeschichtliche Untersuchungen, Historia Enselschriften 72 [Stuttgart,
1992], 115–39) and could thus have been well informed concerning their audience, Rufinus
(De Arrianis, Engelbrecht, ed., 265) was unlikely to know anything about the orations
beyond the texts themselves. See A. Engelbrecht, ed., Tyrannii Rufini Orationum Gregorii
Nazianzeni Novem Interpretatio, CSEL 46, esp. 265.

48. The positions refuted by Gregory in many places—especially where he listed ten
"objections" and then proceeded to demolish them—reflect arguments commonly identified with Eunomians and their methods of questioning. But it is unclear whether these
positions were maintained by a self-styled Eunomian group. The question of how to relate
dogmatic positions and community is a difficult one. In this instance, were all people who
asked such "Eunomian" questions actually Eunomians?

one.[49] Nowhere in the orations do we find a direct reference to an enemy group defined by a common dogmatic position or by a religious label.[50] Instead, Gregory's target audience comprised those who delighted in public disputation of theological issues. Though Eunomius' associates may have formed part of this group, they hardly accounted for the entire category. Gregory would not have been so concerned if the group boundaries were so unambiguously delineated. I acknowledge the many connections between "Eunomians" and Constantinople in later historical works and imperial laws, but maintain that the process of labeling a "heretical" group is highly problematic. The question that instigated the controversy between Basil and Eunomius—do the names of things signify their essences?—might well be asked of doctrinal labels and social entities. Modern historians who rely overmuch on the compendious catalogues of doctrinal tags generated by heresiologists such as Epiphanius, Filastrius, and Augustine run the risk of confusing these labels with social groups.[51]

Though the associates of Aetius and Eunomius epitomized for many orthodox Christians the trait of excessive dialectical questioning in matters of the divine, they were not alone in exhibiting intellectual curiosity and posing theological questions. According to Gregory, his *Oratio 27* was addressed to those whose "cleverness is in words (πρὸς τοὺς ἐν λόγῳ κομψοὺς ὁ λόγος)."[52] He described them as "people . . . who not only have 'itching ears': their tongues, also and now, I see, even their hands itch to attack my arguments." Verbose and vain, they "delight in 'profane and vain babblings and contradictions of the Knowledge falsely so-called,' and in 'strife of words' which lead to no useful result."

49. On the broader context of these orations, see McLynn, "Christian Controversy and Violence," 15–44. The potential multivalence of these sermons is underscored in later manuscript illuminations showing the opponents as Macedonius and Apollinaris; see L. Brubaker, "Politics, Patronage and Art in Ninth-Century Byzantium: The *Homilies* of Gregory of Nazianzus in Paris (B.N. Gr. 510)," *DOP* 39 (1985): 1–14, esp. 4–5.

50. See the helpful discussion in Norris, ed., 85. Among the variants of the major MSS, the *titulus* of *Or.* 27 (see Gallay, ed., 70) indicated that it was written *pros Eunomianous*. It is, however, not known when these titles entered the manuscript tradition.

51. Socrates Scholasticus referred to Epiphanius' *Ancoratus* as a popular compendium of heresies in his own time. On Filastrius, see esp. his *Liber de heresibus* (*PL* 12:1111–302). The works of both authors were used by Augustine for his own *De haeresibus* (*PL* 42:21–50).

52. *Or.* 27.1 (Norris, ed., 217). MS. R of Rufinus' translation (*De Arrianis* 1; Engelbrecht, ed., 265) has the *titulus* "DE ARRIANIS QUOD NON LICET SEMPER ET PUBLICE DE DEO CONTENDERE," while MS. V has "De his qui indecenter de lege contendunt." The latter closely resembles the later title of *Codex Theod.* 16.4: "DE HIS QUI SUPER RELIGIONE CONTENDUNT."

Gregory did not call these people Eunomians or Anomoeans, or invoke any other doctrinal label. Was he simply being circumspect, or was he most concerned with their deeds and traits? These people formed a cohesive social group insofar as they participated in the distinctive praxis of disputing; they also exhibited certain common character flaws. Gregory characterized these objectionable men as eloquent and proud to the point of hubris.[53] Loquacious dialecticians,[54] they devoted their time and energy to

> setting and solving conundrums. They are like the promoters of wrestling-bouts (τὰ παλαίσματα) in the theaters, and not even the sort of bouts which are conducted in accordance with the rules (κατὰ νόμους) of the sport and lead to the victory of one of the antagonists, but the sort which are stage-managed to give the uncritical spectators (τῶν ἀμαθῶν) visual sensations and compel their applause.[55]

Like the promoters who moved wrestling from the palaestra into the public theaters (probably as a form of mud wrestling),[56] these "questioners" showed no respect for rules and boundaries proper to the game. And like a gymnasiarch, a devoted guardian of the dignity of the sport, Gregory railed against such activity spilling out into the streets. His fear that the social order was being upset by the improprieties of the questioners demonstrated a strong locative awareness of established boundaries:

> Every square (πᾶσαν ἀγοράν) in the city has to buzz with their arguments (τοῖς λόγοις), every party must be made tedious by their boring nonsense . . . Even women in the drawing-room, that sanctuary of innocence, are assailed, and the flower of modesty is despoiled by this rushing into controversy (τῇ περὶ λόγων ταχύτητι).[57]

For Gregory, the popularity of debate opened up a Pandora's box in a city already known for the fluidity of its social boundaries, especially given the fact that the new aristocracy boasted diverse backgrounds and religious affiliations. Wanton disputing completely overturned this

---

53. On Gregory's attitude toward eloquence in speech, see J.-M. Szymusiak, "Note sur l'amour des lettres au service de la foi chrétienne chez Grégoire de Nazianze," in *Oikoumene* (Catinia, 1964): 507–13; P. T. Camelot, "Amour des lettres et désir de Dieu chez saint Grégoire de Nazianze: les logoi au service du Logos," *Littérature et religion: Mélanges J. Coppin. MSR* 23 Supplementum (1966): 23–30.

54. Gregory addressed his imaginary adversary in *Or.* 27.8 as "O dialectical and loquacious one (ὦ διαλεκτικὲ καὶ λάλε)!"

55. *Or.* 27.2 (Norris, ed., 217; Gallay, ed., 72).

56. On the use of mud in ancient wrestling, see M. B. Poliakoff, "πήλωμα and κήρωμα: Refinement of the Greco-Roman Gymnasium," *ZPE* 79 (1989): 289–91.

57. *Or.* 27.2 (Norris, ed., 217; Gallay, ed., 72, 74).

fragile social order, even to the point of violating the sanctity of the female quarters![58]

Thus dialectic questioning, a critical intellectual activity to some, was to others a disruption of the community's solidarity and sense of decorum.[59] Questioners lured others into arguments by phrasing their questions (ζητήματα) in a way calculated to be *atopoi* and *paradoxoi*, shocking and controversial. The people who did so within a Christian context were not necessarily opposed to Gregory's orthodox theological formulations; they simply did not believe it inappropriate to discuss theology publicly using the koine of philosophical dialectic, that culturally sanctioned method of applying predicate and propositional logic.[60]

After lamenting this social trend, which he felt powerless to stop, Gregory rhetorically asked his audience: "Why do you conjure up a crop of dialecticians (διαλεκτικῶν ἀνάδοσιν) to attack us, like the Earth-born warriors in the old stories?"[61] The analogy between the dialectical art and Cadmus' warriors was apt: once carelessly sown (σπείρειν), provocative questions would, like the slain dragon's teeth, spontaneously generate fierce *spartoi*, mindless warriors who would fight to the death for no reason.

The bishop attempted his own analysis of the origins of this phenomenon, attributing it to idle curiosity and a spirit of meddling, and accusing the perpetrators of *polupragmosunē*. But meddlesome curiosity was in the eye of the beholder.[62] What was *hē polupragmosunē* to one late antique Christian might have been legitimate theological inquiry to another, and historians should be wary about taking sides prematurely.

In a fiercely competitive environment that valued innovation and agonistic excellence, differing claims to knowledge were a means of structuring a dynamic community of individualists.[63] Whether one ac-

58. On the perceived weakness and passivity of women, and the paternal protection of them in law and custom, see J. Beaucamp, *Le statut de la femme à Byzance, 4–7 siècles*, Travaux et Mémoires du Centre de Recherche d'Histoire et Civilisation de Byzance, Monographies de Collège de France 5 (Paris, 1990): 11–16.

59. See Gregory of Nazianzus, *Or.* 27.5. He pleaded that disputes among Christians be kept within acceptable limits (ἐννόμον). See also Gregory of Nazianzus, *Carmen de vita sua* 1225–59.

60. See generally De Ghellinck, "Quelques appréciations de la dialectique"; idem, "Quelques mentions de la dialectique stoïcienne," 59–67.

61. *Or.* 27.9 (Norris, ed., 223; Gallay, ed., 92).

62. See Gregory of Nazianzus, *Or.* 27.8. See also Gregory of Nyssa, *Contra Eun.* 2.12 (Jaeger, ed., 1:230).

63. See De Witt, "Organization and Procedure in Epicurean Groups," 205–11; Hahn, *Der Philosoph und die Gesellschaft*, 109.

cepted or tolerated these activities depended largely on one's social position and openness to competition. Claims to knowledge, especially to knowledge about the divine world, conferred authority on those who successfully established them.[64]

In terms of method, the *explananda* of this complex scenario are not why so many people were discussing the nature of God in a freewheeling fashion, but rather why some were particularly troubled by it and why they addressed the situation the way they did. In examining some of the strategies Gregory adopted to curb the phenomenon, we must note that, while the short-term effectiveness of his measures is far from clear, they made significant contributions to the subsequent Byzantine evaluation of the rational *logos*.

Credentialism

At issue between Gregory and those he criticized were the definition and validation of the Christian *paideia* that entitled one to philosophize authoritatively about the divine. Gregory imagined that the people he addressed styled themselves the true possessors of *paideia*, and that their misplaced smugness resulted from a deluded sense of their own accomplishments. He argued that the questioners possessed no credentials of serious education, that is, true *paideia;* instead they asked difficult questions, an ability easily gained through cursory study of doctrine and philosophy.

Gregory opposed those who acquired for themselves, and who also helped others to acquire, the ability to ask acute theological questions not through a systematic training in philosophy but through the use of manuals and other shortcuts. They circumvented a system of long and difficult apprenticeship that cultivated a student's sense of social responsibility. Gregory asked these questioners why they interfered so willingly in the lives of others:

> Why do you then try to mold other men into holiness overnight, appoint them theologians (χειροτονεῖς θεολόγους),[65] and as it were, breathe learning into them (ἐμπνεῖς τὴν παίδευσιν), and thus produce ready-made any number of Councils of ignorant intellectuals? Why do

64. See Gregory's reported comment in Jerome, *Ep.* 52.8.
65. Gregory here referred to the Christian practice of laying of hands in a highly ironic fashion. On this tradition, see C. Vogel, "Chirotonie et Chirothesia: Importance et relativité du geste de l'imposition des mains dans la collation des ordres," *Irénikon* 45 (1972): 7–21, 207–38; C. H. Turner, "Χειροτονία, Χειροθεσία, Ἐπίθεσις Χειρῶν (and the Accompanying Verbs)," *JTS* 24 (1923): 496–504, esp. 496–97.

you try to entangle your weaker brethren in your spider's webs, as if it were some brilliant feat?[66]

For Gregory, words were cheap when uttered irresponsibly. He therefore urged the adoption of *bios*, one's deeds or way of life, as a measuring stick for determining one's worthiness to philosophize about God. According to Gregory, the questioners were concerned only with words and cared little for the performance of "true Christian works" such as hospitality, fraternal affection, marital love, virginity, love of the poor, chanting of the Psalms, vigils, fasting, and prayer. In this regard, *praxis* compared favorably with vain discussions.[67]

In effect, Gregory was asserting that Christian philosophers must also be practicing ascetics. Purification of soul and body through meditation became a prerequisite for the contemplation of the divine, as they had been in the traditional training of philosophers. Because spiritual *askesis* or exercise required much leisure, the philosophizing of the divine fell to those who enjoyed *otium* or gentlemanly retirement:[68] "Δεῖ γὰρ τῷ ὄντι σχολάσαι, καὶ γνῶναι θεόν."[69]

Catechesis

No matter how persuasive his orations were, Gregory could not hope to triumph over this social tendency toward disputing by preaching alone. The true test came after the services when, in Christian homes, in the agora, and in the streets, people were confronted with "small questions" and tempted to enter into debates about the divine nature.

Because Gregory could not chaperon his listeners in all situations of controversy, nor realistically hope that they would hold on to the *pistis*, credal formulation, and refuse to enter into controversy, he furnished them with ready-made replies.[70] In *Oratio* 29, Gregory furnished his audience with precise statements, including syllogistic formulations, by which they could confound those who asked theological questions: "Yes, these are the replies one can use to put a brake upon this hasty

---

66. *Or.* 27.9 (Norris, ed., 222–23; Gallay, ed., 92).

67. *Or.* 27.1.

68. *Or.* 27.3. Leisure was a precious commodity. Gregory of Nyssa chided Eunomius for not having enough leisure to produce his *Apologia Apologiae* until many years after Basil of Caesarea had died; see *Contra Eun.* 1, preface. On *otium* and the formation of the gentleman in antiquity, see J.-M. André, *L'otium dans la vie morale et intellectuelle romaine des origines à l'époque augustéenne* (Paris, 1966).

69. *Or.* 27.3 (Gallay, ed., 76).

70. *Or.* 29.21 (Gallay, ed., 224): "ὅταν γὰρ τὸ τοῦ λόγου δυνατὸν προβαλλώμεθα, τὸ πιστεύειν ἀφέντες, καὶ τὸ τοῦ Πνεύματος ἀξιόπιστον ταῖς ζητήσεσι λύσωμεν."

argumentativeness (τὴν περὶ τὸν λόγον αὐτῶν ἑτοιμότητα καὶ ταχύ-τητα), a hastiness that is dangerous in all matters, but especially in theological topics. To censure, of course, is a trivial task—anyone so minded can do it quite easily."[71]

Gregory took his catechetical task seriously, and exhorted his audience to commit his words to memory. As Simonides of Ceos, poet and father of ancient mnemonics, had long ago pointed out, a well-ordered structure is salutary to retention;[72] thus Gregory tried to make memorization easier for his listeners by keeping his statements concise and by building in some basic mnemonic devices: "You want brief explanations here to avoid being swept away by their plausible arguments, and we shall group these explanations in numbered sections (εἰς ἀριθμούς) to aid the memory (διὰ τὸ εὐμνημόνευτον)."[73]

Even if Gregory felt confident that he could successfully fortify his community against the subversive potential of theological debates, he nevertheless lamented the situation. He wished that his catechetical instructions had not become necessary, because true Christians ought to find no delight in logical controversy:

> This is the answer we make perforce to these posers of puzzles (τοῖς αἰνιγματισταῖς). Perforce—because Christian people (τοῖς πιστοῖς: not just Christians, but the upholders of the πίστις) find long-winded controversy (ἀδολεσχία καὶ λόγων ἀντίθεσις) disagreeable and one Adversary enough for them. . . . But may he who "expounds hard questions and solves difficulties," who puts it into our minds to untie the twisted knots of their strained dogmas, may he, above all, change these men and make them believers instead of logicians, Christians instead of what they are currently called (πιστοὺς ἀντὶ τεχνολόγων, καὶ Χριστιανούς, ἀνθ᾽ ὧν νῦν ὀνομάζονται).[74]

Though he too made use of logical arguments, Gregory did not want to be confused with dialecticians, whom he characterized as radical, self-seeking individualists. Further, he reminded his audience that their

71. Or. 29.1 (Norris, ed., 245; Gallay, ed., 176).
72. See Cicero, De oratore 2.87.357.
73. Or. 30.1 (Norris, ed., 262; Gallay, ed., 226). The solicitude for those who might be tempted into a theological debate with adversaries took more and more concrete form. Anastasius of Sinai's Hodegos provides a series of scriptural quotes and physical representations (πραγματικαὶ παραστάσεις or πραγματικαὶ ἀποδείξεις) to enable the orthodox reader to hold his own in the face of challenges; see PG 89:40C–D and the excellent discussion in A. Kartsonis, Anastasis: The Making of An Image (Princeton, 1986), esp. 42–43. I wish to thank the author for bringing this to my attention.
74. Or. 29.21 (Norris, ed., 260; Gallay, ed., 222, 224). See also Or. 31.2, in which Gregory suggested that Christians ought to become bored with theological discussions and avoid them.

pistis remained their best argument and last resort: here the double va-
lence of the noun *pistis*, connoting both faith and credal formula, served
Gregory's point. Holding on to the *pistis* was particularly important because debaters were deceptive to the point of robbing the bible for prooftexts (ten of which Gregory cited and refuted).

Learning

Throughout his orations, Gregory conceded grudgingly that curiosity
and debate were a part of human nature. Activities expressing engrained human traits could not be stopped in toto, only diverted like a
flood.[75] For Gregory, certain kinds of discussions were less perilous than
others; to his restless Constantinopolitan audience he recommended
speculating about the nature of the world, or the worlds, a relatively
benign topic:

> Do you continue to speak even after these charges? Can it be that noth-
> ing else matters for you, but your tongue must always rule you, and
> you cannot hold back words, which, once conceived, must be deliv-
> ered? Well, there are plenty of other fields in which you can win fame.
> Direct your disease there, and you may do good. . . . [Y]ou wish to
> move in your own field, and fulfill your ambitions there: here also I will
> provide you with broad highways. Speculate about the Universe—or
> Universes, about Matter, the Soul, about Natures (good and evil) en-
> dowed with reason. . . . In these questions to hit the mark is not use-
> less, to miss it is not dangerous.[76]

In *Oratio* 28, Gregory specifically drew a connection between the
incomprehensibility of God and the natural world as an aide-mémoire
prompting the beholder to praise God. In fact, the strategy of launching
into an *ekphrasis* of the wonders of the cosmos was a deliberate diver-
sionary strategy used to counter meddling.

It is noteworthy that Gregory drew much of his imagery in *Oratio* 28
from Basil's *Hexaemeron*, a set of sermons about the six days of creation
delivered in Caesarea a few years earlier. This connection may explain
why the genre of *hexaemera* gained popularity from the late fourth century onward.[77] The rationale for introducing sophisticated scientific discussions of elements of the visible world, including man himself, into

75. See John Chrysostom's ideas on the power of sexual impulses and on marriage
as a concession to the frailty of human nature; discussed in Brown, *Body and Society: Men,
Women, and Sexual Renunciation in Early Christianity* (New York, 1988), 308–9.
76. Gregory of Nazianzus, *Or.* 27.9–10 (Norris, ed., 223).
77. F. E. Robbins, *The Hexaemeral Literature: A Study of the Greek and Latin Commentaries
on Genesis* (Chicago, 1912), 42 ff.

the ongoing Christian discourse had much to do with the concern over *polupragmosunē* as curiosity and debate about theology were thought to generate conflicts and divisions among Christians. The Cappadocians, pushing to restrict understanding of human capacities, insisted that if people wanted to grasp the divine nature, they must first grasp the nature of created things.[78] In a letter wrongly attributed to Basil, the author (probably his younger brother Gregory of Nyssa, who also wrote *De opificio hominis*) argued against those who claimed to possess the way and method (ὁδός and ἀκολουθία) for gaining divine knowledge (γνῶσις). Arguing that the normal progression of knowledge was from lower forms to higher, he fashioned a test for those who claimed to know the supramundane: "Now let him who boasts of having apprehended the nature of things actually existing interpret the nature of the most insignificant of phenomena. For instance, let him tell what is the nature of the ant. . . ."[79]

To know God one must first know his creation. This emphasis on scientific knowledge as a prerequisite (though not the only one) for speculation about the divine effectively curtailed debate. Elsewhere, Basil of Caesarea even more forcefully attempted to dampen curiosity concerning the divine essence:

> To know God is to keep His commandments. Surely you do not mean, then, that the essence of God should be investigated thoroughly? Or supramundane things searched out? Or the invisible objects pondered over? "I know mine and mine know me." It should be enough for you to know that there is a good shepherd who gave his soul for His sheep. The knowledge of God is comprised within these limits. How big God is, what His limits are, and of what essence He is, such questions as these are dangerous on the part of the interrogator; they are as unanswerable on the part of the interrogated. Consequently they should be taken care of with silence (σιωπῇ).[80]

Mystification

For Gregory, *polupragmosunē* or "meddlesome curiosity" was a moral flaw that ran the danger (κινδύνευει) of turning the divine *mustērion* into a *technudrion* or a "little finicking profession,"[81] a flaw that he feared was

78. See Basil, *Adv. Eunomium* 3.6 (*PG* 29:668A–B).

79. Pseudo-Basil, *Ep.* 16 (Deferrari, ed., 1:114–17). Cf. Gregory of Nyssa, prologue to *In Hexaemeron explicatio apologetica* (*PG* 44:65A–B).

80. Basil of Caesarea, *Homilia* 23.4 (trans. from Fedwick, *The Church and the Charisma of Leadership in Basil of Caesarea,* 59–60).

81. *Or.* 27.2 (Mason, ed., 3 n. 12); the phrase is also rendered as "mere social accomplishment" (Norris, ed., 217).

not curable by friendly persuasion.[82] Thus he represented the nature of the divine essence as a mystery ringed by taboos. Enumerating the necessary qualities of a theologian, he remarked that "for one who is not pure to lay hold of pure things is dangerous (οὐδὲ ἀσφαλές), just as it is for weak eyes to look at the sun's brightness."[83] Like the emperor Theodosius I, Gregory asserted that theological discussion was an activity fraught with danger:[84] failure to do justice to the exalted topic could incur divine punishment.[85]

In *Oratio* 28, Gregory employed the analogy of Moses' ascent of Mount Sinai to spell out the perils of divine contemplation:

I eagerly ascend the mount—or, to speak truer, ascend in eager hope matched with anxiety for my frailty—that I may enter the cloud and company with God (for such is God's bidding). Is any an Aaron? He shall come up with me. He shall stand hard by, should he be willing to wait, if need be, outside the cloud. Is any a Nadab, an Abihu, or an elder? He too shall ascend, but stand further off, his place matching his purity. Is any of the crowd, unfit as they are, for so sublime contemplation? Utterly unhallowed? —Let him not come near, it is dangerous (Εἰ δέ τις τῶν πολλῶν καὶ ἀναξίων ὕψους τοιούτου καὶ θεωρίας, εἰ μὲν ἄναγνος πάντη, μηδὲ προσίτω, οὐ γὰρ ἀσφαλές).[86]

The locus of the divine was a sanctum, a place both holy and inspiring of dread. It could not be approached (μηδὲ προσίτω) by those who were not worthy of its glory.[87] At the center of this vortex of holiness was a cloud endowed with numinous presence,[88] the composition of which no one could presume to know.

Note also the hierarchical principle implicit in Gregory's portrayal of the ascent. In the past, the prophets and high priests had constituted the privileged few worthy to approach the sanctum; in late antiquity, the bishops and priests were the chosen elite.[89] This new priestly caste coveted the control of the access to the divine: if they themselves could not reach the heights, then neither could those less worthy.

Throughout these orations, concern about the popularity of theo-

82. See *Or.* 27.5.
83. *Or.* 27.3 (Norris, ed., 218; Gallay, ed., 76).
84. Sozomen, *Hist. eccl.* 7.6 (Bidez, ed., 308).
85. See *Or.* 27.9.
86. *Or.* 28.2 (Norris, ed., 224; Gallay, ed., 102).
87. Aetius referred to God as ἀπρόσιτος in the *Syntagmation*, but by that he meant something quite different from the orthodox usage; see Wickham, "*Syntagmation* of Aetius," 565–66.
88. See also Gregory of Nazianzus, *Or.* 28.3 (Norris, ed., 225).
89. On the developing hierarchical order of the Christian church, see A. Faivre, *Naissance d'une hiérarchie: Les premières étapes du cursus clérical* (Paris, 1977).

logical discussion overlaid Gregory's ideas about the mystery of the divine essence. He made it plain that, by outstripping the traditional apophatic claims of philosophers, he deliberately increased the odds against speaking about God:

> To know God is hard, to describe him impossible (θεὸν νοῆσαι μὲν χαλεπόν, φράσαι δὲ ἀδύνατον), as a pagan philosopher taught—subtly suggesting, I think, by the word "difficult" his own apprehension, yet avoiding our test of it by claiming it was impossible to describe. No—to tell of God is not possible (φράσαι μὲν ἀδύνατον), so my argument runs, but to know him is even less possible (νοῆσαι δὲ ἀδυνατώτερον).[90]

Clearly, Gregory was not immediately successful in propagating his views, although eventually his stand prevailed. He made other appeals—for instance, reminding his audience that, with the victorious and threatening Goths roaming not very far from the imperial city, Christians ought to forsake divisiveness of all kinds,[91] including freewheeling theological discussion motivated by meddlesome curiosity.[92]

The unsettled state of affairs, and the rampant theological controversies that it aggravated, saddened a man who preferred to distance himself from the center of intrigues and power struggles. After his deposition in 381, Gregory retired to Cappadocia to a simpler and friendlier world, away from a city polluted by the din of disputation. He professed to have found peace at last in a retreat safe from "evil assemblies and arguments."[93] In a letter to his successor Nectarius (dated late 382)—a polite personal commendation bearing little news—Gregory reflected

90. Or. 28.4 (Norris, ed., 226). See Wolfson, "Knowability and Describability of God," 233–49.

91. See Or. 33.2. On the interconnectedness between church unity and barbarian invasions, see G. F. Chestnut, "Kairos and Cosmic Sympathy in the Church Historian Socrates Scholasticus," Church History 44 (1975): 161–66.

92. See V. Ehrenberg, "Polypragmosune: A Study in Greek Politics," JHS 67 (1947): 46–67; and A. W. H. Adkins, "Polupragmosune and 'Minding One's Own Business': A Study in Greek Social and Political Values," CPhil 71 (1976): 301–27. Adkins quite correctly notes that the accusations of πολυπραγμοσύνη constituted part of a social debate over the definition of and control over ἀρεταί. Thucydides used the same word, πολυπραγμοσύνη, to denote what troubled him about the Athenian radical democracy following Pericles. Both Thucydides and Gregory of Nazianzus felt that their notions of social order were being violated by the common people, who did as they pleased without the suitable guidance of those with παιδεία. What was common to Thucydides and Gregory was not so much the nature of the activities to which their uses of the word πολυπραγμοσύνη referred but rather their assumptions about social order or τάξις: both favored a stable social order over social competition; both loved εὐταξία and preferred ὁμόνοια over discord; both feared the influence of persuasive speech on people whom they thought ill-equipped to judge.

93. Gregory of Nazianzus, Carmen de vita sua 1780.

with satisfaction on the calm life he rediscovered outside the mael-
strom of Constantinople: "Affairs with us are as usual: we are quiet
without strife and disputes, since above all else we honor the privilege
of silence which is without peril (σιωπῆς ἀκίνδυνον γέρας ἀντὶ πάντων
τιμήσαντες)." [94]

Gregory had come to prize quiescent silence. In words that sum-
marized his long and bitter experience with controversy, he said, "It is
better to remain silent, than to speak with malice." [95]

JOHN CHRYSOSTOM ON THE INCOMPREHENSIBLE GOD (ANTIOCH, 386/87)

Gregory's advice and bitter experience were perhaps not lost on Nectarius, an eastern senator and Constantinople's urban prefect when he
was appointed orthodox bishop in 381.[96] Nectarius' episcopate lasted
considerably longer than Gregory's, ending with his death in 397. It is
attractive to imagine that his longevity had to do with his much ma-
ligned "mediocrity": having said and done nothing worthy of note, he
thus occasioned no controversy.

His successor John Chrysostom was not a man of few words, nor one
to adopt a stance of silent neutrality. Nicknamed "the golden mouth,"
he had delivered sermons on the subject of the incomprehensibility of
God, twelve of which are extant.[97] He had already aired some of his
views on the mystical transcendence of the divine essence prior to his

94. Gregory of Nazianzus, *Ep.* 91 (P. Gallay, ed., *St. Grégoire de Nazianze: Lettres*
[Paris, 1964], 1:112). Gregory wrote on behalf of his friend Pancratius; on the network of
patronage, see R. Van Dam, "Emperors, Bishops, and Friends."

95. Gregory of Nazianzus, *De se ipso et episcopis* 257 (PG 37:1184): "καὶ τοῦτο σιγᾶν
κρεῖσσον, ἢ λαλεῖν κακῶς."

96. On Nectarius, see Hauser-Meury, *Prosopographie*, 126–28, s.v. "Nectarius"; and
PLRE 1:621, s.v. "Nectarius 2."

97. The sermons *De incomprehensibili natura Dei* are in PG 48:701–812. For the first
five Antiochene sermons (PG 48:701–48), I refer to J. Daniélou et al., eds., *Jean Chrysostome: Sur l'Incompréhensibilité de Dieu*. Discussions of these sermons can be found in Kopecek, *History of Neo-Arianism*, 2:529–39; E. Amand de Mendieta, "L'incompréhensibilité de
l'essence divine d'après Jean Chrysostome," in *ΣΥΜΠΟΣΙΟΝ: Studies on St. John Chrysostom*, Analekta Vlatadon 18 (Thessaloniki, 1973), 23–40; J. Daniélou, "L'incompréhensibilité
de Dieu," 176–94; M. A. Schatkin, "John Chrysostom as Apologist: With Special Reference
to the *De Incomprehensibili, Quod nemo laeditur, Ad eos qui scandalizati sunt,* and *Adversus
oppugnatores vitae monasticae*" (Th.D. diss., Princeton Theological Seminary, 1982). On the
Nachleben of these sermons in the east, see F. Graffin and A.-M. Malingrey, "La tradition
syriaque des homélies de Jean Chrysostome sur l'incompréhensibilité de Dieu," in J. Fontaine and C. Kannengiesser, eds., *Epektasis: Mélanges patristiques offerts au Cardinal Jean
Daniélou* (Paris, 1972), 603–9.

stay in Constantinople, having done so while still a priest in Antioch (he was ordained in 386). It is likely that a number of his sermons on the incomprehensibility of the divine essence were preached in the small local churches of Antioch in 386 and 387, only a few years after Gregory of Nazianzus had delivered his so-called "Theological Orations" in Constantinople.[98] Other sermons by Chrysostom on the same topic have been associated with the time of his eventful tenure as patriarch of Constantinople eleven years later.[99] It is the former, Antiochene corpus that I examine in this chapter because there the basic patterns of arguments were established.

At the beginning of the first sermon addressing the topic of divine mystery, the priest Chrysostom commended his audience repeatedly for their fine, orderly behavior ($εὐταξία$) while their bishop was away.[100] Yet immediately after the abundant praise in the proem, he directed his address to those who speculated too freely about God's *ousia*. These individuals considered themselves in possession of complete *gnōsis*,[101] believing that they knew the divine *ousia* with precise exactitude ($μετὰ$ $ἀκριβείας$).[102] In response, Chrysostom argued that human beings possess knowledge only in part ($ἐκ$ $μέρους$).[103] Even the ancient prophets did not know God's essence *meta akribeias*.[104] In other words, Chrysostom urged his audience to adhere to a *via media*, steering clear of the extremes of complete ignorance and perfect *gnōsis*.[105]

To whom was Chrysostom directing this diatribe? He rarely made reference in his sermons to adversaries except in rhetorical fashion: "What do you have to say? ($τί$ $λέγεις;$)"[106] If he believed the pre-

98. See W. E. Eltester, "Die Kirchen Antiochias in IV Jahrhundert," *Zeitschrift für neutestamentliche Wissenschaft* 36 (1945): 251–86, esp. 272 ff.; see also C. Baur, *John Chrysostom and His Time*, M. Gonzaga, trans. (London, 1959), 31. The dates of the sermons are inferred from the Jewish feasts (*PG* 48:844D) that Chrysostom referred to in his sermons against the Anomoeans; see R. L. Wilken, *John Chrysostom and the Jews: Rhetoric and Reality in the Late Fourth Century* (Berkeley, Calif., 1983), 34–35. In 386, Rosh Hashanah fell on 9–10 September.

99. Untitled sermon "against the Anomoeans" delivered in Constantinople (*PG* 48: 795–802); *In paralyticum et de Christi divinitate, contra Anomaeos* (*PG* 48:801–12). See F. Van Ommeslaeghe, "Jean Chrysostome et le peuple de Constantinople," *AB* 99 (1981): 329–49.

100. *De incomprehens.* 1.1, 9–10, 13 (Daniélou et al., eds., 92–95).

101. *De incomprehens.* 1.168–69 (Daniélou et al., eds., 112–13): "οἱ γὰρ κατὰ τὸ παρὸν λέγοντες ἀπειληφέναι τὸ πᾶν ἀπειληφέναι τῆς γνώσεως λέγοντες." Here γνῶσις need not connote intimate, revealed knowledge but rather the ability to discourse on the divine nature by knowing the key attribute of the Deity, in this instance ἀγέννητος.

102. See *De incomprehens.* 2.471, 2.487, 4.222.

103. *De incomprehens.* 1.110 (Daniélou et al., eds., 106–7).

104. See *De incomprehens.* 1.195–96 (Daniélou et al., eds., 116–17).

105. See Daniélou et al., eds., 27–29.

106. *De incomprehens.* 1.272 (Daniélou et al., eds., 124–25).

sumptuous individuals to be exclusively Anomoean, he was reticent to say so.[107]

Chrysostom was not addressing strangers. He revealed that those who claimed *gnōsis* regularly attended his services because they enjoyed the oratory.[108] This flattering fact may have inclined Chrysostom to moderate his criticisms. He also said that if he were harsher and more pointed in his remarks, those whom he wished to persuade would simply stay away from church.[109] He thus avoided directly condemning them, instead underscoring the fact that he meant to inflict no harm but to heal their sick, diseased minds.[110]

Chrysostom exhorted the whole audience to exercise restraint in its dealings with the questioners, whom he proposed ought to be treated with care as if afflicted patients.[111] Right-thinking Christians might even attempt to approach their sick peers for conversation, with a view to saving them from the disease of error, like wise and competent physicians (οἱ σοφοὶ τῶν ἰατρῶν) who proceed with gentleness and forbearance rather than in disdain.[112] Yet Chrysostom cautioned that this exhortation applied only to those confirmed in the faith and therefore immune to contagion.[113]

The virtue of headlong flight was a constant refrain of Chrysostom's. Christians were to flee the craze of disputing: "Φεύγειν αὐτῶν τὴν μανίαν."[114] A Christian who was weaker (ἀσθενέστερος) in his faith was to flee (φευγέτω) the company of sick Christians lest he himself come to harm.[115] He must avoid any occasion for discussion with others and

107. Only in *De incomprehens.* 2.1, 2.13, 2.141, 3.10, 3.18. Kopecek again argues that Chrysostom's adversaries belonged to a distinct religious group; see *History of Neo-Arianism*, 2:529–31.

108. *De incomprehens.* 1.334–38 (Daniélou et al., eds., 180–81). On the relationship between the preacher and his audience, see also Chrysostom, *De sacerdotio* 5.1–8; J. Bernardi, *La prédication des pères Cappadociens: Le prédicateur et son auditoire* (Paris, 1969), ch. 4.

109. *De incomprehens.* 1.345–50 (Daniélou et al., eds., 132–33).

110. *De incomprehens.* 1.336–37 (Daniélou et al., eds., 130–31). On the use of the metaphor of sickness for "heresy," see Gregory of Nyssa, *Oratio catechetica* preface. On danger, pollution, and the social order, see M. Douglas, *Purity and Danger* (London, 1966), 94–113.

111. *De incomprehens.* 2.490–508, 3.346–50 (Daniélou et al., eds., 182–83, 214–17). The Anomoeans were associated with the sick because they were regarded as demonically possessed. See F. Van de Paverd, "Zur Geschichte der Messliturgie in Antiocheia und Konstantinopel gegen das Endes des vierten Jahrhunderts: Analyse der Quellen bei Johannes Chrysostomos," *OCA* 187 (1970): 179–83.

112. *De incomprehens.* 2.497–508 (Daniélou et al., eds., 182–83).

113. *De incomprehens.* 2.509–11 (Daniélou et al., eds., 182–85).

114. *De incomprehens.* 1.189 (Daniélou et al., eds., 116–17).

115. *De incomprehens.* 2.511–13, 522–25 (Daniélou et al., eds., 184–85).

must call upon God's mercy[116] rather than yield to the temptation of defending his beliefs. He must run away—"Φεῦγε μόνον, μὴ μάχου, μηδὲ πολέμει"[117]—even from established friendship (φιλία).[118]

Meddling versus Faith

Like Gregory of Nazianzus, Chrysostom expressed deep concern about a widespread tendency to meddle (περιεργάζεσθαι, πολυπραγμονεῖν) in forbidden knowledge of the divine nature.[119] For Chrysostom, *pistis* alone protected against such prying curiosity because it set boundaries without which an investigation could easily degenerate into an infinite regress of questions and responses:[120]

> For they invent and meddle (πραγατεύονται) in everything so that πίστις is excluded from the understanding (διάνοια) of their listeners. . . . [W]henever God reveals something, it is necessary to accept what is said in faith (πιστῶς), not to pry impetuously (οὐ περιεργάζεσθαι τολμηρῶς).[121]

Elsewhere, Chrysostom repeated these themes:

> While (μέν) you would find few people anxious (σπουδάζοντας) about faith (πιστέως) and political constitution (πολιτείας), most of them instead (δέ) are meddling (περιεργαζομένους) and investigating (ζητοῦντας) into questions which one cannot discover and which vex God.[122]

Such unchecked curiosity angered God and brought down chastisement (τιμωρία) in the same way that the disbelief of Zachariah was punished by the affliction of blindness.[123] The asking of how and why—like the use of sophistic devices, syllogistic reasoning, and the posing of *zētēseis*—was not conducive to advancement in the faith but rather obscured the anagogical path.[124]

Yet to advocate strict adherence to the words in the *pistis* was to risk the mistaken notion that merely grasping a credal formula, whether

116. *De incomprehens.* 2.532–33 (Daniélou et al., eds., 184–85): "φεύγωμεν αὐτῶν τὰς συνουσίας, εὐχόμενοι μόνον καὶ παρακαλοῦντες τὸν φιλάνθρωπον Θεόν. . . ."
117. *De incomprehens.* 1.379–80 (Daniélou et al., eds., 134–35).
118. *De incomprehens.* 1.378–79 (Daniélou et al., eds., 134–35): "φεῦγε αὐτῶν τὰς φιλίας, ἄν βλάπτωσι."
119. See index in Daniélou et al., eds., 354–55.
120. See Chrysostom, *In Acta apostolorum* 23.4 (*PG* 60:183).
121. *De incomprehens.* 2.75–80 (Daniélou et al., eds., 148–49).
122. *De sacerdotio* 4.5; A.-M. Malingrey, ed., *Jean Chrysostome: Sur le Sacerdoce (dialogue et homélie),* SC 272 (Paris 1980), 260–63.
123. See esp. *De incomprehens.* 2.141–48 (Daniélou et al., eds., 154–55). This issue is the main theme of the second sermon.
124. *Hom. in Epistulam ad Ephesios* 24.2 (*PG* 62:171). On Chrysostom's view on "curiosity," see his *Ad eos qui scandalizati sunt* (*PG* 52:479–528).

orthodox or not, made one a Christian.[125] Chrysostom faulted the questioners for paying too little attention to correct living, which he thought ought to accompany the profession of the correct *pistis*.[126] Virtue was to be pursued by the performance of deeds (τὰ ἔργα), not by arguing:[127] exercise of reason wrought social fractiousness, whereas charity fostered harmony.[128] Chrysostom urged Christians to become "fools for the sake of Christ" (I Corinthians 4:10): "Restrain our own reasoning, and empty our mind of secular learning, in order to provide a mind swept clean for the reception of the divine words."[129]

At another place, Chrysostom explained why *pistis* provided a safe haven: "Ἄρα πίστις βεβαιοῖ· οὐκοῦν λογισμοὶ σαλεύσιν· ἐναντίον γὰρ ἡ πίστις λογισμῷ."[130] Here, as in Gregory of Nazianzus' orations and elsewhere, the multivalence of the word *pistis* as either an attitude of holy submission or a professed creed must be kept in mind.

Chrysostom, again like Gregory of Nazianzus, was keenly aware that the value of his exhortations rested on events that were to take place beyond the walls of the church, where his listeners faced challenging questions in the course of their daily lives.[131] He too provided solutions to a number of especially popular conundrums in phrases conducive to easy memorization. And he too apologized for arguing back, explaining that the verbal weapons he provided were hurtful only to those who refused to demonstrate goodwill and were already inclined to contentiousness.[132]

The Incomprehensible God and Liturgical Worship

The priest Chrysostom tried every available means to combat rampant theological discussion. He elaborated the idea that knowledge of the

125. See *De incomprehens.* 11.7 (*PG* 48:797).

126. See *De incomprehens.* 10.57 (*PG* 48.793).

127. Chrysostom, *De incomprehens.* 1.32–81 (Daniélou et al., eds., 96–103); idem, *Hom. in Matthaeum* 64.4 (*PG* 58:614): "τὴν ἀπὸ τῶν ἔργων ἀρετὴν ἐπιζητοῦσι. περὶ μὲν γὰρ δογμάτων ὀλιγάκις διαλέγεται."

128. *Hom. in Epistulam ad Colossenes* 5.3 (*PG* 62:335). On the importance of both faith and works for Chrysostom, see *Hom. in Matthaeum* 64.4 (*PG* 58:614–15); *Hom. in Iohann.* 63.3 (*PG* 59:352).

129. See *De incomprehens.* 2.70–75. See also Chrysostom, *Homilia in illud, vidi dominum sedentem in solio excelso* 4.3 (*PG* 56:123) on Peter the apostle as a simple man who silenced sophisticated Greek philosophers with divine help.

130. *Hom. in Epistulam ad Hebraeos* 33.3 (*PG* 63:229): "ἄρα πίστις βεβαιοῖ· οὐκοῦν λογισμοὶ σαλεύσιν· ἐναντίον γὰρ ἡ πίστις λογισμῷ."

131. See Chrysostom, *Hom. in Iohann.* 23.1 (*PG* 59:137–38).

132. *De incomprehens.* 2.6–7. On the value of *logos* for checking "specious reasonings," see Chrysostom, *De sacerdotio* 4.3–5; Baur, *John Chrysostom*, 1:334.

mysterious divine essence was beyond the limits of human cognition.[133] Only the Son knew the Father; other divine beings (οἱ ἄνω δυνάμεις), including angels, did not have complete knowledge of God's *ousia*.[134] In this present context, this statement can only be read as an attempt to deflect curiosity from the subject and to deny competence from people who might otherwise be tempted to discuss and debate the issues.[135]

Chrysostom presented a paradox to strengthen his case: while angels and other divine beings superior to human beings collectively glorified and worshiped God with fear and trembling, men below impiously tried to pry into the secrets of the divine.[136] Chrysostom painted a striking, hyperbolic contrast:

> Did you see how great is the holy dread in heaven and how great the arrogant presumption (καταφρόνησις) here below? The angels in heaven give him glory; these on earth carry on meddlesome investigations (περιεργάζονται). In heaven they honor and praise him; on earth we find curious busybodies (πολυπραγμονοῦσιν). In heaven they veil their eyes; on earth the busybodies are obstinate (φιλονεικοῦσιν) and shamelessly try to hold their eyes fixed on his ineffable glory. Who would not groan, who would not weep for them because of this ultimate madness and folly of theirs?[137]

For Chrysostom, the only proper attitude to assume when approaching the divine presence was humility to the point of fear and trembling.[138] At a minimum, he expected an appropriate spirit of deference before God's superior holiness and wisdom.

A significant aspect of this viewpoint was the implicit comparison between the clergy and the mediating angels,[139] whose exalted status insulated them from the criticism of those below.[140] Priests, like angels,

---

133. See, e.g., J. C. McLelland, *God the Anonymous: A Study in Alexandrian Philosophical Theology*, Patristic Monograph Series 4 (Philadelphia, 1976), 149, on John Chrysostom's emphasis on the inability of human language to capture God's essence: "Apophatic theology is used here as a weapon against the Arian revival of Eunomius."

134. See *De incomprehens.* 1.302 ff.

135. See *De incomprehens.* 1.308–27; see 3–4 passim.

136. See *De incomprehens.* 1.308–12 (Daniélou et al., eds., 126–29). The angelic imagery is also present in his homily against the Judaizers; see *Adversus Judaeos* 1.1. Using angelic analogy to justify Christian conduct was a common ploy of Chrysostom's. In *PG* 56:99, he invoked the angelic hosts to argue against people who frequently attended theatrical plays and dances; see J. Dumortier, "Une assemblée chrétienne au IVᵉ siècle," *MSR* 29 (1972): 15–22.

137. *De incomprehens.* 1.321–27 (Daniélou et al., eds., 128–29), trans. P. Harkins, ed., *St. John Chrysostom On the Incomprehensible Nature of God* (Washington, D.C., 1982), 66.

138. See *De incomprehens.* 3.338–52.

139. On priests as angelic mediators, see Chrysostom, *De sacerdotio* 3.4–6.

140. Chrysostom, *De sacerdotio* 5.5. See H. Chadwick on the silent bishop as an emulator of the Deity in "The Silence of Bishops in Ignatius," *HTR* 43 (1950): 169–72.

mediated between God and ordinary mortals, making possible the spiritual ascent by stages of the faithful.[141]

The dread inspired by the numinous presence was a commonplace in Chrysostom's sermons.[142] Along with other fourth-century leaders such as Cyril of Jerusalem, he gave this theme—rooted in speculation about the heavenly temple in the Jewish tradition—decisive impetus in Christian eucharistic services.[143]

In the face of the overwhelmingly unknowable divine presence, human beings were not entirely bereft of response. They could react most fittingly through common worship. Chrysostom stressed the importance of group prayer and worship, which angels and divine beings continually rendered to God, and which moreover beautifully exemplified communal harmony. The edifying image of humble, united worship was a potent antidote to arrogant, individual questioning.

A DISCIPLINED *LOGOS?*

Had Gregory of Nazianzus delivered his "Theological Orations" after Theodosius I issued his edict *cunctos populos* to the people of Constantinople on 28 February 380, he would have received the authority to take concrete actions against his theological rivals, perhaps even to take possession of their churches with the help of the imperial soldiery.[144] But even the state's coercive powers would not have helped Gregory realize these goals[145] because the questioners were not confined to a rival group with a distinct institutional presence.[146] Gregory's complaint was addressed to an all-pervasive social practice: even rescripts against specific

141. See Pseudo-Dionysius, *De caelesti hierarchia* 4.3 (*PG* 3:179–82). In contrast, see the rabbinic tradition that featured angels who resisted human ascent in P. Schäfer, *Rivalität zwischen Engeln und Menschen: Untersuchungen zur rabbinischen Engelsvorstellung* (Berlin/New York, 1975).

142. See Daniélou et al., eds., 30–39.

143. See J. Quasten, "Mysterium Tremendum: Eucharistische Frömmigkeitsauffassungen des vierten Jahrhunderts," in A. Mayer, J. Quasten, B. Neunheuser, eds., *Vom christlichen Mysterium: Gesammelte Arbeiten zum Gedächtnis von Odo Costel* (Düsseldorf, 1951), 65–75; idem, "The Liturgical Mysticism of Theodore of Mopsuestia," *Theological Studies* 15 (1954): 431–39.

144. *Codex Theod.* 16.1.2 (Krueger, Mommsen, and Meyer, eds., 1.2, 833).

145. On the dangers and difficulties of applying coercion, see Gregory of Nazianzus, *Or.* 33; *Carmen de vita sua* 1290–1304 (*PG* 37:1117–18).

146. On the use of persuasion and compulsion in Christian preaching, see *Carmen de vita sua* 1186–1208, 1290–1304, esp. 1293–94 (*PG* 37:1118): "οὐ γὰρ κατείργειν, ἀλλὰ πείθειν, ἔννομον εἶναι, νομίζω."

"heresies" obtained from well-disposed emperors were of little use in putting an end to curiosity and debate. The only maneuver he could make in this regard was to label the phenomenon as categorically and exclusively Eunomian, and hence heretical, regardless of whether all who posed questions saw themselves as Eunomians.

It is instructive to contrast the concreteness of the concern about debate with the abstract and moral—one might even say ideological— way in which the issue was argued. Ideological mystification was suited to those in a weak position to enforce their will, that is, those whose prescriptive vision was not matched by their real disposable resources.

Gregory's orations, Chrysostom's sermons, and the phenomena discussed in Chapter 4 illustrate the porosity of the boundaries that separated the so-called questioners from orthodox Christians. For some, the issue at hand was the reality of constant "defections": to secure the border regions against "attacks" and "subversion," and to shore up the gradual erosion of dogmatic solidarity, Chrysostom used the only effective means he possessed, ideological mystification. Elsewhere, he rhetorically demonized Jews and Judaism when he found himself powerless to stop his parishioners from attending synagogue services. He likewise preached against public spectacles or *theōria* when sermon attendance dropped because of the theater and hippodrome.

Although the Byzantine tradition later bestowed great authoritative status on Gregory and Chrysostom, their sermons initially were issued from a position of weakness. Many of the advocates of divine mystery were preaching priests and bishops engaged in the task of maintaining the day-to-day solidarity of communities against the threats of those whose claims to knowledge created a two-tiered system of elites and the masses.[147] As a form of *sermo humilis*, the mystification of the divine essence helped to delegitimize a brand of discursive reasoning considered socially divisive.[148] The philosopher Themistius, according to

147. See J. Lebreton, "Le désaccord de la foi populaire et la théologie savantes dans l'Église chrétienne du IIIᵉ siècle," *RHE* 19 (1923): 481–506; 20 (1924): 5–37; P. R. L. Brown, "Pelagius and His Supporters: Aims and Environment," *JTS* n.s. 19 (1968): 93–114; reprinted in *Religion and Society in the Age of Saint Augustine* (London, 1977), 183–207, on the spiritual elitism of the Pelagian movement and its perceived social threat.

148. Not all claims stressing the inability of human language to describe or define divine essence reflected the concerns articulated by Gregory of Nazianzus and John Chrysostom, and many extended their consideration beyond the theological. Ephraem Syrus' objections to Anomoean Arianism has been studied with admirable results by P. Bruns, "Arius hellenizans?—Ephräm der Syrer und die neoarianischen Kontroversen seiner Zeit: Ein Beitrag zur Rezeption des Nizänums im syrischen Sprachraum," *ZKG* 101 (1990): 21–57. Bruns' study is based mostly on Ephraem's *Sermones de fide* (CSCO.SS 88/89) and his *Hymni de fide* (CSCO.SS 73/74). Bruns' statement that Ephraem's rejection of Arius was

Sozomen, expressed the matter somewhat differently.[149] In an oration before the Arian emperor Valens, he argued that the Deity had made Himself not so easily known so that people, robbed of clear understanding, would respond with pious fear and the glorification of divine greatness and providence.

Ideological inculcation was superior to physical coercion because an internalized belief need not be policed from without. A transcendent God shrouded in mystery naturally deflected meddlesome curiosity, because when people realized that they could not know Him they would stop inquiring. Such a belief also helped to preserve social solidarity and order by undermining the legitimacy of any differential claim to precise knowledge about the divine essence; as Gibbon well knew, "Where the subject lies so far beyond our reach, the difference between the highest and the lowest of human understandings may indeed be calculated as infinitely small."[150] Henceforth, claims to virtue and consideration within Christian communities were to be based on the hierarchical factors of birth and ecclesiastical rank.

By emphasizing the vertical gulf between man and his creator, human weakness could be turned into the social glue of earthly communities. The visible manifestation of this came through in liturgical worship, art, and architecture, where the contemplation or *theōria* of the divine was displaced by a communal *theōria* of the created cosmos.[151]

"grounded" on a sense of the unknown God (48) raises the hermeneutical question of whether a historian should accept given reasons as the *only* or the *most fundamental* motivating factors. Further, he finds in Ephraem's strategy of mystification the same connection between the rejection of rationalism and emphasis on worship: "Gerade die Anbetung Christi wird auch in der syrischen Kirche zum Unterscheidungskriterium zwischen Arianismus und Orthodoxie" (52). Finally, he argues (53) that Ephraem's attitude may contain a "nationalist" element in the sense that rejection of the extreme (rational) Arianism represented by Anomoeanism is also a rejection of Hellenism. This insight shows how the Syrian church was distinguishing itself from Greek Christianity partly by mystifying the divine. However, we should remind ourselves that, within the contexts of Nisibis (*Hymni de fide*) and Edessa (*Sermones de fide*), a devaluation of the Greek λόγος was as likely to be at once a theological, national, and political statement, given the fact that the ruling aristocracies were Greek-speaking or bilingual. On possible contacts between Ephraem and the Cappadocians, see O. Rousseau, "Le rencontre de saint Éphrem et de saint Basile," *L'Orient Syrien* 2 (1957): 261–84; 3 (1958): 73–90.

149. Sozomen, *Hist. eccl.* 6.36.

150. Gibbon, *Decline and Fall*, pt. 1: 680–81.

151. See Gregory of Nyssa, *Oratio laudatoria sancti ac magni martyris Theodori* (PG 46:757D) on images as γραφὴ σιωπῶσα. See also E. Kitzinger, "The Cult of Images in the Age before Iconoclasm," *DOP* 8 (1954): 83–150; Basil's *De spiritu sancto* was later used to defend the iconodule position (91), as were writings of the other two Cappadocians, though their interest in the value of icons was strictly incidental (135).

The Cappadocians' insistence on the value of the visible universe for divine contemplation arose from a specific controversial situation, but later led to the worship of icons, which were believed to have anagogical value, especially for the illiterate.[152]

In the high politics and theology of late antiquity, the loci of the exalted increasingly receded from the grasp of the common man. The inner sanctum of the heavenly temple was described with the same language as was applied to the innermost chambers of the palace (guarded by soldiers from the imperial *scholae*) in the so-called "Vision of Dorotheus" contained in Papyrus Bodmer 29.[153] God, like Rome and the emperor himself, was presented as the object of worship and not as the object of theoretical speculation.[154] When access to God and emperor became something only granted through the condescension (συγκατά-βασις) of the powerful[155] and not through the strivings of people from below, *adoratio* became the only fitting response. This emphasis on communal worship as the only appropriate reaction to the incomprehensible divine presence was echoed in one of Cyril of Jerusalem's catechetical lectures:

> For we explain not what God is but candidly confess that we have not exact knowledge concerning him. For in what concerns God to confess our ignorance is the best knowledge. There "magnify the Lord with me, and let us exalt His Name together (Psalm 33:4)"—all of us together, for one alone is hopeless.[156]

"All of us together, for one alone is hopeless." The congregation acted out its appointed role in the liturgical service by following and

152. Basil's *De spiritu sancto* and Gregory of Nyssa's *De opificio hominis* were used by John of Damascus to justify the use of images; see *De imaginibus oratio* 1 (PG 94:1231–84). On the development from scriptural θεωρία to architectural θεωρία, see K. McVey, "The Domed Church as Microcosm: Literary Roots of an Architectural Symbol," *DOP* 37 (1983): 91–121.

153. See A. H. M. Kessels and P. W. Van der Horst, "The Vision of Dorotheus (Pap. Bodmer 29)," *VChr* 41 (1987): 313–59; J. Bremmer, "An Imperial Palace Guard in Heaven: The Date of the Vision of Dorotheus," *ZPE* 75 (1988): 82–88. Bremmer convincingly argues for a date of middle to late fourth century.

154. The lack of theorizing about emperor and empire in late antiquity is noted in connection with the political works of Themistius; see the study by G. Dagron, "L'empire romain d'orient au IVᵉ siècle et les traditions politiques de l'hellénisme: le témoignage de Thémistios," *Travaux et Mémoires du Centre de Recherches d'Histoire et Civilisation du Byzance* 3 (Paris, 1968), 1–242.

155. See Chrysostom, *De incomprehens.* 3.163–66.

156. Cyril of Jerusalem, *Catecheses* 6.2. Cyril digested the theology of Athanasius and Basil; see H. A. Wolfson, "Philosophical Implications of the Theology of Cyril of Jerusalem," *DOP* 11 (1957): 3–19. Cyril's theological reputation was a mixed one; see J. Lebon, "La position de saint Cyrille de Jérusalem dans les luttes provoquées par l'arianisme," *RHE* 20 (1924): 181–210, 357–86; R. C. Gregg, "Cyril of Jerusalem and the Arians," in R. C. Gregg, ed., *Arianism* (Cambridge, Mass., 1985), 85–109.

responding to the words of the celebrant, its unity of purpose manifest in its unity of action.

The intellectual or philosophical *theōria* by which individuals strove to grasp the divine had given way to a more edifying communal *theōria*. Christians rallied unreservedly behind their bishops, worshiping God in humility, together offering up prayers, chants of antiheretical doxologies, and burnt incense. Beyond the narrow walls of the church, in the broader world still ruled over by *tychē* rather than by divine providence, other forms of *theōria* flourished, resoundingly deaf to Christian protestations. There charioteers skillfully piloted their horses around the *spina* in the hippodrome, cheered on by energetic and devoted crowds, and the spectacles of the theater remained a staple of public life.[157] There too the rational *logos* lingered, marginalized, undefeated.

157. See Chrysostom, *De incomprehens.* 11.1 (*P6* 48:796–99). The Anastasia Church stood in the center of Constantinople so that the roaring crowds of the hippodrome would have been clearly audible to the preacher and his audience, perhaps even as Chrysostom delivered his sermons on the incomprehensible God.

SIX

"NON IN SERMONE REGNUM DEI": FIFTH-CENTURY VIEWS ON DEBATE AT NICAEA

The later fourth-century concerns over dialectical debate were inscribed into the subsequent tradition in a number of ways. Sermons on the incomprehensibility of God represented the more subtle expression of the desire that Christian communities not be consumed by mutual testing over propositions about the divine nature; emphasis on the study of the physical cosmos served more directly to stem the flood of arguments concerning the Deity; the emphasis on an anagogic path based on the created order effectively obviated gnostic elitism. Still more direct articulations of the evils of competitive disputation became woven into later recollections of the Constantinian era. One such polemic was associated with the Council of Nicaea in 325.

TOWARD THE COUNCIL OF NICAEA

Soon after Constantine established himself as the sole master of the *oikoumenē* after defeating Licinius in September 324, he called for a congress of his Christian subjects, particularly those from the newly incorporated Greek east. This first universal council, originally planned to meet in Ancyra, eventually took place in the Bithynian city of Nicaea. Though it would be speculative to wonder whether Constantine anticipated the subsequent import of the council and its enduring reputation as a touchstone of orthodoxy, it is easy to see that the emperor had more immediate concerns. He called for the council to meet in May 325, just two months prior to the celebrations of his own *vicennalia*, the twentieth year of his accession, which were scheduled to occur at nearby Nicomedia, the civic rival of Nicaea.[1]

Many Christians journeyed to the council at public expense using the *cursus publicus* both to greet their new patron and to celebrate the good fortunes of church and state, as the council was to last until the end of July and overlap with the *vicennalia*.[2] Though some rancor existed among the participants in the opening days of the council, a more festive mood soon prevailed when, at Constantine's promptings, most attempted to demonstrate goodwill in public. In an irenic gesture, Constantine publicly burned the *libelli* that many Christians had brought for the purpose of accusing each other before their sovereign.[3]

Somber though the business of confronting Christian "heresy" was, it constituted only a portion of the council's agenda. Neither the Arian party of Eusebius of Nicomedia nor the partisans of Alexander of Alexandria dominated the council of more than three hundred bishops, the vast majority of whom, especially those from the Latin west, were not as well-schooled as these two camps and had no strong interest in the prevailing theological controversies. Further, this council, unlike later imperial councils with extant invitation lists, included not only bishops and priests but also those outside the ecclesiastical hierarchy, such as confessors bearing the stigmata of persecution and other lay Christians.[4] It is conceivable that pagan philosophers such as Iamblichus' student Sopater (who visited the court of Constantine in 327) also attended the meeting. In the final tally, nonpartisans were a significant presence at the council.[5]

1. Eusebius, *Vita Constantini* 3.15–16; Socrates, *Hist. eccl.* 1.16; Sozomen, *Hist. eccl.* 1.25; Jerome, *Chronicon* 313F (Helm, ed., 231). See Barnes, *Constantine and Eusebius,* 219. On the rivalry between Nicomedia and Nicaea during the high empire, see L. Robert, "La titulature de Nicée et de Nicomédie: la gloire et la haine," *HSCP* 81 (1977), 1–39.

2. On Nicaea and imperial victory celebrations, see M. McCormick, *Eternal Victory: Triumphal Rulership in Late Antiquity, Byzantium and the Early Medieval West* (Cambridge, 1986), 104–5.

3. Socrates, *Hist. eccl.* 1.8; Sozomen, *Hist. eccl.* 1.17.

4. C. Guarnieri, "Note sulla presenza dei laici ai concili fino al VI secolo," *Vetera Christianorum* 20 (1983): 77–91. Guarnieri argues that there was no general requirement for lay presence in councils in the second and third centuries.

5. Theodoret of Cyrus, *Hist. eccl.* 1.7.6 (Parmentier and Scheidweiler, eds., 31), described the council as an assembly of martyrs (δῆμον μαρτύρων). If we believe Sozomen, *Hist. eccl.* 1.18, a large number of pagans also attended, some to gain more information about the new faith that had found imperial favor and others to sow discord among the ranks of the Christians. The invitation lists to later imperial councils appear to have been

In Constantine's imperial summons, the reason for the council was vague, perhaps deliberately so.[6] The emperor indeed sought to reconcile the feuding parties in the so-called Arian dispute, but it is not clear how he thought the council could contribute to this goal. We can guess more confidently what the council was *not* supposed to do. In earlier attempts to mediate the controversy, the emperor had expressed deep dissatisfaction with philosophical dialectic as a sophistic technique that allowed the worse argument to prevail over the better one. From this we may reasonably deduce that he ruled out open dialectical debate on the contested issues from the council's program.[7]

Perhaps confusion as to the aims of the council explains why no detailed stenographic records of the proceedings appear to have been kept, as was done at other important church synods.[8] The precedents of previous ecclesiastical and secular proceedings, together with the dictates of practical wisdom, would have demanded that some record be maintained, even published, had the predominant goal of the council been to secure a formal refutation of a particular theological position.[9] Thanks largely to the tireless and painstaking efforts of Otto Seeck, Hans Opitz, and other modern scholars engaged in the task of historical reconstruction, we now possess fuller and much more critically assessed knowledge about the Council of Nicaea than has been available since

---

much more selective; see A. Crabbe, "The Invitation List to the Council of Ephesus and Metropolitan Hierarchy in the Fifth Century," *JTS* n.s. 32 (1981): 369–400.

6. In H.-G. Opitz, ed., *Urkunden zur Geschichte des arianischen Streites* 20, in *Athanasius Werke III* (Berlin, 1934–35), 41–42. The summons is extant in Syriac and is published by Schwartz as a retroversion into Greek. Constantine stated merely that he desired a meeting at Nicaea "for many reasons" (the Syriac *metul sagyatha* is rendered by Schwartz as πολλῶν ἕνεκα). On Constantine's belief that the authority of the bishops should supersede established procedural precedents, see *Sirmondian Constitutions* 1, addressed to the notorius praetorian prefect Ablabius.

7. *Oratio ad sanctos* (originally dated 317 by Barnes, now dated 321 by him); see T. D. Barnes, "The Emperor Constantine's Good Friday Sermon," *JTS* n.s. 7 (1976): 414–23. R. Lane Fox has situated this sermon in Antioch on Good Friday of 325; see *Pagans and Christians* (New York, 1987), 627–35, esp. 634–35.

8. Besides the symbol, we possess the twenty canons and the synodal decree that were produced by this first Christian imperial council. On the products of Nicaea, see A. Wickenhauser, "Beiträge zur Geschichte der Stenographie auf den Synoden des vierten Jahrhunderts nach Christus," *Archiv für Stenographie* 59 (1908): 4–9, 33–39; idem, "Zur Frage nach der Existenz von nicaenischen Synodalprotokollen," in F. Dölger, ed., *Konstantin der Grosse und seine Zeit* (Freiburg, 1913), 122–43; P. Batiffol, "Les sources de l'histoire du concile de Nicée," *Échos d'Orient* 24 (1925): 385–402.

9. Constantius later recorded his private audiences with "troublesome" bishops, whom he tried to persuade with threats and cajoling; see the literature cited in T. D. Barnes, *Athanasius and Constantius: Theology and Politics in the Constantinian Empire* (Cambridge, Mass., 1993), 276 n. 56.

the mid– to late–fourth century.[10] Yet even now the exact procedure at Nicaea remains a vexed, and seemingly insoluble, question.[11]

It was certainly not for lack of interest that contemporaries neglected to consult and pass on the records of this council. Many factors contributed to the fact that the meeting's proceedings quickly became obscure even as its outcomes proved (historically and juridically, if not theologically) important.

Though Arius' position and a handful of lesser bishops were condemned, there were few clear winners at Nicaea.[12] Afterward, the dissatisfied parties gave their own conflicting interpretations of the council to promote their own interests.[13] Much of this partisan literature was too deeply invested with immediate polemics and apologetics to be relevant to posterity.[14]

Because the council arose from the failure of discussion, persuasion, and the normative exercise of authority to achieve peaceful resolutions to disputes in a number of important eastern congregations,[15] subsequent overemphasis on unity rendered a set of *acta* unnecessary and undesirable. By contrast, the "products" of the council, the canons even more so than the symbol, were seen by some (especially those who championed a consensual process of decision making) as infinitely more important than the precise processes that led to them because they stood for unity and order.[16]

Even so, the Nicene symbol,[17] which subsequently became the cornerstone of orthodox definition, was not fully crystallized until the

10. O. Seeck, "Untersuchungen zur Geschichte des nicänischen Konzils," *ZKG* 17 (1897): 1–71, 319–62; Opitz, *Urkunden*.

11. See R. E. Person, *The Mode of Theological Decision Making at the Early Ecumenical Councils: An Inquiry into the Function of Scripture and Tradition at the Councils of Nicaea and Ephesus* (Basel, 1978), 44. A possible second session is discussed in C. Luibhéid, "The Alleged Second Session of the Council of Nicaea," *Journal of Ecclesiastical History* 34 (1983): 165–74. Generally, it is wise to observe the caution of Hanson, in *Search for the Christian Doctrine of God*, 172: "The evidence available does not admit of our forming ingenious, elaborate and highly nuanced theories about the Council of Nicaea. Reconstructing the course of the Council is an interesting but rather futile pastime."

12. The deposed bishops were Secundus of Ptolemais and Theonas of Marmarike, both subsequently recalled by Constantine; see Philostorgius, *Hist. eccl.* 1.10.

13. See Socrates, *Hist. eccl.* 1.1; Sozomen, *Hist. eccl.* 1.1.

14. See, e.g., W. D. Hauschild, "Die antinizänische Synodalaktensammlung des Sabinus von Heraklea," *VChr* 24 (1970): 105–26, on Sabinus' *Syntagma* as a homoiousian reaction against Athanasius' *De synodis* (circa 363–67) and the latter's views about the significance of the Council of Nicaea.

15. See Theodoret, *Hist. eccl.* 1.5–6.

16. See Sozomen, *Hist. eccl.* 1.20.

17. In Opitz, ed., *Urkunden* 22:4–6 and 24 (*Athanasius Werke III*, 43 and 51–52). The texts of the two creeds vary greatly.

Council of Constantinople in 381.[18] Furthermore, the reaffirmation of the Nicene formulation as a criterion for orthodoxy in 381, after the promulgation of more than a dozen anti-Nicene creeds between 341 and 360,[19] obscured the less edifying aspects of the first general council (the effects of which were effectively annulled after Constantine's death in 337) by focusing on Nicaea's product rather than on its context and process. The reinterpretation of Nicaea 325 in light of Constantinople 381 was echoed by the recasting of Constantine, the patron of the first general council, into the image of Theodosius I, the patron of the second council.[20] Because of this dialectical relationship, the history of the early fourth century can only be seen through the refracting lens of the late fourth.

By the last quarter of the fourth century, the ranks of the antagonists of the earlier controversies and those who attended Nicaea had been considerably thinned by old age and sickness. The death of Athanasius, who attended the council as a young priest at the side of his bishop Alexander, marked the advent of the post-Nicene age. With all eyewitnesses dead, legends about Nicaea began to emerge.

At the time of the death of Theodosius I in 395, a new generation of Christians born after 325 had already grown to a ripe old age in an empire largely tolerant, if not always decidedly supportive, of the Christian cause. Local traditions, sacramental and liturgical practices, and theological tracts probably kept alive fragmented memories of this past, but there existed no coherent account like Eusebius' *Historia ecclesiastica* to detail the perceived triumph of Christianity under the reign of Constantine.[21]

After Eusebius brought his grand processional narrative to a close with Licinius' defeat by Constantine in 324, the genre of ecclesiastical

18. See R. M. Grant, "Religion and Politics at the Council of Nicaea," *Journal of Religion* 55 (1975): 1–12; F. E. Sciuto, "Dalla Nicea a Costantinopoli: osservazioni sulla prima fase della stabilizzazione teologico-politica cristiana (325–381)," in *La trasformazioni della cultura nella tarda antichità* (Rome, 1985), 1:479–90; A. d'Alès, "Nicée, Constantinople: les premiers symboles de foi," *RSR* 26 (1936): 85–92; A. de Halleux, "La réception du symbole oecuménique, de Nicée à Chalcédoine," *Ephemerides Theologicae Lovanienses* 61 (1985): 5–47. For the creed's subsequent import, see Evagrius Scholasticus, *Hist. eccl.* 3.14, on Zeno's *henotikon* letter of 482.

19. See A. Hahn, *Bibliothek der Symbole und Glaubensregeln der alten Kirche* (Breslau, 1897; 3d ed., Hildesheim, 1962), 183–209; Barnes, *Athanasius and Constantius*, 229–32 (app. 10, "Creeds and Councils 337–361").

20. See J. Taylor, "The First Council of Constantinople (381)," *Prudentia* 13 (1981): 47–54, 91–97.

21. On the rehearsal of past events as part of the process of creating a community and its historical memories, see B. Lewis, *History Remembered, Recovered, Invented* (Princeton, 1975).

history was left largely untended for two to three generations.[22] Then, from the end of the fourth century into the fifth, a blossoming of historical writings interweaved the story of the Christian church with affairs of state and the formerly fallow field yielded an abundant harvest.

The obvious point of departure for these new histories was the reign of Constantine, the Augustus who had done so much to end official persecution against Christians and to promote their interests. Eusebius, having somewhat compromised himself with questionable theological views and by his involvement in the proceedings at Nicaea, had prudently stopped short of the early Arian disputes in his *Historia ecclesiastica*. Thus to others fell the task of explaining why, as the Christian church approached its moment of triumph, bitter divisions arose within its ranks, with the consequences that remained clear to any casual observer in the fifth century.

One of the first of this new generation of histories was Gelasius of Caesarea's *Historia ecclesiastica*, composed circa 386–400. It is no longer extant, but fragments have been gleaned from later works.[23] Gelasius' history quickly became the basis for a number of other works, notably the tenth and eleventh books of Rufinus of Aquileia's *Historia ecclesiastica*, which augmented his translation into Latin of Eusebius' history. Other works soon followed.

Because Nicaea was where Christian leaders from throughout the newly united empire met their patron and self-proclaimed *koinos episkopos*,[24] the council naturally became a focal point for later Christians attempting to understand their past. These legends about Nicaea are inherently interesting to the modern historian, not because accurate information can be mined from them but because they tell us much about the period in which they arose and circulated.

In the following pages, I examine the multiform story of an encounter between a confessor and a philosopher at Nicaea. In the four major versions of the story contained in the later histories (dating from the late

22. See G. F. Chestnut, *The First Christian Histories: Eusebius, Socrates, Sozomen, Theodoret and Evagrius* (Paris, 1977); A. Momigliano, "Pagan and Christian Historiography in the Fourth Century A.D.," in idem, ed., *The Conflict between Paganism and Christianity in the Fourth Century* (Oxford, 1963), 79–99; G. Downey, "The Perspective of the Early Church Historians," *GRBS* 6 (1965): 57–70; F. J. Foakes-Jackson, *A History of Church History: Studies of Some Historians of the Christian Church* (Cambridge, 1939), 71–86; L. Cracco Ruggini, "The Ecclesiastical Histories and the Pagan Historiography: Providence and Miracles," *Athenaeum* n.s. 55 (1977): 107–26.

23. See the discussions of Gelasius of Cyzicus' *Syntagma* and Georgius Monachus' *Chronicon* below.

24. See J. Straub, "Constantine as ΚΟΙΝΟΣ ΕΠΙΣΚΟΠΟΣ: Tradition and Innovation in the Representation of the First Christian Emperor's Majesty," *DOP* 21 (1967): 37–55.

fourth to the fifth century), a "debate" occurs either during or before the formal session of the council. Discounting slight variations for the moment, I can summarize the story as follows: There came to pass a hotly contested debate between a polytheistic philosopher and the assembled bishops at Nicaea. The philosopher was extremely adept at dialectical disputation, and none of the bishops was able to gain advantage over him. After a long series of exchanges, the precise nature or content of which is not given in any of the sources, the stalemate was finally ended when an unlearned and elderly confessor stepped forward to confront the philosopher with a terse credal formula, and simply asked his stunned opponent whether he believed the statement or not. The philosopher assented to the truth of the old man's words, admitted defeat, and (in some versions) accepted baptism at the confessor's hands.

The story appears for the first time in an extant source in Rufinus' *Historia ecclesiastica*, but is conspicuously absent from more contemporary accounts such as the writings of Eustathius of Antioch,[25] Eusebius' *Vita Constantini* and *Letter to His Community about the Council of Nicaea*,[26] and Athanasius' slightly later *Epistula de decretis Nicaenae synodi*.[27] Thus, when we approach this episode in Rufinus, and later in the writings of Socrates Scholasticus, Sozomen, and Gelasius of Cyzicus, we are faced with a complicated historiographical and historical problem.

The story is almost certainly spurious—our first extant attestation is a Latin source composed seventy years after Nicaea—yet it is significant because it crystallized and foregrounded a profound bias against the adoption of public dialectical disputation as a means of settling Christian theological differences. Socrates Scholasticus, whose version departs most significantly from the others', blamed the public discussion of theology for the divisions within the church of his time.[28] Though I do not rule out the stated arguments against debate in these various accounts, I propose that the polemic must be read in light of such post-Nicene developments as the Anomoean controversy and the social and urban conditions of the late fourth (Rufinus), mid–fifth (Socrates, Sozomen), and late–fifth (Gelasius of Cyzicus) centuries.

I will show that, partly because of its placement within the larger works and partly because of the elevation of certain forms of authority

25. In Theodoret, *Hist. eccl.* 1.8.1–5 (Parmentier and Scheidweiler, eds., 33–34). Eustathius' work was composed circa 329; see Batiffol, "Les sources de l'histoire du concile de Nicée," 390–92.

26. In Opitz, ed., *Urkunden* 22 (*Athanasius Werke III*, 42–47).

27. Text in Opitz, ed., *Athanasius Werke II*, 1–45. Dated to 352–53 by Barnes in *Athanasius and Constantius*, 198–99 (app. 4).

28. For example, Socrates, *Hist. eccl.* 2.2, 2.30; more on this point below.

at the expense of others, the story functioned to valorize particular social processes tied to particular social structures and assumptions about power. The story expressed the decisive rejection of a certain form of social contact with religious outsiders, and the preference for the irenic ideology of the *mia ekklēsia*, the unified church of Christ, where disputes were alien and diabolical intrusions.[29]

My examination of how this debate was narrated by the four writers secures a framework for discussing the way this bias operated in the larger context of their histories. Most of the fifth-century histories picked up the thread of the story where Eusebius' *Historia ecclesiastica* left off, and the opening narratives of the council effectively framed the rest of the accounts. By weaving the story of this debate into their reports of a council where many charismatic Christian heroes and bishops came together to express Christian unity (ὁμοφωνία), the authors used the triumph of the simple confessor over the philosopher to drive home a point of deeper import than the mere defeat of arrogance by Christian simplicity.

The only previous study of this episode that examines all the variants is E. Jugie's eight-page article, "La dispute des philosophes païens avec les pères de Nicée," published in 1925.[30] As the title implies, Jugie is primarily interested in the account in Gelasius of Cyzicus' *Syntagma* (see later in this chapter) and describes the other versions only in passing. This is unfortunate, for the shifting shape of the multiform story reveals much about how fifth-century people in different stations of life used the context of Nicaea, around which a tradition had already grown up,[31] to discuss their reception of public dialectical disputation in a Christian culture.

THE *HISTORIAE ECCLESIASTICAE* OF GELASIUS OF CAESAREA AND RUFINUS OF AQUILEIA

Rufinus says in the preface to his *Historia ecclesiastica* that he translated the *Historia ecclesiastica* of Eusebius into Latin at the urgings of Chromatius of Aquileia, with the hope that the product would comfort fellow

29. See Daniélou, "ΜΙΑ ΕΚΚΛΗΣΙΑ," 129–39.

30. See E. Jugie, "La dispute des philosophes païens avec les pères de Nicée," *Échos d'Orient* 24 (1925): 403–10. Contrast with the more ad hoc interpretations of this multiform story in, e.g., G. A. Kennedy, *Greek Rhetoric under Christian Emperors* (Princeton, 1983), 201–2.

31. This happened very early on; see Eusebius, *Vita Constantini* 3.8–9.

Christians at Aquileia, who at that time (circa 401) were threatened by Alaric's Gothic incursions.[32] Scholarly discussion of the relationship between Rufinus' rendition and Eusebius' original is involved and need not be rehearsed here at length.[33] The options of source dependency are best laid out in E. Honigmann's "Gélase de Césarée et Rufin d'Aquilée," though his own hypothesis of an independent Rufinus-Gelasius source (based on Gelasius of Cyzicus' attestation of Ρουφίνος ἤγουν Γελασίος)[34] as distinct from the Greek translation of Rufinus (*Rufin grec*) is questionable because of the uncertainty of statements in Gelasius of Cyzicus and Photius and also because his overly zealous postulation of sources that are no longer extant goes against the scholar's preference for economic

32. Rufinus, *In libros Historiarum Eusebii* (M. Simonetti, ed., [Rome, 1961], CCSL 20:267). Rufinus was himself in the besieged town at the time; see C. P. Hammond, "The Last Ten Years of Rufinus' Life and the Date of His Move South from Aquileia," *JTS* n.s. 28 (1977): 372–429, at 373. The intended audience for the translation was probably the group of ascetics gathered around the figure of Chromatius, Rufinus' friend and loyal supporter; see Rufinus, *Apologia contra Hieronymum* 1.4 (Simonetti, ed., 39).

33. See J. E. L. Oulton, "Rufinus' Translation of the Church History of Eusebius," *JTS* 30 (1929): 150–75. Oulton undertakes a critical comparison of Rufinus' translation with the Greek text of the original and concludes that, although Valois' original negative assessment of the value of Rufinus' rendition remains fundamentally valid, Rufinus' significant departures from his source were in fact newly incorporated material. This assessment is echoed by M. Villain, "Rufin d'Aquilée et l'*Histoire ecclésiastique*," *RSR* 33 (1946): 164–210, who adds that the faithfulness of a translation is a modern scholarly criterion that does not take into account late antique stylistic emphases. Furthermore, the last books in Eusebius' work may have seemed intrinsically unsatisfactory to Rufinus. T. Christensen, "Rufinus of Aquilea and the *Historia Ecclesiastica*, lib. VIII–IX, of Eusebius," *Studia Theologica* 34 (1980): 129–52, argues that the patchy nature of books 7 to 9 was due to his revision of a first draft after Constantine defeated Licinius in 324, and to his use of diverse sources. Given his *ars interpretandi* and his concern for the *Innerzusammenhang* of the narrative, Rufinus had no choice but to deviate significantly. The scholarly consensus now holds that Rufinus was not merely a translator but a redactor of Eusebius' *Hist. eccl.* Besides rearranging book 10, Rufinus added two books, allegedly his own work, to advance the history chronologically to the death of Theodosius I in 395. Such arguments revolve around the nature of the dependence between Rufinus and Gelasius of Caesarea (d. 404), Cyril of Alexandria's nephew, whose *Hist. eccl.* is now lost but exists in fragments contained in the works of others; see A. Glas, *Die Kirchengeschichte des Gelasios von Kaisareia: Die Vorlage für die beiden letzten Bücher der Kirchengeschichte Rufins*, Byzantinisches Archiv 6 (Leipzig/Berlin, 1914); F. Scheidweiler, "Die Kirchengeschichte des Gelasios von Kaisareia," *BZ* 46 (1953): 277–301; E. Honigmann, "Gélase de Césarée et Rufin d'Aquilée," *Bulletin de l'Académie Royale de Belgique*, Classe des lettres et des sciences morales et politiques ser. 5, 40 (1954): 122–61; F. Winkelmann, "Charakter und Bedeutung der Kirchengeschichte des Gelasios von Kaisareia," *Byzantinische Forschungen* 1 (Amsterdam, 1966): 346–85; idem, "Zu einer Edition der Fragmente der Kirchengeschichte des Gelasios von Kaisareia," *Byzantinoslavica* 34 (1973): 193–98; J. Schamp, "The Lost Ecclesiastical History of Gelasius of Caesarea (*CPG*, 3521): Towards a Reconsideration," *Patristic and Byzantine Review* 6 (1987): 146–52; idem, "Gélase ou Rufin: un fait nouveau: sur des fragments oubliés de Gélase de Césarée (*CPG*, no. 3521)," *Byzantion* 57 (1987): 360–90.

34. Gelasius of Cyzicus, *Syntagma* 1.8.1 (Loeschcke and Heinemann, eds., 13).

simplicity.[35] However, any solution to the source dilemma must assume a number of intermediate compilations and sources now lost, a fact that suggests a greater contemporary demand for the history's information than would be the case if one assumed a single line of transmission.

As Rufinus wrote in Latin some seventy-five years after Nicaea,[36] it is tempting to dismiss the story as a spurious invention. But there are some indications that Rufinus may have adapted the story from an earlier, and therefore potentially more reliable, source, namely, Gelasius of Caesarea's *Historia ecclesiastica*.[37] Interestingly, this Gelasius, the uncle of Cyril of Jerusalem, was also the author of a work against the Anomoeans (now lost), according to Photius.[38]

In the present discussion, I set aside the question of source dependency to examine Rufinus' redactional *Tendenz*, which is significant even if his version was lifted from traditional material. As I will illustrate later, there are many resonances between the way Rufinus redacted Eusebius' *Historia ecclesiastica* and his treatment in the tenth and eleventh books of his own *Historia ecclesiastica*.

BOOKS 10 AND 11 OF RUFINUS' *HISTORIA ECCLESIASTICA*

Book 10 of Rufinus' *Historia ecclesiastica* began with the circumstances leading to the Council of Nicaea. The episode of the convocation of the council hinged on the underlying assumption that the protagonists were divided into two camps: Christian priests on one side, and distinguished philosophers and dialecticians—whether all pagans or Christians is not clear from the text—on the other. Immediately, Rufinus explicitly advertised his wish to illustrate the virtue of simplicity in matters of faith:

> We acknowledge how great a merit resides in the simplicity of belief,
> even from those accounts in which the deeds are mentioned. That is,
> when on account of the zeal of the dutiful emperor [Constantine], the
> priests of God came together from every place; likewise, driven by

35. See Rufinus on his own work, in *In libros Historiarum Eusebii* (CCSL 20:267–68): "Decimum uero uel undecimum librum nos conscripsimus partim ex maiorum traditionibus, partim ex his, quae nostrae iam memoria comprehenderat et eos uelut duos pisciculos, supra scriptis panibus addidimus."

36. 402–3 is the estimated date of Rufinus' *Hist. eccl.*; see F. Thélamon, "Une oeuvre destinée à la communauté chrétienne d'Aquilée: L'*Histoire ecclésiastique* de Rufin," *Antichità altoadriatiche* 22 (1982): 255–71.

37. See Rufinus, *Hist. eccl.* 1.3; Winkelmann, "Character und Bedeutung," 351.

38. Photius, *Bibliotheca* 88.

reputation, philosophers and dialecticians, exceedingly elevated and of the highest repute, convened. Among them was a certain person who was distinguished in the dialectical art, who from day to day carried out a contest of supreme rivalry with our bishops, men who were not unlikely similarly learned in the dialectical art. And there arose an enormous spectacle (*ingens spectaculum*) for the learned and lettered men who came to listen. Nevertheless, the philosopher of neither side was able to be boxed in or be trapped by any other. He [the philosopher] confronted the challenges raised with such skill in speaking that, where he was considered to be most confined he would slip out from the narrow spots as if he were greased. But in order that God may show that the kingdom of God consists not in speeches but in virtuous action, a certain one of the confessors, a man of the simplest disposition, and who knew nothing except Jesus Christ and that he was crucified, was present among the rest of the bishops in the audience. This person, when he saw the philosopher insulting us, and boasting in the cunning art of argumentation, begged the floor[39] from all present: he wanted to exchange a few words (*sermonicari*) with the philosopher. . . . He said, "In the name of Jesus Christ, O philosopher, listen to what is true. [He then recited a credal formula.] Do you believe that this is the case, philosopher?" And he, as if he had never said anything to the contrary since he was confounded by the virtue of what was said, became completely quiet, and was only able to say this in response: "Yes, it so appears, truth is none other than what you said." Then the elderly man said, "If you believe that these words are true, rise and follow me to the Lord, and receive the seal of his faith." And the philosopher turned to his disciples, or to those who had come together in order to listen: "Listen," he said, "O learned men. . . ."[40]

Françoise Thélamon, whose exemplary reading of this story from Rufinus' *Historia ecclesiastica* appears within the context of her broader study of the relationship between pagans and Christians, sees this episode as a complete fabrication as well as a typological drama: "All the actors are nameless, none of the protagonists has real existence inasmuch as each represents a type: the confessor, the pagan philosopher, the bishop-dialectician" (Tous les acteurs sont anonymes, chacun des protagonistes n'a d'existence, qu'autant qu'il représente un type: le confesseur, le philosophe païen, les évêques dialecticiens).[41] For her, the tale is a moral one about the encounter of *simplicitas fidei* and *ars dialectica*.

39. The Latin is *locum*; see Glas, *Die Kirchengeschichte des Gelasios von Kaisareia*, 21.
40. Rufinus, *Hist. eccl.* 1.3; translation mine.
41. F. Thélamon, *Païens et chrétiens au IVe siècle. L'apport de l'"Histoire ecclésiastique" de Rufin d'Aquilée* (Paris, 1981), 431 (translation mine). Valois, in *PG* 67:60, also sees it as an invention. But F. X. Murphy argues that the story is not implausible a priori in *Rufinus of Aquileia (345–411): His Life and Works* (Washington, D.C., 1945).

Indeed, Rufinus throughout portrays skill in dialectic as a moral flaw associated with other value-laden words: *dolus, fraus, callidior, simulatio*.[42] But Rufinus did not brand dialectic as categorically un-Christian, because he asserted that many of the bishops debating with the philosophers were themselves well versed in the dialectical art.[43]

For Rufinus, the proper use of dialectic depended on the practitioner's mental attitude, his way of life, and the immediate context of the debate. Rufinus' praise of Didymus the Blind openly proclaimed without apology the dialectical art as one of the many skills in which the Alexandrian excelled.[44] Similarly, though Rufinus in his *Apologia* (401) criticized Jerome for his use of Porphyry's *Eisagogē*, he did not deny his own expertise in the matter[45] but emphasized that knowledge of dialectic should be balanced by the virtue of asceticism.[46]

A proper understanding of Rufinus' version of the episode lies partly in Eusebius' *Historia ecclesiastica:* the two more books that Rufinus appended to his translation of Eusebius' work not only advanced the narrative to the end of the reign of Theodosius I, but also served as a commentary on the Constantinian past for a late-fourth-century Latin-speaking audience that did not have access to the original. In particular, book 7 of Eusebius' *Historia ecclesiastica* containing the famous description of the debate between Paul of Samosata and Malchion in Antioch provides a relevant basis for comparison.[47]

According to Eusebius, after a number of preliminary meetings of bishops gathered from every direction, a final council was held.[48] There Paul of Samosata, derided by Eusebius as no bishop but a sophist and a quack (οὐκ ἐπίσκοπος, ἀλλὰ σοφιστὴς καὶ γόης,),[49] was exposed and later unanimously condemned and excommunicated by the assembled bishops. Though Eusebius did not recount the actual proceedings, he excused this omission by saying that the *acta* from the council were still in wide circulation in his day, thanks to Malchion himself:

Μάλιστα δ᾽ αὐτὸν εὐθύνας ἐπικρυπτόμενον διήλεγξεν Μαλχίων, ἀνὴρ τά τε ἄλλα λόγιος καὶ σοφιστοῦ τῶν ἐπ᾽ Ἀντιοχείας Ἑλληνικῶν παιδευτηρίων διατριβῆς προεστώς, οὐ μὴν ἀλλὰ καὶ δι᾽ ὑπερβάλλουσαν τῆς

42. Thélamon, *Païens et chretiens*, 430–35.
43. Rufinus, *Hist. eccl.* 1.3: "viris, adaeque in dialectica non improbabiliter eruditis."
44. Rufinus, *Hist. eccl.* 2.7.
45. Rufinus, *Apologia contra Hieronymum* 2.9 (Simonetti, ed., 90–91).
46. See Rufinus, *Apologia contra Hieronymum* 2.13–16 (Simonetti, ed., 93–96).
47. See G. Bardy, *Paul de Samosate*, 2d ed. (Louvain, 1929); De Riedmatten, *Les actes du procès de Paul de Samosate*.
48. Eusebius, *Hist. eccl.* 7.28.1–2.
49. Eusebius, *Hist. eccl.* 7.30.9 (Oulton, ed., 2:218–19).

194 PUBLIC DISPUTATION, POWER, AND SOCIAL ORDER

εἰς Χριστὸν πίστεως γνησιότητα πρεσβυτερίου τῆς αὐτόθι παραοικίας ἠξιωμένος· οὗτός γέ τοι ἐπισημειουμένων ταχυγράφων ζήτησιν πρὸς αὐτὸν ἐνστησάμενος, ἥν καὶ εἰς δεῦρο φερομένην ἴσμεν, μόνος ἴσχυ-σεν τῶν ἄλλων κρυψίνουν ὄντα καὶ ἀπατηλὸν φωρᾶσαι τὸν ἄνθρωπον.

Malchion did most to call Paul to account and to refute him, concealed as he was. He was a man of immense learning who was the head of a school of rhetoric, one of the Hellenic institutions of education in Antioch, and who, in view of the exceeding genuineness of his faith in Christ, had been chosen as presbyter of that community. Malchion, by arranging for stenographers to take notes (which we know to be extant to this day) at his disputation with Paul, was the only person who succeeded in exposing him as an evasive and wily man.[50]

The above is my translation based on the Greek text of Eusebius' *Historia ecclesiastica*. Rufinus' Latin translation, apart from stylistic differences, contains two main changes that are noteworthy and telling,[51] shown here in italics:

> Insistente plurimum et disceptationibus valdissimis perurgente Malchione presbytero Antiochenae ecclesiae, viro fidelissimo *et omnibus virtutibus adornato;* cui accedebat etiam hoc, quod erat dissertissimus et potens in verbo atque in omni eruditione perfectus, denique oratoriam in eadem ipsa urbe docuerat. *huic igitur ab omni episcoporum concilio permittitur disputatio cum Paulo,* excipientibus notariis. quae ita magnifice ab eo et adcurate habita est, ut scripta ederetur et nunc quoque in admiratione sit omnibus. solus etenim potuit dissimulantem et occultantem se Paulum confessionibus propriis publicare.

While Rufinus used the ablative absolute (*excipientibus notariis*) to render Eusebius' genitive absolute (*epismeiomenon tachugraphon*), his placement of the phrase significantly understates the importance of this measure to Malchion's eventual success. Rufinus instead chose to augment Eusebius' account in ways that conform to the *Tendenz* already established in his treatment of the Nicene debate discussed earlier. First, Rufinus consistently underscored the vital importance of moral character and ascetic attainments (*omnibus virtutibus adornato*); second, he made it seem that permission to refute erroneous views must be obtained from proper episcopal authority: "The *disputatio* with Paul is thus granted (*permittitur*) by the entire council of bishops."[52]

This implicit restriction on the freedom to debate even a known heretic bespeaks the deep gulf between Rufinus' hierarchizing ecclesi-

50. Eusebius, *Hist. eccl.* 7.29.2 (Oulton, ed., 2:212–13).
51. See E. Schwartz and T. Mommsen, eds., *Eusebius Werke II* (Leipzig, 1908), 705; Rufinus, *Hist. eccl.* 7.29.
52. See Rufinus, *Hist. eccl.* bk. 10.

astical world in the late fourth century and the more autonomous, fluid Christian communities of Origen's and even Arius' time described so well recently by Rowan Williams—when the importance of charismatic figures considerably overshadowed that of church officeholders.[53] Indeed, we certainly do not expect to find debates in which anyone could intervene at will, although Rufinus' confessor at Nicaea requested the floor from all present (*poscit ab omnibus locum*) less in obedience to the protocols of church disputations than in acknowledgment of his own unsuitability for agonistic public debate.

A disputation was a war of words in which a *simplex vir* was normally a source of embarrassment and a liability: this presupposition was stressed in Rufinus' account as well as in later versions of the story. That a theological debate was an event appropriate only for a select few, preferably ordained and educated priests, would have struck a familiar chord with the Aquileian Christians to whom Rufinus was writing. The imposing Ambrose of Milan, the prime mover behind the Council of Aquileia of 381, frustrated his opponent Palladius by arranging for a restricted debate in which only priests were allowed.[54]

Returning to the debate between Paul and Malchion and the light it might shed on the Nicene debate, we note that an important theme of both accounts is the impossibility of defeating even indubitably erroneous opponents by logical argumentation alone. No *elenchos* came about at Nicaea because of the philosopher's crafty ability to argue himself out of tight spots: "Ubi maxime putaretur adstrictus, velut anguis lubricus elaberetur." The eventual outcome was all the more ironic and meaningful in that it required the unlooked-for intervention of a humble confessor, who prevailed because of, not despite, his *sancta simplicitas*.[55]

This, therefore, was a poignant story for readers who might find themselves tempted into disputing with other Christians or pagans using the art of dialectic. Fancy rhetorical tricks were not only inappropriate tools for the settling of differences among Christians but also unreliable weapons with which to confront heretics or unbelievers even for skilled practitioners like Malchion and some of the bishops at Nicaea. Jerome, in 383, before his bitter falling out with Rufinus, regarded so-

53. Williams, *Arius*. See *Dissertatio Maximini* 14.300v (R. Gryson, ed., *Scholies ariennes sur le concile d'Aquilée* SC 267 [Paris, 1980], 216–17) for a proud, classic assertion of the primacy of episcopal authority: "Constat ergo Arrium episcopos secutu(m) fuisse, non episcopos Arrium."

54. See Meslin, *Les ariens d'occident*, 90.

55. This account may be profitably compared with the story of Copres' "debate" with a Manichaean in Rufinus, *Historia monachorum* 9.7 (Schulz-Flügel, ed., 320–21; PL 21: 426C–427B). See Chapter 3 for a fuller discussion of this episode.

phistic arguments and logical acumen as no real defense against the attacks of heretics.[56]

For Rufinus, even records of discussions between Christians were unedifying for Christian readers. In Eusebius' *Historia ecclesiastica*, Malchion specifically arranged to have his debate with Paul noted by stenographers, presumably so that the exchange could be transcribed and disseminated later on. But Rufinus was altogether reluctant to report debates, and not only the understandably embarrassing intra-Christian ones. For example, in his *Historia monachorum* he pointedly left out the discussions of his friend Evagrius of Pontus with pagan philosophers in Alexandria, discussions that clearly existed in his main source, the anonymous Greek *Historia monachorum*.[57]

Guillaumont's analysis of Rufinus' description of Evagrius, based on a comparison of the Greek and Latin texts of the *Historia monachorum*, reveals a consistent editorial bias: "Rufin met moins l'accent sur la science et les activités philosophiques d'Evagre et insiste d'avantage sur ses vertus."[58] Rufinus legitimized his narrative of the Council of Nicaea by enveloping it in the palpable presence of divine pleasure in men of God such as Paphnutius and Spyridon, whose *virtutes* were visibly exhibited in the *mirabilia* that they effected.[59]

Here we witness a shift of emphasis in the definition of virtue. Rufinus' cultural hero was no longer Eusebius' learned, shrewd but faithful Christian presbyter; instead, he was the inexperienced and hence faithful confessor: a *simplicissimae naturae vir*.[60] The confessor's simplicity was singled out as a moral *exemplum* for other Christians to contemplate. Implicitly, Rufinus argued that *simplicitas* was not only a noble trait but

56. *De perpetua virginitate beatae Mariae adversus Helvidium* 2 (*PL* 23:185A): Divine intervention, as expressed through Jerome's inspired exegesis, is preferred to eloquence and dialectic as a means of refuting Helvidius' contentions.

57. See Rufinus, *Historia monachorum* 27 (Schulz-Flügel, ed., 363; *PL* 21:448B–449A); E. Preuschen, *Palladius und Rufinus: Ein Beitrag zur Quellenkunde des ältesten Mönchtums* (Giessen, 1897), 86. On the textual question of dependence, see A.-J. Festugière, "Le problème littéraire de l'*Historia monachorum*," *Hermes* 83 (1955): 257–84; A. Guillaumont, *Les 'kephalaia gnostica' d'Évagre le pontique et l'histoire de l'origénisme chez les grecs et chez les syriens* (Paris, 1962), 71–73, esp. 71 n. 99.

58. Guillaumont, *Les 'kephalaia gnostica*,' 72. See P. Rousseau, *Ascetics, Authority, and the Church in the Age of Jerome and Cassian* (Oxford, 1978), 25–27; Palladius on Didymus in *Historia lausiaca* 4.4; S. N. C. Lieu, "The Holy Men and Their Biographers in Early Byzantium and Medieval China: A Preliminary Comparative Study in Hagiography," in A. Moffatt, ed., *Maistor: Classical, Byzantine, and Renaissance Studies for Robert Browning* (Canberra, 1984), 113–47, at 142–43.

59. See Thélamon, *Païens et chrétiens*, 436–40.

60. On the emphasis on the confessor in the Latin west as a corollary to the widespread concern over the *lapsi*, see M. Lods, *Confesseurs et martyrs* (Neuchâtel, 1958), 66–67.

a pragmatic one, an effective response to opponents and questioners. The best answer to others' taunting challenges was also the simplest one: to recite the words of a creed and ask one's opponent to assent to its truth. One was not to debate but to preach, repeating after the confessor: "O philosopher, in the name of Jesus Christ, listen to the truth."

The lack of reciprocity between what the philosopher was asking and what the confessor said in response is almost absolute. The confessor was decidedly not adhering to the rules of disputation. Thélamon observes that, at this point, "on est passé d'une démarche intellectuelle à une experience religieuse, de la discussion à la conversion."[61] Whether her implication that the philosopher underwent a religious conversion can find support in Rufinus' description is not clear—it can be read as intellectual enlightenment as well. Even so, the eventual conversion of the philosopher became a feature that emerged with marked emphasis in later variants.[62]

Rufinus' portrayal of this scenario is consistent with his advice to Christians concerning the unshakable core of religious belief, the kernel of truth that a Christian must accept without question: "That God is the Father of His only Son Our Lord is something we ought to believe in rather than debate on. Nor is it permitted for a slave to debate the origins of the Master." (Credendus est ergo Deus esse Pater unici Filii sui Dominis nostri, *non discutiendus. Neque* enim *fas* est seruo de natalibus domini *disputare*).[63] In contrast, busybody meddling into the secrets of the divine mystery was a tricky and dangerous business: "De Deo etiam uera dicere periculosum est."[64] One did better to embrace the virtues of humility and simplicity of heart. When interrogated by a polytheist as to the precise manner in which one believed in Christ, one ought to respond simply and straightforwardly, without apology or embarrassment. This was the advice given to Palladius at the Council of Aquileia in 381: "But you will have to declare the liberty of your faith in simplicity. If a nonbeliever were to demand from you in what manner you

61. Thélamon, *Païens et chrétiens*, 433.
62. Within the pagan philosophical tradition there was already a trend to deemphasize protreptic reason in favor of some notion of divine intervention in the conversion of individuals to a life in philosophy; see J.-P. Dumont, "Les modèles de conversion à la philosophie chez Diogène Laërce," *Augustinus* 32 (1987): 79–97. On philosophical conversion in general, see A. D. Nock, *Conversion: The Old and the New in Religion from Alexander the Great to Augustine of Hippo* (Oxford, 1933), 164–86.
63. *Expositio symboli* 4 (Simonetti, ed., *Rufini Opera* CCSL 20:139); emphasis mine. The use of slave/master language is interesting here.
64. *Expositio symboli* 1 (Simonetti, ed., 133).

believed in Christ, you ought not to feel embarrassed to confess it" (Sed deb[e]bis fidei tuae simpliciter prodere libertatem. Si a te gentilis exigeret quemadmodum in Cr(istu)[m cr]ederes, c]onfiteri erubescere non deb[eres]).[65]

This *simplicitas christiana* was based on steadfast adherence to a recited creed,[66] and entailed the good sense to know which topics were fit for discussion and which were out of bounds. Even when challenged, common Christians were not to be lured into debate over the central axioms of the faith. In this respect, ordinary Christians had much to learn from the athletes of God, whose presence in Nicaea was treated as a central theme in Rufinus' *Historia ecclesiastica* as well as in later histories. Among these living exemplars, Paphnutius and Spyridon stood out; they also dominated Rufinus' Nicene narrative to an extent that can only be partly explained by Rufinus' profound interest in heroic Christians, or by his reliance on received traditions.

Rufinus regarded credal statements as immutable truths rooted in local traditions reaching back to the apostolic age.[67] This authority and the charisma of heroic confessors were a winning combination, not only historically—though I think that may be shown—but particularly in a narrative.[68] When interrogated, neither one ventured far from rehearsed formulae (as in *aporiae* literature) to explain theological minutiae.[69]

Thus for Rufinus, hagiography took on the additional role of a polemic against heretics, a perspective (or bias) that unexpectedly reintroduced dogmatic controversies into the mainstream of everyday life, into

65. In *Dissertatio Maximini* 10.299r; Gryson, ed., 210. Upon this, Maximinus comments (in *Dissertatio Maximini* 13.299v; Gryson, ed., 210–13) that Cyprian successfully countered Demetrianus with silence in their dispute. But this validation of Cyprian's tactic was not universally shared; Lactantius, in his *Divine Institutes* 5.4, objects to Cyprian's refusal to use reasoned arguments with Demetrianus because, though Cyprian's stubborn reliance on scriptural prooftexts alone might indeed silence one's enemies, it could not confirm Christians in their belief.

66. *Expositio symboli* 3 (Simonetti, ed., 135–37). See Cyril of Jerusalem, *Catecheses* 18.22, for the public profession of the creed after baptism; see also *Apostolic Constitutions* 8:40–41. When Rufinus himself was accused of heresy, he cleared his name by reaffirming the appropriate creed and by uttering a "negative creed" or anathema; see Rufinus, *Apologia ad Anastasium* 8 (CCSL 20:28).

67. See Rufinus, *Expositio symboli* 1–2 (Simonetti, ed., 133–35).

68. See Thélamon, *Païens et chrétiens*, 437: "Les Confesseurs—Rufin joue sur les différents sens que ce terme a acquis à son époque—sont au nombre des plus fermes opposants d'Arius: le Confesseur est l'antitype de l'évêque arien."

69. Yet Paphnutius was portrayed as speaking on behalf of the legitimacy of married priests before the canons governing church discipline were ratified at Nicaea. He did so by citing Paul's famous *dictum* urging the maintenance of the status quo; see Sozomen, *Hist. eccl.* 1.23.

the heart of the social debates over different forms of authority and the institutions they supported. This story opens up to us a world in which people were expected to find the urbane utterances of sophists and orators not only uninteresting but alien and repugnant. Rufinus was probably correct in supposing that the Christians of northern Italy, living apprehensively in the shadows of pillaging Goths, would prefer the tangible power of charismatic confessors to the subtle verbal power of philosophers. After all, the latter was prized only in a very limited cultural context, a context essentially coterminous with the domain of the classical *polis*.[70]

SOCRATES SCHOLASTICUS'
HISTORIA ECCLESIASTICA

The next extant variant of our story is found in Socrates Scholasticus' *Historia ecclesiastica*, a work that resumes where Eusebius' history leaves off and that continues to 439. The author was born and raised in Constantinople, where he met an elderly Novatian priest who claimed to have been present at the Council of Nicaea.[71] Yet, for his description of the council, Socrates did not rely solely on this oral tradition, but drew liberally from Rufinus' *Historia ecclesiastica*. The first two extant books of Socrates' history come from his revised second edition (circa 440), which he composed after reading Athanasius' writings and becoming dissatisfied with his own previous overindebtedness to Rufinus.[72] Knowing this, we can examine the differences between the treatment in the two books and the treatment in their known precedent to uncover a particular critical reception of Rufinus' *Historia ecclesiastica* in late antiquity.

After encomiastic descriptions of Paphnutius and Spyridon, Socrates digressed to recount our story, contrasting the two charismatics with the simple confessor. Socrates placed the debate prior to the formal session of the council, contradicting his model Rufinus, who had placed it in the midst of the full session. It is unclear whether Socrates made this change on the basis of new information, but rather than postulate unknown sources it is more sound to suppose that he had difficulty accepting Rufinus' attribution of this episode to the formal proceedings of

70. See P. R. L. Brown, "The Rise and Function of the Holy Man in Late Antiquity," *JRS* 61 (1971): 80–101.

71. Socrates, *Hist. eccl.* 1.13; 2.38.

72. See Foakes-Jackson, *History of Church History*, 76. See A. Ferrarini, "Tradizioni orali nella storia ecclesiastica di Socrate Scholastico," *Studia Patavina* 28 (1981): 29–54.

the council. His own experience with the procedures of ecclesiastical councils—procedures by then well established—may have suggested that such a debate was too incompatible with the nature of imperial councils to have been authentic.

Socrates' story also differs radically from Rufinus' in its treatment of details. His narrative is shorter and accords the debate less symbolic weight as a paradigmatic confrontation of good versus evil; it is less an anecdotal, almost folkloric, moral tale. He specifies that the participants in the debate were Christians, but does not associate them with particular doctrinal positions. For Socrates, the precise cognitive (i.e., theological) nature of the issues debated was less important than the form of the debate:

> There were also present among each party (μέρος) many laypeople skilled in dialectic who were eager to plead for their own side. But while Eusebius of Nicomedia (whom I mentioned earlier), and Theognis and Maris (the first was the bishop of Nicaea while the latter, Maris, was the bishop of Bithynian Chalcedon) were in support of the opinion of Arius, Athanasius, who, while still a deacon in the church of Alexandria, was esteemed highly by the bishop Alexander (which made him the target of envy, as we shall narrate), nobly contended (ἀντ-αγωνίζειν) with them. Just before (μικρὸν πρό) the unified meeting of the bishops, the dialecticians conducted preliminary contests of words (προαγῶνες τῶν λόγων) before (πρός) many people.[73]

Casting Athanasius as the hero of Nicaea was anachronistic, though understandable. Socrates did not indicate whether the dialecticians who engaged in preliminary logical skirmishes were connected with Eusebius of Nicomedia or with Athanasius, but the lack of such a distinction hardly lessened the impact of Socrates' story, with its generic and timeless quality. Next, the confessor entered the fray:

> When many were drawn by the lure of the reasoning (λόγος), a certain one of the confessors, a layman and an old man who has good judgment (τὸ φρόνημα), opposed the dialecticians, and said to them: "Did Christ and the apostles hand down to us the dialectical art? . . ."

In this version, the confessor not only enjoyed the respect due his advanced age but was deemed in possession of good judgment, no doubt precisely because he spoke against the exercise of dialectic in Christian debates. Because all the participants were already Christians, Socrates ended this episode not with a conversion but by stressing the confessor's success in putting a felicitous end to harmful disputations.

---

73. Socrates, *Hist. eccl.* 1.8 (*PG* 67:64A); my translation.

The old man's intervention had a decisive outcome: "Then the disruptive uproar (θόρυβος) arising out of dialectic was stopped."[74]

A negative evaluation of disputation shaped Socrates' narrative throughout his *Historia ecclesiastica*. For him, the preeminent cause of the controversies that lasted until his own time was the practice of dialectical debate among Christians. He said that one of his reasons for composing the history was to combat the "dialectical and vain deceit [that] confused and at the same time dispersed the apostolic faith of Christianity"; he wished to narrate in a continuous fashion the historical progress of orthodoxy, so that his readers would not be so easily swayed by the sophistry of the moment.[75]

Socrates' conviction that disputation was the chief cause of Christian theological controversies pervaded his treatment of historical material. According to Socrates, the early Arian dispute began when Alexander of Alexandria attempted to publicly explain the Trinity with more precision than his theological acumen warranted.[76] His imprudent words aroused in Arius, "a man not unlearned in the dialectical art," a spirit of contentiousness (φιλονεικία),[77] and the subsequent disagreement between the two became the catalyst for factionalization throughout eastern Christian communities. When Alexander sent out his circular epistles to bishops of other cities, the recipients of his letters "were thereby excited to contention." Disputation spread like a plague, splitting Christian congregations into warring camps, with "some attaching themselves to one side, others to the other," as congregants witnessed their priests wrangling in debates.[78]

The most striking evidence that Socrates considered disputation a major cause, and not just a manifestation, of Christian controversy lies in his narrative of events following the Council of Constantinople in 381.[79] Socrates praised Theodosius for convoking the synod, noting that the emperor innocently supposed that a fair and open examination of the disputed matters would result in universal agreement. But however noble Theodosius' motives, the proposed discussions would not further the cause of unity. Or so thought Socrates, who demonstrated his skepticism by the manner in which he narrated the episode.

Nectarius was then the orthodox bishop of Constantinople and The-

74. Socrates, *Hist. eccl.* 1.8 (*PG* 67:64B); my translation.

75. Socrates, *Hist. eccl.* 1.8 (*PG* 67:64B).

76. Socrates, *Hist. eccl.* 1.5.

77. Socrates, *Hist. eccl.* 1.5. See R. Williams, "The Logic of Arianism," *JTS* n.s. 34 (1983): 56–81.

78. Socrates, *Hist. eccl.* 1.6 (*PG* 67:52C).

79. Socrates, *Hist. eccl.* 5.10.

odosius' confidant.[80] Informed of the emperor's intentions for the council, the bishop grew uneasy, in part because he lacked the experience to preside over such an event. He conferred with Agelius, the bishop of the Novatian Christians in the city, who confessed that he too was not fit to oversee such a debate because of his ignorance of the art of disputation.[81] He, however, had a reader Sisinnius (who later succeeded him as Novatian bishop) who was well versed in both philosophical knowledge and scriptural exegesis. When consulted, this reader expressed the opinion that "debates (αi $\delta\iota\alpha\lambda\acute{\epsilon}\xi\epsilon\iota\varsigma$) not only do not heal schisms, but they make the heresies even more contentious ($\phi\iota\lambda o\nu\epsilon\iota\kappa o\tau\acute{\epsilon}\rho\alpha\varsigma$). On account of this he offered this advice to Nectarius."[82] This sentiment, echoing the general characterization of the christological controversies by Socrates, himself a Novatian Christian, was highlighted by its attribution to one who allegedly advised Theodosius in the organization of an important imperial Christian council.

The emperor's original designs were represented as commonsensical but misguided. Sisinnius proposed to Theodosius (via Nectarius) that the bishops at the forthcoming council "ought on the one hand to avoid dialectical combats ($\tau\grave{\alpha}\varsigma$ $\delta\iota\alpha\lambda\epsilon\kappa\tau\iota\kappa\grave{\alpha}\varsigma$ $\mu\acute{\alpha}\chi\alpha\varsigma$) and to call instead into witness the ancient authorities."[83] This learned reader's voluntary disavowal of philosophical argumentation as a means of resolving theological disputes conveyed a moral more subtle than that contained in Rufinus' tale of the simple confessor and the philosopher.[84] Here was an accomplished champion in philosophical disputation who nevertheless disapproved of its use in mending Christian theological divisions. A genuine expression of mature and informed judgment, the rejection of formal debate could no longer be dismissed as an expedience allowing the unlearned to hide their ignorance.

Theodosius assented to this wise counsel, and asked the leaders of the sects appearing in Constantinople in June 383 to submit to the views of "those teachers who lived previous to the dissension in the church."[85] This request may be regarded as part of the germinating ideological justification for the patristic florilegia that would play a large role in

80. See Baur, *John Chrysostom,* 1:150–51; E. Gerland, "Die Vorgeschichte des Patriarchates von Konstantinopel," *Byzantinisch-neugriechische Jahrbücher* 9 (1932): 217–30, at 226–28.

81. See T. E. Gregory, "Novatianism: A Rigorist Sect in the Christian Roman Empire," *Byzantine Studies* 2 (1975): 1–18.

82. Socrates, *Hist. eccl.* 5.10 (*PG* 67:585A); my translation.

83. Socrates, *Hist. eccl.* 5.10 (*PG* 67:585A); my translation.

84. See De Ghellinck, "Quelques appréciations de la dialectique," 9–10.

85. Socrates, *Hist. eccl.* 5.10 (*PG* 67:585B). "Previous to the period of dissension" refers to the time before 318.

Christian councils. Here, the reaction of Theodosius to Christian controversy recalls Socrates' earlier characterization of Constantine's attitude
toward the disputing parties during the opening phases of the Arian
controversy.[86]

The emperor's decision put the disputing parties in a quandary, for
they had come with their champions in dialectical disputation (οἱ παρ'
ἑκάστοις αὐτῶν διαλεκτικοί).[87] They had clearly expected the council to
be a dialectical contest (πρὸς τὸν ἀγῶνα τῆς διαλέξεως), and were utterly at a loss when that prospect did not materialize. Perceiving that the
attending bishops' fear that an appeal to traditional authorities would
undermine their causes, Theodosius, to eliminate trickery and evasion,
ordered each of the sects to submit in writing a statement of its dogmatic
beliefs, which he would then use as the basis of *his* final decision.[88] On
the appointed day, bishops representing each of the *sectae* were called to
the imperial palace to deliver their creeds,[89] after which the emperor

> betook his own counsel, and began praying assiduously that God would
> help him make the true decision. Then after reading each of the written
> doctrinal statements, he accepted and praised only the one which con-
> tained the *homoousion;* all the rest he condemned on account of the fact
> they introduced a separation of the Trinity.[90]

In this manner, the creed from the Council of Nicaea, after a number
of setbacks at regional councils, again received its formal reinstatement
at Constantinople. The happy outcome was attributed strictly to the
agency of a pious emperor who, praying to God for the wisdom of dis-
cernment, had the good sense to halt destructive theological debates.[91]

Socrates' distrust of verbal disputation was probably informed by
his perspective as a professional lay Christian.[92] Ammianus Marcellinus,

86. See a letter from Constantine to Alexander of Alexandria and Arius quoted in
Eusebius' *Vita Constantini* 2.64–72.

87. Socrates, *Hist. eccl.* 5.10 (PG 67:585–94).

88. See F. Dvornik, "Emperor, Popes and General Councils," *DOP* 6 (1951): 3–23.

89. Socrates, *Hist. eccl.* 5.10 (PG 67:588A).

90. Socrates, *Hist. eccl.* 5.10 (PG 67:589A–92A); my translation. On Constantine's
daily secluded prayers, see Eusebius, *Vita Constantini* 4.22.

91. See *Codex Theod.* 16.4.1 (386), 16.4.2 (388), in Krueger, Meyer, and Mommsen,
eds., 1:853–54. On the importance of the emperor's prayer, see Socrates' account about
Theodosius' prayer before the Battle of Frigidus, in *Hist. eccl.* 5.25.

92. See Foakes-Jackson, *History of Church History,* 77:

> Socrates was by profession a lawyer (*scholasticus*), and was on the side of all
> which made for peace and good government. He notices that whenever the
> Church is distracted, civil disturbances ensue, and he has the practical objection
> of a layman to disputes on theological subtleties being allowed to disturb public
> tranquility.

an army officer and a polytheist, shared Socrates' view to a remarkable degree when he criticized Constantius for importing complexity and subtlety into Christian quarrels, arguing that the frequent meetings of the bishops made a bad situation worse.[93] On his part, Socrates was aware of pagan criticisms of Christian disunity and sought to rebut them in his work.[94]

Socrates believed in a bond of cosmic sympathy between the affairs of state and church, and that Christian quarrels could bring down on the empire such calamities as barbarian invasions. This theory does much to explain Socrates' wish for peace and *eutaxia* in the church: he was troubled by Christian factionalism not only for sectarian reasons but because it affected the very well being of Rome and its people.[95] Belief in a close causal connection between ecclesiastical unity and the manifestation of *pax Dei* could easily lead to a totalitarian vision of ecclesiastical affairs. Surprisingly, Socrates was one of the most tolerant of late antique church historians in his treatment of those ordinarily considered unorthodox.[96]

We must remember that, according to the prevailing orthodoxy of his time, Socrates himself belonged to a schismatic sect, the Novatians. He pleaded not for the forceful suppression of religious dissidents but for a *consensus gentium* that was moderate, tolerant, and conducive to the common good of the Roman world. The goal of polite coexistence was often hurt when opposing sides articulated their differences clearly and publicly, whereas a measure of mutual ignorance could help the cause of peace. This profoundly pragmatic and secular perspective left little room for debates on complex theological issues, which our author confessed not to understand in any case. A peace-loving attitude counted for more than precise knowledge: the new emperor Jovian, besieged by bishops competing for his favor, declared his hatred of contentiousness, adding that he would favor those individuals who promoted concord.[97]

93. Ammianus Marcellinus, *Res gestae* 21.16.18. See also, in *Anecdota* 13, the similar reservation shown later by Procopius in his characterization of the disastrous consequences of Justinian's excessive zeal in pursuing religious controversy.

94. See Downey, "Perspectives of the Early Church Historians," 59–63.

95. See, e.g., Socrates, *Hist. eccl.* 2.10, where he connected the pro-Arian council of Antioch with the invasion of the Franks and an earthquake near Antioch. See also Chestnut, "Kairos and Cosmic Sympathy."

96. Socrates' treatment of fellow Novatians such as Agelius and Sisinnius is generous to a fault. In contrast, his negative judgment of Nestorius stemmed from his hatred of the man both as a troublemaker and a "busybody" heresy hunter; see Socrates, *Hist. eccl.* 7.29; Foakes-Jackson, *History of Church History*, 78.

97. Socrates, *Hist. eccl.* 3.25.

A trained *scholastikos* in the late Roman Empire, Socrates had little reason to regard argumentation as a necessary, let alone healthy, component of sound government, whether secular or ecclesiastical.[98]

SOZOMEN'S *HISTORIA ECCLESIASTICA*

Salamanes Hermeias Sozomenos began writing his ecclesiastical history circa 439 and dedicated the completed work to Theodosius II in 443–44.[99] He was born in Bethelea near Gaza circa 380, and later moved to Constantinople.[100]

For Sozomen, monks and confessors represented the ideological antithesis to reliance on eloquence and dialectic for authority by earning their claim to respectful consideration through ascetic practices and suffering. Their virtuous deeds guaranteed the truth of their beliefs, making verbal articulation or defense unnecessary.[101] Sozomen prefaced his discussion of the controversies of the church by describing the edifying lives of these ascetic Christians, who demonstrated

> the truth of their doctrines by their virtuous way of life. In fact the most useful gift that man had received from God is their philosophy. They ignore many aspects of mathematics and the contrived argumentation of the dialectical art ($\delta\iota\alpha\lambda\epsilon\kappa\tau\iota\kappa\tilde{\eta}\varsigma$ $\tau\epsilon\chi\nu\omega\lambda\omega\gamma\iota\alpha\varsigma$) because they viewed such pursuits as meddling ($\pi\epsilon\rho\iota\epsilon\rho\gamma\omega\nu$), and a profitless waste of time since they contribute nothing to living uprightly. . . . For they do not

98. In 426, Valentinian III issued the "Law of Citations" (*Codex Theod.* 1.4.3) to regulate the function of juristic opinion in legal decision making. Thenceforth, court rulings were to be based on a corpus of five authorities: Gaius, Julius Paulus, Ulpianus, Modestinus, and Papinianus. Judges were instructed to follow the five jurists where they were in consensus, to follow the majority view when opinion was divided, and, when equally divided, to adopt the decision of Papinianus. This rule has been regarded by scholars as a prime indicator of the decline of Roman jurisprudence in late antiquity because the "tyranny of the majority" was set over juristic rationalization; see P. Dalloz, *Institutions politiques et sociales de l'antiquité* (Paris, 1984), 428; W. W. Buckland, *A Text-book of Roman Law from Augustus to Justinian*, 2d ed. (Cambridge, 1932), 27. Under this law, there was no longer room for local discussion or individual judgment in matters already ruled upon by the ancient jurists. Suggesting that this law ought to be seen as part of a broader and more persistent trajectory toward authoritarianism, Dalloz (428) traces the development back to around 325, when the *Sententiae Pauli*, a collection of decisions by the famous jurist Julius Paulus (fl. circa 210) was compiled *sans* argumentation.

99. See C. Roueché, "Theodosius II, the Cities, and the Date of the 'Church History' of Sozomen," *JTS* n.s. 37 (1986): 130–32.

100. He probably also attended the school of law at Gaza; see B. Grillet's introduction to A.-J. Festugière and G. Sabbah, eds., *Sozomène: Histoire ecclésiastique livres I–II*, SC 306 (Paris, 1983), 19 n. 1.

101. Sozomen, *Hist. eccl.* 1.1.

use demonstration to show their virtue (οὐ γὰρ ἐπιδείκνυται ἀρε-τήν), but they practice it, dismissing as nothing the reputation before men.[102]

Sozomen's preface to his Nicene account describes the lives and deeds of confessors and monks more fully than did the work of Socrates.[103] This may be seen as a function of Sozomen's general belief, expressed later in his discussion of the Anomoean controversy, that all the "monk-philosophers" were faithful supporters of the Nicene creed. It was through the widely admired, heroic, and god-loving Christians that the common people also came to hold the right belief.[104]

Sozomen also told a story about Spyridon not found in Socrates' *Historia ecclesiastica*. At a meeting of the local bishops on Cyprus, a certain Triphyllius,[105] the bishop of the Ledri and a *scholastikos*, quoted the scriptural phrase "Take up the bed and walk" but substituted the literary word for "bed," *skimpous*, for the humbler *krabbatos* in the original. Hearing this, Spyridon flew into a rage and reproached Triphyllius for daring to improve the scriptures. He made this outburst so that all present might learn a lesson, for according to Sozomen,

> he was teaching them to keep a man who was proud in words within bounds (μετριάζειν); and he was worthy to give this rebuke because he was reverenced and enjoyed the highest reputation from his deeds, also at the same time he happened to be more advanced in age and in priestliness.[106]

Eloquence was not in and of itself an evil art,[107] unless employed in a spirit of contention or in the persistent investigation of out-of-bounds topics. For Sozomen, the close examination of a subject by its very nature led to differences: "οἷα δὲ εἰκὸς εἰς διαφόρους ζητήσεις περιϊσ-

102. Sozomen, *Hist. eccl.* 1.12 (Festugière and Sabbah, eds., 162–63). See pp. 85–86 on Sozomen's preference for the monks' simplicity and ignorance.

103. For Sabinus of Heraclea's account of Nicaea, see Socrates, *Hist. eccl.* 1.8. For Sozomen's use of Sabinus' account of Nicaea, see G. Schoo, *Die Quellen Kirchenhistorikers Sozomenos* (Berlin, 1911).

104. Sozomen, *Hist. eccl.* 6.27 (Bidez, ed., 276): "καὶ τοὺς ἄλλως φρονοῦντας οἷά γε μὴ καθαρεύοντας νόθων δογμάτων ἀπεστρέφοντο." He attached this statement to his list of ascetic Christians and his discussion of the Anomoean controversy. Thus it may be argued that Sozomen's views of the history of early Arianism and the Council of Nicaea were to a large extent informed by his more abundant and contemporary knowledge of the later Anomoean controversy.

105. See Jerome, *De viris illustribus* 92.

106. Sozomen, *Hist. eccl.* 1.11 (Festugière and Sabbah, eds., 160–61).

107. According to Sozomen, *Hist. eccl.* 1.20, the emperor Constantine, after listening to speeches by the respective parties in the palace, "applauded those who spoke well, [and] rebuked those who displayed a tendency to altercation." The definition of "speaking well" was of course at issue here.

ταμένης τῆς διασκέψεως."[108] He thus shared Socrates' assessment of debate as an unhelpful, even unhealthy, process. He also unabashedly professed his own lack of understanding of the controverted issues.[109]

Writing his *Historia ecclesiastica* about a decade after Socrates had finished his, Sozomen often used his description of theological debates to emphasize the superiority of the Christian life and the manifestation of divine grace.[110] Sozomen either deliberately chose not to use Socrates' idiosyncratic second edition, or he based his work on the latter's unrevised books 1 and 2, which may have represented the debate at Nicaea much as in Rufinus' version. In effect, Rufinus' version resurfaced in Sozomen's work; Sozomen also developed one of the potential trajectories of Rufinus' story into an exemplary demonstration of Christian *aretē* by linking the confessor's triumph over the philosopher with another story in which a pious Christian confounded pagan sophistry.

At a meeting before the day the council was to be formally convoked, many bishops and their accompanying clergy, all of them skilled in debate (δεινοὶ διαλέγεσθαι) and trained in the rules of disputation (μεθόδους τῶν λόγων), met to conduct a public debate.[111] Foremost among the participants was Athanasius, who even as a deacon took a leading position in the deliberating process (βουλή). Having told this much, Sozomen digressed into two "miraculous" stories before proceeding with the account of the disputation. The first is a variant of the multiform story we have been discussing:

> While these disputations were being carried on, certain of the pagan philosophers became desirous of taking part in them; some, because they wished for information as to the doctrine that was inculcated; and others, because, feeling incensed against the Christians on account of the recent suppression of the pagan religion, they wished to convert the inquiry about doctrine into a strife about words, so as to introduce dissensions among them, and to make them appear as holding contradictory opinions (τὴν περὶ τοῦ δόγματος ζήτησιν εἰς ἔριδας λόγων ἐνέβαλλον, ὥστε πρὸς ἑαυτὸ στασιάζειν καὶ ἐναντίον δοκεῖν).[112]

Of Sozomen's two explanations for the presence of pagan philosophers at a Christian convention, the first—sheer curiosity about the upstart religion—seems reasonable enough, although mere plausibility

108. Sozomen, *Hist. eccl.* 1.17 (Festugière and Sabbah, eds., 196–97); see also *Hist. eccl.* 3.13 on the disruptive effects of verbal contests.

109. Sozomen, *Hist. eccl.* 7.17 (Festugière and Sabbah, eds., 41, 48–49, esp. n. 5).

110. See Festugière and Sabbah, eds., 41.

111. Sozomen, *Hist. eccl.* 1.17 (Festugière and Sabbah, eds., 196–97).

112. Sozomen, *Hist. eccl.* 1.18 (trans. from NPNF 253; Greek text in Festugière and Sabbah, eds., 198–99); see Festugière and Sabbah, eds., 37–41 on Sozomen's treatment of miracles.

does not prove its authenticity. The second explanation—a scheme to undermine Christian unity and discredit the religion by introducing dialectical disputation—appears much more insidious, as it reiterates a prejudice against philosophical reasoning as the primary cause for discord within the church catholic. Following this expository introduction, Sozomen adhered more closely to his source, Rufinus' *Historia ecclesiastica*, in depicting the confrontation between the philosopher and the confessor:

> It is related that one of these philosophers, priding himself on his acknowledged superiority of eloquence (λόγων κομπάζων), began to ridicule the priests, and thereby roused the indignation of a simple old man, highly esteemed as a confessor, who, although unskilled in logical refinements and wordiness, undertook to oppose him. The less serious of those who knew the confessor, raised a laugh at his expense for engaging in such an undertaking; but the more thoughtful felt anxious lest, in opposing so eloquent a man, he should only render himself ridiculous (μὴ παρὰ ἀνδρὶ τεχνίτῃ λόγων γέλοιος φανείη); yet his influence was so great, and his reputation was so high among them, that they could not forbid his engaging in the debate.[113]

The confessor stepped into the fray, recited his credo, and exhorted the philosopher not to waste his time in attempting to understand what could only be grasped with humble, unmeddling faith (ἀπεριέργως). The philosopher, dumbfounded by the confessor's words (πρὸς ταῦτα καταπλαγείς), assented to their truth. He even professed that his enlightenment had been brought about by nothing less than divine intervention (οὐκ ἀθεεί).[114]

It is significant that Sozomen chose to reject Socrates' shorter and more idiosyncratic variant in favor of Rufinus'.[115] But unlike Rufinus' story, which Thélamon characterizes as a typological drama, Sozomen's account was transformed by the second "miraculous" story into a folk tale.

Sozomen introduced the second tale as a similar marvel (παραπλήσιον θαῦμα), a bit of hearsay (λέγεται) most likely picked up in the bustling streets of Constantinople.[116] It certainly had a strong local flavor. After Constantine founded his new imperial capital, a number of the philosophers from the incorporated pagan city of Byzantium approached Alexander, the first bishop of Christian Constantinople, to find out whether he dared to debate with them. Although Alexander, a

---

113. Sozomen, *Hist. eccl.* 1.18 (trans. from NPNF 253–54; Greek text in Festugière and Sabbah, eds., 200, and Bidez, ed., 39–40).
114. Sozomen, *Hist. eccl.* 1.18 (Festugière and Sabbah, eds., 200–201).
115. See Schoo, *Die Quellen Kirchenhistorikers Sozomenos*, 19, 26.
116. Sozomen, *Hist. eccl.* 1.18 (Festugière and Sabbah, eds., 200–201).

virtuous man (καλὸς καὶ ἀγαθός), was untrained in the philosophical discourse of the schools (ὧν τοιαύτης λόγων ἀτριβής), he agreed to meet their challenge, perhaps because he considered his upright way of life a sufficient guard against subtle words.[117] The philosophers gathered, eager for debate (πάντες διαλέγεσθαι ἐβούλοντο), but before their chosen spokesman could say a word Alexander said: "In the name of Jesus Christ, I command you to be silent (μὴ λαλεῖν)." After these words, the philosopher could not utter a sound.[118] An anticlimactic ending perhaps, but telling in its crude abruptness.

From dialectical debate to quiet virtue to the silencing of adversaries: this movement was for Sozomen the outline of a Christian miracle and triumph.[119] His high regard for the self-chosen ignorance and virtuous silence of Christian ascetics informed Sozomen's choice to favor Rufinus' version as well as the particulars of his own treatment of the story.[120]

Sozomen's respect for asceticism was born of close personal involvement. The entire city of Bethelea, where Sozomen's family was among the first of the aristocratic families to become Christian, had been converted when Hilarion, an anchorite from the Egyptian desert, cast a demon out of Alaphion, a citizen of Bethelea and possibly Sozomen's relative.[121] To one who grew up in a tradition validating the miraculous power of charismatic Christian ascetics, the power of persuasion naturally paled by comparison.[122]

GELASIUS OF CYZICUS' *SYNTAGMA*

Gelasius of Cyzicus' version of the episode in his *Syntagma*, written circa 475–76, contains two separate confrontations between philosophers and

117. Sozomen, *Hist. eccl.* 1.18 (Festugière and Sabbah, eds., 200–201).

118. Sozomen, *Hist. eccl.* 1.18 (Festugière and Sabbah, eds., 200–201). Compare this scenario with the abject fate of Julia in Pseudo-Mark the Deacon's *Vita Porphyrii* as discussed in Chapter 3.

119. See Sozomen, *Hist. eccl.* 1.18 (Festugière and Sabbah, eds., 200–203). The miracle doublet (one occurring at Nicaea and the other at Constantinople) are favorably compared to pagan propaganda about Julian the Chaldean, who reputedly cleft stones with bare hands.

120. Festugière and Sabbah, eds., 85–86: "[Sozomène est un] fervent admirateur de la simplicité des moines, de cette ignorance volontaire qu'il déclare être la suprême sagesse."

121. See Sozomen, *Hist. eccl.* 3.14, 21–28 (Bidez, ed., 121–22) and Valois' comments in *PG* 67:1259n. 11. See also Jerome, *Vita Hilarionis* (*PL* 23:29–54); Van Dam, "From Paganism to Christianity," 8–10.

122. Sozomen may not have been simply pandering to his audience, the character of which remains a matter for discussion; see F. Paschoud, *Cinq études zur Zosime* (Paris, 1975), 212; Festugière and Sabbah, eds., 78n. 1. The former argues for an elevated audience, the latter a popular one.

bishops.[123] The first is the multiform story we have been examining; the second, more substantial segment is a dialogue between a philosopher named Phaidon and a number of bishops at Nicaea. The connection between the debate and the dialogue is one of the two major textual questions of this tradition; the other is the relationship of the versions of Rufinus and Gelasius of Caesarea. Gelasius of Cyzicus claimed that his detailed book 2 derived from a record made of the Council of Nicaea by Dalmatius, the bishop of Cyzicus who had attended the meeting. The *Liber Dalmatii*, purportedly transcribed from the stenographic notes of the proceedings at Nicaea, later passed into the keeping of Gelasius' father, a presbyter of the Cyzican church.

The question of whether a set of stenographic *acta* at Nicaea ever existed is too complex to be treated here. Suffice it to say that while Loeschcke,[124] the editor of Gelasius' *Syntagma*, is inclined to acknowledge the authenticity of the dialogue fragment, the majority of scholars have decided against this judgment.[125] The strongest arguments against its authenticity are the lack of attestation of the existence of stenographic records from the Nicene proceedings, and the fact that the theological content of the dialogue clearly indicates a polemic against both Anomoean and Macedonian views, suggesting a date of redaction, if not outright composition, in the late fourth or early fifth century. The dialogue records verbatim a series of acerbic interchanges between a pagan philosopher named Phaidon and a number of prominent bishops, including Eustathius of Antioch, the council president Ossius, Eusebius of Caesarea, and Leontius of Caesarea. While not impossible, it is highly implausible that a pagan was chosen as spokesman for the Arian "opposition" and engaged so many famous bishops in a lengthy debate based on scriptural premises. Furthermore, the assertion that the bishops spoke on behalf of the entire synod has the air of an ex post facto

123. This section from book 2 of Gelasius of Cyzicus' late-fifth-century compilation of the history of Nicaea, the *Syntagma*, was, according to the author's own report, derived from a source called the *Liber Dalmatii*, containing two accounts of philosophers who argued Arius' case before an assembly of pious bishops in full council. The first is the multiform story that appeared in the *Historiae ecclesiasticae* of Rufinus, Socrates, and Sozomen, and is told in the third person. The second debate, comprising the bulk of the *Liber*, purports to be a transcription of a stenographic record of the proceedings of the Council of Nicaea in 325, a record not noted in any contemporary sources. This section was marked off according to the convention of a dialogue, with alternating remarks by the philosopher Phaidon and various bishops speaking on behalf of the entire synod.

124. G. Loeschcke, "Das *Syntagma* des Gelasius Cyzicenus," *RhM* 60 (1905): 594–613; 61 (1906): 34–77; idem, *Das Syntagma des Gelasius von Cyzicus* (Bonn, 1906).

125. See Jugie, "La dispute des philosophes païens," who sees a later tradition, *contra* Loeschcke, *Das Syntagma des Gelasius von Cyzicus*.

conception of what Nicaea was all about: the unified consensus of the fathers in stout opposition to the provocations of self-seeking and wrong-thinking individuals.

The dialogue itself is an exegetical contest, with both sides pitting scriptural arguments (*martyria*) against each other. Thus even a pagan philosopher accepted scriptural proofs as adequate premises for his *apodeixeis*. One rather suspects the adaptation of one or more florilegia or patristic catenae to a dialogue form bearing greater resemblance to question-and-answer dialogues (*erōteseis kai apokriseis*) than to literary or philosophical ones. The level of the reasoning is not very high: the coup de grâce that brought the philosopher to confess Christ is a clumsy analogical argument comparing the persons of the Trinity to fire, emanation, and light.

Thus it is understandable that the scholarly consensus questions the authenticity of Gelasius of Cyzicus' *Syntagma*, particularly the *Liber Dalmatii*, and its value as an independent source for Nicaea.[126] Most recently, Ehrhardt has argued that Gelasius' *Syntagma*, though worthless as a source for the fourth century, is useful as a document about more contemporary controversies.[127] This conclusion is sufficient here because we are primarily interested in the document as evidence for the reception of Nicaea in the fifth century.

The multiform story opens with a new characterization of the philosopher as a hireling (ὁ μισθωτός) of the Arians. According to Gelasius of Cyzicus, the debate occurred during the formal session of the council:

> A certain person, among those who were in the hire of Arius, was a philosopher admired above all others. He stoutly maintained many and numerous contentions for Arius' sake against our bishops for a good number of days in front of all the rest who were exceedingly astounded. This resulted in a large audience every day on account of the encounter (συμβολή) of words (διὰ λόγων), with the majority of the assembled crowd thrown into confusion, while the philosopher was advancing the impious blasphemies of Arius against those who were arguing on behalf of the holy synod, and saying concerning the Son of God that "there was a time (πότε) when he was not" and "he is a fashioned and created being made out of nothing and from other substances (οὐσίαι) and *hypostases*." He put forth [lit., "there was to him"] a great contest (ἀγών) for the sake of the polluted teachings of Arius and showers of speeches (λόγοι). He fought against the Son of God and inveighed against the χορός of those saintly priests.[128]

126. See Person, *Mode of Theological Decision Making*, 53.

127. See C. T. H. R. Ehrhardt, "Constantinian Documents in Gelasius of Cyzicus' *Ecclesiastical History*," *JAC* 23 (1980): 48–57.

128. Gelasius of Cyzicus, *Syntagma* 2.13.1–2 (Loeschcke and Heinemann, eds., 61).

The implicit connection in Rufinus' *Historia ecclesiastica* between the philosopher and the Arian cause has now been made explicit.[129] This description mobilized in one stroke two deeply ingrained late Roman prejudices against the philosopher and his cause: he acted on the base motive of material gain, and his position as a hireling suggested a low social station.

During the debate, the philosopher abandoned all sense of decorum, behaving like a Corybant, with the abandon normally associated with frenzied females in Greek culture. This portrayal discredited the philosopher as lacking the self-restraint so important to late antique elites, and tarnished the practice of disputation itself as conducive to a loss of self-control.[130]

The philosopher's zeal was insufficient for helping him carry the day. As in the other versions, the philosopher was destined to be worsted by the confessor. Struck dumb and humbled, he conceded defeat and was led by the old man to a church to be baptized.[131] Faced with this felicitous and unexpected outcome, "the entire synod rejoiced" (ἡ σύνοδος ἔχαιρεν).[132]

From the typological drama of Rufinus to the miracle story of Sozomen, this story had evolved almost imperceptibly[133] into an account of exorcism in Gelasius' *Syntagma*. Here the word *dynamis* was given back one of its concrete meanings as the power to effect miracles; God, "in order to show that his kingdom consists not in speech (λόγος) but in power (δύναμις), not only silenced but also forcibly cast out (ἐξέβαλεν) the evil spirit speaking through (ἐν) the philosopher by means of one of his servants there."[134]

This episode marked the complete demonization of the process of verbal argumentation, now termed the "diabolical skill of words (ἡ τῶν λόγων διαβολικὴ εὐτεχνία)."[135] The philosopher even told his disciples that, though he formerly opposed *logoi* with *logoi*, "when a certain di-

---

129. Gelasius of Cyzicus, *Syntagma* 2.13.1 (Loeschcke and Heinemann, eds., 61): "Εἶς δέ τις τῶν μισθωτῶν Ἀρείου φιλόσοφος."

130. Chrysanthius of Sardis also associated disputation with the rousing of one's *thumos*; see Eunapius, *VS* 502. The disciples of Chrysanthius who delighted in disputation were specifically described as behaving like Corybants.

131. "εἰς τὴν ἐκκλησίαν." According to Gelasius, the synod was held at the imperial palace, a fact implying direct imperial supervision and the exclusion of undesirable hoi polloi.

132. Gelasius of Cyzicus, *Syntagma* 2.13.15 (Loeschcke and Heinemann, eds., 64).

133. Jugie does not seem to have noticed this addition in his "La dispute des philosophes païens."

134. Gelasius of Cyzicus, *Syntagma* 2.13.6 (Loeschcke and Heinemann, eds., 62).

135. Gelasius of Cyzicus, *Syntagma* 2.13.4 (Loeschcke and Heinemann, eds., 14).

vine power (δύναμίς τις θεῖα) proceeded from the mouth of the questioner in the place of words (ἀντὶ λόγων), words are unable to withstand the power any further, for man is not able to withstand God."[136]

SOME LATER TRADITIONS

As authentic records of the events that took place at Nicaea, the above traditions contain little to commend themselves. However, as records of the reception of Nicaea and of the conciliar process in general, they speak volumes about how particular authors construed the role of disputation in settling Christian theological differences.[137]

Our multiform story was to enjoy a long and varied life beyond the fifth century. It resurfaced in various compilations, including Theodore the Reader's *Historia tripartita*, an "ecclesiastical history from the time of Constantine to the reign of Justinian," according to the Suidas.[138] In this writing, Sozomen's second story has completely usurped the place of the Nicene debate: Alexander, the bishop of Byzantium, confronted by one of several philosophers who wished to debate (διαλεχθῆναι) him concerning his faith (περὶ πίστεως), silenced his challenger with the words, "In the name of Jesus Christ the Son of God, I command you to be silent and not to utter a sound (ἐπιτάττω σοι σιωπᾶν καὶ μὴ φθέγγεσθαι)."[139]

In the *Chronicon* of Georgius Monachus the Sinner (ὁ ἁμαρτωλός), the role of the simple intervener is played by none other than Spyridon, the Cyprian bishop.[140] He also appears as a refuter of heretics at Nicaea

136. Gelasius of Cyzicus, *Syntagma* 2.13.14 (Loeschcke and Heinemann, eds., 64).

137. See Ehrhardt, "Constantinian Documents."

138. Suidas, *Lexicon*, s.v. Θεόδωρος (θ 153).

139. Theodore the Reader, *Historia tripartita* 1, epitome 14 (G. C. Hansen, ed., *Theodoros Anagnostes Kirchengeschichte* GCS [Berlin, 1971], 7):

Κωνσταντίνου τοῦ βασιλέως ὑπὸ Ἑλλήνων φιλοσόφων ὀνειδισθέντος εἰς τὸ Βυζάντιον, ὡς οὐ πράττοι καλῶς παρὰ τὰ ἔθη τῶν παρὰ Ῥωμαίοις βασιλευσάντων διαγινόμενος, ἀλλὰ νεωτερίζοι τὴν θρησκείαν μεταθέμενος, ἔδοξεν ἕνα τῶν φιλοσόφων διαλεχθῆναι Ἀλεξάνδρῳ τῷ ἐπισκόπῳ τοῦ Βυζαντίου περὶ τῆς πίστεως. λόγων δὲ ἄπειρος ὢν Ἀλέξανδρος, τὰ δὲ ἄλλα θεῖος, ἐν τῇ ἡμέρᾳ τῆς διαλέξεως εἶπε τῷ διαλεκτικῷ φιλοσόφῳ· "ἐν ὀνόματι Ἰησοῦ Χριστοῦ τοῦ θεοῦ ἐπιτάττω σοι σιωπᾶν καὶ μὴ φθέγγεσθαι." ἅμα δὲ τῷ λόγῳ ἐφιμώθη καὶ ἔμεινεν ἄλαλος.

See J. Bidez, *La tradition manuscrite de Sozomène et la Tripartite de Théodore le Lecteur* (Leipzig, 1908).

140. In C. de Boor, ed., *Georgii Monachi chronicon* (Leipzig, 1904), 506. See Paul Van den Ven, *La légende de Saint Spyridon, évêque de Trimithonte* (Louvain, 1953). He discusses

in the illuminated manuscript of the London Psalter.[141] In the *Chronicon,* Spyridon commanded the philosopher to listen, "in the name of Jesus Christ," to the doctrines of truth (τὰ τῆς ἀληθείας δόγματα). As before, the dogmata turned out to be a credal formula.

The identification of the simple confessor with Spyridon only made concrete a connection hinted at in Rufinus' *Historia ecclesiastica,* where the debate was placed adjacent to stories of charismatic confessors, signifying the natural alliance between Christian virtue and holy simplicity against the empty sophistry of words. In contrast, Spyridon's status as a bishop suggests a shift from a world of freewheeling charismatic Christians to a more settled and hierarchical Christian empire.

In the west, the story was preserved not only through Rufinus but also in Cassiodorus' Latin *Historia tripartita,* comprising excerpts from the works of Socrates, Sozomen, and Theodoret. Understandably, Cassiodorus juxtaposed Sozomen's two stories with Socrates' markedly different version without trying to harmonize them,[142] separating them by "fertur enim et aliud."[143]

Why is this interesting episode absent from Theodoret's *Historia ecclesiastica,* and what can explain his decision to omit it from his account of Nicaea? It may be that he was suspicious of the story's authenticity; more likely, he did not share the bias against public debate that was a hallmark of all versions of the story. Theodoret, the author of a treatise that demonstrated the truth of Christian dogma with syllogisms, reported that Eustathius of Antioch attributed the Council of Nicaea's failure to condemn the Eusebians to the absence of thorough discussion.

---

mostly earlier sources: Athanasius, Rufinus, Socrates, Sozomen, Gelasius of Caesarea (whom he accepts as *"Rufin-grec,"* 31) and Gelasius of Cyzicus (30–33). See 27–30 on whether or not Spyridon was a confessor. The ambiguity caused by the confessor's lack of a concrete rank in the ecclesiastical hierarchy is now resolved in the story; see also E. R. Hardy, "The Decline and Fall of the Confessor-Presbyter," *SP* 15 (1984): 221–25; *Apostolic Constitutions* 8.23.

141. London Psalter folio 107v. See C. Walter, *L'iconographie des conciles dans la tradition byzantine,* Archives de l'Orient Chrétien 13 (Paris, 1970), 256–57 and fig. 121.

142. Cassiodorus, *Historia ecclesiastica tripartita* 2.3.1–2 (CSEL 71:87) (= Socrates, *Hist. eccl.* 1.8):

> Cumque plurimi disputationis delectatione traherentur, unus quidam ex confessoribus laicis simplicem habens sensum dialecticis obviavit dicens: "Audite igitur, Christus et apostolici non nobis artem dialecticam tradiderunt vanamque verborum fallaciam, sed puram scientiam fide et operibus bonis observandam." Haec dicente iuvene et animo sene praesentes quidem mirati sunt dictumque probaverunt, dialectici vero satisfactione suscepta cessarunt rationem quippe simplicem veritatis audientes.

143. Cassiodorus, *Historia ecclesiastica tripartita* 2.3.3 (CSEL 71:87).

This was because, we are told, crypto-Eusebians at the council, "under the pretext of maintaining peace, silenced all who were deemed to be the best speakers (τοὔνομα προβαλλόμενοι τῆς εἰρηνῆς, κατεσίγησαν μὲν ἅπαντας τοὺς ἄριστα λέγειν εἰωθότας)," for fear that a rational discussion would expose their heretical ideas before a hostile "majority."[144] This attitude blamed the ability of the Eusebian party to evade detection at Nicaea, and ultimately the failure of the conciliar process, on a lack of serious and critical debate.

The many versions of this Nicene tradition can be explained in part by the authors' different narrative strategies and redactional biases. Yet a remarkably consistent theme emerges—a matrix linking the Christian bias against public disputation to stories about charismatic ascetics, to irreducible credal formulatiöns, and to the ideology of Christian unity (ὁμόνοια) expressed liturgically through vocal expressions of consensus (ὁμοφωνία).

Another consistent theme that surfaces in these variants is a hint that perhaps theological and philosophical differences were given insufficient opportunity for discussion at Nicaea. Such a suspicion would certainly not be unjustified in light of Constantine's opening address urging unanimity and harmony: "Having forsaken contentious dispute (ἔρις), let us find the solution to the matters under investigation from the inspired words."[145]

Even our incomplete records make clear that the Council of Nicaea was no meeting of a debating society; as Murphy points out in his study on Rufinus, debates most likely did not take place at Nicaea in a "democratic" fashion.[146] Subsequent councils were even less "democratic," the more so because they emulated traditional Roman senatorial proceedings with their emphasis on correct procedure, seniority in the offering of sententiae, written documents such as creeds and hupographai, traditional authorities, and even acclamations.[147]

The fear that a single dialectician could disrupt an imperial Christian council by engaging the assembled bishops in disputation may well have

144. Theodoret, Hist. eccl. 1.8.3 (Parmentier and Scheidweiler, eds., 34).
145. Theodoret, Hist. eccl. 1.7.12 (Parmentier and Scheidweiler, eds., 32). See also Constantine's letter to Alexander in Eusebius, Vita Constantini 2.64–72. After the synod, Constantine emphasized in a letter (with perhaps too much zeal to be convincing) that all the controverted points had indeed (rumor notwithstanding) been given careful consideration. For a discussion of Constantine's prominence at the council and his many interventions in the process, see Barnes, Constantine and Eusebius, 215–19.
146. See Murphy, Rufinus of Aquileia, 345–411.
147. See H. Gelzer, "Die Konzilien als Reichsparlamente," in idem., Ausgewählte Kleine Schriften (Leipzig, 1907), 142–55. For a fuller exposition of these conciliar trappings, see Chapter 7.

appeared reasonable in the late fourth and early fifth centuries, a transitional period when much was uncertain. Once a consensual conciliar tradition was firmly rooted, the bishops were able to hold their own, and the temporary services of a charismatic confessor were no longer required to confront an equally charismatic dialectician-philosopher. In this respect, one might say that, although the bishops in the story lost, the victory ultimately belonged to them. As if to drive this point home, a letter of Ambrose, himself a vocal advocate of the dangers of relying on dialectic in Christian disputes,[148] was read at the Council of Ephesus in 431 as part of the patristic *testimonia*. In it, the bishop of Milan freely paraphrased I Corinthians 2:4:

> Sileant igitur inanes de sermonibus quaestiones, quia regnum dei, sicut scriptum est, non in persuasione verbum est, sed in ostensione virtutis.[149]

> Let the empty questions regarding speech cease now, for the Kingdom of God, as it is written, consists not in the persuasion of words but in the exhibition of virtuous deeds.

148. See *Palladii Ratairensis fragmenta* (R. Gryson, ed., *Scholies ariennes sur le concile d'Aquilée*, SC 267 [Paris, 1980]), where Ambrose discussed the character of Arian Christians, including the Anomoeans: "Omnem enim vim venenorum suorum in dialectica disputatione constituunt, quae filosoforum sententia definitur, non adstruendum habentes studium, sed studium destruendi. sed in dialectica conplacuit d(e)o salvum facere populum suum."

149. *ACO* 1.2, 17.25 (Schwartz, ed., 56). Latin text from *Collectio Veronensis*; Greek text from *Collectio Vaticana* in *ACO* 1.1.2, 54 (Schwartz, ed., 42–43).

· SEVEN ·

THE CONTAINMENT
OF THE *LOGOS*

The first council of Persian bishops, under the auspices of Yazdigird I, met on 6 January 410 at the Sasanid capital of Ctesiphon. The synod, named after Mar Isaac, *katholikos* and bishop of Seleucia and Ctesiphon, was convoked to receive a letter dispatched by eastern Roman bishops to Mar Maruta of Maipherqat. Bishop Maruta addressed the assembly of his peers, informed them of the letter detailing the outcome of Nicaea, and exhorted them to sign an agreement affirming the conclusions reached by their Roman counterparts.[1] According to the surviving Syriac *acta*, the bishops readily concurred and collectively sealed the pact with acclamations and an official statement recorded by notaries. The rationale behind committing their decision to writing is elucidated for us in canon 17: it was thought to help Christians avoid uncertainty and confusion in the future. In other words, the Persian bishops found a well-kept written record critical to the establishment of a definitive statement of orthodoxy for all time.[2]

1. J.-B. Chabot, ed., *Synodicon Orientale ou recueil de synodes nestoriens* (Paris, 1902), 21–22 (Syriac text), 260–62 (French). On the perceived benefits of holding such a meeting, see 19 (Syriac) and 257 (French): "Par leur venue et leur réunion, les disputes cessassent, les schismes et les divisions n'existassent plus." On the role of the *katholikos,* see C. Detlef and G. Müller, "Stellung und Bedeutung des Katholikos-Patriarchen von Seleukeia-Ktesiphon im Altertum," *Oriens Christianus* 53 (1969): 227–45.

2. Chabot, ed., *Synodicon Orientale*, 30 (Syriac), 269 (French). The Synod of Mar Isaac became a touchstone for later Syrian Christian councils; see the proceedings of the Synod of Mar Yahbalaha I in 420, in Chabot, ed., *Synodicon Orientale*, 39, 279–80.

This sentiment toward the written word would have been warmly received by many of the Persian bishops' Roman brethren, who met the following year in Carthage to deliberate on the disagreements between catholic and Donatist Christians in North Africa. The famous Council of Carthage of 411 left a rare, almost complete record of its proceedings, a record scrupulously authenticated by both sides of the controversy.[3]

The synodal tradition of the Latin west had developed differently from the customs of Greek-speaking churches, especially before Constantine and the rise of an imperial conciliar tradition.[4] Even then, a clear preference for procedural norms resembling the reading of *relationes* and the expression of *sententiae* in the Roman Senate is clearly evident from the stenographic records of African councils;[5] the technical terminology used to describe Roman senatorial and conciliar proceedings passed effortlessly into the vocabulary of the synods of Latin-speaking Christians.[6] In the Greek east, however, the language describing councils maintained a link to the public disputations of the schools.[7] The interrelatedness of the two traditions took a striking form at the Council of Sirmium in 351, when Photinus reacted to a conciliar decision to depose him by challenging his rival bishops, especially Basil of Ancyra, to a public disputation presided over by a good number of senators (τῶν

3. *Gesta Conlationis Carthaginensis anno 411* (CCSL 149a, S. Lancel, ed. [Turnholt, 1974]). On the use of stenography in this council, see especially the studies by E. Tengström, *Die Protokollierung der Collatio Carthaginensis. Beiträge zur Kenntnis der römischen Kurzschrift nebst einem Exkurs über das Wort scheda (schedula)* (Göteborg, 1962); H. C. Teitler, *Notarii et Exceptores*. See a valuable analysis of the performative dynamics of this council in B. Shaw, "African Christianity: Disputes, Definitions, and 'Donatist,'" in M. R. Greenshields and T. A. Robinson, eds., *Orthodoxy and Heresy in Religious Movements: Discipline and Dissent* (Lewiston-Queenston-Lampeter, 1992), 5–34, at 16 ff.

4. P. Batiffol, "Le règlement des premiers conciles africains et le règlement du sénat romain," *Bulletin d'ancienne littérature et d'archéologie chrétienne* 11 (1913): 3–19; Gelzer, "Konzilien als Reichsparlamente." Gelzer compares the senatorial proceedings set out in the *gesta* accompanying the adoption of the *Theodosian Code* with the imperial councils, especially the Council of Chalcedon. See also now the critique of Batiffol's thesis by P. Amidon, "The Procedure of St. Cyprian's Synods," *VChr* 37 (1983): 328–39.

5. See the nature of the proceedings of the Council of Carthage in 256, which dealt with the issue of the rebaptism of heretics, in *Sententiae episcoporum numero LXXXVII de haereticis baptizandis* (CSEL 3.2:435–61); the Council of Carthage in 345–48 entailed the confirmation of the statement of the leading bishops' opinions by universal acclamations, see *Concilia Africae anno 345–anno 525* (CCSL 149, C. Munier, ed. [Turnholt, 1974], 3–10). The same occurred at the councils of Carthage in 390 and Hippo in 393, in ibid., 12–19, 20–21.

6. On late imperial senatorial proceedings, see P. de Francisci, "Per la storia del senato romano e della Curia," *Rendiconti della Pontificia Accademia di Archeologia* 22 (1946–47): 275–317. On the councils of the imperial court, see J. A. Crook, *Consilium Principis: Imperial Councils and Counsellors from Augustus to Diocletian* (Cambridge, 1955).

7. See Gelzer, "Konzilien als Reichsparlamente," on the proliferation of local municipal councils in the Greek east after Diocletian and Constantine.

συγκλητικῶν οὐκ ὀλίγοι).[8] The staff of seven stenographers who recorded the event was borrowed from the imperial administration.[9]

Disputation was officially ruled out at the Council of Aquileia in 381.
It was noteworthy to his opponents that Ambrose of Milan delivered a
short tirade on the bane of dialectical sophistry—according to the *Palladii Ratiarensis fragmenta*, the Arian version of the conciliar proceedings—
in which he roundly denounced his rivals' characteristic facility with
disputation.[10] Instead, the council proceeded as an interrogation of the
Arian bishops Palladius and Secundianus, with Ambrose acting in the
role of magistrate for which his background had prepared him. Palladius
objected to his opponents' arrogation of the role of judges,[11] and claimed
that their monopoly over the stenographers would render the subsequent conciliar *acta* very one-sided.[12] Palladius' complaints show that he
regarded the event as an unfair trial, with no *exceptores* from his own
side or *auditores* who might be sympathetic to his cause.[13] In the face of
these repeated protestations, Ambrose refused to budge and, by means
of a timely request for the *sententiae* by the bishops, secured an anathema of Palladius.[14] Ambrose, a former lawyer and imperial governor,
was thus able to mobilize the same authoritative resources available to
a Roman magistrate to secure the victory of the catholic cause at the
council.

8. Socrates, *Hist. eccl.* 2.30. See also Sozomen, *Hist. eccl.* 4.6; Epiphanius, *Adversus
haereses* 71.1.4; Nicephorus, *Hist. eccl.* 9.31. Discussed in A. Wickenhauser, "Die Stenographische Aufnahme der Disputation zwischen Photinus und Basilius auf der Synode zu
Sirmium im Jahre 351," *Korrespondenzblatt: Amtliche Zeitung des könig. Stenographischen Instituts zu Dresden* 51 (1906): 259–65. For the confusing plurality of fourth-century councils
held in Sirmium, see Barnes, *Athanasius and Constantius*, 231–32.

9. See Epiphanius, *Adversus haereses* 71.1; Wickenhauser, "Stenographische Aufnahme," 263–65. There were an imperial secretary, an *exceptor* of the praetorian prefect,
three *memoriales* from the *scrinium memoriae*, and two imperial *notarii*.

10. *Palladii Ratiarensis fragmenta* 81 (Gryson, ed., 264–65).

11. *Gesta episcoporum Aquileia adversus haereticos Arrianos* 42 (Gryson, ed., 360–63).
Palladius protested that "ego te iudicem non patior quem impietatis arguo." Later (48;
Gryson, ed., 366–67): "Cum impietatis te argui, te iudice non utor. Transgressor es."

12. *Gesta episcoporum Aquileia* 43 (Gryson, ed., 362–63):

Palladius dixit: Non tibi respondeo, quia quaecumque ego dixi non sunt scripta.
Uestra tantummodo scribuntur uerba, non uobis respondeo. Ambrosius episcopus dixit: Omnia uides scribi. Denique quae scripta sunt abundant ad tuae
impietatis indicium. . . . Palladius dixit: Si uultis, exceptores nostri ueniant et sic
totum excipiatur.

13. *Gesta episcoporum Aquileia* 51 (Gryson, ed., 368–69): "Palladius dixit: Date auditores, ueniant et ex utraque parte exceptores. Non potest esse iudices si auditores non
habuerimus et ex utraque parte uenerint qui audiant."

14. *Gesta episcoporum Aquileia* 54 (Gryson, ed., 370–71): "Quoniam omnes consistunt
uiri christiani et Deo probati fratres et consacerdotes nostri, dicat unusquisque quod sibi
uidetur."

When stenographers recorded the words spoken in council and later wrote them out in verbatim transcriptions, the speakers became directly accountable for what they said. During the Council of Aquileia, Palladius was extremely cautious, often refusing to respond to questions. The dynamics of public debate were altered dramatically when one could be held responsible for everything one said in the heat of discussion. Clever argumentation in rapid-fire debate became less important than ensuring that one's statements were internally coherent and inoffensive to public sentiment. The attendance of stenographers tended to retard the pace of the proceedings considerably.

The presence of imperial commissioners, increasingly common after the reign of the "activist" emperor Constantius, likewise affected the atmosphere of the councils. Concomitant with this burgeoning imperial interest in their outcome, church councils became more and more concerned with the ratification or rejection of written documents.[15] The living voice of public disputation was nearly silenced by the insistent voice of written authorities at the Council of Ephesus in 431.[16] From then on, the sway of the *logos* in formal councils was eclipsed by consensual procedures that centered on written evidence read aloud by *notarii* and episcopal *sententiae* reacting to those documents.

This shift in emphasis came to the forefront during the Nestorian controversy.[17] The period preceding the Council of Ephesus in 431 was one of intense but diffused rivalry, during which Cyril of Alexandria attempted to consolidate his position by corresponding with Pope Celestine in Rome, with the imperial court at Constantinople, and with Nestorius. These letters did not help to resolve the conflict. Indeed, the wide publicity attending the reception of these controversial and polemical documents tended to make the dispute more intractable. To some, it appeared that a decisive face-to-face encounter between the antagonists would be necessary to reach a settlement. It was probably no coincidence that the bishops were to meet on the day of Pentecost, 7 June 431, thus symbolically associating the council with the onrush of inspiration by the Holy Spirit.

The avowed goal of the council, which Nestorius may have put into the mind of Theodosius II, was to examine and resolve the disputed issues through dispassionate research. This intention was sternly expressed in the letter Theodosius II and Valentinian dispatched to Cyril:

15. See the evidence collected by Wickenhauser, "Beiträge zur Geschichte," 4–9, 33–39, beginning with the Council of Antioch in 330.

16. See Socrates, *Hist. eccl.* 7.34.

17. See H. Chadwick, "Eucharist and Christology in the Nestorian Controversy," *JTS* n.s. 2 (1951): 145–64.

It is necessary that priests be admired both for the goodness of their morals and for the rigor of their faith; that they daily manifest the simplicity of their life and know the nature of any problem and betake themselves to discover the true doctrine with respect to religion chiefly by means of research rather than by arrogant disputations concerning words. Everyone knows that religion owes its security to consent rather than to orders.[18]

The emperors were rightly concerned about the goodwill of the disputing parties: history provided little assurance of spontaneous cooperation. The *comes domesticorum* Candidianus, the imperial commissioner sent to ensure order in the city and to preside over the meeting, conveyed a message to the council from the emperors:

With patience each shall hear whatsoever is said and each shall be ready to reply or for reply to be made to him and thus by questions and by replies and by solution the inquiry touching the true faith shall be judged without any dispute and by the common examination of your Saintliness it will reach a happy agreement without dispute.[19]

The emperors took pains to recognize the autonomy of the bishops in settling their own disputes. They desired that agreement be achieved without compulsion or undue outside influence. Candidianus was instructed to abstain from an active role in the debates; he was to preside over the proceedings simply to assure their smooth operation.

A notion of "consent" was used in contradistinction to resolution through argumentation, which could ironically enable the will of a few to prevail over that of the many. This emphasis on consent was reiterated at the opening proceedings at Ephesus: Theodotus of Ancyra stated that "matters of religion ought to be established by common consent and agreement."[20] But what actually transpired at Ephesus in 431 was not what the emperors and Nestorius had in mind.[21]

Cyril directly violated the conciliatory purpose of the meeting when he convened the council without waiting for the arrival of John of Antioch, openly disregarding the understandable objections of Candidianus.[22] With good reason, Nestorius absented himself from this irregular procedure. Nonetheless, Cyril pushed on, and was able to prescribe the

18. *ACO* 1.1, 8 (Schwartz, ed., 73–74); my translation.
19. Nestorius, *Bazaar of Heraclides* 167 (trans. from Driver and Hodgson, eds., *Nestorius' Bazaar*, 111). See also F. Nau, ed., *Nestorius: Le livre d'Héraclide de Damas* (Paris, 1910), 102–3.
20. *ACO* 1.1.2, 37 (Schwartz, ed., 9): "ὥστε τὰ τῆς εὐσεβείας στῆναι ἐκ κοινῆς γνώμης καὶ συναινέσεως."
21. See T. Gregory, *Vox Populi*, pp. 100–108 on the social unrests and violence leading up to the event.
22. On the *Contestatio* of Candidianus, see Nestorius, *Bazaar of Heraclides* 170–74.

eventual direction of the meeting. He was even able to suppress the reading of the imperial letter that Candidianus had brought, thereby turning the council to his own purposes.

The "consensual" procedures that Cyril and his party imposed were in fact majoritarian bully tactics, partly because his hand had been strengthened by the promise of support by Pope Celestine, and partly because his initial position was insecure and he needed to snatch a quick victory. First, Cyril arranged for the Nicene creed to be read aloud by Peter, presbyter of the church of Alexandria and *primicerius* of the notaries.[23] Then Cyril's letter to Nestorius was read out. The ensuing procedure had the elegance of simplicity: 126 bishops, beginning with Juvenal of Jerusalem, spoke in turn in favor of Cyril's views, claiming that his doctrine agreed ($\sigma\nu\mu\phi\omega\nu\epsilon\hat{\imath}\nu$) with those expressed by the "three hundred and eighty fathers" who met at Nicaea.[24] Nestorius' letter was then read aloud in his absence and the procedure of offering *sententiae* was repeated. However, the bishops found little in the letter that corresponded to the Nicene creed. After all, Nestorius' views were said to be consonant ($\sigma\nu\mu\phi\omega\nu\omega\varsigma$) not with those of the *patres* but with those of a condemned heretic, Paul of Samosata.[25] He was anathematized forthwith without debate.

The order in which the bishops offered their *sententiae* is instructive about the nature of authority at the meeting (see table 1).[26] The overarching collective *auctoritas* of the foremost bishops shaped the proceedings. Although no exact speaking order was prescribed, we can clearly discern the bishops of the first rank.[27] Once the first ten or so senior bishops had offered their weighty *sententiae*, there was little room for discussion, let alone dissent.[28] After the creed and the two letters had been read and received, the reading of Pope Celestine's letter and a long series of patristic florilegia refuting Nestorius' views served only to confirm

23. *ACO* 1.1.2, 43 (Schwartz, ed., 12–13).

24. *ACO* 1.1.2, 45 (Schwartz, ed., 13–31). Cyril had already intimated his use of Nicaea and the language of harmony against Nestorius in their correspondence prior to Ephesus; see L. R. Wickham, *Cyril of Alexandria: Select Letters* (Oxford, 1983), 2–33.

25. *ACO* 1.1.1, 18 (Schwartz, ed., 101). Such a comparison served an apparent propagandistic purpose; see *Obtestatio publice proposita* in *ACO* 1.1.1, 18 (Schwartz, ed., 101–2).

26. *ACO* 1.1.2, 62 (Schwartz, ed., 55). Generally on the importance of ecclesiastical hierarchy at this council, see Crabbe, "Invitation List," 369–400.

27. As in the Roman senate, the presiding officer solicited the participants' opinions in descending rank, though not necessarily in order within the ranks; see L. R. Taylor and R. T. Scott, "Seating Space in the Roman Senate and the *senatores pedarii*," *TAPA* 100 (1969): 529–82, at 534.

28. On the superior weight of the *sententiae* of the powerful, see gloss on Ulpian, *Digest* 1.19.12.1. More generally on the issue of authority in similar settings, see F. G. Bailey, "Decision by Consensus in Councils and Committees," in *Political Systems and the Distribution of Power* (London, 1965), 1–20.

Table 1. Foremost Bishops at the Council of Ephesus, 431

First Speakers after Cyril's Letter[a]	First Speakers after Nestorius' Letter[b]	Names Listed at Top of *Acta* Roster[c]
		Cyril of Alexandria
Juvenal of Jerusalem	Juvenal of Jerusalem	Juvenal of Jerusalem
Firmus of Caesarea	Flavianus of Philippi	Memnon of Ephesus
Memnon of Ephesus	Firmus of Caesarea	Flavianus of Philippi
Theodotus of Ancyra	Valerian of Iconium	Theodotus of Ancyra
Flavianus of Philippi	Iconius of Gortyn	Firmus of Caesarea
Acacius of Melitene	Hellanicus of Rhodes	Acacius of Melitene
Iconius of Gortyn	Acacius of Melitene	Iconius of Gortyn
Hellanicus of Rhodes	Memnon of Ephesus	Perigenes of Corinth
Palladius of Amaseia	Theodotus of Ancyra	Cyrus of Aphrodisias
Cyrus of Aphrodisias	Palladius of Amaseia	Valerian of Iconium
		Hesychius of Nicopolis
		Hellanicus of Rhodes

SOURCE: *ACO* 1.1.2, 62 (Schwartz, ed., 55).

[a]The first ten bishops who spoke after the reading of Cyril's letter. On the leading role of Juvenal of Jerusalem at the council, see E. Honigmann, "Juvenal of Jerusalem," *DOP* 5 (1950): 213–79, esp. 223–24. Generally, see Crabbe, "Invitation List."

[b]The first ten bishops who spoke after the reading of Nestorius' letter. Valerius of Iconium spoke here instead of Cyrus of Aphrodisias, but otherwise the names in the first two columns are the same.

[c]The first thirteen bishops listed on the roster at the beginning of the *acta*.

a decision already reached.[29] The bishops at Ephesus pronounced an anathema on Nestorius. There was no attempt to open a theological debate ab ovo; the rationale for this was that the inspired council of 325 had settled the issue of orthodox formulation once and for all. Clearly, to triumph in such proceedings, one needed to mobilize social and political support beforehand; skill in argument contributed little to the final outcome.[30]

This choreographed procedure openly flouted the imperial wish stated in the letter calling for the council, as Nestorius later pointed out. His *Bazaar of Heracleides*, penned after his receipt of the *acta* that came out of the events at Ephesus, aimed to counteract the one-sidedness of the council, and to protest Cyril's strong-arm tactics and his suppression

29. *ACO* 1.1.2, 54–59 (Schwartz, ed., 39–45). On the growth of the tradition of patristic florilegia in a conciliar setting, see M. Richard, "Les florilèges diphysites du Ve et VIe siècle," in A. Grillmeier and H. Bacht, eds., *Das Konzil von Chalkedon* (Würzburg, 1951), 1:721–48.

30. The two distinct types of communal leaders exercised different kinds of power; see M. Hobart, "Orators and Patrons: Two Types of Political Leader in Balinese Village Society," in M. Bloch, ed., *Political Language and Oratory in Traditional Society* (London/New York, 1975), 66–92.

of legitimate discussion. Seeking to redress the wrongs done to him, Nestorius expressed grave misgivings about Cyril's abuse of the conciliar process, and characterized the published transcripts of the proceedings as so highly partisan as to amount to being Cyril's *acta:*[31]

> Will then a sincere inquiry be settled [even] by sincere inquirers through division and through that which causes dispute, or through impartiality and patience on the part of the hearers towards what is said? And [will a sincere inquiry be settled] by merely laying down the subject of inquiry, or by the giving and receiving of replies on either side, and their being examined by questioning and unravelling, until the inquiry which is being examined is [settled] without dispute? Shall we with haste or without haste find a solution and an answer in harmony therewith when we are asked a question? Which of these things has been said untruly? But this command was not pleasing unto thee [Cyril] because thou didst wish to conquer and not to discover the truth.[32]

In the name of truth, discussion ought to be allowed free rein: this was Nestorius' position, stated in retrospect. Perhaps it was merely the rhetorical self-justification of the vanquished. In any event, considerations other than truth weighed more heavily with the imperial authorities. Theodosius II was initially quite upset by Cyril's outrages, but popular demonstrations orchestrated by Cyril's partisans and the flow of Alexandrian gold to members of the imperial court soon tilted the balance in Cyril's favor.[33] Once the council had become a fait accompli, Theodosius II attempted to minimize the social disorder of an ongoing controversy by ordering the books of Nestorius sought out and burned and his name banished from mention even in "religious disputations."[34]

Cyril outsmarted and outmaneuvered Candidianus at Ephesus, usurping the presidency of the council on 22 June 431. At the Council of Chalcedon in 451, to ensure that imperial wishes prevailed, more commissioners presided than had in 431. In the published *acta,* these dignitaries were referred to by the formula "οἱ ἐνδοξότατοι ἄρχοντες καὶ ἡ ὑπερφυὴς σύγκλητος."[35] These *gloriossimi* did not just lend decorum and weight to the proceedings; though they did not participate in the dogmatic controversy itself, they directed the procedures of the council, and

31. Nestorius, *Bazaar of Heraclides* 186.
32. Nestorius, *Bazaar of Heraclides* 169 (Driver and Hodgson, eds., *Nestorius' Bazaar,* 112).
33. See Gregory, *Vox Populi,* 108–16 and nn.; Batiffol, "Les présents de saint Cyrille," 154–79.
34. *Codex Theod.* 16.5.66 issued on 3 August 435.
35. *ACO* 2.1.1, 15, 17 (Schwartz, ed., 66–67).

the language of their preliminary instruction to the participants was decidedly judicial.[36] In their view, an accusation (κατηγορία) had been made and they were there officially to investigate the charge.[37] Dioscurus of Alexandria, the mover of the council, seconded by Eusebius of Dorylaius, was obliged to petition the *archontes* for permission to have his side's dossiers read. The *archontes* consented with the stipulation that the documents be read in their proper order (κατὰ τάξιν).[38]

The promise of dignified and orderly conduct was short-lived; when Theodoret of Cyrus was invited to join the proceedings, the bishops from Egypt, Illyria, and Palestine (who sat together)[39] cried out in unison: "Mercy upon us! The faith is destroyed! The rules of faith cast this man out! Cast this man outside! Cast the teaching of Nestorius outside!"[40] The bishops of the dioceses of Asia Minor and Thrace, supporters of Theodoret, responded by calling their adversaries Manichaeans and enemies of the faith, chanting: "Cast out Dioscurus the murderer! Who doesn't know Dioscurus' deeds?"[41] The partisans of Dioscurus then reminded all of their support from Pulcheria: "Long live the Empress!" and "The Empress cast Nestorius out, long live the orthodox one!"[42] The shouting continued after the *archontes* had granted Theodoret permission to join the council. These histrionic gestures clearly did not find favor with the secular notables, who reprimanded the bishops, instructing them that "popular acclamations are not suitable for bishops and the factions (τὰ μέρη) shall incur a penalty."[43] The *archontes* were accustomed to acclamations in senatorial proceedings, but those were affirmations rather than accusations in the manner of popular petitions.[44] The commissioners unmistakably moved the church council in the direction of formal procedures and consensual agreement.

The touchstones of Chalcedon were the formulations of Nicaea and Ephesus, just as Nicaea had been the touchstone of Ephesus 431: "The Fathers defined everything perfectly; he who transgresses this is anath-

36. *ACO* 2.1.1, 13 (Schwartz, ed., 66): "Εἰ δικαστοῦ ἐπέχεις πρόσωπον, ὡς δικαζόμενος οὐκ ὀφείλεις δικαιολογεῖσθαι."
37. *ACO* 2.1.1, 22 (Schwartz, ed., 67).
38. *ACO* 2.1.1, 20 (Schwartz, ed., 67).
39. *ACO* 2.1.1, 4 (Schwartz, ed., 65).
40. *ACO* 2.1.1, 27 (Schwartz, ed., 69).
41. *ACO* 2.1.1, 28, 30 (Schwartz, ed., 69).
42. *ACO* 2.1.1, 31, 33 (Schwartz, ed., 69).
43. *ACO* 2.1.1, 45 (Schwartz, ed., 70). Not only bishops but their attendants also participated in these acclamations; see *ACO* 2.1.1, 72–76 (Schwartz, ed., 78). On another case in which spontaneous accusations were made by acclamations, see Socrates, *Hist. eccl.* 6.14.
44. See *Codex Theod.* 1.16.6.

ema; no one adds, no one takes away." [45] Dioscurus invoked the primacy of the Nicene formulation by anathematizing any who "asks questions, meddles or undermines the faith (ἢ ζητεῖ ἢ πολυπραγμονεῖ ἢ ἀνασκευάζει, ἀνάθεμα ἔστω)." [46]

Clearly, he who controlled which documents were read was well-positioned to influence the outcome of the council. Dioscurus even forcibly ejected all notaries but his own, hoping to ensure that his version of events was the only one communicated to the emperor and the outside world.

However intense the behind-the-scenes political jostlings and bitter the mutual rivalry, the value of the councils themselves was largely affirmed by subsequent authorities. A tradition had begun to take root, and as late antique religious competitors repeatedly invoked conciliar precedents on their own behalf, they became increasingly bound by the parameters of these norms when they engaged in controversy.

The results of Chalcedon became sacrosanct to Chalcedonian Christians, and were guaranteed by imperial law; a law of 455 deemed punishable any discussion or writing contrary to the council's conclusions. [47] The later *henotikon* letter of the emperor Zeno placed an anathema on anyone who questioned the decisions of Chalcedon. [48] Both Nicaea and Chalcedon were eventually memorialized with liturgical celebrations in the later Byzantine tradition. [49] Indeed, shedding their complexities and messiness, entire councils were reduced to icons encapsulating simple lessons. The Council of Nicaea, for example, endured as the triumph of orthodoxy and Arius' Waterloo. The number 318 became the canonical number of the saintly fathers who formulated the Nicene creed, the touchstone of orthodoxy, though that tally surely does not correspond exactly to the number of bishops who attended Nicaea. [50] The power of patristic consensus exhibited in various florilegia can only be fully appreciated in light of their visual representations in early Byzan-

45. *ACO* 2.1.1, 142 (Schwartz, ed., 89): "'Απαραλείπτως πάντα ὥρισαν οἱ πατέρες· ὁ παραβαίνων ταῦτα ἀνάθεμα. οὐδεὶς προστίθησιν, οὐδεὶς ἀφαιρεῖ."
46. *ACO* 2.1.1, 143 (Schwartz, ed., 89).
47. *Codex Iustinianus* 1.5.8.9–11 (Krueger, ed., *Corpus Iuris Civilis*, 2:52): "Nulli etiam contra venerabilem Chalcedonensem Synodum liceat aliquid vel dictare vel scribere vel edere atque e mittere aut aliorum scripta super eadem re proferre."
48. See Pseudo-Leontius of Byzantium, *De sectis* 5 (PG 86.1:1228–30).
49. See S. Salaville, "La fête du concile de Nicée et les fêtes de conciles dans le rite byzantin," *Échos d'Orient* 24 (1925): 445–70; idem, "La fête du concile de Chalcédoine dans le rite byzantin," in A. Grillmeier and H. Bacht, eds., *Das Konzil von Chalkedon* (Würzburg, 1953), 2:677–95.
50. See Socrates, *Hist. eccl.* 1.9.

tine frescoes and illuminated manuscripts,[51] in which solid phalanxes of saintly bishops in serried ranks vividly embody the principle of *homonoia*. Against this overwhelming consensus, dissent and debate were literally swept aside.[52]

The gathering of authority gained momentum. The Syriac *acta* of the Latrocinium in 449 required prospective priests to swear not to discuss theological doctrine.[53] Bishops and other Christian authorities no longer had to demonstrate that opponents held heterodox views to impose censure; they had only to prove participation in public theological debate. Thus resistance to disputation became an issue of the nature of authority in the church: in 452, a year after Chalcedon, the pro-Nestorius Marcian expanded the restrictions against public discussion of doctrine to various classes of people.[54]

Such expressive bans on discussion accorded well with the ruling

51. See Walter, *L'iconographie des conciles*, e.g., 34, fig. 7.

52. See Walter, *L'iconographie des conciles*, 252–60, on the representations of heretics.

53. In J. Flemming, ed., *Akten der ephesinischen Synode vom 449, in Abhandlungen der königlichen Gesellschaft der Wissenschaften zu Göttingen*, Phil.-hist. Klasse, n.s. 15.1 (Berlin, 1917), 86–89:

> Sie selber nämlich machten und setzen eine Eidesschrift auf, verleumdeten darin gewisse Leute, die mit mir Umgang haben, und waren so vermessen, einen Entwurf eines Glaubens-[bekentnisses] nach ihrem Gutdünken zu machen, ohne sich auch nur ein bischen vor jener, dieser eurer heiligen vorangegangenen Synode zu fürchten, welche deutlich das Gegenteil befohlen hat: (fol. 59v) "Niemand solle Vollmacht haben, außer dem Glauben der heligen und seligen Väter: weder zu schreiben, noch auszulegen, noch auszufassen"; und fügten sogar hinzu, ich dürfte weder öffentlich vor jedermanns Augen disputieren, noch wagen, heimlich zu unterweisen, welche zu lernen wünschten. . . . "Auch befehlen wir dir dringend an: disputier nicht im Namen Iesu."

54. *Codex Iustinianus* 1.1.4 (Krueger, ed., *Corpus Iuris Civilis*, 2:6):

> Nemo clericus vel militans vel alterius cuiuslibet condicionis de fide Christiana publice turbis coadunatis et audientibus tractare conetur in posterum, ex hoc tumultus et perfidiae occasionem requirens. Nam iniuriam facit iudicio reverentissimae synodi, si quis semel iudicata ac recte disposita revolvere et publice disputare contendit, cum ea, quae nunc de Christiana fide a sacerdotibus, qui Chalcedone convenerunt, per nostra praecepta statuta sunt, iuxta apostolicas expositiones et instituta sanctorum patrum trecentorum decem et octo et centum quinquaginta definita esse noscuntur. Nam in contemptores huius legis poena non deerit, quis non solum contra fidem vere expositam veniunt, sed etiam Iudaeis et paganis ex huiusmodi certamine profanant veneranda mysteria. Igitur si clericus erit, qui publice tractare de religione ausus fuerit, consortio clericorum removebitur: si vero milita praeditus sit, cingulo spoliabitur: ceteri etiam huiusmodi criminis rei, si quidem liberi sint, de hac sacratissima urbe pellentur, pro vigore iudiciario, etiam competentibus suppliciis subiugandi, sin vero servi, severissimis animadversationibus plectentur.

elites' unembellished authoritarianism in a time of consolidation and the self-conscious formation of tradition. This was an age of compendia and epitomes. Authority, whether personal, textual, or institutional, began to be gathered, hierarchized, and centralized by those who favored a visibly stable social order. The preeminent task of the fifth century was to summarize and define the accomplishments of previous ages. This effort was achieved in the field of Roman law through the publication of the *Theodosian Code* in 438 by the emperors Theodosius II and Valentinian, whose *novella* explaining the code remind us that the desire to limit freewheeling local initiatives governed secular and ecclesiastical deliberations alike:

> In order that this matter may not be further discussed by anyone with zealous ambiguity, as there occurs to Our minds the boundless multitudes of books, the diversity of actions and the difficulty of cases, and finally the mass of imperial constitutions which shut off from human ingenuity a knowledge of themselves by a wall, as though they were submerged in a thick cloud of obscurity, We have completed a true undertaking of Our Time (*negotium temporis*); We have dispelled the darkness and given the light of brevity to the laws by means of a compendium. We have selected noble men of proved fidelity and renowned learning, to whom had been delegated the responsibilities of civil offices. The decrees of previous Emperors have been purged of interpretations and published by Us, in order that no further may the jurisconsults dissimulate their ignorance by a pretended severity, while their formidable responses are awaited as though they proceed from the innermost shrines. . . .[55]

55. *Novellae Theodosiani* 1.1 (Pharr, *Theodosian Code*, 487). Latin text in Krueger, Mommsen and Meyer, eds., 3–4:

> Quod ne a quoquam ulterius sedula ambiguitate tractetur, si copia inmensa librorum, si actionum diversitas difficultasque causarum animis nostris occurrat, si denique moles constitutionum divalium, quae velut sub crassa demersae caligine obscuritatis vallo sui notitiam humanis ingeniis interclusit, verum egimus negotium temporis nostri et discussis tenebris conpendio brevitatis lumen legibus dedimus, electis viris nobilibus exploratae fidei, famosae doctrinae, quibus delegata causa civilis officii, purgata interpretatione, retro principium scita vulgavimus, ne iurisperitorum ulterius, severitate mentita dissimulata inscientia, velut ab ipsis adytis expectarentur formidanda responsa . . .

On the argument that the code was produced to ease the task of imperial judges, see W. Turpin, "The Purpose of the Roman Law Codes," *Zeitschrift der Savigny-Stiftung für Rechtsgeschichte* 104 (1987): 620–30. The same concern over confusion and abuse arising from a multiplication of legal cases and regulations led to efforts at compilation, simplification, and distribution in early modern China; see T. A. Metzger, *The Internal Organization of the Ch'ing Bureaucracy: Legal, Normative, and Communication Aspects* (Cambridge, Mass., 1973), 131.

The emperors had spoken truly in their statement of intent, eloquently conveying the paramount concerns of people in authority during that period. It is, however, the task of the modern historian to turn this process on its head with the hope of finding under the monolithic summations not a cloud of obscurity, darkness, or a stone wall, but light in abundance. If my present attempt at a social history of public disputation in late antiquity has made it any easier to achieve this goal, I will have succeeded.

EPILOGUE

The book is about the peculiar power of words. It is about their power to persuade, to influence public behavior, and to constitute social authority; it is only marginally about their ability to articulate ideas and to form abstract intellectual edifices. In a traditional society, *logos* mediated the relations of social life and introduced a dimension of competitive fluidity that was not always welcomed. Rational *logoi* simultaneously furnished the tools of argument and created discursive universes that shaped perceptions about the relationship of human discourse to "the world," especially to the divine world. In late antiquity, *logoi* about the nature of deity, when articulated by certain actors familiar with the terms of logic and philosophy, became a focus for the intense fear and loathing of others, particularly those whose standing was grounded on notions of social order potentially threatened by verbal competition. Some responded with ad hoc rebuttals of particular arguments, while others denounced the competitive verbal culture wholesale; all condemned particular writings and persons for promoting curiosity, meddling, and disrupting the social order.

A thread that weaves through this book is the importance of certain controversial texts, including question-and-answer dialogues and debate stories, generated by philosophical and religious disputation in a dialectical fashion. Deservedly or not, Aristotle's *Categories* became a prime villain in the tradition. In the introduction to the *Organon*, the late antique compilation of Aristotelian logical treatises, this little tractate laid out an easily popularized technical vocabulary ideally suited to the theological and philosophical discussions of divine attributes and essences. The appeal of the little book, beginning with Andronicus' edition in the first century B.C.E., transcended sectarian boundaries: philosophers of all stripes used and commented on it; Augustine read it avidly as a young Manichaean auditor; Aetius and Eunomius, as well as their inveterate foes Basil of Caesarea and Gregory of Nyssa, were thought to have resorted to its formulations in their intra-Christian controversy; much later, Anastasius of Sinai associated the ten horns of the dragon in Revelation with the ten heresies stemming from the ten Aristotelian categories. Writings such as the *Categories* were considered dangerous because they furnished a precise, respected philosophical vocabulary for constructing propositions about the divine, which, in situations of open disputation, threatened to upset established patterns of social authority when appropriated by self-taught men who had not been socialized into an ethos subordinating individual advantage to "the common good."

Inextricably linked with the controversial text was the dialectician-philosopher. Men of this type represent another strand that binds together the chapters. The career of Aetius the Syrian, for instance, brought him into contact (and sometimes conflict) with many key figures and groups: he joined in the discussions of Alexandrian physician-philosophers, allegedly impressing them with his innovative syllogistic application of the categories to divine speculation; he challenged to debate and defeated a charismatic Manichaean leader in the same city; he grappled with other Christians over the suitability and implications of a strict logical method for describing the divine nature in the so-called Anomoean controversy. He not only defeated well-known and respected bishops in formal debates, but in his role as teacher and author he also allegedly made popular a culture of dialectical questioning, greatly magnifying his threat to others. The connection between controversial text and disruptive dialectician was reinforced by the traditional association of Aetius—whose claim to fame rested on his power with words—with Aristotle's *Categories*.

Against subversive texts and dangerous dialecticians, a number of defenses were thrown up by those who defined themselves as the pastors of stable, peaceable communities. I have examined a number of strategies that, whether used self-consciously or not, aimed to tame the agonistic rivalry of words. These contrivances can be divided roughly into three kinds: individual, ideological, and institutional.

An individual's skill with words was a charismatic virtue, with a long-established claim to social consideration, particularly in Hellenic culture, which nevertheless might be neutralized in a number of ways: by juxtaposing it with the impressive deeds of confessors and ascetics;

by branding it as a relatively humble attainment in a hierarchical ranking of philosophical and theological virtues; by categorizing it as baneful
skill belonging to the domain of the Evil One.

The ideological response was an apophatic stance of mystical silence
that limited the human capacity to know, with perspicuity and exactitude, the divine nature.

Institutional responses were various, among them the privileging of
a particular model of truth that had until then been one of several competing options. The rise of traditional authority and hierarchical tendencies in philosophical and ecclesiastical bodies rendered clever words
harmless by attributing more weight to written documents, and by favoring acclamatory (synchronic) and traditional (diachronic) consensus, thus returning the settlement of Christian disputes to the province
of old-style power politics, away from the unpredictable sway of *tychē*
in which fortune might favor talent and daring. Dialecticians, the *ars
dialectica*, controversial texts, debate narratives, church councils, consensual ideology: all comprised this complex game of social competition and differentiation; it has been my task to spell out how each related to the other and to chart the historical consequences of particular
configurations.

Though it is my hope that nonspecialists can read this work with
profit and interest, I remind readers that the sources, figures, and events
treated here are already well-known to students of late antiquity. My
aim in writing has been not so much to offer these *zēlōtai* facts and materials previously ignored, but rather to "re-dress" the familiar in unfamiliar garb. The social histories of philosophical rivalry and Christian
controversies have long languished partly because of the isolation of
specialists laboring in disparate fields of inquiry. The mild aversion to
a social approach is also itself cultural. Students of ancient philosophy,
studying an intellectual discourse of great complexity and internal con-
sistency, often approach their subjects as philosophers. When they move—
and they rarely do—from intellectual history to the praxis of ancient
philosophers, they do so from within the parameters of judgment established by the Graeco-Roman philosophical tradition. Thus, cognitive argument tends to be treated as precisely that and nothing more, while
the social dimensions of philosophical practice lie in relative obscurity.
Likewise, students of early Christian controversies tend to immerse
themselves in the scriptural exegeses and philosophical enterprises of
revered *patres*. Erudite, conscientious scholars who have learned patristic scholarship by mimesis and through painstaking apprenticeship discuss the doctrinal and philosophical disputes in terms that would not be

entirely unfamiliar to the original protagonists; oftener still, they use the very terms employed by the victors of ancient struggles. The shades of the ancestors cast long shadows. Yet I know of no modern historical scholar who proposes to adhere as steadfastly to the logic and perspectives of ancient heresiography.

My goal here has been to join others in opening up these fields to modes of inquiry that have already been fruitfully applied to less sanctified realms of human life and history. The theoretical probings of anthropologists and sociologists have much to contribute to the study of classical intellectual discourse because of their emphasis on the ties between articulated ideologies and group structures, between language, discourses, and the constitution of social order. In this book, I have aimed to bring together the two traditions of intellectual and social historical scholarship in the hope of narrowing the gap, at least for historians.

It is only fitting that this book should end with the posing of questions. The processes that contributed to the formation of tradition in the late antique and early Byzantine periods invite examination in terms of their relationship to social competition. Such historical developments have all too often been explained in essentially ahistorical terms, by appealing to a prevailing *Zeitgeist* or the *mentalité* of an age; yet essentialist discourses are fundamentally tautological, explaining little. I believe the present study of how disputation and dialectic—as defined by interested actors—were used to claim authority in competitive settings affords a gainful perspective from which to chart the connections between changes in social and intellectual currents from the third to the sixth centuries.

Another area of interest lies in the historical significance of the philosophical polarity of speech versus silence. I have begun, in Chapter 5, to argue for a causal link between the culture of competitive speech and the seemingly antithetical growth of apophatic mystical theology. The fuller historical documentation of this matrix, particularly in the fifth-century context, awaits a more comprehensive examination of the connection between Christian preaching and the *via negativa* as a function of the shifting relationship between Christian elites and non-elites.

A third area warranting future study is the growth and articulation of the consensual tradition both within and outside of the Christian church, and the mechanisms that contributed to the sanctification of both synchronic and diachronic consensus. The acceptance of *homonoia* as ideology ought to be viewed in the context of its dialectical relationship with competing modes of social order, for without understanding the rejected or marginalized alternatives along with the concrete interests at stake in this process, we cannot fully grasp the import of its eventual triumph.

Finally, we need a fuller understanding of parallel developments in the Christian conciliar tradition and in jurisprudential rationality and legal codification, a subject on which I am able to comment only en passant. These two bodies of material invite a comparative study, both in sociohistorical terms with respect to their genesis, and in the ideological correspondences between their discourses. Roman legal scholars who study the *Theodosian Code,* for instance, should find much of interest in the construction of authority in nearly contemporaneous church councils, since the legal and conciliar authorities of the time were fashioned by an elite that was, if not identical in composition, then at least of like temperament. Their habits of mind and discourses on power, seldom articulated in theoretical terms, must yet remain one of the central concerns of any student of late antiquity.

APPENDIX:
CHRONOLOGICAL CHART

Timeline scale: 125 | 150 | 175 | 200 | 225 | 250 | 275 | 300 | 325 | 350

Imperial Reigns
- 161——180 Marcus Aurelius
- 270—275 Aurelian
- 284—305 Diocletian
- 324——337 Constantine

Italy and North Africa
- *c.135 Justin Martyr's *Dialogue with Trypho*
- c.160 ——— Tertullian ——— c.225
- 244———270 Plotinus in Rome

Greece and Asia Minor
- 129———Galen———199
- *Celsus' *Alēthēs Logos*
- 330——— Basil of
- c.329 ——— Gregory of
- 335———
- *325 Council of Nicaea; *Vicennalia* of Constantine

Syria and Palestine
- 260 ——— Iamblichus ——— 330
- 232——— Porphyry ———303
- c.260——— Eusebius of Caesarea ——— c.340 347———
- *c.272–275 Aurelian arbitrated Christian dispute in Antioch
- *c.313 Birth of Aetius
- *350 Aetius began teaching in Antioch

Egypt and Arabia
- c.185——— Origen of Alexandria ———254
- *c.245 debated with Heraclides
- 296——— Athanasius
- 247———c.264 Dionysius bishop of Alexandria
- *248 *Contra Celsum*
- 250——— Arius of Alexandria ———336

Persia
- 216——— Mani ———277
- 240——— Shāpūr I ———277

Timeline

350 375 400 425 450 475 500 525 550 575

Imperial Reigns

361
Constantius II
379———395 408——————450   527————————565
360–363 Theodosius I   Theodosius II   474—491——518   Justinian
Julian   Zeno Anastasius

Italy and North Africa

354 ————Augustine of Hippo———— 430
*381
Council of Aquileia

*392
Augustine
debated Fortunatus

*397
Confessions

*404
Augustine
debated Felix

*411 Council of
Carthage

Greece and Asia Minor

Caesarea ——378   411——   Proclus   ————485
Nazianzus ————389   *431   *475/76 Gelasius of Cyzicus' HE
Eunomius ———— 394   C. of Ephesus
                              *438   *c.500 Pseudo-Dionysius
379–381   Cod. Theod.   the Areopagite
Gnaz bishop of Constantinople   *451   *c.527
*c.370   *399 Eurapius wrote VS   C. of Chalcedon   Paul the Persian
death of   *383 Council of   *c.439–450 Sozomen's HE   debated Photinus
Aetius   Constantinople   *440 Socrates completed HE   *c.529 Justinian closed Academy

Syria and Palestine

*395 Porphyry
bishop of Gaza

John Chrysostom ————407
*386/7 Chrysostom's sermons
De Incomprehens.
*386— 400 Gelasius of Caesarea's HE
*c.402 Julia in Gaza

Egypt and Arabia

Athanasius ——373
357 ———————— 361
George of Cappadocia
bishop of Alexandria
370 ———————— 414
Synesius of Cyrene
412———————— 444
Cyril of Alexandria bishop

Persia

*410
Synod of
Mar Isaac

SELECT BIBLIOGRAPHY
OF SECONDARY SOURCES

Adam, A. *Texte zum Manichäismus*. Berlin, 1969.

Adkins, W. "*Polupragmosune* and 'Minding One's Own Business': A Study in Greek Social and Political Values." *CPhil* 71 (1976): 301–27.

Alfaric, P. *Les écritures manichéennes*. 2 vols. Paris, 1918/19.

———. "Un manuscrit manichéen." *RHLR* n.s. 6 (1920): 62–94.

Amand, D. *L'ascèse monastique de saint Basile*. Paris, 1949.

Amand de Mendieta, E. "L'incompréhensibilité de l'essence divine d'après Jean Chrysostome." In *ΣΥΜΠΟΣΙΟΝ: Studies on St. John Chrysostom*, Analekta Vlatadon 18. Thessaloniki, 1973.

Amidon, P. "The Procedure of St. Cyprian's Synods." *VChr* 37 (1983): 328–39.

Anastos, M. "Basil's KATA EYNOMIOY: A Critical Analysis." In Fedwick, ed., *Basil of Caesarea* 1:67–136.

André, J.-M. *L'otium dans la vie morale et intellectuelle romaine des origines à l'époque augustéenne*. Paris, 1966.

Andreas, F. C., and W. B. Henning. "Mitteliranische Manichaica aus Chinesisch-Turkestan II." *SPAW* Phil-hist. Klasse 5 (1933): 294–363.

Armstrong, A. H. "Elements in the Thought of Plotinus at Variance with Classical Intellectualism." *JHS* 93 (1973): 13–22.

———. "Pagan and Christian Traditionalism in the First Three Centuries, A.D." *SP* 15 (1984): 414–31.

———. "The Background of the Doctrine 'That the Intelligibles are not Outside the Intellect.'" In *Les sources de Plotin*. Entretiens sur l'antiquité classique 5. Vandoeuvres-Genève.

Armstrong, C. B. "The Synod of Alexandria and the Schism of Antioch in A.D. 362." *JTS* 21 (1920/21): 206–21.

Asmussen, J. P. *Manichaean Literature: Representative Texts Chiefly from Middle Persian and Parthian Writings*. Persian Heritage Series 22. Delmar, N.Y., 1975.

Auerbach, E. *Literary Language and Its Public in Late Latin Antiquity and in the Middle Ages*. London, 1965.

Austin, J. L. *How to Do Things with Words*. Oxford, 1962.

Avotins, I., and M. M. *Index in Eunapii vitas sophistarum*. Hildesheim, 1983.

Bailey, F. G. "Decision by Consensus in Councils and Committees." In *Political Systems and the Distribution of Power*. London, 1965.

Bardy, G. "La littérature patristique des "*quaestiones et responsiones*" sur l'écriture sainte." *Revue Biblique* 41 (1932): 210–36, 340–69, 515–37; 42 (1933): 14–30, 211–29, 328–52.

———. *Paul de Samosate*. 2d ed. Louvain, 1929.

———. "Pour l'histoire de l'école d'Alexandrie." *Vivre et Penser* 2 (1942): 80–109.

———. *Recherches sur saint Lucien d'Antioche et son école*. Paris, 1936.

———. "L'héritage littéraire d'Aétius," *RHE* 24 (1928): 809–27.

Barnard, L. W. *Justin Martyr: His Life and Thought*. Cambridge, 1967.

Barnes, T. D. *Athanasius and Constantius. Theology and Politics in the Constantinian Empire*. Cambridge, Mass., 1993.

———. "The Chronology of Plotinus' Life." *GRBS* 17 (1976): 65–70.

———. *Constantine and Eusebius*. Cambridge, Mass., 1981.

———. "The Emperor Constantine's Good Friday Sermon." *JTS* n.s. 7 (1976): 414–23.

———. *The New Empire of Diocletian and Constantine*. Cambridge, Mass., 1982.

Bartelink, G. J. M. "Eunape et le vocabulaire chrétien." *VChr* 23 (1969): 293–303.

———. "The Use of the Words *electio* and *consensus* in the Church until about 600." *Concilium* 77 (1972): 147–54.

Batiffol, P. "Les présents de saint Cyrille à la cour de Constantinople." In *Études de liturgie et d'archéologie chrétienne*. Paris, 1919.

———. "Le règlement des premiers conciles africains et le règlement du sénat romain." *Bulletin d'ancienne littérature et d'archéologie chrétienne* 3 (1913): 3–19.

———. "Les sources de l'histoire du concile de Nicée." *Échos d'Orient* 24 (1925): 385–402.

Bauchich, T. M. "The Date of Eunapius' *Vitae sophistarum*." *GRBS* 25 (1984): 183–92.

Bauer, F. X. *Proklos von Konstantinopel: Ein Beitrag zur Kirchen- und Dogmengeschichte des fünften Jahrhunderts*. Munich, 1919.

Bauman, R. A. *Lawyers and Politics in the Early Roman Empire: A Study of Relations between the Roman Jurists and the Emperors from Augustus to Hadrian*. Munich, 1989.

Baur, C. *John Chrysostom and His Time*. M. Gonzaga, trans. 2 vols. London, 1959.

Baynes, N. H. *Constantine the Great and the Christian Church*. London, 1931.

Benko, S. "Pagan Criticism of Christianity during the First Two Centuries, A.D." *ANRW* 2.23.2 (Berlin, 1980): 1055–1118.

Bernardi, J. *La prédication des pères cappadociens: Le prédicateur et son auditoire*. Paris, 1969.

———. "Nouvelles perspectives sur la famille de Grégoire de Nazianze," *VChr* 38 (1984): 352–59.

Bers, V. "Dikastic *thorubos*." In P. A. Cartledge and F. D. Harvey, eds., *Crux: Essays in Greek History Presented to G. E. M. de Ste Croix on His 75th Birthday*. Exeter, 1985.

Beskow, P. "The Theodosian Laws against Manichaeism." In P. Bryder, ed., *Manichaean Studies I*, (Lund, 1988): 1–11.

Bidez, J. "Le philosophe Jamblique et son école." *REG* 32 (1919): 29–40.

———. *La tradition manuscrite de Sozomène et la Tripartite de Théodore le Lecteur.* Leipzig, 1908.

———. *Vie de Porphyre: Le philosophe néo-platonicien.* Gand/Leipzig, 1913.

Binder, G. "Eine Polemik des Porphyrios gegen die allegorische Auslegung des Alten Testaments durch die Christen." *ZPE* 3 (1968): 81–95.

Bloch, M., ed. *Political Language and Oratory in Traditional Society.* London/New York, 1975.

Blockley, R. C. *The Fragmentary Classicising Historians of the Later Roman Empire: Eunapius, Olympiodorus, Priscus and Malchus.* ARCA Classical and Medieval Texts, Papers and Monographs 6. Liverpool, 1981.

Bonis, C. G. "The Problem Concerning Faith and Knowledge, or Reason and Revelation, as Expounded in the Letters of Basil the Great to Amphilochius of Iconium." *The Greek Orthodox Theological Review* 5 (1959): 27–44.

Booth, E. *Aristotelian Aporetic Ontology in Islamic and Christian Thinkers.* Cambridge, 1983.

Bourdieu, P. *Distinction: A Social Critique of the Judgement of Taste.* Cambridge, Mass., 1984.

———. *Homo Academicus.* Stanford, 1984.

———. *Outline of a Theory of Practice.* Cambridge, 1977. Originally published as *Esquisse d'une théorie de la pratique* (Geneva, 1972).

Bousset, W. *Jüdisch-christlicher Schulbetrieb in Alexandria und Rom: Literarische Untersuchungen zu Philo und Clemens von Alexandria, Justin und Irenäus.* Göttingen, 1915.

Bowersock, G. W. "From Emperor to Bishop: The Self-Conscious Transformation of Political Power in the Fourth Century A.D." *CPhil* 81 (1986): 298–307.

———. *Greek Sophists in the Roman Empire.* Oxford, 1969.

Bowie, E. L. "The Importance of Sophists." *Yale Classical Studies* 27 (1982): 29–59.

Bowman, A. K. "Landholding in the Hermopolite Nome in the Fourth Century, A.D." *JRS* 75 (1985): 137–63.

Bremmer, J. "An Imperial Palace Guard in Heaven: The Date of the Vision of Dorotheus." *ZPE* 75 (1988): 82–88.

———. "Scapegoat Rituals in Ancient Greece." *HSCP* 87 (1983): 299–320.

Brière, M. "Une homélie inédite d'Atticus, patriarche de Constantinople." *Revue de l'Orient Chrétien* 29 (1933–34): 160–80.

Brisson, L., M. O. Goulet-Cazé, R. Goulet, and D. O'Brien, eds. *Porphyre: La vie de Plotin.* Paris, 1982.

Brown, P. R. L. *Augustine of Hippo: A Biography.* Berkeley, 1969.

———. "The Diffusion of Manichaeism in the Roman Empire." *JRS* 59 (1969): 92–103.

———. *The Making of Late Antiquity.* Cambridge, Mass., 1978.

———. "Pelagius and His Supporters: Aims and Environment." *JTS* n.s. 19 (1968): 93–114. Reprinted in *Religion and Society in the Age of Saint Augustine* (London, 1977).

———. "The Philosopher and Society in Late Antiquity." In *Protocol of the 34th Colloquy*, Center for Hermeneutical Studies. Berkeley, 1980.

———. *Power and Persuasion in Late Antiquity: Towards a Christian Empire*. Madison, Wisc., 1992.

———. "Religious Coercion in the Later Roman Empire: The Case of North Africa." *History* 48 (1963): 283–305.

———. "The Rise and Function of the Holy Man in Late Antiquity." *JRS* 61 (1971): 80–101.

———. "St. Augustine's Attitude to Religious Coercion." *JRS* 65 (1964): 107–16. Reprinted in *Religion and Society in the Age of St. Augustine* (London, 1977).

Browning, R. "The Riot of A.D. 387 in Antioch: The Role of the Theatrical Claques in the Later Empire." *JRS* 42 (1952): 13–20.

Brubaker, L. "Politics, Patronage, and Art in Ninth-Century Byzantium: The *Homilies* of Gregory of Nazianzus in Paris (B.N. Gr. 510)." *DOP* 39 (1985): 1–14.

Bruck, E. F. *Kirchenväter und soziales Erbrecht*. Berlin/Göttingen/Heidelberg, 1956.

Bruckner, A. *Faustus von Mileve: Ein Beitrag zur Geschichte des abendländischen Manichäismus*. Basel, 1901.

Bruns, P. "Arius hellenizans?—Ephräm der Syrer und die neoarianischen Kontroversen seiner Zeit: Ein Beitrag zur Rezeption des Nizänums im syrischen Sprachraum." *ZKG* 101 (1990): 21–57.

Buch, D. F. "Eunapius of Sardis and Theodosius the Great." *Byzantion* 58 (1988): 36–53.

Buckley, J. J. "Mani's Opposition to the Elchasaites: A Question of Ritual." In P. Slater, D. Wiebe, M. Boutin, and H. Coward, eds., *Traditions in Contact and Change*. Waterloo, 1983.

———. "Tools and Tasks: Elchasaite and Manichaean Purification Rituals." *Journal of Religion* 66 (1986): 399–411.

Burkitt, F. C. *The Religion of the Manichees*. Cambridge, 1925.

Bury, J. B. *Constitution of the Later Roman Empire*. Cambridge, 1910.

Camelot, P. T. "Amour des lettres et désir de Dieu chez saint Grégoire de Nazianze: les logoi au service du Logos." *Littérature et religion: Mélanges J. Coppin. MSR* 23 supp. (1966): 23–30.

Cameron, Al. "A Disguised Manuscript of Rufinus, Translation of Eusebius' Ecclesiastical History." *Scriptorium* 18 (1964): 270–71.

———. "The Last Days of the Academy at Athens." *Proceedings of the Cambridge Philological Society* n.s. 15 (1969): 7–29.

———. "Wandering Poets: A Literary Movement in Byzantine Egypt." *Historia* 14 (1965): 470–509.

Cameron, Av. *Christianity and the Rhetoric of Empire: The Development of Christian Discourse*. Sather Classical Lectures 1986. Berkeley, Calif., 1991.

———. "The Language of Images: the Rise of Icons and Christian Representation." In D. Wood., ed., *The Church and the Arts*. Studies in Church History 28. Oxford, 1992.

———. "New and Old in Christian Literature." In *Major Papers of the 17th International Byzantine Congress*. New York, 1986.

Carawan, E. M. "*Erōtesis*: Interrogation in the Courts of Fourth-Century Athens." *GRBS* 24 (1983): 209–26.

Carpenter, H. J. "Popular Christianity and the Theologians in the Early Centuries." *JTS* n.s. 14 (1963): 294–310.

Carter, R. E. "Chrysostom's *Ad Theodorum lapsum* and the Early Chronology of Theodore of Mopsuestia." *VChr* 16 (1962): 87–101.

Cavalcanti, E. *Studi Eunomiani. OCA* 202. Rome, 1976.

———. "Y a-t-il des problèmes eunomiens dans la pensée trinitaire de Synésius?" *SP* 13 (1975): 138–44.

Cavallera, F. *Le schisme d'Antioche, IVᵉ–Vᵉ siècles.* Paris, 1905.

Chabot, J.-B., ed. *Synodicon Orientale ou recueil de synodes nestoriens.* Paris, 1902.

Chadwick, H. "Eucharist and Christology in the Nestorian Controversy." *JTS* n.s. 2 (1951): 145–64.

———. "Faith and Order at the Council of Nicaea." *HTR* 53 (1960): 171–95.

———. "The Fall of Eustathius of Antioch." *JTS* 49 (1948): 27–35.

———. "The Role of the Christian Bishop in Ancient Society." In *Protocol of the 35th Colloquy,* Center for Hermeneutical Studies. Berkeley, Calif., 1980.

———. "The Silence of Bishops in Ignatius." *HTR* 43 (1950): 169–72.

Châtillon, F. "Adimantus Manichaei discipulus." *Revue de Moyen Age Latin* 10 (1954): 191–203.

Chestnut, G. F. *The First Christian Histories: Eusebius, Socrates, Sozomen, Theodoret and Evagrius.* Paris, 1977.

———. "Kairos and Cosmic Sympathy in the Church Historian Socrates Scholasticus." *Church History* 44 (1975): 161–66.

Christensen, T. "Rufinus of Aquilea and the *Historia Ecclesiastica, lib.* VIII–IX, of Eusebius." *Studia Theologica* 34 (1980): 129–52.

Cirillo, L., A. Concolino Mancini, and A. Roselli, eds. *Codex Manichaicus Coloniensis "Concordanze".* Cosenza, 1985.

Clark, E. A. *The Origenist Controversy: The Cultural Construction of an Early Christian Debate.* Princeton, 1992.

Clay, D. "The Cults of Epicurus." *Cron Ercol* 16 (1986): 11–28.

Colin, J. *Les villes libres de l'orient gréco-romain et l'envoi au supplice par acclamations populaires.* Collection Latomus 82. Brussels, 1965.

Coman, J. "La démonstration dans le traité sur le saint Esprit de saint Basile le grand." *SP* 9 (1966): 172–209.

Constantelos, D. J. "Kyros Panopolites, Rebuilder of Constantinople." *GRBS* 12 (1971): 451–64.

Corrigan, K. "Body's Approach to Soul: An Examination of a Recurrent Theme in the *Enneads.*" *Dionysius* 9 (1985): 37–52.

Coser, L. A. *The Functions of Social Conflict.* New York, 1956.

Coster, C. H. "Synesius, a *curialis* of the Time of the Emperor Arcadius." *Byzantion* 15 (1940–41): 10–38.

Courcelle, J. and P. "Quelques illustrations du 'contra Faustum' de saint Augustin." In *Oikoumene* (Catinae, 1964): 1–21.

Crabbe, A. "The Invitation List to the Council of Ephesus and Metropolitan Hierarchy in the Fifth Century." *JTS* n.s. 32 (1981): 369–400.

Cracco Ruggini, L. "The Ecclesiastical Histories and the Pagan Historiography: Providence and Miracles." *Athenaeum* n.s. 55 (1977): 107–26.

Crehan, J. H. "Patristic Evidence for the Inspiration of Councils." *SP* 9 (1966): 210–15.

Crook, J. A. *Consilium Principis: Imperial Councils and Counsellors from Augustus to Diocletian.* Cambridge, 1955.

Crouzel, H. "Origène et Plotin élèves d'Ammonios Saccas." *Bulletin de Littérature Ecclésiastique* 57 (1956): 193–214.

Cumont, F. "La propagation du manichéisme dans l'Empire romain." *RHLR* n.s. 1 (1910): 31–43.

———. "Comment Plotin détourna Porphyre du suicide." *REG* 32 (1919): 113–20.

Dagron, G. *L'empire romain d'orient au IVᵉ siècle et les traditions politiques de l'hellénisme: le témoignage de Thémistios. Travaux et Mémoires du Centre de Recherches d'Histoire et Civilisation de Byzance, 3.* Paris, 1968.

Daly, L. W. "Altercatio Hadriani Augusti et Epicteti Philosophi." *Illinois Studies in Language and Literature* 24 (1939): 11–94.

Daniel, R. W., and F. Maltomini. *Supplementum Magicum I.* Papyrologica Coloniensia 16.1. Wiesbaden, 1989.

Daniélou, J. "Eunome l'arien et l'exégèse néo-platonicienne du Cratyle." *REG* 69 (1956): 412–32.

———. "L'incomprehensibilité de Dieu d'après saint Jean Chrysostome." *RSR* 37 (1950): 176–94.

———. "Les pères de l'église et l'unité des chrétiens." *SP* 7 (1966): 23–32.

———. "ΜΙΑ ΕΚΚΛΗΣΙΑ chez les pères grecs des premiers siècles." In *l'Église et les églises: Études et travaux offerts à Dom Lambert Beauduin.* Vol. 1. Chevetogne, 1954.

———. *Platonisme et théologie mystique: Essai sur la doctrine spirituelle de saint Grégoire de Nysse.* Paris, 1944.

Dawes, E. A. S., and N. H. Baynes. *Three Byzantine Saints: Contemporary Biographies of St. Daniel the Stylite, St. Theodore of Sykeon and St. John the Almsgiver.* New York, 1977.

Decret, F. *L'Afrique manichéenne (IVᵉ–Vᵉ siècles). Étude historique et doctrinale.* 2 vols. Paris, 1978.

———. *Aspects du manichéisme dans l'Afrique romaine: Les controverses de Fortunatus, Faustus et Felix avec saint Augustin.* Paris, 1970.

———. "Basile le Grand et la polémique antimanichéenne en Asia Mineure au IVᵉ siècle." *SP* 17 (1983): 1060–64.

———. "Du bon usage du mensonge et du parjure: Manichéens et Priscillianistes face à la persécution dans l'Empire chrétien (IVᵉ–Vᵉ siècles)." In *Mélanges P. Lévêque.* Vol. 4. Paris, 1990.

De Francisci, P. "Per la storia del senato romano e della curia." *Rendiconti della Pontificia Academia di Archeologia* 22 (1946–47): 275–317.

De Ghellinck, J. "Quelques appréciations de la dialectique d'Aristote durant les conflits trinitaires du IVᵉ siècle." *RHE* 26 (1930): 5–42.

———. "Quelques mentions de la dialectique stoïcienne dans les conflits doctrinaux du IVᵉ siècle." In *Abhandlungen über die Geschichte der Philosophie I: Philosophia Perennis.* Regensberg, 1930.

De Halleux, A. "La réception du symbole oecuménique, de Nicée à Chalcédoine." *Ephemerides Theologicae Lovanienses* 61 (1985): 5–47.

De Labriolle, P. *La réaction païenne. Étude sur la polémique antichrétienne du Iᵉʳ au VIᵉ siècle.* Paris, 1934.

Delacy, P. H. "Stoic Categories as Methodological Principles." *TAPA* 76 (1945): 246–63.

De Lange, N. *Origen and the Jews: Studies in Jewish-Christian Relations in Third-Century Palestine.* Cambridge, 1976.

Delcambre, E. "Les procès de sorcellerie en Lorraine: psychologie des juges." *Revue d'Histoire du Droit* 21 (1953): 408–15.

Delehaye, H. "Vita S. Danielis Stylitae." *AB* 32 (1913): 121–229.

De Riedmatten, H. *Les actes du procès de Paul de Samosate: Étude sur la christologie du IIIe au IVe siècle.* Fribourg, 1952.

Der 'Nersessian, S. "The Illustrations of the Homilies of Gregory of Nazianzus Paris GR. 510." *DOP* 16 (1962): 197–228.

Déroche, V. "L'authenticité de l'apologie contre les juifs.'" *BCH* 110 (1986): 655–69.

De Romilly, J. *Magic and Rhetoric in Ancient Greece.* Cambridge, Mass., 1975.

———. "Vocabulaire et propagande, ou les premiers emplois du mot ὁμόνοια." In *Mélanges de linguistique et de philologie grecques offerts à Pierre Chantraine.* Études et Commentaires 79. Paris, 1972.

De Stoop, E. *Essai sur la diffusion du manichéisme dans l'empire romain.* Ghent, 1909.

Détienne, M., and J.-P. Vernant. *Cunning Intelligence in Greek Culture and Society,* trans. J. Lloyd. Atlantic Highlands, N.J., 1978.

Detlef, C., and G. Müller. "Stellung und Bedeutung des Katholikos-Patriarchen von Seleukeia-Ktesiphon im Altertum." *Orien Christianus* 53 (1969): 227–45.

Devos, P. "S. Grégoire de Nazianze et Hellade de Césarée en Cappadoce." *AB* 79 (1961): 91–101.

Dewey, J. *Markan Public Debate.* Society of Biblical Literature Dissertation Series 48. Chico, Calif., 1980.

De Witt, N. W. "Organization and Procedure in Epicurean Groups." *CPhil* 31 (1936): 205–11.

Diekamp, F. "Literargeschichtliches zu der eunomianischen Kontroverse." *BZ* 18 (1909): 1–13.

Diertele, R. *Platons Laches und Charmides: Untersuchungen zur elenktisch-aporetischen Struktur der platonischen Frühdialoge.* Freiburg, 1966.

Dillon, J. M. "Iamblichus of Chalchis (c. 240–325 A.D.)," *ANRW* 2.36.2 (Berlin, 1987): 862–909.

———. *The Middle Platonists 80 B.C. to A.D. 220.* Ithaca, 1977.

———. "Self-Definition in Later Platonism." In B. F. Meyers and E. P. Sanders, eds., *Jewish and Christian Self-Definition.* Vol. 1. Philadelphia, 1982.

Dispaux, G. *La logique et le quotidien: une analyse dialogique des mechanismes de l'argumentation.* Paris, 1984.

Dodds, E. R. *The Greeks and the Irrational.* Berkeley, Calif., 1951.

———. *Pagan and Christian in an Age of Anxiety: Some Aspects of Religious Experience from Marcus Aurelius to Constantine.* Cambridge, 1965.

———. *Proclus: The Elements of Theology.* 2d ed. Oxford, 1963.

———. "Numenius und Ammonius." In *Les sources de Plotin.* Entretiens sur l'antiquité classique 5. Vol. 1. Vandoeuvres-Genevè, 1957.

———. "Tradition and Personal Achievement in the Philosophy of Plotinus." *JRS* 50 (1960): 1–7.

Douglas, M. *How Institutions Think.* Syracuse, New York, 1986.

———. *Natural Symbols: Explorations in Cosmology.* New York, 1970.

———. *Purity and Danger*. London, 1966.

Downey, G. "The Perspectives of the Early Church Historians." *GRBS* 6 (1965): 57–70.

Drijvers, H. J. "Addai und Mani: Christentum und Manichäismus im dritten Jahrhundert in Syrien." *OCA* 221 (1983): 173–85.

———. "Conflict and Alliance in Manichaeism." In H. G. Kippenberg, ed., *Struggles of the Gods*. Berlin/New York/Amsterdam, 1984.

Dumont, J.-P. "Les modèles de conversion à la philosophie chez Diogène Laërce." *Augustinus* 32 (1987): 79–97.

Dumortier, J. "Une assemblée chrétienne au IVe siècle." *MSR* 29 (1972): 15–22.

Dupréel, E. "Le problème sociologique du rire." *Revue Philosophique* 106 (1928): 228–60.

Duval, Y. M. "Un nouveau lecteur de l'*Histoire Ecclésiastique* de Rufin d'Aquilée, l'auteur du *liber promissionum et praedictorum Dei*." *Latomus* 26 (1967): 175–91.

———. "Le sens des débats d'Aquilée pour les nicéens. Nicée-Rimini-Aquilée." *Antichità Altoadriatiche* 21 (1981): 67–97.

Dvornik, F. "De auctoritate civili conciliis oecumenicis." *Acta Conventus Velehradensis* 6 (1935): 156–67.

———. "Emperors, Popes and General Councils." *DOP* 6 (1951): 1–27.

Edlow, R. B. *Galen on Language and Ambiguity: An English Translation of Galen's 'De captionibus (On Fallacies).'* Leiden, 1977.

Edwards, M. J. "On the Platonic Schooling of Justin Martyr." *JTS* n.s. 42 (1991): 17–34.

———. "Two Episodes in Porphyry's *Life of Plotinus*." *Historia* 40 (1991): 456–64.

Ehrenberg, V. "Polypragmosune: A Study in Greek Politics." *JHS* 67 (1947): 46–67.

Ehrhardt, C. T. H. R. "Constantinian Documents in Gelasius of Cyzicus' *Ecclesiastical History*." *JAC* 23 (1980): 48–57.

Eisenstadt, S. N., and L. Roniger. *Patrons, Clients and Friends: Interpersonal Relations and the Structure of Trust in Society*. Cambridge, 1984.

Eltester, W. E. "Die Kirchen Antiochias in IV Jahrhundert." *Zeitschrift für neutestamentliche Wissenschaft* 36 (1945): 251–86.

Ernesti, J. C. T. *Lexicon Technologiae Graecorum Rhetoricae*. Hildesheim, 1962.

Evangeliou, C. *Aristotle's Categories and Porphyry*. Leiden, 1988.

———. "The Plotinian Reduction of Aristotle's Categories." *Ancient Philosophy* 7 (1987): 147–62.

Evans, E. C. "Physiognomics in the Ancient World." *Transactions of the American Philosophical Society* n.s. 59 (1969): 5–97.

Faivre, A. *Naissance d'une hiérarchie: Les premières étapes du cursus clérical*. Paris, 1977.

Fedwick, P. J. *The Church and the Charisma of Leadership in Basil of Caesarea*. Toronto, 1979.

———, ed. *Basil of Caesarea: Christian, Humanist, Ascetic*. 2 vols. Toronto, 1981.

Feldmann, E. *Die "Epistula Fundamenti" der nordafrikanischen Manichäer: Versuch einer Rekonstruktion*. Altenberge, 1987.

Ferrarini, A. "Tradizioni orali nella storia ecclesiastica di Socrate Scholastico." *Studia Patavina* 28 (1981): 29–54.

Festugière, A.-J. *Antioche païenne et chrétienne*. Paris, 1959.

——. "Le problème littéraire de l'*Historia monachorum*." *Hermes* 83 (1955): 257–84.

——, ed. *Historia monachorum in Aegypto*. Subsidia Hagiographica 53. Brussels, 1971.

Flemming, J., ed. *Akten der ephesinischen Synode vom 449*. In *Abhandlungen der königlichen Gesellschaft der Wissenschaften zu Göttingen*. Phil.-hist. Klasse, n.s. 15.1. Berlin, 1917.

Foakes-Jackson, F. J. *A History of Church History: Studies of Some Historians of the Christian Church*. Cambridge, 1939.

Fonkič, B. L., and F. B. Poljakov. "Paläographische Grundlagen der Datierung des Kölner Mani-Kodex." *BZ* 83 (1990): 22–29.

Fowden, G. "Bishops and Temples in the Eastern Roman Empire." *JTS* n.s. 29 (1978): 53–78.

——. *The Egyptian Hermes: A Historical Approach to the Late Pagan Mind*. Cambridge, 1986.

——. "The Pagan Holy Man in Late Antique Society." *JHS* 102 (1982): 33–59.

——. "Pagan Philosopher in Late Antique Society: With Special Reference to Iamblichus and His Followers." D.Phil. diss. University of Oxford, 1979.

——. "The Platonist Philosopher and His Circle in Late Antiquity." Φιλοσοφία 7 (Athens, 1977): 359–83.

Frankfurter, D. M. *Elijah in Upper Egypt: The Apocalypse of Elijah and Early Egyptian Christianity*. Studies in Antiquity and Christianity 7. Minneapolis, 1993.

Frazee, C. A. "Anatolian Asceticism in the Fourth Century: Eustathios of Sebastea and Basil of Caesarea." *Catholic Historical Review* 66 (1980): 16–33.

Frede, M. "On Galen's Epistemology." In V. Nutton, ed., *Galen: Problems and Prospects*. London, 1981.

Frend, W. H. C. *The Donatist Church: A Movement of Protest in Roman North Africa*. Oxford, 1952.

——. "The Gnostic-Manichaean Tradition in Roman North Africa." *Journal of Ecclesiastical History* 4 (1953): 13–26.

——. "Manichaeism in the Struggle between Saint Augustine and Petilian of Constantine." In *Augustinus Magister*. Paris, 1954.

——. "Popular Religion and Christological Controversy in the Fifth Century." In G. J. Cuming, ed., *Popular Belief and Practice*. Studies in Church History 7. Cambridge, 1971.

Fuhrer, T. "Das Kriterium der Wahrheit in Augustins *contra Academicos*." *VChr* 46 (1992): 257–75.

Gager, J. G. *Kingdom and Community: The Social World of Early Christianity*. (Englewood Cliffs, N.J., 1975).

——. *Moses in Greco-Roman Paganism*. Society of Biblical Literature Monograph Series no. 16. Nashville, Tenn., 1972.

——. *The Origins of Anti-Semitism*. Oxford, 1983.

Gain, B. *L'Église de Cappadoce au IVe siècle d'après la correspondance de Basile de Césarée (330–379)*. OCA 225. Rome, 1985.

Gallay, P. *La vie de saint Grégoire de Nazianze*. Lyon/Paris, 1943.

Gardner, D. K. "Modes of Thinking and Modes of Discourse in the Sung: Some Thoughts on the *Yü-lu* ('Recorded Conversations') Texts." *Journal of Asian Studies* 50 (1991): 574–603.

Gardner, J. A. "Proofs of Status in the Roman World." *Bulletin of the Institute of Classical Studies* 33 (London, 1986): 1–14.

Garfinkel, H. "Conditions of Successful Degradation Ceremonies." *American Journal of Sociology* 61 (1956): 420–24.

Garnsey, P. D. A. *Social Status and Legal Privilege in the Roman Empire*. Oxford, 1970.

Garsoïan, N. G. "Nersês le grand, Basile de Césarée et Eustathe de Sébaste." *Revue des Études Armeniennes* 17 (1983): 145–69.

Gelzer, H. "Die Konzilien als Reichsparlamente." In *Ausgewählte Kleine Schriften*. Leipzig, 1907.

Gendle, N. "Cappadocian Elements in the Mystical Theology of Evagrius Ponticus." *SP* 16 (1985): 373–84.

Geppert, F. *Die Quellen des Kirchenhistorikers Socrates Scholasticus*. Leipzig, 1898.

Gerland, E. "Die Vorgeschichte des Patriarchates von Konstantinopel." *Byzantinisch-neugriechische Jahrbücher* 9 (1932): 217–30.

Gero, S. "Galen on the Christians: A Reappraisal of the Arabic Evidence." *OCA* 56 (1990): 371–411.

Gersch, S. E. *From Iamblichus to Eriugena: An Investigation of the Prehistory and Evolution of the Pseudo-Dionysian Tradition*. Leiden, 1978.

Gibbon, E. *Decline and Fall of the Roman Empire*. New York, n.d.

Giet, S. *Les idées et l'action sociales de saint Basile*. Paris, 1941.

———. "Saint Basile et le concile de Constantinople de 360," *JTS* n.s. 6 (1955): 94–99.

Gigli, G. *L'ortodossia l'arianesimo e la politica di Constanzo II (337–361)*. Rome, 1949.

Gilliard, F. D. "The Social Origins of Bishops in the Fourth Century." Ph.D. diss., University of California at Berkeley, 1966.

Giradet, K. M. *Kaisergericht und Bischofsgericht: Studien zu den Anfängen des Donatistenstreites (313–315) und zum Prozeß des Athanasius von Alexandrien (328–346)*. Bonn, 1975.

Girardi, M. "Nozione di eresia, scisma e parasinagoga in Basilio di Cesarea." *Vetera Christianorum* 17 (1980): 49–77.

———. "'Semplicità' e ortodossia nel dibattito antiariano di Basilio de Cesarea: la raffigurazione dell'eretico." *Vetera Christianorum* 15 (1978): 51–74.

Glas, A. *Die Kirchengeschichte des Gelasios von Kaisareia: Die Vorlage für die beiden lezten Bücher des Kirchengeschichte Rufins*. Byzantinisches Archiv 6. Leipzig/ Berlin, 1914.

Gluckman, M. *The Judicial Process among the Barotse of Northern Rhodesia*. Manchester, 1955.

Goldschmidt, V. *Les dialogues de Platon: Structure et méthode dialectique*. 2d ed. Paris, 1963.

Goulet, R. "Eunape et ses devanciers. À propos de *Vitae sophistarum*, p. 5.4–17 G." *GRBS* 20 (1979): 161–72.

———. "Les intellectuels païens dans l'empire chrétien selon Eunape de Sardes." *Annuaire: École Pratique des Hautes Études*, Section de Sciences Religieuses, 87 (1978–79): 289–93.

————. "Sur la chronologie de la vie et des oeuvres d'Eunape de Sardes." *JHS* 100 (1980): 60–72.

————. "Variations romanesques sur la mélancholie de Porphyre." *Hermes* 110 (1982): 443–57.

Goulet-Cazé, M.-O. "L'école de Plotin." In L. Brisson et al., eds., *Porphyre: La vie de Plotin.* Vol. 1. Paris, 1982.

Graffin, F., and A.-M. Malingrey. "La tradition syriaque des homélies de Jean Chrysostome sur l'incompréhensibilité de Dieu." In J. Fontaine and C. Kannengiesser, eds., *Epektasis: Mélanges patristiques offerts au Cardinal Jean Daniélou.* Paris, 1972.

Grant, R. M. "Paul, Galen and Origen." *JTS* n.s. 34 (1983): 533–36.

————. "Religion and Politics at the Council of Nicaea." *Journal of Religion* 55 (1975): 1–12.

Greenslade, S. L. *Church and State from Constantine to Theodosius.* Westport, Conn., 1954.

————. "Heresy and Schism in the Later Roman Empire." In D. Baker, ed., *Schism, Heresy and Religious Protest.* Cambridge, 1972.

————. *Schism in the Early Church.* London, 1953.

Gregg, R. C., and D. E. Groh, "The Centrality of Soteriology in Early Arianism." *Anglican Theological Review* 59 (1977): 260–78.

————. *Early Arianism: A View of Salvation.* Philadelphia, 1981.

Gregory, T. E. "Novatianism: A Rigorist Sect in the Christian Roman Empire." *Byzantine Studies* 2 (1975): 1–18.

————. "The Remarkable Christmas Homily of Kyros Panopolites." *GRBS* 16 (1975): 317–24.

————. *Vox Populi: Popular Opinion and Violence in the Religious Controversies in the Fifth Century A.D.* Columbus, Ohio, 1979.

Grondys, L. H. "La diversità delle sette Manichee." In *Silloge Bizantina in onore di Silvio Giuseppe Mercati.* Rome, 1957.

Guarnieri, C. "Note sulla presenza del laici ai concili fino al VI secolo." *Vetera Christianorum* 20 (1983): 77–91.

Guillaumont, A. *Les 'kephalaia gnostica' d'Évagre le pontique et l'histoire de l'origénisme chez les grecs et chez les syriens.* Paris, 1962.

Haas, C. J. "Late Roman Alexandria: Social Structure and Intercommunal Conflict in the Entrepôt of the East." Ph.D. diss. University of Michigan, 1988.

Hadot, P. *Marius Victorinus: Recherches sur sa vie et ses oeuvres.* Paris, 1971.

————. "Philosophie, dialectique, rhétorique dans l'antiquité." *Studia Philosophica* 39 (1980): 139–66.

Hahn, A. *Bibliothek der Symbole und Glaubensregeln der alten Kirche.* Breslau, 1897; 3d ed., Hildesheim, 1962.

Hahn, J. *Der Philosoph und die Gesellschaft: Selbstverständnis, öffentliches Auftreten und populäre Erwartungen in der hohen Kaiserzeit.* Stuttgart, 1989.

Hällstrom, G. af. *Fides simpliciorum according to Origen of Alexandria.* Helsinki, 1984.

Haloun, G., and W. B. Henning. "The Compendium of the Doctrines and Styles of the Teaching of Mani, The Buddha of Light." *Asia Major* n.s. 3 (1952): 184–212.

Hammond, C. P. "The Last Ten Years of Rufinus' Life and the Date of his Move South from Aquileia." *JTS* n.s. 28 (1977): 372–429.

Hanke, M. *Der maieutische Dialog.* Aachen, 1986.

Hanson, R. P. C. *The Search for the Christian Doctrine of God: The Arian Controversy, 318–381.* Edinburgh, 1988.

Hardy, E. R. "The Decline and Fall of the Confessor-Presbyter." *SP* 15 (1984): 221–25.

Harris, W. V. *Ancient Literacy.* Cambridge, Mass., 1989.

———. "Literacy and Epigraphy I." *ZPE* 52 (1983): 87–111.

Hathaway, R. F. *Hierarchy and the Definition of Order in the Letters of Pseudo-Dionysus: A Study in the Form and Meaning of Pseudo-Dionysian Writings.* The Hague, 1969.

Hauschild, W. D. "Die anti-nizänische Synodalaktensammlung des Sabinus von Heraklea." *VChr* 24 (1970): 105–26.

Hauser-Meury, M.-M. *Prosopographie zu den Schriften Gregors von Nazianz.* Theophaneia 13. Bonn, 1960.

Hefele, C. J. *Histoire des conciles.* Vols. 1, 2. Paris, 1907–8.

Heinrici, C. F. G. "Griechisch-byzantinische Gesprächsbücher und Verwandtes aus Sammelhandschriften." *Abhandlungen der königlich sächsischen Gesellschaft der Wissenschaften.* Phil.-hist. Klasse 28 (1911): 3–97.

———. "Zur patristischen Aporienliteratur." *Abhandlungen der königlich sächsischen Gesellschaft der Wissenschaften.* Phil.-hist. Klasse 27 (1909): 843–60.

Henrichs, A. "Mani and the Babylonian Baptists: A Historical Confrontation." *HSCP* 77 (1973): 23–59.

———. "Pagan Ritual and the Alleged Crimes of the Early Christians: A Reconsideration." In P. Granfield and J. A. Jungmann, eds., *Kyriakon: Festschrift Johannes Quasten.* Vol. 1. Münster, 1970.

Henrichs, A., and E. M. Husselman. "Christian Allegorizations (P. Mich. Inv. 3718)." *ZPE* 3 (1968): 175–89.

Henrichs, A., and L. Koenen, eds. "Der Kölner Mani-Codex (P. Colon. inv. nr. 4780) ΠΕΡΙ ΤΗΣ ΓΕΝΝΗΣ ΤΟΥ ΣΩΜΑΤΟΣ ΑΥΤΟΥ, Edition der Seiten." *ZPE* 19 (1975): 1–85; 32 (1978): 87–199; 44 (1981): 201–318; 48 (1982): 1–59.

Henry, P. "The Oral Teaching of Plotinus." *Dionysius* 6 (1982): 4–12.

———. "Trois apories orales de Plotin sur les Categories d'Aristote." In *Zētēsis: Album Amicorum.* Antwerp/Utrecht, 1973.

Heron, A. "The Two Pseudo-Athanasian Dialogues against the Anomoeans." *JTS* n.s. 24 (1973): 101–22.

Hess, H. *The Canons of the Council of Sardica, A.D. 343: A Landmark in the Early Development of Canon Law.* Oxford, 1958.

Hirzel, R. *Der Dialog: Ein literarhistorischer Versuch.* 2 vols. Leipzig, 1895.

Hobart, M. "Orators and Patrons: Two Types of Political Leader in Balinese Village Society." In M. Bloch, ed., *Political Language and Oratory in Traditional Society.* London/New York, 1975.

Hoffmann, M. *Der Dialog bei den christlichen Schriftstellern der ersten vier Jahrhunderte.* TU 96. Berlin, 1966.

Holl, K. *Amphilochius von Ikonium in seinem Verhältnis zu den grossen Kappadoziern.* Tübingen/Leipzig, 1904.

Holland, D. L. "The Creeds of Nicaea and Constantinople Revisited." *Church History* 38 (1969): 248–61.

Hollemann, J. F. *Issues in African Law*. The Hague, 1974.

Hollum, K. G. *Theodosian Empresses: Women and Imperial Dominion in Late Antiquity*. Berkeley, Calif., 1982.

Honigmann, E. "Gélase de Césarée et Rufin d'Aquilée." *Bulletin de l'Académie Royale de Belgique*. Cl. des lettres et des sciences morales et politiques, 40 (1954): 122–61.

————. "Juvenal of Jerusalem." *DOP* 5 (1950): 213–79.

Hopkins, K. "Conquest by Book." In J. H. Humphrey, ed., *Literacy in the Roman World*. Journal of Roman Archaeology, supp. ser. 3. Ann Arbor, 1991.

————. "Elite Mobility in the Roman Empire." In M. Finley, ed., *Studies in Ancient Society*. London, 1974.

————. "Social Mobility in the Later Roman Empire: The Evidence of Ausonius." *CQ* n.s. 11 (1961): 239–49.

Hudson William, H. L. "Conventional Forms of Debate and the Melian Dialogue." *AJP* 71 (1950): 156–69.

Hyldahl, N. *Philosophie und Christentum: Eine Interpretation der Einleitung zum Dialog Justins*. Copenhagen, 1966.

Instinsky, H. U. "*Consensus universorum*." *Hermes* 75 (1940): 265–78.

Jacques, F. *Le privilège de liberté: Politique impériale et autonomie municipale dans les cités de l'occident romain (161–244)*. Rome, 1984.

Jaeger, W. *Early Christianity and Greek Paideia*. Cambridge, Mass., 1961.

Janin, R. *Le siège de Constantinople et le patriarchat oecuménique*. Vol. 1 of *La géographie ecclésiastique de l'Empire byzantin*. Paris, 1953.

Jayyusi, L. *Categorization and the Moral Order*. Boston/London, 1984.

Jerphagnon, L. *Vivre et philosopher sous l'empire chrétien*. Toulouse, 1983.

Jones, A. H. M. *The Later Roman Empire 284–602*. Oxford, 1964.

Jones, C. P. *The Roman World of Dio Chrysostom*. Cambridge, Mass., 1978.

Jugie, E. "La dispute des philosophes païens avec les pères de Nicée." *Échos d'Orient* 24 (1925): 403–10.

Kaden, E. H. "Die Edikte gegen die Manichäer von Diokletian bis Justinian." In *Festchrift für Hans Lewald*. Basel, 1953.

Karayannopoulos, I. "St. Basil's Social Activity: Principles and Praxis." In P. J. Fedwick, ed., *Basil of Caesarea: Christian, Humanist, Ascetic*. Vol. 1. Toronto, 1981.

Kartsonis, A. D. *Anastasis: The Making of an Image*. Princeton, 1986.

Kaster, R. A. *The Guardians of Language: The Grammarian and Society in Late Antiquity*. Berkeley, Calif., 1988.

Kennedy, G. A. *The Art of Persuasion in Greece*. Princeton, 1963.

————. *The Art of Rhetoric in the Roman World 300 B.C.–A.D. 300*. Princeton, 1972.

————. *Classical Rhetoric and Its Christian and Secular Tradition from Ancient to Modern Times*. Chapel Hill, N.C., 1980.

————. *Greek Rhetoric under Christian Emperors*. Princeton, 1983.

Kessels, A. H. M., and P. W. Van der Horst. "The Vision of Dorotheus (Pap. Bodmer 29)." *VChr* 41 (1987): 313–59.

King, N. Q. *The Emperor Theodosius and the Establishment of Christianity*. London, 1961.

Kinzig, W. *In Search of Asterius: Studies on the Authorship of the Homilies on the Psalms*. Göttingen, 1990.

Kitzinger, E. "The Cult of Images in the Age before Iconoclasm." *DOP* 8 (1954): 83–150.

Klausner, A. T. "Akklamation." *RAC* 1:216–33.

Kleijwegt, M. *Ancient Youth: The Ambiguity of Youth and the Absence of Adolescence in Greco-Roman Society.* Amsterdam, 1991.

Klein, R. *Constantius II und die christliche Kirche.* Darmstadt, 1977.

Koenen, L., and C. Römer, eds. *Der Kölner Mani-Kodex: Über das Werden seines Leibes.* Papyrologica Coloniensia 14. Wiesbaden, 1989.

Kollesch, J. *Untersuchungen zu den ps.galenischen Definitiones Medicae.* Berlin, 1973.

Kopecek, T. A. *A History of Neo-Arianism.* 2 vols. Philadelphia, 1979.

———. "Neo-Arian Religion: The Evidence of the *Apostolic Constitutions.*" In R. C. Gregg, ed., *Arianism: Historical and Theological Reassessments.* Cambridge, Mass., 1985.

———. "The Social Class of the Cappadocian Fathers." *Church History* 42 (1973): 453–66.

Koster, W. J. W. "De Arii et Eunomii sotadeis." *Mnemosyne* ser. 4, no. 16 (1963): 135–41.

Krauss, S. "The Jews in the Works of the Church Fathers." *Jewish Quarterly Review* 5 (1893): 123–30.

Kretschmar, G. "Origenes und die Araber." *Zeitschrift für Theologie und Kirche* 50 (1953): 258–79.

Kudlien, F. "Dialektik und Medizin in der Antike." *Medizinhistorisches Journal* 9 (1974): 187–200.

Kuper, A. "Council Structure and Decision-making." In A. Richards and A. Kuper, eds., *Councils in Action.* Cambridge Papers in Social Anthropology 6. Cambridge, 1971.

L'Orange, H. P. *Art Forms and Civic Life in the Late Roman Empire.* Princeton, 1965.

Laistner, M. L. W. *Christianity and Pagan Culture in the Later Roman Empire.* Ithaca, 1951.

Lane Fox, R. *Pagans and Christians.* New York, 1987.

Langerbeck, H. "The Philosophy of Ammonius Saccas." *JHS* 77 (1957): 67–74.

Le Boulluec, A. *La notion d'hérésie dans la littérature grecque, IIe–IIIe siècles.* 2 vols. Paris, 1989.

Lear, J. *Aristotle and Logical Theory.* Cambridge, 1980.

———. *Aristotle: The Desire to Understand.* Cambridge, 1988.

Lèbe, L. "Saint Basile et ses règles morales." *Revue Bénédictine* 75 (1965): 193–200.

Lebon, J. "Discours d'Atticus de Constantinople 'sur la sainte Mère de Dieu,'" *Le Muséon* 46 (1933): 167–202.

———. "La position de saint Cyrille de Jérusalem dans les luttes provoquées par l'arianisme." *RHE* 20 (1924): 181–210, 357–86.

Lebreton, J. "Le désaccord de la foi populaire et de la théologie savantes dans l'Église chrétienne du IIIe siècle." *RHE* 19 (1923): 481–506; 20 (1924): 5–37.

Lee Tae-Soo. *Die griechische Tradition der aristotelischen Syllogistik in der Spätantike: Eine Untersuchung über die Kommentare zu den analytica priora von Alexander Aphrodisiensis, Ammonius und Philoponus.* Hypomnemata, Untersuchungen zur Antike und zu ihrem Nachleben 79. Göttingen, 1984.

Lentz, T. M. "Spoken versus Written Inartistic Proof in Athenian Courts." *Philosophy and Rhetoric* 16 (1983): 242–61.

Levesque, G. "Consonance chrétienne et dissonance gnostique dans Irénée 'Adversus haereses' IV, 18, 4 à 19, 3." *SP* 16 (1985): 193–96.

Lieu, S. N. C. "An Early Byzantine Formula for the Renunciation of Manichaeism: the *capita VII contra Manichaeos of <Zacharias of Mytilene>*." *JAC* 26 (1983): 152–218.

———. "Fact and Fiction in the *Acta Archelai*." In P. Bryder, ed., *Manichaean Studies*. Vol. 1. Lund, 1988.

———. *Manichaeism in the Later Roman Empire and Medieval China: A Historical Survey*. Manchester, 1985.

———. "The Holy Men and Their Biographers in Early Byzantium and Medieval China: A Preliminary Comparative Study in Hagiography." In A. Moffatt, ed., *Maistor: Classical, Byzantine, and Renaissance Studies for Robert Browning*. Canberra, 1984.

Lieu, S. N. C., and J. "'Felix conversus ex Manichaeis': A Case of Mistaken Identity." *JTS* n.s. 32 (1981): 173–76.

Lim, R. "The Auditor Thaumasius in the *Vita Plotini*." *JHS* 113 (1993): 157–60.

———. "Manichaeans and Public Disputation in Late Antiquity." *RecAug* 24 (1992): 233–72.

———. "The Politics of Interpretation in Basil of Caesarea's *Hexaemeron*." *VChr* 44 (1990): 351–70.

———. "Religious Disputation and Social Disorder in the Later Roman Empire." *Historia* (forthcoming).

———. "Theodoret of Cyrus and the Speakers in Greek Dialogues." *JHS* 111 (1991): 181–82.

———. "Unity and Diversity among the Western Manichaeans: A Reconsideration of Mani's *sancta ecclesia*." *REAug* 35 (1989): 231–50.

Lizzi, R. *Il potere episcopale nell'oriente romano: Rappresentazione ideologica e realtà politica (IV–V sec. d. C.)*. Rome, 1987.

Lloyd, A. C. *The Anatomy of NeoPlatonism*. Oxford, 1990.

———. "Neoplatonic Logic and Aristotelian Logic." *Phronesis* 1 (1955): 58–72, 146–60.

Lloyd, G. E. R. *Magic, Reason and Experience: Studies in the Origins and Development of Greek Sciences*. Cambridge, 1979.

———. *Polarity and Analogy*. Cambridge, 1966.

———. *The Revolutions of Wisdom: Studies in the Claims and Practice of Ancient Greek Science*. Berkeley, Calif., 1987.

Lods, M. *Confesseurs et martyrs*. Neuchâtel, 1958.

Loeschcke, G. "Das *Syntagma* des Gelasius Cyzicenus." *RhM* 60 (1905): 594–613; 61 (1906): 34–77.

———. *Das Syntagma des Gelasius von Cyzicus*. Bonn, 1906.

Louth, A. "Envy as the Chief Sin in Athanasius and Gregory of Nyssa." *SP* 15 (1984): 458–60.

Luibhéid, C. "The Alleged Second Session of the Council of Nicaea." *Journal of Ecclesiastical History* 34 (1983): 165–74.

———. *Eusebius of Caesarea and the Arian Crisis*. Dublin, 1981.

Lyman, R. "Arians and Manichees on Christ." *JTS* n.s. 40 (1989): 493–503.

Lynch, J. P. *Aristotle's School: A Study of a Greek Educational Institution*. Berkeley, Calif., 1972.

Maas, P. "Metrische Akklamationen der Byzantiner." *BZ* 21 (1912): 28–51.

MacCormack, S. G. *Art and Ceremony in Late Antiquity.* Berkeley, Calif., 1981.

MacCoull, L. S. B. "Anastasius of Sinai and the Ten-Horned Dragon." *Patristic and Byzantine Review* 9 (1990): 193–94.

MacDowell, D. M. *The Law in Classical Athens.* Ithaca, N.Y., 1978.

MacMullen, R. *Changes in the Roman Empire: Essays in the Ordinary.* Princeton, 1990.

———. *Enemies of the Roman Order: Treason, Unrest, and Alienation in the Empire.* Cambridge, 1966.

———. "A Note on *sermo humilis*." *JTS* n.s. 16 (1966): 108–12.

———. "Personal Power in the Roman Empire." *AJP* 107 (1986): 513–24.

———. "The Preacher's Audience (AD 350–400)." *JTS* n.s. 40 (1989): 503–11.

———. *Roman Government's Response to Crisis, A.D. 235–337.* New Haven/London, 1976.

———. "Social Mobility and the Theodosian Code." *JRS* 54 (1964): 49–53.

———. "Two Types of Conversion to Early Christianity." *VChr* 37 (1983): 174–92.

Mandouze, A., ed. *Prosopographie de l'Afrique chrétienne.* Vol. 1 of *Prosopographie chrétienne du Bas-Empire.* Paris, 1982.

Maraval, P. "La date de la mort de Basile de Césarée." *REAug* 34 (1988): 25–38.

Marrou, H. I. ΜΟΥΣΙΚΟΣ ΑΝΗΡ. 2d ed. Rome, 1964.

———. "Synesius of Cyrene and Alexandrian Neoplatonism." In A. D. Momigliano, ed., *The Conflict between Paganism and Christianity in the Fourth Century.* Oxford, 1963.

Mason, A. J., ed. *The Five Theological Orations of Gregory of Nazianzus.* Cambridge Patristic Texts. Cambridge, 1899.

Mason, H. J. *Greek Terms for Roman Institutions: A Lexicon and Analysis.* Toronto, 1974.

Mates, B. *Stoic Logic.* Berkeley, Calif., 1961.

Mazzarino, S. *Aspetti sociali del quarto secolo.* Rome, 1951.

McCormick, M. *Eternal Victory: Triumphal Rulership in Late Antiquity, Byzantium and the Early Medieval West.* Cambridge, 1986.

McKeon, R. "Greek Dialectics: Dialectic and Dialogues, Dialectic and Rhetoric." In C. Perelman, ed., *Dialectics.* The Hague, 1975.

McLelland, J. C. *God the Anonymous: A Study in Alexandrian Philosophical Theology.* Patristic Monograph Series 4. Philadelphia, 1976.

McLynn, N. "Christian Controversy and Violence in the Fourth Century." *Kodai* 3 (1992): 15–44.

McVey, K. "The Domed Church as Microcosm: Literary Roots of an Architectural Symbol." *DOP* 37 (1983): 91–121.

Mentz, A. "Die hellenistische Tachygraphie." *Archiv für Papyrusforschung* 8 (1927): 34–59.

Mercati, G. "Per la vita e gli scritti di 'Paolo il Persiano': Appunti de una disputa di religione sotto Giustino e Giustiniano." In *Note di letteratura biblica e cristiana antica.* Studi e Testi 5. Rome, 1901.

Meredith, A. "Orthodoxy, Heresy and Philosophy in the Latter Half of the Fourth Century." *Heythrop Journal* 16 (1975): 5–21.

———. "Traditional Apologetic in the *Contra Eunomium* of Gregory of Nyssa." *SP* 14 (1976): 315–19.

Méridier, L. *L'influence de la second sophistique sur l'oeuvre de Grégoire de Nysse.* Paris, 1906.

Meslin, M. *Les ariens d'occident 335–430.* Patristica Sorbonensia 8. Paris, 1967.

Meyendorff, J. *Imperial Unity and Christian Divisions: The Church 450–680 A.D.* New York, 1987.

Meyer, M. "Dialectic and Questioning: Socrates and Plato." *American Philosophical Quarterly* 17 (1980): 281–89.

Meyer, T. *Geschichte des römischen Ärztestandes.* Kiel, 1907.

Millar, F. G. B. "Paul of Samosata, Zenobia and Aurelian: the Church, Local Culture and Political Allegiance in Third-century Syria." *JRS* 61 (1971): 1–17.

Milne, H. J. M. *Greek Shorthand Manuals: Syllabary and Commentary; edited from Papyri and Waxed Tablets in the British Museum and from the Antinoë Papyri in the Possession of the Egypt Exploration Society.* London, 1934.

Minio-Paluello, L. "The Text of the 'Categoriae': the Latin Tradition." *CQ* 39 (1945): 63–74.

Mitsis, P. "Epicurus on Friendship and Altruism." *Oxford Studies in Ancient Philosophy* 5 (1987): 126–53.

Moles, J. L. "The Career and Conversion of Dio Chrysostom." *JHS* 94 (1978), 79–100.

Momigliano, A. D. "La libertà di parola nel mondo antico." *Rivista Storia Italiana* ser. 4, no. 83 (1971): 499–524.

———. "Pagan and Christian Historiography in the Fourth Century A.D." In idem, ed., *The Conflict between Paganism and Christianity in the Fourth Century.* Oxford, 1963.

Monceaux, P. *Le manichéen Faustus de Milève: Restitution de ses Capitula.* Mémoires de l'Institut National de France, Académie des Inscriptions et Belles-Lettres 43. Paris, 1933.

Montes-Peral, L. A. *Akataleptos Theos: Der unfassbare Gott.* Leiden, 1987.

Moraux, P. *Galen de Pergame: Souvenirs d'un médecin.* Paris, 1985.

———. "La joute dialectique d'après le VIIIᵉ livre des *Topiques.*" In G. E. L. Owen, ed., *Aristotle on Dialectic: The Topics.* Oxford, 1968.

Mortley, R. A. *From Word to Silence.* 2 vols. Bonn, 1986.

———. "The Fundamentals of the via negativa." *AJP* 103 (1982): 429–39.

Mueller, R. "La sofistica e la democrazia." *Discorsi* 6 (1986): 7–23.

Müri, W. "Das Wort Dialektik bei Platon." *Museum Helveticum* 1 (1944): 152–68.

Murphy, F. X. *Rufinus of Aquileia (345–411): His Life and Works.* Washington, D.C., 1945.

Nader, L. *Harmony Ideology: Justice and Control in a Zapotec Mountain Village.* Stanford, 1990.

Nau, F. "Analyse de la seconde partie inédite de l'*Histoire Ecclésiastique* de Jean d'Asie, patriarche jacobite de Constantinople (d. 585)." *Revue de l'Orient Chrétien* 2 (1897): 455–93.

Nencei, G. "Eunapio, *Vitae sophistarum* II, 2, 6-8 e la periodizzazione della φιλό-σοφος ἱστορία." *Annali della Scuola Normale Superiore di Pisa,* Classe di Lettere e Filosofia 3 (1973): 95–102.

Newman, D. "Pleading Guilty for Considerations: A Study of Bargain Justice." *Journal of Criminal Law, Criminology and Police Science* 46 (1956): 780–90.

Nock, A. D. *Conversion: The Old and the New in Religion from Alexander the Great to Augustine of Hippo.* Oxford, 1933.

Norden, E. *Agnostos Theos.* Leipzig/Berlin, 1913.

———. *Die Antike Kunstprosa.* 2 vols. Leipzig, 1898.

Norman, A. F. "Gradations in Later Municipal Society." *JRS* 48 (1958): 79–85.

———. "Magnus in Ammianus, Eunapius and Zosimus: New Evidence." *CQ* n.s. 7 (1957): 129–33.

———. "Note on Eunapius P. 485B, *Vitae sophistarum* 10.1.5, Prohaeresius." *Liverpool Classical Monthly* 4 (1979): 135–36.

Norris, F. W. "Gregory Nazianzen's Opponents in *Oration* 31." In R. Gregg, ed., *Arianism: Historical and Theological Reassessments.* Cambridge, Mass., 1985.

———, ed. *Faith Gives Fullness to Reasoning: The Five Theological Orations of Gregory Nazianzen.* Supplements to Vigiliae Christianae 13. Leiden, 1991.

Nutton, V. "Ammianus and Alexandria." *Clio Medica* 7 (1972): 165–76.

———. "*Archiatri* and the Medical Profession in Antiquity." *PBSR* 32 (1977): 191–226.

O'Connor, D. K. "The Invulnerable Pleasures of Epicurean Friendship." *GRBS* 30 (1989): 165–86.

O'Donnell, J. *Augustine: Confessions.* 3 vols. Oxford, 1992.

O'Meara, D. J. *Pythagoras Revived: Mathematics and Philosophy in Late Antiquity.* Oxford, 1989.

Oehler, K. "Aristotle in Byzantium." *GRBS* 5 (1964): 133–46.

———. "Der Consensus Omnium als Kriterium der Wahrheit in der antike Philosophie und der Patristik: Eine Studie zur Geschichte des Begriffs der allgemeinen Meinung." *Antike und Abendland* 10 (1961): 103–30.

Ohlmann, D. "Die Stenographie im Leben des heiligen Augustin." *Archiv für Stenographie* 56 (1905): 273–79, 312–19.

Optiz, H.-G., ed. *Urkunden zur Geschichte des arianischen Streites* 20. In *Athanasius Werke III.* Berlin, 1934–35.

Ort, L. J. R. *Mani: A Religio-historical Description of His Personality.* Leiden, 1967.

Ortiz de Urbina, I. *Nicée et Constantinople.* Paris, 1963.

Oulton, J. E. L. "Rufinus' Translation of the Church History of Eusebius." *JTS* n.s. 30 (1929): 150–75.

Owen, G. E. L. "Philosophical Invective." *Oxford Studies in Ancient Philosophy* 1 (1983): 1–25.

P.-H. Poirier. "Le *contra Manichaeos* de Titus de Bostra." *Annuaire: École Pratique des Hautes Études,* Section de Sciences Religieuses 98 (1989–90): 366–68.

Parkes, D. "The Rhetoric of Responsibility." In M. Bloch, ed., *Political Language and Oratory in Traditional Society.* London/New York, 1975.

Parmentier, L. "Eunomius tachygraphe." *Revue de Philologie* 33 (1909): 238–46.

Paschoud, F. *Cinq études sur Zosime.* Paris, 1975.

Pearson, B. A., and Goehring, J. E., eds. *The Roots of Egyptian Christianity.* Philadelphia, 1986.

Pedersen, F. S. *Late Roman Public Professionalism.* Odense University Classical Studies 9. Odense, 1976.

———. "On Professional Qualifications for Public Posts in Late Antiquity." *Classica et Mediaevalia* 31 (1975): 161–213.

Peeters, H. "La vie géorgienne de saint Porphyre de Gaza." *AB* 59 (1941): 65–216.

Penella, R. J. *Greek Philosophers and Sophists in the Fourth Century, A.D.: Studies in Eunapius of Sardis.* ARCA. Classical and Medieval Texts, Papers and Monographs 28. Leeds, 1990.

Pépin, J. *Saint Augustin et la dialectique.* The Saint Augustine Lecture 1972. Villanova, 1976.

———. "La vraie dialectique selon Clément d'Alexandrie." In *Epektasis: Mélanges offerts à Jean Daniélou.* Paris, 1972.

Person, R. E. *The Mode of Theological Decision Making at the Early Ecumenical Councils: An Inquiry into the Function of Scripture and Tradition at the Councils of Nicaea and Ephesus.* Basel, 1978.

Petit, P. *Les étudiants de Libanius.* Paris, 1956.

Pinborg, J. "Das Sprachdenken der Stoa und Augustinus." *Classica et Mediaevalia* 23 (1962): 149–50.

Pitt-Rivers, J. "The Stranger, the Guest and the Hostile Host: Introduction to the Study of the Laws of Hospitality." In J.-G. Peristiany, ed., *Contributions to Mediterranean Sociology: Mediterranean Rural Communities and Social Change.* Paris, 1968.

Plagnieux, J. *Saint Grégoire de Nazianze théologien.* Paris, 1951.

Pocock, J. G. A. "The Classical Theory of Deference." *AHR* 81 (1976): 516–23.

Poliakoff, M. B. "πήλωμα and κήρωμα: Refinement of the Greco-Roman Gymnasium." *ZPE* 79 (1989): 289–91.

Pollard, T. E. "The Exegesis of Scripture and the Arian Controversy." *Bulletin of the John Rylands Library* 41 (1959): 414–29.

Praetcher, K. "Richtungen und Schulen im Neuplatonismus." In *Genethliakon: Carl Robert zum 8 Marz 1910.* Berlin, 1910. Reprinted in H. Dörrie, ed., *Kleine Schriften.* Hildesheim, 1973.

Prestige, G. L. *St. Basil the Great and Apollinaris of Laodicea.* London, 1956.

Preuschen, E. *Palladius und Rufinus: Ein Beitrag zur Quellenkunde des ältesten Mönchtums.* Giessen, 1897.

———. "Die Stenographie im Leben des Origens." *Archiv für Stenographie* 56 (1905): 6–14.

Puech, H.-C. *Le manichéisme, son fondateur, sa doctrine.* Paris, 1949.

Quasten, J. "The Liturgical Mysticism of Theodore of Mopsuestia." *Theological Studies* 15 (1954): 431–39.

———. "Mysterium Tremendum: Eucharistiche Frömmigkeitsauffassungen des vierten Jahrhunderts." In A. Mayer, J. Quasten, B. Neunheuser, eds. *Vom christlichen Mysterium: Gesammelte Arbeiten zum Gedächtnis von Odo Costel.* Düsseldorf, 1951.

Ravenhil, P. L. "Religious Utterances and the Theory of Speech Acts." In W. J. Samarin, ed., *Languages in Religious Practice.* Rowley, Mass., 1976.

Rebenich, S. *Hieronymus und sein Kreis.* Historia Einzelschriften 72. Stuttgart, 1992.

Reisman, K. "Contrapunctal Conversations in an Antiguan Village." In R. Bauman and J. Scherzer, eds., *Explorations in the Ethnography of Speaking.* Cambridge, 1974.

Reitzenstein, R. "Alexander von Lykopolis." *Philologus* 86 (1930–31): 185–98.

Remus, H. "Justin Martyr's Argument with Judaism." In S. G. Wilson, ed., *Anti-Judaism in Early Christianity II: Separation and Polemic*. Waterloo, Ont., 1986.

Rescher, N. *Dialectics: A Controversy-oriented Approach to the Theory of Knowledge*. Albany, N.Y., 1977.

Richard, M. "Les florilèges diphysites du Vᵉ et VIᵉ siècle." In A. Grillmeier and H. Bacht, eds., *Das Konzil von Chalkedon*. Vol. 1. Würzburg, 1951.

———. "Malchion et Paul de Samosate: Le témoignage d'Eusèbe de Césarée." *Ephemerides Theologicae Lovanienses* 35 (1959): 325–38.

Richter, G. *Die Dialektik des Johannes von Damaskos: Eine Untersuchung des Textes nach seinen Quellen und seiner Bedeutung*. Ettal, 1964.

Rist, J. M. "Basil's 'Neoplatonism': Its Background and Nature." In P. Fedwick, ed., *Basil of Caesarea: Christian, Humanist, Ascetic*. Vol. 1. Toronto, 1981.

———. "The Importance of Stoic Logic in the *Contra Celsum*." In H. J. Blumenthal and R. A. Markus, eds., *Neoplatonism and Early Christian Thought: Essays in Honour of A. H. Armstrong*. London, 1971.

Robbins, F. E. *The Hexaemeral Literature: A Study of the Greek and Latin Commentaries on Genesis*. Chicago, 1912.

Robert, L. "Les juges étrangers dans la cité grecque." In idem, *Opera Minora Selecta*. Vol. 5. Amsterdam, 1989.

———. "La titulature de Nicée et de Nicomedie: la gloire et la haine." *HSCP* 81 (1977): 1–39.

Roberts, C. H. *Manuscript, Society and Belief in Early Christian Egypt*. London, 1979.

Roberts, L. "Origen and Stoic Logic." *TAPA* 101 (1970): 433–44.

Robinson, L. *Freedom of Speech in the Roman Republic*. Baltimore, 1940.

Rochow, I. "Zum Fortleben des Manichäismus im byzantinischen Reich nach Justinian I." *Byzantinoslavica* 40 (1979): 13–21.

Roethe, G. *Zur Geschichte der römischen Synoden im II und V Jahrhunderten: Geistige Grundlage römischer Kirchenpolitik*. Stuttgart, 1937.

Roques, R. *L'univers dionysien: Structure hiérarchique du monde selon le pseudo-Denys*. Paris, 1954.

———. "Pierre l'Ibérien et le 'corpus' dionysien." *RHR* 145 (1954): 69–98.

Roueché, C. "Acclamations in the Later Roman Empire: New Evidence from Aphrodisias." *JRS* 74 (1984): 181–99.

———. "Theodosius II, the Cities, and the Date of the 'Church History' of Sozomen." *JTS* n.s. 37 (1986): 130–32.

Rousseau, O. "La rencontre de saint Éphrem et de saint Basile." *L'Orient Syrien* 2 (1957): 261–84; 3 (1958): 73–90.

Rousseau, P. *Ascetics, Authority, and the Church in the Age of Jerome and Cassian*. Oxford, 1978.

———. "Basil of Caesarea, *Contra Eunomium*: the Main Preoccupations." *Prudentia* Supplementary Number (1988): 77–94.

Rousselle, A. "Aspects sociaux du recrutement ecclésiastique au IVᵉ siècle," *Mélanges d'Archéologie et d'Histoire de l'École Française de Rome* 89 (1977): 333–70.

Ruether, R. R. *Gregory of Nazianzus: Rhetor and Philosopher*. Oxford, 1969.

Runia, D. T. "Festugière Revisited: Aristotle in the Greek Patres." *VChr* 43 (1989): 1–34.

————. "Philosophical Heresiography: Evidence in Two Ephesian Inscriptions." *ZPE* 72 (1988): 241–43.

Ryle, G. "Dialectic in the Academy." In G. E. L. Owen, ed., *Aristotle on Dialectic: The Topics*. Oxford, 1968.

Saffrey, H. D. and O. P. "Nouveaux liens objectifs entre le pseudo-Denys et Proclus." *Revue des Sciences Philosophiques et Théologiques* 63 (1979): 3–16.

Salaville, S. "La fête du concile de Chalcédoine dans le rite byzantin." In A. Grillmeier and H. Bacht, eds., *Das Konzil von Chalkedon*. Vol. 2. Würzburg, 1953.

————. "La fête du concile de Nicée et les fêtes de conciles dans le rite byzantin." *Échos d'Orient* 24 (1925): 445–70.

Schamp, J. "Gélase ou Rufin: un fait nouveau: sur des fragments oubliés de Gélase de Césarée (*CPG*, no. 3521)." *Byzantion* 57 (1987): 360–90.

————. "The Lost Ecclesiastical History of Gelasius of Caesarea (CPG, 3521): Towards a Reconsideration." *Patristic and Byzantine Review* 6 (1987): 146–52.

Schatkin, M. A. "John Chrysostom as Apologist: With Special Reference to the *De Incomprehensibili, Quod nemo laeditur, Ad eos qui scandalizati sunt*, and *Adversus oppugnatores vitae monasticae*." Th.D. diss., Princeton Theological Seminary, 1982.

Scheidweiler, F. "Die Kirchengeschichte des Gelasios von Kaisareia." *BZ* 46 (1953): 277–301.

Schemmel, F. "Die Hochschule von Alexandria im IV. und V. Jahrhundert p. Ch. n." *Neue Jahrbücher für das klassische Altertum* 24 (1909): 438–57.

Scherer, J. *Entretien d'Origène avec Héraclide et les évêques ses collègues, sur le père, le fils, et l'âme*. Publications de la Société Fouad Ier de Papyrologie, Textes et Documents 9. Cairo, 1949.

Schmidt, C., and H. J. Polotsky. "Ein Mani-Fund in Ägypten: Originalschriften des Mani und seiner Schüler." *SPAW*, Phil.-hist. Klasse 1 (1933): 4–90.

Schoo, G. *Die Quellen des Kirchenhistorikers Sozomenos*. Berlin, 1911.

Sciuto, F. E. "Dalla Nicea a Costantinopoli: osservazioni sulla prima fase della stabilizzazione teologico-politica cristiana (325–381)." In *La trasformazioni nella cultura della tarda antichità*. 2 vols. Rome, 1985.

Seeberg, R. *Die Synode von Antiochen im Jahre 324/25*. Berlin, 1913.

Seeck, O. "Untersuchungen zur Geschichte des nicänischen Konzils." *ZKG* 17 (1897): 1–71, 319–62.

Seston, W. "Constantine as Bishop." *JRS* 37 (1947): 127–31.

————. "L'Égypte manichéene." *Chronique d'Égypte* 14 (1939): 362–72.

Setton, K. M. *The Christian Attitude Towards the Emperor in the Fourth Century*. New York, 1941.

Shaw, B. "African Christianity: Disputes, Definitions, and 'Donatist.'" In M. R. Greenshields and T. A. Robinson, eds., *Orthodoxy and Heresy in Religious Movements: Discipline and Dissent*. Lewinston-Queenston-Lampeter, 1992.

Sheppard, A. R. R. "*Homonoia* in the Greek Cities of the Roman Empire." *Ancient Society* 15/17 (1984/86): 229–52.

Shils, E. *Center and Periphery: Essays in Macrosociology*. Chicago, 1975.

Siddals, R. "Logic and Christology in Cyril of Alexandria." *JTS* n.s. 38 (1987): 341–67.

Sider, R. D. *Ancient Rhetoric and the Art of Tertullian*. Oxford, 1971.

Simon, M. "From Greek *hairesis* to Christian Heresy." In W. R. Schoedel and R. L. Wilken, eds., *Early Christian Literature and the Classical Intellectual Tradition*. Paris, 1979.

Simonetti, M. *La crisi ariana nel IV secolo*. Rome, 1975.

Skarsaune, O. *The Proof from Prophecy: A Study in Justin Martyr's Proof-text Tradition*. Leiden, 1987.

Smith, A. *Porphyry's Place in the Neoplatonic Tradition: A Study in Post-Plotinian Neoplatonism*. The Hague, 1974.

Smith, J. Z. *Map is Not Territory: Studies in the History of Religions*. Leiden, 1978.

Smith, R. R. R. "Late Roman Philosopher Portraits from Aphrodisias." *JRS* 80 (1990): 127–55.

———. "Late Roman Philosophers." In R. R. R. Smith and K. T. Erim, eds., *Aphrodisias Papers 2: The Theatre, A Sculptor's Workshop, Philosophers, and Coin-Types*. Journal of Roman Archaeology Supplementary Series 2. Ann Arbor, 1991.

Snee, R. "Valens' Recall of the Nicene Exiles and Anti-Arian Propaganda." *GRBS* 25 (1985): 395–419.

Solmsen, F. "Aristotle and Cicero on the Orator's Playing Upon the Feelings." *CPhil* 33 (1938): 390–404.

———. "Early Christian Interest in the Theory of Demonstration." In *Romanitas et Christianitas*. Studia J. H. Waszink oblata. Amsterdam/London, 1973.

Sorabji, R. *Philoponus and the Rejection of Aristotelian Science*. London, 1987.

Stanton, G. R. "Sophists and Philosophers: Problems of Classification." *AJP* 94 (1973): 350–64.

Stead, G. C. "The *Thalia* of Arius and the Testimony of Athanasius." *JTS* n.s. 29 (1978): 20–52.

Stein, J. A. *Encomium of Saint Gregory Bishop of Nyssa, on His Brother Saint Basil Archbishop of Cappadocian Caesarea*. The Catholic University of America Patristic Studies 17. Washington, D.C., 1928.

Strange, S. K. "Plotinus, Porphyry, and the Neoplatonic Interpretation of the 'Categories,'" *ANRW* 2.36.2 (Berlin, 1987): 955–74.

Straub, J. "Constantine as ΚΟΙΝΟΣ ΕΠΙΣΚΟΠΟΣ: Tradition and Innovation in the Representation of the First Christian Emperor's Majesty." *DOP* 21 (1967): 37–55.

Stroumsa, G. "The Manichaean Challenge to Egyptian Christianity." In B. A. Pearson and J. E. Goehring, eds., *The Roots of Egyptian Christianity*. Philadelphia, 1986.

———. "Manichéisme et marranisme chez les manichéens d'Égypte." *Numen* 29 (1983): 184–201.

Sundermann, W., ed. *Mitteliranische manichäische Texte kirchengeschichtlichen Inhalts*. Berliner Turfantexte 11. Berlin, 1981.

Süss, W. *Ethos*. Leipzig, 1910.

Szymusiak, J.-M. "Note sur l'amour des lettres au service de la foi chrétienne chez Grégoire de Nazianze." In *Oikoumene*. Catinae, 1964.

———. "Pour une chronologie des discours de S. Grégoire de Nazianze." *VChr* 20 (1966): 183–89.

Talbert, R. J. A. *The Senate of Imperial Rome*. Princeton, 1984.

Tardieu, M. "Gnose et manichéisme." *Annuaire: École Pratique des Hautes Études*, Section de Sciences Religieuses 96 (1987–88): 297–301.

———. "Les manichéens en Égypte." *Bulletin de la Société Française d'Égyptologie* 94 (1982): 5–19.

Tarrant, H. *Scepticism or Platonism?: The Philosophy of the Fourth Academy.* Cambridge, 1985.

Taylor, J. "The First Council of Constantinople (381)." *Prudentia* 13 (1941): 47–54, 91–97.

Taylor, L. R., and R. T. Scott. "Seating Space in the Roman Senate and the *senatores pediarii.*" *TAPA* 100 (1969): 529–82.

Teitler, H. C. *Notarii and Exceptores: An Inquiry into Role and Significance of Shorthand Writers in the Imperial and Ecclesiastical Bureaucracy of the Roman Empire (from the Early Principate to c. 450 A.D.).* Amsterdam, 1985.

Tengström, E. *Die Protokollierung der Collatio Carthaginensis: Beiträge zur Kenntnis der römischen Kurzschrift nebst einem Exkurs über das Wort scheda (schedula).* Göteborg, 1962.

Tentler, T. N. "The Summa for Confessors as an Instrument of Social Control." In C. Trinkaus and H. A. Oberman, eds., *The Pursuit of Holiness in Late Medieval and Renaissance Religion.* Leiden, 1974.

Thélamon, F. "Une oeuvre destinée à la communauté chrétienne d'Aquilée: l'*Histoire ecclésiastique* de Rufin." *Antichità altoadriatiche* 22 (1982): 255–71.

———. *Païens et chrétiens au IVᵉ siècle: L'apport de l' "Histoire ecclésiastique" de Rufin d'Aquilée.* Paris, 1981.

Thompson, E. P. *Customs in Common.* London, 1991.

———. "Patrician and Plebeian Society." *Journal of Social History* 7 (1974): 382–405.

Thromm, H. *Die Thesis: Ein Beitrag zu ihre Enstehung und Geschichte.* Rhetorische Studien 17. Freiburg, 1932.

Tod, M. N. "Sidelights on Greek Philosophers." *JHS* 77 (1957): 132–41.

Turner, C. H. "Notes on the *Apostolic Constitutions.*" *JTS* 16 (1914–15): 54–61.

Turpin, W. "The Purpose of the Roman Law Codes." *Zeitschrift der Savigny-Stiftung für Rechtsgeschichte* 104 (1987): 620–30.

Uthemann, K.-H. "Syllogistik im Dienst der Orthodoxie: Zwei unedierte Texte byzantinischer Kontroverstheologie des 6. Jahrhunderts." *JÖB* 30 (1981): 103–12.

Vaggione, R. P. *Eunomius: The Extant Works.* Oxford, 1987.

———. "Some Neglected Fragments of Theodore of Mopsuestia's *Contra Eunomium.*" *JTS* n.s. 31 (1980): 403–70.

Van Dam, R. "Emperors, Bishops, and Friends in Late Antique Cappadocia." *JTS* n.s. 37 (1986): 53–76.

———. "From Paganism to Christianity in Late Antique Gaza." *Viator* 16 (1985): 1–20.

Van de Paverd, F. "Zur Geschichte der Messliturgie in Antiocheia und Konstantinopel gegen das Endes des vierten Jahrhunderts: Analyse der Quellen bei Johannes Chrysostomos." *OCA* 187 (1970): 179–83.

Van den Broek, R., T. Baarda, and J. Mansfield, eds. *Knowledge of God in the Graeco-Roman World.* Études Préliminaires aux Réligions Orientales dans l'Empire Romain 44. Leiden, 1988.

Vandenbusschen, E. "La part de la dialectique dans la théologie d'Eunomius 'le technologue,'" *RHE* 40 (1944–45): 47–72.

Van den Ven, P. *La légende de saint Spyridon, évêque de Trimithonte.* Louvain, 1953.

Van der Lof, L. J. "Mani as the Danger from Persia in the Roman Empire." *Augustiniana* 24 (1974): 74–84.

Van Eemeren, F., and R. Grootendorst. *Speech Acts in Argumentative Discussions: A Theoretical Model for the Analysis of Discussions Directed Towards Solving Conflicts of Opinion.* Dordrecht, 1984.

Van Esbroeck, M. "Jean II de Jérusalem et les cultes de saint Étienne de la Sainte-Sion et de la Croix," *AB* 102 (1984): 99–134.

Van Ommeslaeghe, F. "Jean Chrysostome et le peuple de Constantinople." *AB* 99 (1981): 329–49.

Vecchi, A. "L'antimanicheismo nelle 'confessioni' di sant'Agostino." *Giornale di metafisica* 20 (1965): 91–121.

Villain, M. "Rufin d'Aquilée et l'*Histoire ecclésiastique.*" *RSR* 33 (1946): 164–210.

Vogel, C. "Primaliatié et synodalité dans l'église locale durant la periode anténicéene." In M. Simon, ed., *Aspects de l'orthodoxie: Structure et spiritualité.* Paris, 1982.

Von Campenhausen, H. *Ecclesiastical Office and Spiritual Power in the Church in the First Three Centuries.* Stanford, 1969. Originally published as *Kirchliches Amt und geistliche Vollmacht in den ersten drei Jahrhunderten.* Tübingen, 1953.

Von Harnack, A. *Marcion: Das Evangelium vom fremden Gott.* TU 45. Leipzig, 1921.

Von Heintze, H. "*Vir sanctus et gravis:* Bildniskopf eines spätantiken Philosophen." *JAC* 6 (1963): 35–53, and plates 1–9.

Voss, B. R. *Der Dialog in der frühchristlichen Literatur.* Munich, 1970.

Walter, C. *L'iconographie des conciles dans la tradition byzantine.* Archives de l'Orient Chrétien 13. Paris, 1970.

Walzer, R. *Galen on Jews and Christians.* London, 1949.

Weitman, S. R. "Intimacies: Notes towards a Theory of Social Inclusion and Exclusion." *Archives Européennes de Sociologie* 11 (1970): 348–67.

Weitzmann, K. "Illustration for the Chronicles of Sozomenos, Theodoret and Malalas." *Byzantion* 16 (1942–43), 87–134.

Westerink, L. G. *The Anonymous Prolegomena to Platonic Philosophy.* Amsterdam, 1962.

———. "Philosophy and Medicine in Late Antiquity." *Janus* 51 (1964): 169–77.

Wickenhauser, A. "Beiträge zur Geschichte der Stenographie auf den Synoden des vierten Jahrhunderts nach Christus." *Archiv für Stenographie* 59 (1908): 4–9, 33–39.

———. "Die Stenographische Aufnahme der Disputation zwischen Photinus und Basilius auf der Synode zu Sirmium im Jahre 351." *Korrespondenzblatt: Amtliche Zeitung des könig. Stenographischen Instituts zu Dresden* 51 (1906): 259–65.

———. "Zur Frage nach der Existenz von nicaenischen Synodalprotokollen." In F. Dölger, ed., *Konstantin der Grosse und seine Zeit.* Freiburg, 1913.

Wickham, L. R. *Cyril of Alexandria: Select Letters.* Oxford, 1983.

———. "The Date of Eunomius' Apology: a Reconsideration." *JTS* n.s. 20 (1969): 231–40.

———. "The *Syntagmation* of Aetius the Anomean." *JTS* n.s. 19 (1968): 532–69.

Wiles, M. "Eunomius: Hair-splitting Dialectician or Defender of the Accessibility of Salvation?" In R. Williams, ed., *The Making of Orthodoxy: Essays in Honour of Henry Chadwick.* Cambridge, 1989.

Wilken, R. L. *The Christians as the Romans Saw Them.* New Haven, Conn., 1984.
———. "The Jews and Christian Apologetics after Theodosius' *Cunctos Populos.*" *HTR* 73 (1980): 451–71.
———. *John Chrysostom and the Jews: Rhetoric and Reality in the Late Fourth Century.* Berkeley, Calif., 1983.
William, A. L. *Adversus Judaeos: A Bird's-Eye View of Christian Apologiae until the Renaissance.* Cambridge, 1935.
Williams, R. *Arius: Heresy and Tradition.* London, 1987.
———. "The Logic of Arianism." *JTS* n.s. 34 (1983): 56–81.
———, ed. *The Making of Orthodoxy: Essays in Honour of Henry Chadwick.* Cambridge, 1989.
Winkelmann, F. "Charakter und Bedeutung der Kirchengeschichte des Gelasios von Kaisareia." *Byzantinische Forschungen* 1 (1966): 346–85.
———. "Zu einer Edition der Fragmente der Kirchengeschichte des Gelasios von Kaisareia." *Byzantinoslavica* 34 (1973): 193–98.
Winslow, D. F. *The Dynamics of Salvation: A Study in Gregory of Nazianzus.* Patristic Monograph Series 7. Philadelphia, 1979.
Wipszycha, E. "Le degré d'alphabetisation en Égypte byzantine." *REAug* 30 (1984): 279–96.
Wolf, E. "Die Entstehung der kaiserlichen Synodengewalt unter Konstantin der Grossen, ihre theologischen Begründung und ihre kirchliche Reception." In G. RihBack, ed., *Kirche angesichts der konstantinischen Wende.* Darmstadt, 1976.
Wolf, P. *Vom Schulwesen der Spätantike: Studien zu Libanius.* Baden-Baden, 1952.
Wolfson, H. A. "The Knowability and Describability of God in Plato and Aristotle." *HSCP* 56/57 (1947): 233–49.
———. *Philo.* 2 vols. Cambridge, Mass., 1947–48.
———. "The Philosophical Implications of Arianism and Apollinarianism." *DOP* 12 (1958): 3–28.
———. "Philosophical Implications of the Theology of Cyril of Jerusalem." *DOP* 11 (1957): 3–19.
Youtie, H. C. "ΑΓΡΑΜΜΑΤΟΣ: An Aspect of Greek Society in Egypt." *HSCP* 75 (1971): 161–76.
———. "ΥΠΟΓΡΑΦΕΥΣ: the Social Impact of Illiteracy in Graeco-Roman Egypt." *ZPE* 17 (1975): 201–21.

INDEX

Abgar, King of Edessa, 77
Academy. *See* Plato, Academy of
Acclamations, 28, 215, 217
  at debates, 78, 80–81
  in councils, 217, 218n5, 225
acta, 217
  at African councils, 104, 218
  at Aquileia (381), 219–20
  at Chalcedon (451), 224
  at Ephesus (431), 223–24
  at Nicaea (325), 184, 185, 210, 210n123
  debate between Origen and Heracleides, 18
  debate between Paul and Malchion, 23–24
Addai, 81n46
Addas, 74–75
Adimantus, 8
adversus Judaeos literature, 4, 5, 9–10, 15–16, 106
adversus Manichaeos literature, 76–78, 102, 102n155, 103, 106, 107
Aedesius of Cappadocia, circles of, 50–53
Aetius the Syrian
  as debater, 87–88, 119, 120, 232
  as seen by others, 111, 143–144
  career and character, 112–15, 117–18, 141, 143
  circles of, 129–30, 132
  contacts with Gallus and Julian, 52n113, 122
  reliance on Aristotle, 131, 231, 232
  Syntagmation, 130, 132–33
Agapetus, 147
Age qualification for disputation, 35, 65.
  See also Youth
Agelius, Novatian bishop of Constantinople, 202
akribeia. See Precision
akroatai
  and *zēlōtai*, 66, 130
  in Plotinus' circles, 38, 38nn41, 42
Alaphion of Bethelea, 209
Alexander of Alexandria, 183, 201
Alexander of Constantinople, 208–9, 213
Alexander III of Macedon, 54, 62
Alexandria
  Aetius and Eunomius in, 87–88, 119, 232
  Arians in, 27, 201
  medical and Aristotelian learning in, 115–17
  Origen in, 16
  philosophers and gnostics in, 49–50, 87–88, 196
Altercatio Heracliani, 137
Altercatio Jasonis et Papisci, 15–16
Alypius of Alexandria, 49–50
Ambrose of Milan, 195, 216, 219
Ambrose the Valentinian Christian, 17
Amelius Gentilianus, 38, 43, 44, 53
Ammianus Marcellinus
  interest in physiognomy, 58n139

Julia the Manichaean, 82–87, 88
Julian of Cappadocia, 63
Julian of Eclanum, 101
Julian, Emperor, philosophical interests
     of, 51–53, 60
Jurists, Roman
     Law of Citations, 205n98
     tendency to disagree, 26
Justin Martyr, 6–7
Justinian I, Emperor, 105
Juvenal of Jerusalem, 222

Knowledge, certain
     claims to, 12, 34, 62, 67, 135
     definition of *gnōsis*, 168, 172, 173

Latrocinium (449), 227
Law, Roman. *See* Imperial law
Lawyer. See *scholasticus*
Learning
     as credential, 92, 98
     importance to bishops, 140
     need for, in divine contemplation,
        167–71
Leisure, 10
     need for, in divine contemplation, 165,
        165n8
Leontius of Antioch, 114
Leontius of Caesarea, 210
Leontius of Neapolis, 106
Libanius of Antioch, 63–64
libelli, 183
Liber Dalmatii, 210
Licinius, 182
Literacy as means of social mobility, 112,
     112n19
Literary style
     criticism of, as invective, 44–45, 142
     distinction between sophists and phi-
        losophers, 124–25
London Psalter, 213–14
Longinus
     dispute with Plotinus, 44–45
     teacher of Porphyry, 44
Lucian of Antioch, students of, 114
Lucian of Samosata, 31–32
Luke-Acts, 11
Lysimachus, school of, 44

MacMullen, R., 110
Macrobius, 143n181
Macrosocial elites, 28
Magnus of Nisibus, 116–17

Malchion of Antioch, 23–24, 193–94,
     195, 196
Mani
     among the Elchasaites, 71–72
     as Persian stranger, 77
     as seducer of the young, 83
     debating Archelaus, 76–78, 103
     early life and career, 71–74
     spiritual companion of, 73, 74
     writings of, 74–75, 77
Manichaeans
     accusations against, 94–95
     as monastics in Central Asia, 108
     as peripatetics, 78
     as seducers of the young, 82–83
     challenge to other religions, 29, 71
     Christians' fear of, 75–76, 79
     engaging in set disputation, 70–71,
        72–73, 77–78, 80–81, 84–86, 88, 92,
        93–96, 99–102, 105–7
     laws against, 99–100, 103, 104–5
     pagan critics of, 75, 87n71
     posing aporetic questions, 70–71, 89,
        91–92, 103
     presence in Mesopotamia, 71–73,
        75–78
     presence of, in Alexandria and Egypt,
        74–75, 79–81, 87–88
     presence of, in Gaza, 82–87
     presence of, in North Africa, 88–102
     proselytizing tendency of, 29
     reject the Hebrew bible, 75, 88–89
     relying on scriptural premisses of,
        95–96
     reworking texts, 75, 89
     two kinds of public disputation of,
        70–71, 86
     young elect, 77, 84, 95
Manichaeism
     as cult of rationalism, 89
     authoritative texts, 74–75, 77, 99–100
     doctrine of two principles, 75, 103
     pagan converts to, 87
Mar Isaac, *katholikos* of Seleucia and
     Ctesiphon, 217
Mar Maruta, Bishop of Maipherqat, 217
Marcellus, correspondent of Mani in the
     Acta Archelai, 128
Marcian, Emperor, 227
Marcion of Sinope, 75, 89
Marcus Aurelius, Emperor, 14, 32nn5, 6
Marinus of Neapolis, 67
Mark the Deacon, 82–87

Designer:	Ina Clausen
Compositor:	G&S Typesetters, Inc.
Text:	10/13 Palatino
Display:	Palatino
Printer:	Thomson-Shore, Inc.
Binder:	Thomson-Shore, Inc.

.